Managing the Partners in Strategic Alliances

A volume in
Research in Strategic Alliances
T. K. Das, *Series Editor*

Research in Strategic Alliances

T. K. Das, *Series Editor*

Published

Researching Strategic Alliances: Emerging Perspectives (2010)
Edited by T. K. Das

Strategic Alliances in a Globalizing World (2011)
Edited by T. K. Das

Behavioral Perspectives on Strategic Alliances (2011)
Edited by T. K. Das

Strategic Alliances for Value Creation (2012)
Edited by T. K. Das

Management Dynamics in Strategic Alliances (2012)
Edited by T. K. Das

Managing Knowledge in Strategic Alliances (2013)
Edited by T. K. Das

Interpartner Dynamics in Strategic Alliances (2013)
Edited by T. K. Das

Managing Public–Private Strategic Alliances (2014)
Edited by T. K. Das

Strategic Alliances for Innovation and R&D (2014)
Edited by T. K. Das

Managing Multipartner Strategic Alliances (2015)
Edited by T. K. Das

Strategic Alliances for SME Development (2015)
Edited by T. K. Das

Governance Issues in Strategic Alliances (2016)
Edited by T. K. Das

Managing Alliance Portfolios and Networks (2017)
Edited by T. K. Das

Managing Trust in Strategic Alliances (2018)
Edited by T. K. Das

Managing Interpartner Risks in Strategic Alliances (2019)
Edited by T. K. Das

Managing the Partners in Strategic Alliances (2021)
Edited by T. K. Das

In Development

Managing Interpartner Cooperation in Strategic Alliances
Edited by T. K. Das

Managing the Partners in Strategic Alliances

edited by

T. K. Das

City University of New York

IAP

INFORMATION AGE PUBLISHING, INC.

Charlotte, NC • www.infoagepub.com

Library of Congress Cataloging-in-Publication Data

A CIP record for this book is available from the Library of Congress
http://www.loc.gov

ISBN: 978-1-64802-590-7 (Paperback)
978-1-64802-591-4 (Hardcover)
978-1-64802-592-1 (E-Book)

Printed and bound by CPI Group (UK) Ltd, Croydon, CR0 4YY

CONTENTS

FOREWORD TO THE SERIES

Relationships have been important to commercial activity and economic transactions for thousands of years. Yet, the development of a competitive global landscape has substantially enhanced the importance of partnerships between economic entities. These partnerships, referred to as strategic alliances, provide access to resources and capabilities that allow firms to gain economies of scope and to increase their productivity and innovation. The economies, productivity, and innovations are necessary to at least maintain competitive parity, and especially to achieve a competitive advantage in the often highly competitive global markets. Strategic alliances have also become a prominent means of entering new markets, especially foreign markets. Therefore, alliances and the networks of firms of which they are a part, have become essential to conducting business for all types of firms: large, small, established and new.

Because of their growing importance, research on strategic alliances has increased markedly in the last two decades. Yet, there is a need for an authoritative compendium of strategic alliance research and knowledge. This book series on *Research in Strategic Alliances* fills this critically important gap in the field. It provides a thorough examination of significant topics that provide complete and up-to-date knowledge on strategic alliances. This book series can serve as a catalyst for the more effective management of strategic alliances, and will guide future research on them. I commend it to you.

—Michael A. Hitt
Distinguished Professor and Joe B. Foster Chair in Business Leadership at Texas A&M University, and Past President of the Academy of Management and the Strategic Management Society.

Managing the Partners in Strategic Alliances, page vii

ABOUT THE SERIES

The globalization of markets has led to an increased interdependence among business firms, resulting in an explosion in the number of strategic alliances. Strategic alliances, briefly, are cooperative arrangements aimed at achieving the strategic objectives of two or more partner firms. These interfirm arrangements can range from joint R&D to equity-based joint ventures. However, the scholarship relating to strategic alliances remains largely dispersed in the literatures of traditional academic disciplines such as strategic management, marketing, economics, and sociology.

This book series on strategic alliances covers the essential progress made thus far in the literature and elaborate upon fruitful streams of scholarship. More importantly, the book series focuses on providing a robust and comprehensive forum for new scholarship in the field of strategic alliances. In particular, the books in the series cover new views of interdisciplinary theoretical frameworks and models (dealing with resources, risk, trust, control, cooperation, learning, opportunism, governance, developmental stages, performance, etc.), significant practical problems of alliance organization and management (such as alliance capability, interpartner conflict, internal tensions, use of information technology), and emerging areas of inquiry. The series also includes comprehensive empirical studies of selected segments of business, economic, industrial, government, and non-profit activities with wide prevalence of strategic alliances. Through the ongoing release of focused topical titles, this book series seeks to disseminate theoretical insights and practical management information that will enable interested professionals to gain a rigorous and comprehensive understanding of the field of strategic alliances.

—T. K. Das
City University of New York
Series Editor, *Research in Strategic Alliances*

Managing the Partners in Strategic Alliances, page ix

CHAPTER 1

DETERRING DECEITFUL BEHAVIORS OF ALLIANCE PARTNERS

T. K. Das

ABSTRACT

The purpose of this chapter is to provide decision makers in strategic alliances a risk-time framework to (a) categorize types of potential deceitful behaviors by partners, and (b) adopt appropriate deterrence mechanisms to curb and control such behavior. The chapter identifies four types of deceitful behavior, based on: the degree of relational risk that characterizes interactions of a firm with its alliance partner; and the length of the deceit horizon. It also suggests a number of deterrence mechanisms for controlling the different types of deceitful behavior, with the aim of enhancing confidence in partner cooperation in alliances. The chapter provides a practical template for alliance managers to decide what kinds of deterrence mechanisms to adopt on the basis of the type of perceived deceitful behavior of alliance partners. It also responds to an unmet need of managers with alliance responsibilities for a framework to help select the most effective mechanisms to deter different kinds of potential deceitful behavior of alliance partners.

Managing the Partners in Strategic Alliances, pages 1–18

INTRODUCTION: NEED FOR VIGILANCE ABOUT ALLIANCE PARTNERS

Like thorns on the stems of roses, the popularity of strategic alliances has been plagued by potential for deceitful behavior by partners. We know that alliances, or cooperative arrangements among businesses, have been growing very rapidly in recent years. However, alliances have also failed at remarkably high rates, owing to the deceitful behavior of the member firms. Deceitful behavior refers to the self-interest seeking behavior of alliance firms that involve deceit. The threat of potential deceitful behavior hinders the collaborative efforts of member firms in alliances, destroys interpartner trust and confidence, injects uncertainties about alliance performance, and leads, eventually, to alliance termination.

Writing on the subject of cooperative behavior of alliance partners, experts have commented along the following lines:

> Given that it is often impossible to identify who is likely to act opportunistically, the interesting question is what enables alliance partners to garner enough confidence in partner cooperation so that they are not overwhelmed by the potential hazards in alliances. (Das & Teng, 1998, p. 491)

Low confidence levels arising from deceitful behavior not only discourage the formation of alliances but also perpetuate suspicion among partners even after the alliances are formed. However, not much is known about how deceitful behavior affects confidence in partner cooperation and how it might be controlled and managed. A framework is presented in this article that business executives involved with alliances can use to employ deterrence mechanisms to curb and control the incidence of deceitful behavior.

DECEITFUL BEHAVIOR IN ALLIANCES

The objective of deceitful behavior by a partner firm is to seek gain for itself at the expense of other members in the alliance. Withholding or distorting information and shirking or failing to fulfill promises or obligations are examples of deceitful behavior. Williamson observes that "opportunism extends the conventional assumption that economic agents are guided by considerations of self-interest to make allowance for *strategic* behavior" (Williamson, 1975, p. 26; emphasis in original). Therefore, those who are least principled are likely to be most deceitful, and would likely exploit those who are more principled (Williamson, 1985, p. 64). In fine, the potential for deceit characterizes an alliance partner's behavior, and should be distinguished from other forms of self-interest seeking behavior.

It is widely recognized that all alliance members have potential for deceitful behavior to some degree. However, the tendencies for deceit may be latent or dormant. Most member firms refrain from behaving deceitfully for fear that they may be found out, resulting in possible contractual termination, loss of reputation, and so on. Nevertheless, when a firm enters into an alliance with a partner, it needs to be wary of its partner's attitude, regardless of its own behavior. Especially when making alliance-specific investments, a firm becomes vulnerable to its partner's future behavior (which may have little resemblance to its initial behavior).

RISK-TIME FRAMEWORK OF DECEITFUL BEHAVIOR

Deceitful behavior has generally been conceived in relatively simplistic terms. It is rare to find a sophisticated conceptualization of deceitful behavior, although some suggestions have been made on the related topics of opportunism and strategic risk behavior (Das, 2006; Das & Rahman, 2010; Das & Teng, 2001a). Wathne and Heide (2000) have proposed a framework of four different forms of opportunism (evasion, refusal to adapt, violation, and forced renegotiation). We suggest that deceitful behavior in strategic alliances has two fundamental dimensions: risk and time-horizon of deceitful behavior. The risk dimension captures the degree of the potential adverse impact of deceitful behavior in terms of the apprehension that a partner may not be committed to mutual interests in an alliance. Risk in alliances is made up of relational risk and performance risk (Das & Teng, 1996, 1999). Briefly, relational risk in an alliance is the probability that the partner will not cooperate fully. Performance risk refers to the probability of not attaining the performance goals even when the partner cooperates fully. Clearly, deceitful self-interest seeking generates only relational risk. Performance risk, by definition, does not relate to deceit because it is based on the given condition of full partner cooperation. Thus, performance risk in inter-firm alliances is no different from that in single firms. Relational risk, however, is unique to strategic alliances. The potential deceitful behaviors of the partner firm that may not cause any substantial harm to an alliance member can be said to entail low relational risk, whereas the behaviors that may severely damage the member would pose high relational risk.

The time dimension relates to the duration of potential adverse impact of deceitful behavior on inter-firm cooperation. This temporal dimension is thus the time-span of deceit, or deceit horizon. Deceit horizon can be considered as somewhat akin to the well-known notion of time-span of decisions (Jaques, 1979).

An appreciation of the role of both these dimensions is necessary for an adequate understanding of the essential nature of deceitful behavior.

The risk consequences of deceitful behavior can be better understood and more effectively controlled and prevented if they are recognized in terms of specific time-based categories.

Figure 1.1 lays out the four types of deceitful behavior that can be used as a template to discuss how specific deterrence mechanisms can be used to control deceitful partner behavior in strategic alliances (see Das, 2004). The four types of deceitful behavior are:

Type 1: low relational risk, short deceit horizon;
Type 2: high relational risk, short deceit horizon;
Type 3: low relational risk, long deceit horizon; and
Type 4: high relational risk, long deceit horizon.

DETERRENCE MECHANISMS FOR CONTROLLING DECEITFUL BEHAVIOR

In using the risk-time framework of deceitful behavior, alliance managers should incorporate appropriate deterrence mechanisms to curb and control such behavior in order to enhance confidence in partner cooperation. Given that there are a number of mechanisms available for the purpose, alliance managers need to assess the applicability of particular mechanisms for specific purposes. The more significant deterrence mechanisms are: contracts, governance structure, mutual hostages, monitoring, participatory decision making, and staffing and training.

A summary of our discussion is given in Table 1.1. Managers should note that each of these mechanisms, used properly, would achieve desired results within the limited circumstances of potential partner intentions, but none of them would be effective on a consistent basis because of the ever-present potential for deceitful partner behavior. Thus, for synergistic benefits, alliance managers should consider adopting tailored sets of deterrence mechanisms, depending on the type of potential deceitful behavior that is perceived.

Contracts

Contracts determine and influence the policies and procedures that are to be followed in alliances. As Williamson (1999) observes, "Credible contracting is very much an exercise in farsighted contracting, whereby the parties look ahead, recognize hazards, and devise hazard mitigating responses—thereby to realize mutual gain" (p. 1090). Prespecified rigorous contracts are important because they reduce the risk of defection and facilitate legal enforcement. According to Crocker and Reynolds (1993, p. 127), the parties to a contract may mitigate post-formation cheating and

Deceit Horizon

Risk Level	Short	Long
Low Relational Risk	Type 1 • "Misrepresenting one's abilities" (Deeds & Hill, 1998, p. 143) • "Reluctance of members to fulfill commitments to partners in cooperative arrangements" (Gassenheimer, Baucus, & Baucus, 1996, p. 70) • Shirking "involves the withholding of full effort and cooperation in an ongoing relationship. Shirking, free riding, and stonewalling are examples of such behaviors" (Griesinger, 1990, p. 487) • "Shirking or failing to fulfill promises or obligations" (John, 1984, p. 278) • Providing products that are of an inferior quality than originally agreed upon (Provan & Skinner, 1998, p. 507) • Non-adherence "to the explicit or implicit controls governing the relationship" (Weaver & Dickson, 1998, p. 507)	Type 3 • "Withholding...information" (Deeds & Hill, 1998, p. 143; John, 1984, p. 278) • Reacting dishonestly in response to contractual specifications to cause moral hazards (Klein, 1996, pp. 461–462) • "Calculated efforts to…confuse"; "incomplete…disclosure of information" (Williamson, 1985, p. 47) • "Strategic manipulation of information" (Williamson, 1975, p. 26)
High Relational Risk	Type 2 • "Expropriation of tacit technological knowledge" (Dutta & Weiss, 1997, p. 347) • Infidelity "results when an agreement is abrogated or a relationship abandoned to the advantage of the instigator but without provision or remedy for the other party" (Griesinger, 1990, p. 486) • "Hold-up" (Klein, 1996, p. 461) • "Stealing"; "Cheating" (Williamson, 1985, p. 47)	Type 4 • "Distorting information" (Deeds & Hill, 1998, p. 143; John, 1984, p. 278) • "Willful deception" (Gassenheimer, Baucus, & Baucus, 1996, p. 69) • Dishonesty "comes into play when one party to an excange possesses information about a transaction that could significantly alter the other party's assessment of the outcomes," and such information is concealed, misrepresented, or not contributed. (Griesinger, 1990, p. 486) • "Defect…while pretending to be trustworthy" (Nootboom, 1996, p. 989)

Figure 1.1 Risk-time framework of deceitful behavior.

TABLE 1.1 Deterrence Mechanisms for Different Types of Deceitful Behavior in Alliances

Deterrence Mechanisms	Level of Effectiveness			
	Type 1 Low Relational Risk/ Short Deceit Horizon	Type 2 High Relational Risk/Short Deceit Horizon	Type 3 Low Relational Risk/ Long Deceit Horizon	Type 4 High Relational Risk/ Long Deceit Horizon
1. Contracts	*High* Possible to address near future contingencies	*Moderate* Possible to address near future contingencies	*Low* Not possible to address distant future contingencies	*Low* Not possible to address distant future contingencies
2. Governance structure	*High* Harms the alliance, not the firm	*Low* Harms the firm, not the alliance	*Low* Retaliation not feasible	*High* Retaliation feasible
3. Mutual hostages	*Low* Retaliation not justified—self-defeating if alliance is the focus of retaliation	*High* Retaliation justified—not self-defeating	*Moderate* Wearing off of hostage value	*Low* Illusion of hostage exchange
4. Monitoring	*High* Deterrence possible after detection, and useful if deceit has low impact	*Low* Deterrence not possible after detection, if deceit has high impact	*Low* Secretive nature makes detection difficult	*Moderate* Deterrence possible if detection is early enough for counter measures
5. Participatory decision making	*High* Genuine goal alignment possible	*High* Genuine goal alignment possible	*High* Genuine goal alignment possible	*Low* Goal alignment of partners may be deceiving
6. Staffing and training	*High* Recruitment and training of appropriate personnel possible	*Moderate* Temptation of grand gains makes staffing and training ineffective, although staffing may help in securing critical information	*High* Recruiting people who believe in full disclosure, and training to devalue withholding	*High* Persuading people against deceit, and training to detect such deceit

investment distortions by the use of more complete agreements, but only at the expense of a great deal of resources dedicated to crafting the document. The higher the degree of contractual completeness, the lower the marginal benefits and the higher the marginal cost associated with crafting the contract. Contracts need to be rigorous in such a way that it retains flexibility even while providing adequate guidelines for the operation of an alliance. According to Klein (1996), "rather than attempting to determine all of the many events that might occur during the life of a contractual relationship and writing a pre-specified response to each, the gains from exchange are increased by the use of incomplete contracts" (p. 447). It would be unrealistic to expect comprehensive contracts that insure against future surprises. Indeed, contractual rigor and flexibility need to be balanced.

Littler and Leverick (1995) argue that policies and procedures can control the behaviors of alliance members. Different instances of Type-1 deceitful behavior (low relational risk/short deceit horizon) can be addressed in contract provisions to enhance confidence in partner cooperation. Although a comprehensive contract can help a firm minimize the risk of hold-up by a deceitful partner, this may not always be feasible. Birnberg (1998) argues that "while the parties contract and those contracts provide incentives that direct their behavior, rules and co-operation also are necessary to allow for greater levels of uncertainty that makes the writing of a complete contract inappropriate" (p. 424). For instance, Tabeta (1998) refers to Type-2 deceit (high relational risk/short deceit horizon) when suggesting that

> after a contract has been struck and a specialized machine has been developed and installed, the supplier could threaten to hold up production to coerce the buyer into offering a higher price. Because of the specificity of the machine, the buyer cannot switch suppliers without costly delay. (p. 2)

Therefore, rigorous contracts at best will be moderately effective in deterring Type-2 deceitful behavior. Contractual provisions may not be effective against partners engaging in long-horizon deceitful behavior (Types 3 and 4), because formal provisions cannot comprehensively capture the possibility of occurrence of these types of deceitful behavior. Contractual terms cannot cover distant-future contingencies, because the number of possible outcomes becomes far too many to grasp or conjecture (Das, 1991). Thus, rigorous contracts will not be effective against Types 3 and 4 deceitful behavior, such as disclosing incomplete information and misrepresenting intentions.

Managers need to realize that contracts tend to be more effective in the short term. Whereas it is impractical to try to address all future contingencies in a contract, managers should nevertheless try to identify as many of them as possible (Das, 2006, 2019). However, they should not seek an overly comprehensive contract because, after all, contracts per se do not ensure compliance.

Governance Structure

Governance arrangements in alliances range from joint ventures, minority-equity exchanges, supplier relationships, R&D agreements, technology licensing, and so on. Alliance structures are commonly classified into equity and nonequity alliances. The literature generally suggests that, as compared to nonequity alliances, equity alliances are more effective in restraining deceitful behavior. A governance structure based on equity will serve to curb Type-1 deceitful behavior because of a heightened concern for alliance performance. A potentially deceitful partner with a high equity stake in an alliance will be disinclined to shirk, waste alliance resources, and so on (Type-1 deceitful behavior), because such behavior will likely harm alliance performance. This deterrence mechanism will not be very effective against Type-2 deceitful behavior, in which a firm (not so much the alliance) is taken advantage of by a deceitful partner to secure unfair gains. For example, a member firm is directly affected by its partner's stealing and cheating, but the larger alliance is much less so. However, the idea behind equity structure is to increase a potential deceitful partner's concern for the alliance, which in effect will curb deceitful behavior. Of course, a Type-2 deceitful partner will steal and cheat whenever there is scope, irrespective of its share of equity in the alliance.

An alliance partner that engages in Type-3 deceitful behavior may withhold critical information from the focal firm. The latter usually does not have the option to retaliate because of the intangible and ambiguous nature of Type-3 deceitful behavior. As a result, the firm will have to dissolve the alliance when it realizes the presence of Type-3 deceitful behavior. In such a situation, an equity alliance may leave it with little choice but to tolerate the partner's Type-3 deceitful behavior. In such circumstances, a firm is better off with a nonequity alliance, because that will allow it to leave the alliance without much loss immediately on learning about a partner's Type-3 deceitful behavior. On the other hand, an equity alliance will be an effective deterrent for Type-4 deceitful behavior, such as pretending to be trustworthy while actually being deceitful. An equity structure binds the deceitful partner to a significant level of commitment. A Type-4 deceitful partner may also risk retaliation from the affected firm, because it will still be around, given the long-span character of this kind of deceitful behavior.

Managers should try to control potential deceitful behavior through appropriate governance structure of alliances if they fear that the alliance itself is the primary target of deceit. In some cases, an equity structure provides some retaliatory power to a member firm. However, this power may diminish over time. Thus, the structural choice should not be made solely to gain retaliatory power against the potential deceit of an alliance partner.

Mutual Hostages

The notion of mutual hostages suggests the exchange of critical resources between partners, such that each member firm becomes vulnerable to potential losses, thereby materially demonstrating credible commitment to each other and to the alliance. Unless parties make similar amounts of transaction-specific investments, there would be a strong incentive for parties making less transaction-specific investments to behave deceitfully. Thus, the possibility of deceitful behavior will be proportional to the differences in transaction-specific investments by alliance members.

The notion of mutual hostages suggests the exchange of critical resources between partners, such that each partner becomes vulnerable to potential losses, thereby materially demonstrating credible commitment to each other and to the alliance. According to Hwang and Burgers (1997), "alliance-specific investments provide the credible commitment that buttresses mutual assurance. Thus, mutual commitment offers a way of enhancing the robustness of cooperation and diminishing the attractiveness of defection" (p. 105). Unless parties make similar amounts of transaction-specific investments, there would be a strong incentive for parties making less transaction-specific investments to behave deceitfully. Thus, the possibility of deceitful behavior will be proportional to the differences in transaction-specific investments by alliance members.

Due to this vulnerability on both sides, a partner will hesitate to engage in deceitful behavior for fear of losing its own critical resources held hostage by the presumptive "victim" firm. Unless the gain from deceit is considered greater than the loss of the hostage resources, a partner will refrain from deceitful behavior even if there is scope for it. However, credible commitments will not always have a significant effect on deterring deceitful behavior.

For Type-1 deceitful behavior, such as failing to fulfill commitments and supplying inferior quality products, this mechanism will not be very effective. Since Type-1 deceitful behavior of a partner adversely affects principally the alliance and not the focal firm, a reprisal can be problematic. On the one hand, a counteraction will antagonize the deceitful partner, jeopardizing the prospects of a continuing cooperative relationship. On the other hand, if a retaliatory action (i.e., an attempt at retribution with an act similar to that of the deceitful partner) of Type-1 deceit harms the alliance instead of the partner, the whole idea of using hostages as a counterbalance becomes self-defeating. After all, the proximate reason for such retaliation is the partner's Type-1 deceit that negatively impinges on the alliance. Thus, it does not make sense to retaliate if it further hurts the alliance. The use of mutual hostages may be effective in deterring Type-2 deceit because the partner's purpose is to take advantage of the affected firm, and the firm can retaliate against the partner as long as it holds critical resources as hostage. Implementing this mechanism will deter Type-2 deceit because the partner will be in fear of the affected firm's retaliatory power in terms of the mutual hostages.

In the case of Type-3 deceitful behavior, such as calculated efforts to confuse and obfuscate alliance situations, mutual hostages may be useful only during the initial stages when the deceitful partner values its own hostage resources. It is possible that over time the criticality of the hostage resources provided by the deceitful partner may wear off. The potential victim firm cannot then successfully retaliate in response to partner deceit. The efficacy of this mechanism is doubtful in deterring Type-4 deceitful behavior. For example, distorting results and misrepresenting information may lead a focal firm from the outset to be under the illusion that it holds certain critical resources of its partner as hostage. However, it could well be that not only does the so-called hostage resources cease to retain its importance to the partner, but the member firm's genuinely critical resources may remain with its partner as hostage. This kind of situation will worsen the vulnerability of the affected firm. Thus, this mechanism will not be effective against Type-4 deceit and, thus, should not be used as a deterrence mechanism.

When potential partners discuss the exchange of hostages to establish credible commitments, managers of alliancing firms should beware of fake hostages. Even genuine hostages are likely to lose their value over time. Therefore, mutual hostages need to be exchanged periodically. That way, even if a prior hostage begins to lose its value, the new one will be a suitable replacement. Also, managers should be open and candid about the critical resources that they are willing to commit as hostage. A firm can only hope that its partner will reciprocate such transparency. The advantage of openness is that it increases the probability of the partner acting in a trustworthy manner. However, managers need to be cautious in assessing the genuineness of their counterpart's hostage offer, notwithstanding their own candid approach.

Monitoring

Monitoring can restrict the deceitful tendencies of alliance partners once a contract is signed. Monitoring suggests close, firsthand supervision of activities of partners and the alliance. The idea is to discourage a partner from being deceitful, on the reasoning that it will be difficult for it to behave deceitfully when other alliance members are monitoring it.

Since the nature of Type-1 deceitful behavior, for example, delaying payments, supplying inferior goods, and so on, is usually clearly discernible, an alliance member can identify this kind of deceit through the monitoring mechanism. The effects of Type-1 deceit are relatively less serious vis-à-vis the effects of other types of deceitful behavior. Therefore, a firm can take preventive actions once its monitoring reveals possible Type-1 deceitful behavior. Accordingly, a deceitful alliance partner will not be able to easily gain from Type-1 deceit if this deterrence mechanism is in place. Monitoring can be potentially effective in detecting Type-2 deceit, such as stealing proprietary technology. However, because of the grave impact of Type-2 deceit, its detection after the fact will not be of much help to the affected firm. Some other deterrence measures, such as using mutual hostages and setting up an equity structure for the alliance, can better restrain Type-2 deceit once monitoring has successfully revealed its presence.

Type-3 deceitful behavior is usually secretive in character, such as in withholding critical information from alliance members. For that reason, monitoring may not be sufficient for detecting all instances of Type-3 deceitful behavior. At least during the initial stages, Type-3 deceitful behavior is not very serious in its impact because it allows a focal firm to take corrective measures whenever the monitoring mechanism successfully detects it. However, Type-4 deceitful behavior (high relational risk/long deceit horizon) is not as secretive in nature as Type-3 deceitful behavior, such as distorting information. As a result, a firm will be able to detect Type-4 deceitful behavior through monitoring, such as when distorted information does not match actual operations and performance. The timing of detecting Type-4 deceitful behavior is critical though, because a firm may become misguided by its partner's Type-4 deceit if it goes on for an extended period.

An alliance member may consider monitoring its partner to make sure it abides by contractual provisions and mutually understood roles and expectations. However, excessive monitoring may jeopardize mutual trust-building efforts because monitoring requires close scrutiny, which often detracts from trusting behavior. Monitoring should be done as unobtrusively as possible. Ideally, continuous monitoring would ensure the detection of deceitful behavior. However, continuous monitoring is ordinarily expensive. An alternative is periodic monitoring, which, however, will not be effective if its timing is predictable. Therefore, managers of a focal firm need to monitor partner behavior in a random fashion to ensure that the partner will be always on guard about engaging in deceitful behavior.

Participatory Decision Making

Participatory decision making processes help align the visions and values of alliance members. According to Johnson et al. (1996), "shared decision making has positive consequences in the IJV [international joint venture] relationship in that it inhibits opportunistic tendencies" (p. 91). As Saxton (1997) also notes,

> The close interaction and the investment partners make through shared decision making signify two things: (1) a commitment to and interest in outcomes, which decrease the perceived likelihood of opportunistic behavior and (2) the likelihood that a partner's opportunistic behavior will be recognized. (p. 446)

This mechanism will be responsive to potential conflicts and facilitate goal congruence. Continuous goal congruence is necessary for smooth alliance functioning, for otherwise it could create conflicts and jeopardize the cooperative environment needed in an alliance. Besides the economic aspects, the social aspects also need to be managed for controlling potential deceitful behavior (Das & Teng, 1998). Scholars have argued that similar backgrounds among alliance partners are helpful in achieving and sustaining goal congruence. For example, Deeds and Hill (1998) hypothesize that "a congruence between the backgrounds of the partners in a research alliance will decrease perceived opportunism" (p. 146).

This mechanism will be a successful deterrent of deceitful behavior as long as it leads to goal congruence between partners. Short horizon deceit with both low and high risks (Types 1 and 2), as well as Type-3 deceitful behavior (low relational risk/long deceit horizon), do not presuppose long-term deceit for dishonest gains. For example, when a deceitful partner delays payment to a firm, exploits its quasi-rents, and withholds certain information, these do not involve any prolonged or high levels of deceitful behavior. Participatory decision making processes can effectively help coalesce the interests of all members, thereby neutralizing many of the factors responsible for these kinds of dishonest intentions. However, this mechanism may not be useful in deterring Type-4 deceitful behavior, since it involves willful deception, distortion of intention, and so on. For example, a Type-4 deceitful partner may falsely claim that its own goals are compatible with the member firm's goals, and render the latter more vulnerable.

Negotiation skills are a basic necessity to implement this mechanism. Managers of an alliance firm should search for the root causes for differences in their own goals and those of their partner's. Listening carefully to the partner's arguments is extremely important for this mechanism to work. Once the partner's major issues have been clearly identified, the member firm's managers should attend to those issues within the framework of the participatory decision making processes to achieve goal congruence. However, even when goal congruence is achieved, managers should not be complacent, because such congruence may turn out to be deceptive. Managers should weigh, on a continuous basis, how much credence to place on the congruence of goals.

Staffing and Training

Staffing and training serve to regulate and standardize behavior within alliances. While staffing allows alliance members to select managers and lower-level employees for the alliance following certain criteria, training enables alliance members to impress certain behavioral norms on the alliance staff and nurture desired skills. Through training, an alliance member can persuade the alliance staff to behave in an appropriate fashion. Also, staffing and training are comparatively more effective when the alliance structure leans toward hierarchical governance.

This mechanism will be effective in controlling most types of deceitful behavior because it can create a culture of trust, efficiency, high performance, and so on (Das & Teng, 2001b). In so doing, it will be able to deter Type-1 deceitful tendencies, such as making insufficient efforts, delaying payments, and so on. Training can further condition the alliance staff to avoid these deceitful tendencies. However, Type-2 deceitful behavior, such as exploiting partner's transaction-specific investments, has a strict economic rationale with very little behavioral aspect to it. Therefore, staffing and training will not be effective in curbing Type-2 deceitful behavior when suitable occasions arise for the partner. Usually, the unfair gain from Type-2 deceitful behavior is very substantial, and it is quite possible that the temptation of this gain may overwhelm the trustworthiness and behavioral training of personnel. One exception to this is the use of staffing to place trusted member firm employees to control the dissemination of certain types of information, so as to prevent the partner firm from expropriating any critical know-how or technology.

Through proper training, a firm can attempt to inculcate in the personnel the practice of full disclosure of information and results. In a joint venture, the alliance staff from the parent firm can also be trained similarly, so that they reinforce the value of being open with critical information of relevance to the partner. Thus, this mechanism may serve to discourage Type-3 deceitful behavior. Training can also deter various types of distortion, an example of Type-4 deceitful behavior. Behavioral training can persuade the alliance staff (particularly those of the partner) not to practice Type-4 deceitful behavior by repeatedly demonstrating the desirability of sharing pertinent information. Moreover, training should include the development of skills to detect possible Type-4 deceitful tendencies and possibilities.

A firm should only assign its more competent and astute managers to work with its partner. This is important because these people will be the only direct link between the firm and its partner. It must also be noted that senior managers, if left without proper controls for too long in an alliance, may run the risk of being socialized in the partner's ways and, possibly, enticed away. To reduce the potential dangers of such eventualities, a firm should be careful in assigning technical experts or individuals who know a great deal of a firm's proprietary information.

Managers of an alliance firm, given the potential of partner deceit, should try to have a say in recruiting alliance employees. In the staffing process, they should be able to call the shots or at least veto the partner's choice in who gets recruited and placed in what position. Similarly, the training curriculum should also be jointly decided with the partner.

GUIDELINES FOR ALLIANCE MANAGERS

Identify the Types of Potential Deceitful Behavior

Identify the specific types of potential deceitful behavior that an alliance firm anticipates from its partner in different situations, keeping in mind the four types of such behavior in the risk-time framework. This selection has been problematic heretofore because managers have had to consider deceitful behavior as a relatively simple, if jumbled, phenomenon, so that they had no clear idea about which deterrence mechanism to deploy for what type of potential deceitful behavior. The conventional advice to managers of alliance firms has been to consider using some precautions if and when a particular threat of deceit is perceived.

Select Appropriate Deterrence Mechanisms

Select one or more of the deterrence mechanisms discussed here, to achieve the desired level of prevention and control of deceit. The approach to implementing deterrence mechanisms proposed here is based on different types of deceitful behavior. The six selected deterrence mechanisms should be understood in terms of how each of these will have varying deterrence effects on different types of deceitful behavior. In other words, a specific deterrence mechanism will be effective for certain types of deceitful behavior and not so for other types. This contingent approach should help in the selective deployment of available deterrence mechanisms.

Evaluate Effectiveness of the Selected Deterrence Mechanisms

Managers need to recognize that even among these mechanisms not every one will be compatible with the others. On the one hand, if a firm applies incompatible deterrence mechanisms, the effectiveness of all the mechanisms will be reduced. On the other hand, the effectiveness of particular deterrence mechanisms may be enhanced when certain compatible mechanisms are used in tandem. This conscious calculation will also help managers to avoid the use of deterrence mechanisms that may be ineffective for specific types of deceit. Although we have discussed a robust set of deterrence mechanisms, our understanding of which one to use when with others remains less than satisfactory. With the refined categories of deceitful behavior proposed here, managers should be in a position to get more purchase on specific deterrence mechanisms that would be appropriate in different situations. Managers need to explore the calculus of effectiveness with different sets of deterrence mechanisms to determine the most viable combinations of mechanisms for particular types of deceitful behavior.

Consider the Appropriateness of Deterrence Mechanisms for Each Alliance Stage

It would be worthwhile to identify the appropriate deterrence mechanisms for each stage of the alliance making process. Researchers have studied the evolution of alliances in terms of various stages (Das & Teng, 2002). The deterrence mechanisms can be easily identified as belonging to either pre-agreement and post-agreement categories, so that one category will be more relevant during the pre-formation and early stages of the alliance making process, while another in the implementation or later operating stages. For instance, decisions on contractual rigor and governance structure are more relevant for the early stages of negotiating an alliance agreement, whereas decisions concerning monitoring and participatory decision making are more applicable to the later stages of setting-up and operating the alliance. Plainly, proper timing of implementation of various deterrence mechanisms is critical for maximum effectiveness.

Understand and Keep in Mind the Contingent Character of the Effectiveness of Deterrence Mechanisms

Managers of alliancing firms should also be careful in implementing specific deterrence mechanisms in conjunction with others, because, as we noted earlier, the effectiveness of some mechanisms may be constrained by the presence of other mechanisms. For example, certain aspects of monitoring mechanisms may conflict with contractual provisions that permit flexibility in decision making by alliance members. The objectives of monitoring may also contradict the spirit of participatory decision making. Given that deterrence mechanisms are expensive to implement, alliance managers should aim for optimal effectiveness of these mechanisms in their totality. The risk-time framework and the discussion of deterrence mechanisms should be helpful in the systematic understanding and management of potential deceitful behavior in strategic alliances.

CONCLUSION

In conclusion, the most significant obstacle in developing confidence in partner cooperation in strategic alliances is the potential for deceit. Although the hazards of deceitful behavior are well known, they need to be assessed in a fairly sophisticated manner. The deterrence mechanisms employed to curb and control deceitful behavior also need to be considered in a contingent manner to optimally address the different kinds of deceitful behavior. The approach suggested here has clear advantages over the traditional approach to controlling deceitful behavior. By treating each type of deceitful behavior differently, and deterring them in different ways, alliance managers can significantly improve the chances of success. The careful assessment of each type of deceitful behavior would reduce the redundant and ineffective use of deterrence mechanisms.

ACKNOWLEDGMENT

This chapter, save some minor changes, was earlier published as Das, T. K. (2005). Deceitful behaviors of alliance partners: Potential and prevention. *Management Decision, 43*(5), 706–719.

REFERENCES

Birnberg, J. G. (1998). Control in interfirm co-operative relationships. *Journal of Management Studies, 35*(4), 421–428.

Crocker, K. J., & Reynolds, K. J. (1993). The efficiency of incomplete contracts: An empirical analysis of air force engine procurement. *RAND Journal of Economics, 24*(1), 126–146.

Das, T. K. (1991). Time: The hidden dimension in strategic planning. *Long Range Planning, 24*(3), 49–57.

Das, T. K. (2004). Time-span and risk of partner opportunism in strategic alliances. *Journal of Managerial Psychology, 19*(8), 744–759.

Das, T. K. (2006). Strategic alliance temporalities and partner opportunism. *British Journal of Management, 17*(1), 1–21.

Das, T. K. (2019). Future orientation in strategy making. In Das, T. K. (Ed.), *Time issues in strategic and organization* (pp. 1–25). Charlotte, NC: Information Age.

Das, T. K., & Rahman, N. (2010). Determinants of partner opportunism in strategic alliances: A conceptual framework." *Journal of Business and Psychology, 25*, 55–74.

Das, T. K., & Teng, B. (1996). Risk types and inter-firm alliance structures. *Journal of Management Studies, 33*(6), 827–843.

Das, T. K., & Teng, B. (1998). Between trust and control: Developing confidence in partner cooperation in alliances. *Academy of Management Review, 23*(3), 491–512.

Das, T. K., & Teng, B. (1999). Managing risks in strategic alliances. *Academy of Management Executive* [renamed *Academy of Management Perspectives*], *13*(4), 50–62.

Das, T. K., & Teng, B. (2001a). Strategic risk behavior and its temporalities: Between risk propensity and decision context. *Journal of Management Studies, 38*(4), 515–534.

Das, T. K., & Teng, B. (2001b). Trust, control, and risk in strategic alliances: An integrated framework. *Organization Studies, 22*(2), 251–283.

Das, T. K., & Teng, B. (2002). The dynamics of alliance conditions in the alliance development process. *Journal of Management Studies, 39*(5), 725–746.

Deeds, D. L., & Hill, C. W. L. (1998). An examination of opportunistic action within research alliances: Evidence from the biotechnology industry. *Journal of Business Venturing, 14*(2), 141–163.

Dutta, S., & Weiss, A. M. (1997). The relationship between a firm's level of technological innovativeness and its pattern of partnership agreements. *Management Science, 43*(3), 343–356.

Gassenheimer, J. B., Baucus, D. B., & Baucus, M. S. (1996). Cooperative arrangements among entrepreneurs: An analysis of opportunism and communication in franchise structure. *Journal of Business Research, 36*(1), 67–79.

Griesinger, D. W. (1990). The human side of economic organization. *Academy of Management Review, 15*(3), 478–499.

Hwang, P., & Burgers, W. P. (1997). The many faces of multi-firm alliances: Lessons for managers. *California Management Review, 39*(3), 101–117.

Jaques, E. (1979). Taking time seriously in evaluating jobs. *Harvard Business Review, 57*(5), 124–132.

John, G. (1984). An empirical investigation of some antecedents of opportunism in a marketing channel. *Journal of Marketing Research, 21*(3), 278–289.

Johnson, J. L., Cullen, J. B., & Sakano, T. (1996). Opportunistic tendencies in IJVs with the Japanese: The effects of culture, shared decision making, and relationship age. *International Executive, 38*(1), 79–94.

Klein, B. (1996). Why hold-ups occur: the self-enforcing range of contractual relationships. *Economic Inquiry, 34*(3), 444–463.

Littler, D., & Leverick, F. (1995). Joint ventures for product development: learning from experience. *Long Range Planning, 28*(3), 58–67.

Nooteboom, B. (1996). Trust, opportunism and governance: A process and control model. *Organization Studies, 17*(6), 985–1010.

Provan, K. G., & Skinner, S. J. (1989). Interorganizational dependence and control as predictors of opportunism in dealer-supplier relations. *Academy of Management Journal, 32*(1), 202–212.

Saxton, T. (1997). The effects of partner and relationship characteristics on alliance outcomes. *Academy of Management Journal, 40*(2), 443–461.

Tabeta, N. (1998). The *Kigyo Keiretsu* organization and opportunism in the Japanese automobile manufacturing industry. *Asia Pacific Journal of Management, 15*, 1–18.

Wathne, K. H., & Heide, J. B. (2000). Opportunism in interfirm relationships: Forms, outcomes, and solutions. *Journal of Marketing, 64*(4), 36–51.

Weaver, K. M., & Dickson, P. H. (1998). Outcome quality of small- to medium-sized enterprise-based alliances: The role of perceived partner behaviors. *Journal of Business Venturing, 13*(6), 505–522.

Williamson, O. E. (1975). *Markets and hierarchies: Analysis and antitrust implications.* New York, NY: Free Press.

Williamson, O. E. (1985). *The economic institutions of capitalism.* New York, NY: Free Press.

Williamson, O. E. (1999). Strategy research: Governance and competence perspectives. *Strategic Management Journal, 20*(12), 1087–1108.

CHAPTER 2

PARTNER SELECTION IN STRATEGIC ALLIANCES FOR INNOVATION

An Individual-Level Framework for Assessing Goodwill and Competence

Diana Rus
Nadine Roijakkers

ABSTRACT

Partner choice in strategic innovation alliances determines the extent to which effective collaboration and value creation is possible. Therefore, choosing a suitable partner is critical for alliance management and success. Yet, the partner selection process requires careful balancing of a complex set of criteria under time pressure and with limited information. We propose that an understanding of the psychological processes underlying alliance managers' subjective evaluations of potential partners' suitability in the alliance formation phase could provide valuable insights into the partner selection process. By drawing upon work in social cognition and organizational behavior, we present a framework that identifies the key dimensions (warmth and compe-

Managing the Partners in Strategic Alliances, pages 19–50

tence) used by alliance managers to evaluate potential partner firm's trustworthiness based on their interactions with the individuals representing these firms. We advance propositions linking initial evaluations of potential partner firms' representatives to firm attractiveness, selection, and the development of interpersonal trust as a precursor of interorganizational trust.

INTRODUCTION

Strategic alliances for innovation constitute an essential element in how firms seek to accelerate the pace of product development, market entry, and innovation in the 21st century. As firms enter strategic innovation alliances, they need to collaborate across organizational boundaries under inherently uncertain conditions (Lumineau & Quélin, 2012) while reconciling inevitable mixed motives over longer time horizons (Ness, 2009). This requires a continuous, open information flow to ensure integration of core competencies and flexibility in handling the myriad of unanticipated issues arising during the course of the alliance (Ariño, Ragozzino, & Reuer, 2008; Cummings & Holmberg, 2012; Shah & Swaminathan, 2008). For instance, firms need to safeguard against potential partner opportunistic behavior; initial alignment conditions may change over the course of the alliance's life cycle requiring adjustments (Das & Teng, 2000); and differences in organizational cultures, mindsets, expectations, and behavior may lead to conflicts (Hanson & Lackman, 1998; Tse, Francis, & Walls, 1994). It is therefore not surprising that strategic alliances for innovation are difficult to manage and many fail to fulfill their envisioned potential (Cartwright & Cooper, 2011; Gulati, Wohlgezogen, & Zhelyazkov, 2012).

A considerable amount of work at the organizational level of analysis addresses the motivations for strategic alliance formation, their governance structures, and the drivers of alliance success and failure. Whereas alliance failures can be attributed to a number of reasons, two of the most common identified causes are poor partner selection and inappropriate alliance management (Dev, Klein, & Fisher, 1996; Emden, Calantone, & Droge, 2006; Shah & Swaminathan, 2008). The choice of partner determines the raw material or the foundation for potential collaboration; and even superior alliance management capabilities cannot compensate for the lack of this initial foundation (Holmberg & Cummings, 2009). Yet, selecting the right partner goes beyond simply choosing the one with the best skills or resources (Lambe, Spekman, & Hunt, 2002). It is a complex process that requires weighting evaluations on several more or less tangible criteria. Research has shown that strategic alignment and complementarity in terms of resources and capabilities is critical for alliance viability and sustainability (Das & Teng, 2000; Lambe et al., 2002). Additionally, a partner firm must also satisfy more intangible criteria such as being compatible, committed to the relationship, and trustworthy (Kale & Singh, 2009). Our current understanding of the underlying processes involved in determining partner suitability based on balancing this complex set of criteria is limited. This might, at least in part, be due to a curious omission: assessments of partner suitability at the organizational level hinge on (sometimes subjective) judgments made by individual alliance managers with limited time and information (Ariño et al., 2008; Luvison & Cummings, 2017; Schilke & Cook, 2013). Therefore, we argue that a focus on understanding the psychological processes underlying alliance managers' evaluations of potential partners' suitability is critical to our understanding of macro-level processes such as partner selection and effective alliance management (cf. Barney & Felin, 2013; Felin, Foss, & Ployhart, 2015).

In this chapter, we take an individual-level perspective and focus on the largely understudied psychological processes (Ahuja, Soda, & Zaheer, 2012; Casciaro et al., 2015; Porter & Woo, 2015) underlying alliance managers' evaluations of potential partners' suitability. Although firms enter alliance formation negotiations in mutuality, the decision to partner is typically initiated by one firm. Therefore, we take the perspective of the focal firm's alliance manager and focus on the alliance formation phase, where a set of potential partner firms that fulfill complementarity criteria has been identified. Drawing from research in organizational behavior and social cognition (i.e., how people perceive and evaluate others), we argue that alliance managers' evaluations of potential partner firms' suitability will hinge (at least in part) on their evaluations of the individuals representing these firms. Specifically, when interacting with potential partners' representatives, we argue that they will first try to determine their trustworthiness by answering two fundamental sets of questions: (a) "Are these the kinds of people we would like to work with and do we trust their intentions?" and (b) "Are these the kinds of people that have the will and the skill to contribute to long-term alliance goals?" We will provide a framework that illustrates how the answers to these two sets of questions shape alliance managers' evaluations of the individuals representing potential partner firms, and by extension, of the firms they represent.

The chapter is structured as follows. First, we provide an overview as to why partner selection is important for alliance success and advance reasons as to why a micro-foundational approach (Foss, 2011) in general, and a focus on the psychological processes underlying alliance managers' subjective evaluations of potential partners in particular, is valuable. Second, we present a framework that identifies the key dimensions used by alliance managers to evaluate potential partner firm's trustworthiness based on their interactions with individuals representing these firms. We also advance propositions linking initial evaluations of potential partner firms' representatives to firm attractiveness, selection, and the development of interpersonal trust as a precursor of interorganizational trust.

THE IMPORTANCE OF PARTNER SELECTION AND THE ADDED VALUE OF A MICRO-FOUNDATIONAL APPROACH

Strategic innovation alliances are not a new phenomenon: firms in high-tech sectors such as ICT and pharmaceutical biotechnology were already collaborating on R&D projects as early as the 1970s. Strategic innovation alliances are collaborative agreements between two or more firms, who temporarily join forces with the purpose of jointly creating new or improved ideas, knowledge, products, or services (Hagedoorn, 1993). These inter-organizational relationships follow a number of distinct phases in their evolution including (a) the *alliance formation phase* wherein a firm searches for potential partners to jointly develop a new product/service, engages in initial negotiations and determines fit in terms of strategies, goals, and resources; (b) *the design phase* wherein a firm and its partner set up governance mechanisms to oversee the alliance; (c) *the post-formation/operational phase* wherein a firm manages the alliance to create value; and (d) *the dissolution phase* where the alliance is wrapped up, results are evaluated, and potential new areas for collaboration are identified (Schreiner, Kale, & Corsten, 2009). A strategic alliance for innovation is considered successful once its goals (e.g., the creation of the new knowledge or product) are reached. Given that the development of innovations typically takes years, requires high levels of integration, transparency, flexibility, open communication, and the creation of synergies, it is important that partners can ensure the health of the partnership until objectives are achieved (Pangarkar, 2003; Sivadas & Dwyer, 2000).

A large percentage of strategic alliances are discontinued prematurely, neither meeting the goals of their parent companies, nor delivering the benefits they purported to provide (Bamford, Gomes-Casseres, & Robinson, 2004), and even leading to shareholder value destruction for the partners (Kale, Dyer, & Singh, 2002). The success of any single alliance depends on several inter-related factors linked to the different stages of alliance evolution (Gulati, 1998). However, the two most frequently identified causes of alliance failure are poor partner selection and ineffective alliance management (Dev et al., 1996; Emden et al., 2006; Shah & Swaminathan, 2008). It has been argued that the choice of partner determines the foundation for collaboration and that even effective alliance management capabilities cannot compensate for choosing an unsuitable partner (Holmberg & Cummings, 2009). The partner chosen determines the extent to which effective collaboration and value creation during the alliance is possible and thereby is critical for alliance management and success (Dekker, 2008; Duisters, Duysters, & De Man, 2011; Shah & Swaminathan, 2008).

Research on partner selection has shown that achieving strategic alignment via a clear partnering strategy and the identification of value creation areas at the level of the alliance is crucial for alliance effectiveness (Das & Teng, 2000). Additionally, four partner characteristics have been identified as positively influencing alliance success: partner complementarity, compatibility, commitment, and trustworthiness (Das & Teng, 2001; Kale & Singh, 2009; Shah & Swaminathan, 2008). Complementarity refers to the extent to which the partner brings non-overlapping resources, such as knowledge, expertise, and innovative capabilities to the table. Partner compatibility represents the extent to which there is chemistry or an overall fit between the partners in goals, culture, collaborative capability, mindset, working, and decision making styles. Partner commitment refers to the extent to which the partner is willing to not only contribute required resources to the alliance, but to go the extra mile and make short-term sacrifices to achieve long-term alliance benefits (Gundlach, Achrol, & Mentzer, 1995; Kale & Singh, 2009). Partner trustworthiness represents the extent to which the partner appears benevolent (showing goodwill and refraining from opportunistic behavior) and competent (having expertise and being reliable; Das & Teng, 2001; Nooteboom, 2002). Strategic alignment and partner complementarity may trigger the decision to enter an alliance, yet they are insufficient for alliance success. Partner compatibility, commitment and trustworthiness must also be present (Kale & Singh, 2009; Shah & Swaminathan, 2008).

In the design phase, the assessment of a partner's trustworthiness has been linked to the selected governance mechanisms (control-based, contractual vs. trust-based, relational governance mechanisms). Firms tend to choose more control-based governance models if they have little alliance experience and judge the potential of their partner's opportunistic behavior as high, whereas they tend to opt for more relational, trust-based governance models if they have had previous positive experiences with this partner or if they judge the potential of their opportunistic behavior as low (De Man & Roijakkers, 2009). Note that there are different views as to the relationship between control-based and trust-based governance mechanisms (whether they act as substitutes or as complements; see Kale & Singh, 2009).

The need to select partners that are trustworthy, committed to the relationship, and compatible is important when it comes to effectively managing innovation alliances. These are risky endeavors characterized by potentially opportunistic partner behavior, high uncertainty regarding project outcomes, and a highly interdependent collaboration process requiring intensive communication, coordination, integration, and flexibility in handling unanticipated issues (Emden et al., 2006). Hence, building interorganizational trust is critical and has been shown to be crucial for the success of strategic innovation alliances (Ariño, de la Torre, & Ring, 2001; Das & Teng, 1998, 2001; Zaheer, McEvily, & Perrone, 1998). Relational alignment between partners, in terms of compatible cultures, collaborative abilities, mindsets, a propensity to be flexible and a long-term orientation, plays a key role not only in building interorganizational trust (Emden et al., 2006), but also in avoiding conflicts due to incompatible management styles, misaligned priorities, differences in decision making procedures, cultures, or mindsets (Hanson & Lackman, 1998). Moreover, research shows that partners who develop interorganizational trust and experience working together as mutually beneficial, tend to formulate new joint objectives and engage in future collaborations (sometimes referred to as repeated ties in the strategic alliance literature).

The choice of partner in a strategic innovation alliance seems to have important consequences not only for the type of governance mechanism chosen but also for the effective management of the alliance, and ultimately its success. Nevertheless, our understanding of the processes underlying firms' assessment of potential partner suitability in these initial interaction phases is limited. Below, we argue that taking a micro-foundational approach might provide valuable insights.

The Added Value of a Micro-Foundational Approach

With some exceptions, the strategic innovation alliance literature has focused on understanding the macro-level foundations of alliance formation, governance, management, and success. In contrast, our understanding of their micro-foundations—the processes and dynamics surrounding the individuals and teams who are effectively engaged in interorganizational collaboration—is lagging behind. Following calls for investigations at the individual and team levels of analysis (Felin et al., 2015; Foss, 2011; Liu, Sarala, Xing, & Cooper, 2017), some recent studies have explored emotions, commitment, trust, and role expectations in strategic alliances (Cullen, Johnson, & Sakano, 2000; Kumar, van Kleef, & Higgins, 2019; Luvison & Cummings, 2017). Despite these advances, the individual and team levels of analysis remain the most under-investigated areas in the strategic alliance domain. Yet, there are several reasons why a micro-foundational approach in general, and a specific focus on the psychological processes underlying alliance managers' subjective evaluations of potential alliance partners' suitability, is essential and in need of more attention.

First, strategic alliances for innovation are underpinned by foundations on two levels: (a) the *macro-level foundations* of alliance formation, governance, and management of potentially risky collaborations with external partners and (b) the *micro-level foundations* of boundary-spanning individuals evaluating, negotiating, navigating complex issues, resolving disagreements, and building relationships with their external counterparts. However, macro-level processes, such as the management of strategic alliances, often find their foundations at the micro-level. It is individuals that decide whether to trust/distrust, cooperate with or deceive other individuals, not organizations (Foss, Husted, & Michailova, 2010). In this respect, alliance managers' actions tend to disproportionately impact alliance viability (Spekman, Isabella, MacAvoy, & Forbes, 1996). They are the primary actors evaluating and deciding on potential partners under conditions of limited time and information. In addition, they are the linchpins coordinating alliance efforts, negotiating deals, balancing competition with cooperation, attempting to resolve potential disagreements, and managing the risks inherent in alliances (Albers, Wohlgezogen, & Zajac, 2016; Currall & Judge, 1995; Das & Teng, 1999; Hamel, 1991; Marchington & Vincent, 2004). Given that individuals are the driving force behind all interorganizational processes (Senge, 1990), a micro-foundational approach focusing on alliance managers is essential to further our understanding of macro-level strategic alliance processes and outcomes (Barney & Felin, 2013; Liu et al., 2017).

Second, our understanding of the psychological processes underlying alliance managers' evaluations of potential partners' suitability is limited (Ahuja et al., 2012; Casciaro et al., 2015; Porter & Woo, 2015). A micro-foundational approach focusing on these psychological processes might help us understand macro-level processes in the alliance formation phase, such as partner selection decisions, which are critical to effective alliance management and success. We argue that alliance managers' evaluations of potential partner suitability will hinge—at least in part—on the extent to which they see potential partner firms' representatives as trustworthy (benevolent and competent) during initial interactions. We base this contention on research showing that individuals tend to form stereotypical impressions of groups based on the impressions they form of individual members seen as representative of these groups (Fiske, Cuddy, Glick, & Xu, 2002). During initial interactions, alliance managers will form a trustworthiness assessment of the individuals representing potential partner firms. The positive or negative characteristics ascribed to these individuals (e.g., their goodwill, likeability, motivations, skill) will also be attributed to the organizations they represent. We posit that alliance managers' subjective evaluations of the individuals representing potential partner firms, will shape, to a certain extent, the potential partner firm's overall attractiveness (i.e., the extent to which they are seen as appealing and useful), which, in turn, will impact the partner selection decision. By understanding the processes underlying these evaluations, we might gain insights into factors that help or hinder optimal partner selection.

Third, alliance managers' initial evaluations of the individuals representing potential partner firms will determine the extent to which interpersonal trust (i.e., goodwill- and competence-based trust; cf. Colquitt, Scott, & LePine, 2007; Das & Teng, 2001) can develop with these individuals, provided their firm is selected. Interpersonal trust has been shown to facilitate effective coordination, open communication and shared decision making processes, to create a sense of loyalty and cooperation, reduce the risk of opportunistic behavior, facilitate mutual knowledge sharing, and effective conflict management (for reviews see Costa, Fulmer, & Anderson, 2018; Fulmer & Gelfand, 2012). Understanding the conditions under which interpersonal trust is likely to develop is all the more important, since it is one of the main drivers for the development of interorganizational trust (Barney & Felin, 2013; Schilke & Cook, 2013).

A FRAMEWORK FOR PARTNER EVALUATIONS IN THE ALLIANCE FORMATION PHASE

Organizing Scheme of Our Proposed Framework

We advance a psychological framework for how alliance managers evaluate the individuals representing potential partners in the alliance formation phase. In doing so, we do not claim to be exhaustive; we simply aim to show how a focus on the psychological processes underlying alliance managers' evaluations of the individuals representing potential partner firms may help us understand partner selection and alliance management processes at the macro-level.

In our framework, we take the perspective of the focal firm's alliance manager in the alliance formation phase. Specifically, once a set of potential partners that are deemed valuable and fulfill complementarity criteria has been identified, the alliance manager needs to predict their trustworthiness in order to determine their suitability as partners. To this end, she first gathers clues regarding the firms' trustworthiness based on, for instance, prior interorganizational interactions and general reputation. Next, she engages in initial conversations with individual counterparts in these organizations to determine trustworthiness firsthand. During these initial interactions, she seeks information about these individuals' goodwill- and competence-based trustworthiness (cf. Das & Teng, 2001) by assessing them on two dimensions: *warmth* (i.e., "Can we get along and can I trust their intentions?") and *competence* (i.e., "Do they have the will and the skill to contribute to long-term alliance goals?"). We base this contention on a large body of research in social cognition and organizational behavior showing that all initial interpersonal and intergroup assessments are underpinned by judgments on these two core dimensions: warmth and competence (for reviews see Abele & Wojciszke, 2014; Fiske, Cuddy, & Glick, 2007; Judd, James-Hawkins, Yzerbyt, & Kashima, 2005).

The resulting evaluations on these two orthogonal criteria (warmth and competence; Fiske et al., 2002) combine to produce four overall archetypes

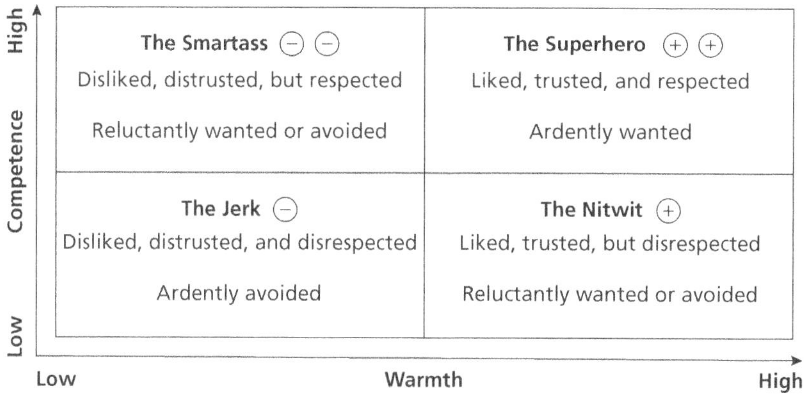

Figure 2.1 Four archetypes of potential collaboration partners.

of high/low warmth and high/low competence (see Figure 2.1), which influence subsequent trustworthiness assessments, emotions, intentions, and behaviors (Cuddy, Fiske, & Glick, 2008). Alliance managers form an extremely positive or negative assessment, if they judge their interaction partners as being high or low on both dimensions: the *superhero* who is competent, driven, affable, and well-intentioned and the *jerk* who is incompetent, lazy, obnoxious, and ill-intentioned. Critically, alliance managers can—and often do—form ambivalent or mixed impressions that include positive content on the one dimension and negative content on the other: the *smartass* who is competent and driven but obnoxious and ill-intentioned and the *nitwit* who is affable, well-intentioned but unfortunately useless. We deem these combinations particularly interesting, given that the effects of warmth and competence judgments on the global impression are asymmetrical and non-additive. Warmth perceptions determine whether the global impression is positive or negative; competence perceptions only determine the intensity of the positive or negative impression (i.e., how positive or negative it is). Hence, competence judgments amplify the valence of the global impression formed based on warmth: a negative impression based on low warmth becomes more negative with low competence; a positive impression based on high warmth becomes more positive with high competence (Abele & Wojciszke, 2014; Fiske et al., 2007).

These archetypes are clearly over-exaggerated, yet, people in any organization can roughly be classified by using this simple matrix. We argue that the specific archetype associated with the representatives of different potential partner firms will color the global positive or negative impression associated with their respective firms: the trustworthiness perception of the firms' representatives will influence the trustworthiness perception of their firm. All other things being equal, this will shape the firms' attractiveness, likelihood to be selected, and the potential development of interpersonal trust (i.e., goodwill- and competence-based trust) between partnering firms' representatives.

In the following, we define warmth and competence and describe their effects; present an overview of the sources of information alliance managers use to evaluate potential partner firms' representatives on these two dimensions; and engage in a detailed discussion of the four resulting archetypes (*superhero, jerk, smartass, and nitwit*) paired with the advancement of specific propositions.

Warmth and Competence: Two Core Dimensions of Social Perception

Researchers have long been interested in understanding the core dimensions on which people judge others when forming first impressions. In order to successfully navigate the social world, individuals need to routinely and rapidly make accurate assessments of people and groups they encounter. Is a stranger likely to help or harm? Is a person a suitable friend or colleague? Is a potential collaborator worthy of trust? Is this person really an expert? To answer such questions, individuals need to quickly determine another's intentions and their ability to act on them. Although these assessments may be based on different factors, more than 5 decades of research suggests that two core dimensions govern the content of all social judgments: *warmth* and *competence* (Abele & Wojciszke, 2014; Cuddy et al., 2008; Fiske et al., 2007; Judd et al., 2005). People across cultures, spontaneously and unconsciously, assess strangers they encounter by judging whether their intentions are good or bad and whether they are competent or incompetent. The pervasiveness and automaticity of these evaluations has been explained from an evolutionary perspective: upon encountering an unfamiliar person (or group), our ancestors had to quickly answer two fundamental types of questions to ensure survival: (a) "What are this person's intentions towards me? Am I in danger of being exploited or cheated?" and (b) "Does this person possess the skills, the will, and the resources to enact these intentions?" (Cuddy, Glick, & Beninger, 2011; Fiske et al., 2007).

These judgments of warmth and competence account for about 82% of the variance in the global positive or negative impression formed of a person or group (Wojciszke, 2005), and they influence subsequent trustworthiness assessments, emotions, intentions, and behaviors (Cuddy et al., 2008). Individuals use similar pairs of dimensions to judge countries, cultures (Oyserman, Coon, & Kemmelmeier, 2002), and even companies and brands (Fournier & Alvarez, 2012). The labels used for these two dimensions have varied over time and across theoretical domains and traditions, ranging from socially good–bad vs. intellectually good–bad (Rosenberg, Nelson, & Vivekananthan, 1968), communion vs. agency (Abele & Wojciszke, 2014; Bakan, 1966), getting along vs. getting ahead (Hogan, 1983), other-profitability vs. self-profitability (Peeters & Czapinski, 1990), to warmth vs. competence (Fiske et al., 2002). Importantly, all these different labels have been shown to share a common core (see Abele & Wojciszke, 2014 for a review). Hence, for the sake of simplicity, we will refer to them as warmth and competence.

Warmth is an overarching label reflecting others' perceived sociability and intentions (good vs. bad) and it can be further decomposed into two sub-dimensions: friendliness and trustworthiness (Abele, Cuddy, Judd, & Yzerbyt, 2008; Fiske, 2018; Fiske et al., 2002), which are akin to the notions of getting along (Hogan, 1983) and other-profitability (Peeters & Czapinski, 1990). As such, warmth reflects traits relevant to the establishment and maintenance of social relationships, which hinge on behaviors that are on the one hand warm and friendly and on the other hand fair and reliable. Warmth encompasses being both benevolent towards others in ways that facilitate cooperative relationships with them and being benevolent in ways that facilitate fair relationships by adhering to ethical principles and social values (Abele & Wojciszke, 2014; Brambilla & Leach, 2014). Positive traits such as warm, friendly, helpful, kind, sociable, generous, understanding, trustworthy, honest, sincere, fair, good-natured, and tolerant (vs. negative traits such as cold, unfriendly, dishonest, deceitful etc.), are different ways to describe a person's or group's overall warmth (Abele & Wojciszke, 2014; Cuddy et al., 2008; Judd et al., 2005). In sum, positive traits associated with the warmth dimension signal an accommodating orientation in social interactions as well as benevolent intent or trustworthiness (cf. Abele et al., 2008; Cuddy et al., 2008; Fiske, 2018) and serve as the basis for assessments of goodwill-based trustworthiness.

Competence is an overarching label reflecting others' perceived ability and agency in pursuing their intentions. It can be further decomposed into two sub-dimensions: capability and assertiveness (Abele et al., 2008; Fiske, 2018; Fiske et al., 2002), which are akin to the notions of self-profitability (Peeters & Czapinski, 1990) and getting ahead (Hogan, 1983). As such, competence reflects traits relevant to effective goal-pursuit, which hinges on having the skills and the drive to perform (Abele & Wojciszke, 2014; Brambilla & Leach, 2014). Competence is characterized by positive traits relevant for goal-attainment such as capable, skillful, intelligent, effective, talented, ingenious, knowledgeable, foresighted, creative, active, energetic, agentic, assertive, ambitious, strong, confident, independent, determined, competitive (vs. negative traits such as incapable, unskilled, passive, lazy, etc.; Abele & Wojciszke, 2014; Cuddy et al., 2008; Judd et al., 2005). In sum, positive traits associated with the competence dimension signal capability as well as agency or assertiveness in goal-pursuit (cf. Abele et al., 2008; Cuddy et al., 2008; Fiske, 2018) and serve as the basis for assessments of competence-based trustworthiness.

When interacting with the representatives of potential partner firms with the goal of finding a suitable partner for collaborative innovation, the focal alliance manager tries to determine their goodwill- and competence-based trustworthiness (Das & Teng, 2001; Nooteboom, 2002) which have been shown to be critical antecedents to the development of (goodwill- and competence-based) interpersonal and interorganizational trust in strategic innovation alliances (Barney & Felin, 2013; Schilke & Cook, 2013). Based on our framework, a focal alliance manager determines her counterparts' trustworthiness by automatically trying to answer two types of questions: "Are these the kinds of people we would like to work with? Are we in danger of being deceived or exploited?" (i.e., warmth; goodwill-based trustworthiness); and "Are these the kinds of people that have the will, skill and resources to contribute to long-term alliance goals?" (i.e., competence; competence-based trustworthiness). That is, she tries to assert whether the individuals she interacts with, and by extension, the firms they represent, are likely to be pleasant, benevolent, collaboration partners that are competent and driven to achieve alliance goals.

Beyond affecting assessments of goodwill- and competence-based trustworthiness, warmth and competence judgments have been shown to influence both the quality and outcomes of a variety of interpersonal interactions relevant in the context of strategic innovation alliances (Cuddy et al., 2008). For instance, judging someone as warm (vs. cold) results in a tendency to actively engage with and collaborate with this person (vs. a tendency to avoid them; Cuddy et al., 2008; Van't Wout & Sanfey, 2008). It also increases liking (Wojciszke, Abele, & Baryla, 2009), facilitates trust (Delgado, Frank, & Phelps, 2005), and promotes cooperative behavior in negotiation contexts (Steinel & De Dreu, 2004). In contrast, judging someone as competent leads to increased respect and a desire to be associated with this person (vs. disrespecting and neglecting the incompetent person; Cuddy et al., 2008; Fiske et al., 2002; Wojciszke et al., 2009). Additionally, people want to work with and cooperate with those they deem competent, but not with those they deem incompetent (Hinds, Carley, Krackhardt, & Wholey, 2000; Van Lange & Kuhlman, 1994).

Yet, how do these warmth and competence judgments come about? Below, we outline the main sources of information used by alliance managers when evaluating others' warmth and competence.

How Do Alliance Managers Evaluate Potential Partner Firms' Representatives on Warmth and Competence?

When assessing the representatives of potential partner firms on warmth, an alliance manager looks for cues indicating whether the other is sincere, sociable, cooperative, well-intentioned, fair, and tolerant. In contrast, when assessing their competence, she searches for cues indicating whether the other is capable, experienced, effective, creative, influential, confident, driven, and energetic. In making these judgments, alliance managers can rely on a variety of information sources such as physical appearance, nonverbal cues, conversations, observed behavior, status, and reputation (Cuddy et al., 2011; Uleman, Adil Saribay, & Gonzalez, 2008). The first judgments (or misjudgments) are made based on physical appearance and nonverbal cues. These are automatic, fast (often elicited in a matter of milliseconds) and consistent across genders and cultures (Willis & Todorov, 2006; Zebrowitz, 2017).

Even in the absence of prior knowledge, an alliance manager is likely to judge a counterpart that is older, male, taller, or stronger as more influential and competent than a counterpart that is younger, female, shorter, or weaker (Anderson & Brion, 2014). A person whose face looks familiar (vs. unfamiliar) will be judged as warm and trustworthy (DeBruine, 2002), whereas a person whose face is more babyish than average will be assessed as trustworthy but incompetent (Zebrowitz, Fellous, Mignault, & Andreoletti, 2003). A male counterpart with a higher (vs. lower) facial width-to-height ratio will (correctly) be judged as more dominant, less trustworthy and more prone to engaging in deception (Haselhuhn, Wong, & Ormiston, 2013). Alliance managers may also infer warmth and competence from nonverbal cues. They will assess a counterpart whose face expresses happiness as warm and competent; one who expresses anger as competent but cold; and one who expresses sadness as incompetent (Montepare & Dobish, 2003). An interaction partner who smiles genuinely (vs. not smiling at all or fake-smiling), will be judged as warm, kind, sociable, tolerant, and honest (Cuddy et al., 2011). Moreover, a conversation partner, who leans forward during interactions and orients their body towards the focal alliance manager, nods and makes eye-contact, will be evaluated as warm and trustworthy (Cuddy et al., 2011; Kraft-Todd et al., 2017). In contrast, a counterpart who physically expands to take up more space, seats herself to occupy a central or more elevated position or moves deliberately, will be judged as agentic, dominant and competent; whereas she will be seen as passive, submissive and incompetent if she physically slumps, contracts her body to take up less space, or fidgets (Cuddy et al., 2011).

During interactions with representatives of potential partner firms, alliance managers will also infer warmth and competence from how these individuals describe themselves and how they behave. In social interactions, people tend to engage in impression management or self-presentation (Schlenker, 2012). This is especially the case in work settings, such as a meeting with a potential partner, where the stakes are high and creating a favorable impression is crucial to seal the deal. Research has identified two major types of self-presentation styles: a self-focused (agentic or self-promoting) and other-focused (communal or ingratiating) style (Paulhus & Trapnell, 2008). Individuals using self-focused presentation styles describe their and their company's past achievements in terms that emphasize their talent, capabilities, successful risk-taking and ability to master challenges. Alliance managers faced with conversation partners confidently and dominantly self-promoting in this manner are likely to see them as competent but also as cold and ruthless, especially if they ascribe their successes to innate talent or intelligence (Steinmetz, 2018). Individuals using other-focused self-presentation styles attempt to get along and gain their interaction partner's trust by emphasizing their goodwill and fairness (Paulhus & Trapnell, 2008). Alliance managers faced with counterparts acting in ingratiating ways, emphasizing their sense of fairness and goodwill, are likely to judge them as being warm (Barrick, Schaffer, & DeGrassi, 2009). In terms of observed behavior, research indicates that we judge people as more competent if they behave assertively and forcefully (Anderson & Kilduff, 2009). An alliance manager is likely to judge an interaction partner who verbally expresses anger, violates social norms of polite behavior by talking more or interrupting others as being competent and powerful (Anderson & Brion, 2014). In contrast, she will judge counterparts as warm (friendly and trustworthy) if they actively listen and ask questions, acknowledge and address any concerns, express gratitude and generally show signs of empathy and caring (Howe, Leibowitz, & Crum, 2019; Williams & Bartlett, 2015).

Judgments of warmth and competence are also influenced by contextual factors such as status and reputation. Status cues are one of the strongest predictors of perceived competence, with status and competence judgments correlated at 0.77 across 19 countries (Cuddy et al., 2008). Alliance managers will judge representatives of potential partner firms as more competent if their firm is prestigious (vs. non-prestigious) and if their job title indicates high status within their home organizations: a global vice-president of Innovation Alliances will be judged as more competent than a manager of Innovation Alliances. Other status indicators leading to assessments of high competence are the individual's economic success, education level, power, clothing, car, and so on. (Anderson & Brion, 2014; Brambilla, Sacchi, Castellini, & Riva, 2010; Cuddy et al., 2011). Importantly, alliance managers will make automatic trade-offs in these evaluations: they will judge a high-status interaction partner as competent but less warm, while judging a low-status counterpart as warm but less competent (Fiske et al., 2002,

2007). Reputation is yet another predictor of an individual's warmth and competence. For instance, if a third party provides positive information about the interaction partner on only one dimension (e.g., warmth) but completely omits information concerning the other dimension (e.g., competence), the alliance manager will automatically develop a negative evaluation for the omitted dimension. An alliance manager hearing that their counterpart is "very nice, sociable, and outgoing" will conclude that this person is probably incompetent, whereas if they were described as "very smart, hard-working, and competent" they would conclude that they are probably cold. This effect is stronger in contexts where the omitted information is expected, like information on competence in the work context. Presumably, information recipients account for the unwritten rule of communication "If you don't have anything nice to say, don't say anything at all" (Kervyn, Bergsieker, & Fiske, 2012).

THE FOUR ARCHETYPES

To recap, after first gathering clues regarding the potential partner firms' trustworthiness based on third-party information such as the firms' reputations, the focal alliance manager engages with these firms' representatives to establish trustworthiness firsthand. As a result of these interactions, she forms a subjective evaluation of their counterparts' overall warmth (goodwill-based trustworthiness) and competence (competence-based trustworthiness). These resulting evaluations combine into four overall impression archetypes (*superhero, jerk, smartass, and nitwit*), and the different potential partner firm representatives are categorized as falling into one of these four archetypes (see Figure 2.1). Below, we discuss these four archetypes and develop propositions relating them to the overall impression formed of the potential partner firm, the firms' attractiveness, likelihood to be selected, and the potential development of interpersonal trust between the partnering firms' representatives.

The Superhero

An alliance manager that judges a potential partner firm's representative as high in both competence and warmth sees this individual as trustworthy on both dimensions and forms an extremely positive impression. This individual embodies all the qualities one wishes to see in a collaborative innovation partner: someone who is capable and skilled, experienced and effective, creative and confident, motivated to collaborate and with the stamina to go the distance, is influential and likeable, socially skilled and cooperative, empathetic and well-intentioned, generous and fair, trustworthy and genuine. Working with this person not only bodes well for achieving shared objectives, but also for enjoying the process of working with them. Besides simple common sense dictating that one would respect, admire, and be attracted to this type of potential partner, research has shown that people prefer to work with others who are friendly, helpful, and benevolent, besides being skillful and ambitious (Casciaro & Lobo, 2008); that leaders who simultaneously project competence and interpersonal concern are more effective (Fransen, Delvaux, Mesquita, & Van Puyenbroek, 2018); and that employees who show both expertise and approachability are effective in their teams and with clients (Barrick, Stewart, Neubert, & Mount, 1998).

Given that individuals form stereotypical impressions of groups based on the impressions they form of individual members seen as representative of these groups (Cuddy et al., 2008; Fiske et al., 2002), it is likely that this extremely positive impression of the representative of a potential partner firm will also transfer to the impression formed of their firm. The focal alliance manager will see the potential partner firm as embodying the characteristics associated with their representative: being benevolent, trustworthy, collaborative, compatible, committed to contribute to long-term alliance goals and as having the required capabilities to contribute to value creation in the alliance. This (potentially biased) positive impression of the firm may also lead to selectively attending to evidence confirming this positive impression (i.e., prior reputation information suggesting the firm is trustworthy) and discounting potential disconfirming evidence (i.e., prior reputation information suggesting the firm may not be trustworthy; see work on the confirmation bias; Nickerson, 1998). Hence, the initial positive impression formed of a potential partner firm's representative is likely to have a halo effect and be transferred to the firm at large; selective attention to external information might further amplify this positive impression. This will positively influence the firm's perceived attractiveness and may shape the partner selection decision:

Proposition 1: *High warmth and competence evaluations of a potential partner firm's representative positively influence the firm's attractiveness and potential to be selected as a partner.*

These positive evaluations of warmth and competence of the potential partner firm's representative, also set the foundation for the development of interpersonal trust, provided the two firms indeed enter an alliance. Evaluations of high warmth signal that the counterpart has goodwill and will refrain from opportunistic behavior (i.e., goodwill-based trustworthiness) and evaluations of high competence signal that the counterpart has the necessary expertise and is committed (i.e., competence-based trustworthiness). These initial assessments of trustworthiness set positive expectations regarding the counterpart's intentions and future behavior and represent the basis for the development of interpersonal trust:

> **Proposition 2:** *High warmth and competence evaluations of a potential partner firm's representative set the foundation for the development of interpersonal trust.*

Provided that these positive expectations do not get disconfirmed, this could lead to a low level of perceived relational risk, which could result in more trust-based alliance governance mechanisms and the development of interorganizational trust. Downstream and over time, this could have a positive effect on successfully resolving potential mixed-motive situations, reaching alliance objectives, and the creation of repeated ties. Yet, a false positive, that is, a judgment of a potential partner firm's representative as being trustworthy—when they are not to be trusted—can have costly consequences not only for the development of interpersonal trust, but also for the viability of the alliance at large (Kale & Singh, 2009). Trust grows with increased evidence of the trustee's qualities, a positive relationship history and increased knowledge and predictability of the other's behavior (Lewicki, Tomlinson, & Gillespie, 2006). In contrast, repeated instances of unmet expectations, opportunistic behavior, or other trust violations lead to soured relationships, particularly if deception was involved (Schweitzer, Hershey, & Bradlow, 2006). Hence, it is important to identify factors that might lead to an unwarranted positive impression of a partner firm's representative and we deem dark triad personality traits, such as narcissism (Paulhus & Williams, 2002), as critical for a number of reasons. First, those scoring high on dark triad traits, such as narcissism, are prevalent in leadership positions, including alliance management positions (O'Boyle, Forsyth, Banks, & McDaniel, 2012), and their impact on their employees and organizations is largely negative (Furnham, Richards, & Paulhus, 2013). Second, in initial interactions, they successfully come across as energetic, competent, interesting, warm, trustworthy, and entertaining given their mastery at combining a forceful, glorifying agentic self-presentation style with the use of ingratiation techniques (Jonason & Fletcher, 2018). Whereas they are initially successful at gaining others' trust, with the passage of time, their arrogance and self-entitlement come to the fore (Küfner, Nestler, & Back, 2013): they consider themselves superior and belittle others; exhibit little empathy or perspective-taking in social interactions and show few signs of accommodation in conflict situations (O'Boyle et al., 2012). They behave selfishly and create poor-quality social exchanges, which result in being disliked and distrusted. Therefore, we argue that a narcissistic representative of a potential partner firm will succeed in creating an unwarranted positive impression:

Proposition 3: *High warmth and competence evaluations of a potential partner firm's representative may be biased due to her narcissistic personality traits.*

In sum, evaluating a potential partner firm's representative as high in both competence and warmth results in an overall positive trustworthiness assessment of the individual. All other things being equal, this positive impression will be positively related to the firm's attractiveness and to its potential to be selected as an alliance partner. It also sets the foundation for building interpersonal trust between the partners' representatives, which is a precursor of interorganizational trust. Yet, these initial positive impressions might be erroneous, which can have disastrous consequences not only for the development of interpersonal relationships but also for the effective management of the alliance. Future research might benefit from considering factors that might bias the initial impression formed.

The Jerk

An alliance manager that judges a potential partner firm's representative as low in both competence and warmth sees this individual as being untrustworthy on both dimensions and forms an extremely negative impression. This person doesn't have any redeeming qualities that would make them a desirable collaboration partner: they are neither capable nor skilled, are inexperienced, passive and not very motivated to go the extra mile. They are cold, unfriendly, selfish, dishonest, and deceitful. Choosing to work with this person would be irrational: a collaboration would not bode well for achieving shared goals and the actual process of working with them would be a nightmare. Besides simple common sense dictating that one would disrespect, feel contempt towards, and try to avoid this person as a potential collaboration partner, research indicates that the most desperately avoided colleague at work is one embodying these characteristics: someone that is incompetent, dishonest, and obnoxious (Casciaro & Lobo, 2008).

The extremely negative impression formed of this individual boundary-spanner is likely to be transferred to the global impression of their firm. The focal alliance manager is likely to see the potential partner firm as embodying the negative characteristics associated with their representative: being dishonest, opportunistic, competitive, unlikely to contribute in good faith to long-term alliance goals and as lacking the required capabilities to contribute to value creation in the alliance. This (potentially biased) negative impression of the firm may lead to selectively attending to evidence confirming this negative impression (i.e., prior reputation information suggesting the firm is untrustworthy) and discounting potential disconfirming evidence (e.g., prior reputation information suggesting the firm may be trustworthy;

cf. Nickerson, 1998). Hence, the initial negative impression formed of the potential partner firm's representative, is likely to have a horn effect and be transferred to the firm at large; selective attention to external information might further amplify this negative impression. Unless there is very strong and credible evidence (e.g., prior collaborations with this firm that were mutually beneficial) to overrule this impression, this will negatively influence the firm's perceived attractiveness and potential to be selected as a partner:

> **Proposition 4:** *Low warmth and competence evaluations of a potential partner firm's representative negatively influence the firm's attractiveness and potential to be selected as a partner.*

If for whatever other reasons, the two firms enter an alliance, these negative evaluations of the partner firm's representative in terms of goodwill- and competence-based trustworthiness, set negative expectations regarding their intentions and future behavior and will hamper the development of interpersonal trust:

> **Proposition 5:** *Low warmth and competence evaluations of a potential partner firm's representative will hamper the development of interpersonal trust.*

Downstream, provided that these negative expectations do not get disconfirmed, this would lead to a high level of perceived relational risk, which could result in more control-based alliance governance mechanisms and might also hamper the development of interorganizational trust. Potentially opportunistic behavior could result in conflict and ineffective resolution of mixed-motive situations; the premature disbanding of the alliance and potential financial losses.

In sum, evaluating a potential partner firm's representative as low in both competence and warmth results in an extremely negative trustworthiness assessment of the individual. All other things being equal, this assessment will be negatively related to the firm's attractiveness and to its potential to be selected as an alliance partner. If for whatever other reasons, the two firms form an alliance, this negative impression will hamper the development of interpersonal trust and can have disastrous consequences for the viability of the alliance.

The Smartass

An alliance manager that judges a potential partner firm's representative as high in competence yet as low in warmth is ambivalent about this individual. On the one hand, they possess superstar qualities that inspire respect such as being capable and skilled, experienced and effective, creative and confident, influential and full of energy. On the other hand, they come across as unpleasant, ruthless, competitive, selfish, dominant, and dishonest. The alliance manager is likely torn: choosing to enter a collaboration with this superstar promises to be associated with sizeable returns given the qualities they bring to the table; yet, it also entails a high level of risk (since their intentions are not to be trusted) and requires considerable effort (given that they are dominant and unpleasant). The alliance manager likely feels a mix of respect and wariness coupled with a strong intuition to not ignore the nagging feeling signaling the threat of selfish and opportunistic behavior (Cuddy et al., 2008). The global impression formed is predominantly negative: the information signaling a potential partner's selfishness and likely opportunistic behavior (low warmth) is weighted more heavily in the global impression than the positive competence information (Abele & Wojciszke, 2014; Fiske et al., 2007). This is because negative evaluations on the warmth dimension are assumed to be diagnostic of who the person is (a person who acts dishonestly even once is a dishonest person) and, therefore, present a greater threat to the self, especially if the other is not only untrustworthy in their intentions but also highly competent (Kenworthy & Tausch, 2008; Skowronski & Carlston, 1989).

Generally, people prefer working with those who are both competent and warm and are less inclined to work with those who are competent, yet selfish and obnoxious (Casciaro & Lobo, 2008; Fiske et al., 2007). Yet, the attractiveness of the *smartass* as a potential collaboration partner will depend on whether the alliance manager values both warmth and competence in a partner or whether she deems competence to be sufficient. Alliance managers who are older or more experienced (vs. younger or less experienced) will see this type of collaboration partner as unattractive (Garbers & Konradt, 2014). They know that successful collaboration not only requires high competence, but also the pursuit of shared goals, refraining from opportunistic behavior, a will to sacrifice short-term selfish benefits for long-term alliance goals, honesty, and cooperation. Even if the individual has the requisite competence to create value in the project, the risk and effort involved in working with them is too high.

However, under certain circumstances, the potential benefits of high competence may overshadow the threat associated with selfishness and opportunistic behavior. If the alliance manager is younger or inexperienced (Garbers & Konradt, 2014), has high status (Cislak, 2013), feels a high sense of power/control or thrives on risk-taking (Fast, Gruenfeld, Sivanathan, & Galinsky, 2009), the threat posed by potential partner selfishness will be less salient than the potential benefits associated with their superior capabilities. Also, if the alliance manager has an instrumental mindset (i.e., thinks in an instrumental, calculated strategic fashion) and sees potential personal benefits (e.g., an internal promotion, a large bonus) in being associated with this individual or their firm, they will place a greater emphasis on their competence than on their selfishness or unpleasantness (Belmi & Pfeffer, 2018). This preference for a partner who is highly competent, yet ruthless and selfish is likely to be stronger if the focal alliance manager's firm has an individualistic, performance-oriented culture (Cameron & Freeman, 1991) where competitiveness and individual achievements are emphasized and valued.

It is likely that the predominantly negative impression formed of the potential partner firm's representative will also transfer to the impression formed of the firm: whereas, it has superior resources and capabilities to contribute to value creation in an alliance, its intentions are untrustworthy and the risk of opportunistic behavior is high. Its attractiveness as a potential partner will depend on a number of things. First, if other potential partner firms have been identified that are both trustworthy and have the required capabilities for value creation, those will automatically be more attractive. Second, the attractiveness of the firm as a potential partner is also shaped by the alliance manager's preference: "Does she value both warmth and competence, or does competence overshadow the potential threat involved in working with a partner whose intentions can't be trusted?" An alliance manager valuing both warmth and competence in a partner firm, will be sensitive to the high stakes of making either an error of commission (i.e., entering an alliance with a competent, yet untrustworthy partner and thereby incurring a financial loss due to partner opportunistic behavior) or an error of omission (i.e., missing the opportunity to enter an alliance with a competent and trustworthy partner and thereby forfeiting a financial gain resulting from a successful alliance). She is likely to devote special effort and care to form an accurate impression (Carrier, Dompnier, & Yzerbyt, 2019) of this firm, by displaying heightened sensitivity to and engaging in an effortful search for disambiguating information: third-party information signaling the firm's (un)trustworthiness. Depending on whether this additional information disconfirms or confirms the initial low trustworthiness assessment, the potential partner firm will be deemed more or less attractive. In contrast, an alliance manager that deems the benefits associated with competence in a partner firm to be more important than the threat of potential opportunistic behavior, will likely see this firm as an attractive partner. She is likely to engage in a motivated information search by investing effort in selectively heeding third-party information that confirms their beliefs about the firm's unique capabilities and potential for value creation, while discounting or neglecting information signaling the firm's potential lack of trustworthiness:

> **Proposition 6:** *The impact of low warmth and high competence evaluations of a potential partner firm's representative on the firm's attractiveness and*

potential to be selected as a partner depends on (a) the availability of more attractive partnering options and (b) the focal alliance manager's preference for both high warmth and high competence vs. high competence alone.

If the two firms enter an alliance, the evaluation of the partner firm's representative as being high in competence-based trustworthiness sets positive expectations regarding their future performance and will favor the development of competence-based trust. Their being seen as low in goodwill-based trustworthiness sets negative expectations regarding their intentions and will hamper the development of goodwill-based trust. Changing this initial negative assessment of the individual's trustworthiness will be difficult, even if it was initially biased. Even if their future behavior is friendly, honest, cooperative, this initial assessment of low warmth will be largely resistant to change, given that warmth information is seen as highly diagnostic of who the person is (Skowronski & Carlston, 1989). A person seen as cold will continue to be seen as unfriendly and untrustworthy, despite acting in ways that communicate trustworthiness. Positive deviations from the initial assessment are explained by situational demands: after all, even dishonest people can be nice, if it suits them.

Proposition 7: *Low warmth and high competence evaluations of a potential partner firm's representative will hamper the development of goodwill-based interpersonal trust but will set the foundation for the development of competence-based interpersonal trust.*

Whereas in the short term, working with a highly competent partner might be instrumental and deliver tangible benefits, over time, a lack of goodwill-based trust could lead to a high level of perceived relational risk. This could result in more control-based alliance governance mechanisms and may hamper the development of interorganizational trust. In the long term, potentially opportunistic partner behavior could lead to information hoarding or stealing, conflict, ineffective resolution of mixed-motive situations, the premature disbanding of the alliance, and financial losses.

In sum, evaluating a potential partner firm's representative as high in competence and low in warmth results in a predominantly negative impression of the individual. The impact of the high competence and low warmth evaluation of the boundary-spanner on the firm's attractiveness and likelihood to be selected as a partner depends on the availability of more attractive potential partner firms and on the focal alliance manager's preference for both warmth and competence vs. competence alone. If the two firms enter an alliance, goodwill-based interpersonal trust will be difficult to develop, which may also hamper the development of interorganizational trust.

The Nitwit

An alliance manager that judges a potential partner firm's representative as high in warmth yet as low in competence has a mixed opinion of this individual. On the one hand, they are good-natured, trustworthy, friendly, and sincere. On the other hand, they are neither capable nor skilled, are inexperienced and lack the necessary drive and influence to be able to positively contribute to value creation in the alliance. The alliance manager likely feels a mix of pity and sympathy coupled with a lack of respect (Fiske et al., 2007). The global impression is predominantly positive given that the person is likeable and trustworthy (Abele & Wojciszke, 2014; Fiske et al., 2007). In a personal context, the alliance manager might feel inclined to socialize with or help this person. Yet, in a work context, especially in the context of choosing a suitable partner to create joint value in a strategic innovation alliance, competence is required. Whereas she might trust this person and enjoy working with them, choosing them as a collaboration partner would neither be wise nor instrumental to achieving alliance goals. Research indeed suggests that, in interdependent work contexts, people value competence in others and choose to work with colleagues that can contribute to mutually shared goals (Abele & Wojciszke, 2007; Porter & Rigby, 2019).

It is likely that the assessment of high warmth and low competence associated with the potential partner firm's boundary spanner will transfer to the impression formed of the firm. The focal alliance manager is likely to see the potential firm as embodying the characteristics associated with their representative: trustworthy yet lacking the drive and internal capabilities necessary to contribute to value creation in the alliance. Depending on the extent to which the focal alliance manager likes and is personally motivated to work with or help the representative of the potential partner firm, she might engage in a more thorough third-party information search to find potential evidence signaling the firm's competence and capabilities in an attempt to disconfirm their initial low competence assessment of the firm. Unless strong and credible evidence to overrule this initial impression emerges, the firm's perceived attractiveness and potential to be selected as a partner is low:

> **Proposition 8:** *High warmth and low competence evaluations of a potential partner firm's representative negatively influence the firm's attractiveness and potential to be selected as a partner.*

If the two firms enter an alliance, the evaluation of the partner firm's representative as being high in goodwill-based trustworthiness sets positive expectations regarding their intentions and will set the foundation for the development of goodwill-based trust. Their being assessed as low in competence-based trustworthiness sets negative expectations regarding their future performance and will hamper the development of competence-based trust. Although initial negative assessments of competence may be biased, they generally tend to be accurate given that they rely on relatively objective sources of information (Kenworthy & Tausch, 2008). Yet, they are less resistant to change than low warmth evaluations; there is potential for them to be overturned with repeated interactions (Skowronski & Carlston, 1989):

> **Proposition 9:** *High warmth and low competence evaluations of a potential partner firm's representative will set the foundation for the development of goodwill-based interpersonal trust but will hamper the development of competence-based interpersonal trust.*

Over time, the development of interpersonal goodwill-based trust could bode well for effective coordination, open communication, and shared decision making processes, creating a sense of loyalty and cooperation, reducing the risk of opportunistic behavior, facilitating mutual knowledge sharing and effective conflict management. Yet, if the partner's boundary-spanner doesn't have the requisite skills to effectively manage the alliance or lacks the internal clout and influence to push initiatives through in their home organization, this can result not only in frustration but also ineffective alliance management, potentially threatening its viability.

In sum, evaluating a potential partner firm's representative as low in competence and high in warmth results in a predominantly positive impression of the individual. The inferred lack of competence renders the individual unattractive as a potential collaboration partner. All other things being equal, this assessment will be negatively related to the firm's attractiveness and to its potential to be selected as an alliance partner. If the two firms enter an alliance, goodwill-based interpersonal trust is likely to develop yet competence-based interpersonal trust is unlikely to form.

CONCLUSION

We argue that a micro-foundational approach focusing on the psychological processes underlying alliance managers' evaluations of potential partner suitability in the alliance formation phase is indispensable for an adequate understanding of partner selection processes, and ultimately might also prove informative for effective alliance management. We draw upon work in social cognition and organizational behavior and present a framework identifying two key dimensions (warmth and competence) used by alliance managers to evaluate potential partner firm's trustworthiness and suitability based on their interactions with the individuals representing these firms. We advance specific propositions linking initial evaluations of potential partner firms' representatives to firm attractiveness, selection and the development of interpersonal trust as a precursor of interorganizational trust.

As stated previously, our discussion of alliance managers' evaluations of potential partners' suitability in the alliance formation phase is not meant to be exhaustive, but we hope to have underscored the importance of acknowledging and accommodating for the potential impact of psychological processes in the study of strategic innovation alliances. Certainly, other factors such as market conditions, strategic alignment, resource complementarity, and compatibility at the firm level affect partner attractiveness and selection. Although different authors may stress the importance of one factor over the others, it is critical to think of them as being interlocking parts of a larger system and not as stand-alone issues that can be addressed in isolation. Therefore, we deem it important to also focus on the potential impact that micro-foundational processes may have on macro-level processes such as partner selection or effective alliance management. As such, we hope to have opened an avenue for alliance researchers to also consider the potential effects of micro-foundational processes and test our propositions within comprehensive, empirical settings.

REFERENCES

Abele, A. E., & Wojciszke, B. (2007). Agency and communion from the perspective of self versus others. *Journal of Personality and Social Psychology, 93*(5), 751–763.

Abele, A. E., & Wojciszke, B. (2014). Communal and agentic content in social cognition: A dual perspective model. In J. M. Olson, & M. P. Zanna (Eds.), *Advances in experimental social psychology* (Vol. 50; pp. 195–255), San Diego, CA: Elsevier Academic Press.

Abele, A. E., Cuddy, A. J. C., Judd, C. M., & Yzerbyt, V. (2008). Fundamental dimensions of social judgment. *European Journal of Social Psychology, 38*(7), 1063–1065.

Ahuja, G., Soda, G., & Zaheer, A. (2012). The genesis and dynamics of organizational networks. *Organization Science, 23*(2), 434–448.

Albers, S., Wohlgezogen, F., & Zajac, E. J. (2016). Strategic alliance structures: An organization design perspective. *Journal of Management, 42*(3), 582–614.

Anderson, C., & Brion, S. (2014). Perspectives on power in organizations. *Annual Review of Organizational Psychology and Organizational Behavior, 1*(1), 67–97.

Anderson, C., & Kilduff, G. J. (2009). The pursuit of status in social groups. *Current Directions in Psychological Science, 18*(5), 295–298.

Ariño, A., de la Torre, J., & Ring, P. S. (2001). Relational quality: Managing trust in corporate alliances. *California Management Review, 44*(1), 109–131.

Ariño, A., Ragozzino, R., & Reuer, J. J. (2008). Alliance dynamics for entrepreneurial firms. *The Journal of Management Studies, 45*(1), 147–168.

Bakan, D. (1966). *The duality of human existence: Essays on psychology and religion.* Chicago, IL: Rand McNally.

Bamford, J., Gomes-Casseres, B., & Robinson, M. (2004). *Mastering alliance strategies.* San Francisco, CA: Jossey-Bass.

Barney, J., & Felin, T. (2013). What are microfoundations? *Academy of Management Perspectives, 27*(2), 138–155.

Barrick, M. R., Schaffer, J. A., & DeGrassi, S. W. (2009). What you see may not be what you get: Relationships among self-presentation tactics and ratings of interview and job performance. *Journal of Applied Psychology, 94*(6), 1394–1411.

Barrick, M. R., Stewart, G. L., Neubert, M. J., & Mount, M. K. (1998). Relating member ability and personality to work-team processes and team effectiveness. *Journal of Applied Psychology, 83*(3), 377–391.

Belmi, P., & Pfeffer, J. (2018). The effect of economic consequences on social judgment and choice: Reward interdependence and the preference for sociability versus competence. *Journal of Organizational Behavior, 39*(8), 990–1007.

Brambilla, M., & Leach, C. W. (2014). On the importance of being moral: The distinctive role of morality in social judgment. *Social Cognition, 32*(4), 397–408.

Brambilla, M., Sacchi, S., Castellini, F., & Riva, P. (2010). The effects of status on perceived warmth and competence: Malleability of the relationship between status and stereotype content. *Social Psychology, 41*(2), 82–87.

Cameron, K. S., & Freeman, S. J. (1991). Cultural congruence, strength, and type: Relationships to effectiveness. *Research in Organizational Change and Development, 5,* 23–58.

Carrier, A., Dompnier, B., & Yzerbyt, V. (2019). Of nice and mean: The personal relevance of others' competence drives perceptions of warmth. *Personality and Social Psychology Bulletin, 45*(11), 1549–1562.

Cartwright, S., & Cooper, C. L. (2011). *Managing mergers, acquisitions, and strategic alliances: Integrating people and cultures* (2nd ed.). Abingdon, England: Routledge.

Casciaro, T., Barsade, S. G., Edmondson, A. C., Gibson, C. B., Krackhardt, D., & Labianca, G. (2015). The integration of psychological and network perspectives in organizational scholarship. *Organization Science, 26*(4), 1162–1176.

Casciaro, T., & Lobo, M. S. (2008). When competence is irrelevant: The role of interpersonal affect in task-related ties. *Administrative Science Quarterly, 53*(4), 655–684.

Cislak, A. (2013). Effects of power on social perception: All your boss can see is agency. *Social Psychology, 44*(2), 139–147.

Colquitt, J. A., Scott, B. A., & LePine, J. A. (2007). Trust, trustworthiness, and trust propensity: A meta-analytic test of their unique relationships with risk taking and job performance. *Journal of Applied Psychology, 92*(4), 909–927.

Costa, A. C., Fulmer, C. A., & Anderson, N. R. (2018). Trust in work teams: An integrative review, multilevel model, and future directions. *Journal of Organizational Behavior, 39*(2), 169–184.

Cuddy, A. J. C., Fiske, S. T., & Glick, P. (2008). Warmth and competence as universal dimensions of social perception: The stereotype content model and the BIAS Map. In M. P. Zanna (Ed.), *Advances in experimental social psychology* (Vol. 40; pp. 61–149). San Diego, CA: Elsevier Academic Press.

Cuddy, A. J. C., Glick, P., & Beninger, A. (2011). The dynamics of warmth and competence judgments and their outcomes in organizations. *Research in Organizational Behavior, 31*, 73–98.

Cullen, J. B., Johnson, J. L., & Sakano, T. (2000). Success through commitment and trust: The soft side of strategic alliance management. *Journal of World Business, 35*(3), 223–240.

Cummings, J. L., & Holmberg, S. R. (2012). Best-fit alliance partners: The use of critical success factors in a comprehensive partner selection process. *Long Range Planning, 45*(2/3), 136–159.

Currall, S. C., & Judge, T. A. (1995). Measuring trust between organizational boundary role persons. *Organizational Behavior and Human Decision Processes, 64*(2), 151–170.

Das, T. K., & Teng, B. (1998). Between trust and control: Developing confidence in partner cooperation in alliances. *Academy of Management Review, 23*(3), 491–512.

Das, T. K., & Teng, B. (1999). Managing risks in strategic alliances. *Academy of Management Executive, 13*(4), 50–62.

Das, T. K., & Teng, B. (2000). A resource-based theory of strategic alliances. *Journal of Management, 26*(1), 31–61.

Das, T. K., & Teng, B. (2001). Trust, control, and risk in strategic alliances: An integrated framework. *Organization Studies, 22*(2), 251–283.

De Man, A-P., & Roijakkers, N. (2009). Alliance governance: Balancing control and trust in dealing with risk. *Long Range Planning, 42*(1), 75–95.

DeBruine, L. M. (2002). Facial resemblance enhances trust. *Proceedings of the Royal Society Biological Sciences, 269*(1498), 1307–1312.

Dekker, H. C. (2008). Partner selection and governance design in interfirm relationships. *Accounting, Organizations and Society, 33*(7/8), 915–941.

Delgado, M. R., Frank, R. H., & Phelps, E. A. (2005). Perceptions of moral character modulate the neural systems of reward during the trust game. *Nature Neuroscience, 8*(11), 1611–1618.

Dev, C. S., Klein, S., & Fisher, R. A. (1996). A market-based approach for partner selection in marketing alliances. *Journal of Travel Research, 35*(1), 11–17.

Duisters, D., Duysters, G. M., & De Man, A-P. (2011). The partner selection process: Steps, effectiveness, governance. *International Journal of Strategic Business Alliances, 2*(1/2), 7–25.

Emden, Z., Calantone, R. J., & Droge, C. (2006). Collaborating for new product development: Selecting the partner with maximum potential to create value. *Journal of Product Innovation Management, 23*(4), 330–341.

Fast, N. J., Gruenfeld, D. H., Sivanathan, N., & Galinsky, A. D. (2009). Illusory control: A generative force behind power's far-reaching effects. *Psychological Science, 20*(4), 502–508.

Felin, T., Foss, N. J., & Ployhart, R. E. (2015). The microfoundations movement in strategy and organization theory. *Academy of Management Annals, 9*(1), 575–632.

Fiske, S. T. (2018). Stereotype content: Warmth and competence endure. *Current Directions in Psychological Science, 27*(2), 67–73.

Fiske, S. T., Cuddy, A. J. C., & Glick, P. (2007). Universal dimensions of social cognition: Warmth and competence. *Trends in Cognitive Sciences, 11*(2), 77–83.

Fiske, S. T., Cuddy, A. J. C., Glick, P., & Xu, J. (2002). A model of (often mixed) stereotype content: Competence and warmth respectively follow from the perceived status and competition. *Journal of Personality and Social Psychology, 82*(6), 878–902.

Foss, N. J. (2011). Invited editorial: Why micro-foundations for resource-based theory are needed and what they may look like. *Journal of Management, 37*(5), 1413–1428.

Foss, N. J., Husted, K., & Michailova, S. (2010). Governing knowledge sharing in organizations: Levels of analysis, governance mechanisms, and research directions. *Journal of Management Studies, 47*(3), 455–482.

Fournier, S., & Alvarez, C. (2012). Brands as relationship partners: Warmth, competence, and in-between. *Journal of Consumer Psychology, 22*(2), 177–185.

Fransen, K., Delvaux, E., Mesquita, B., & Van Puyenbroeck, S. (2018). The emergence of shared leadership in newly formed teams with an initial structure of vertical leadership: A longitudinal analysis. *Journal of Applied Behavioral Science, 54*(2), 140–170.

Fulmer, C. A., & Gelfand, M. J. (2012). At what level (and in whom) we trust: Trust across multiple organizational levels. *Journal of Management, 38*(4), 1167–1230.

Furnham, A., Richards, S. C., & Paulhus, D. L. (2013). The dark triad of personality: A 10 year review. *Social and Personality Psychology Compass, 7*(3), 199–216.

Garbers, Y., & Konradt, U. (2014). The effect of financial incentives on performance: A quantitative review of individual and team-based financial incentives. *Journal of Occupational and Organizational Psychology, 87*(1), 102–137.

Gulati, R. (1998). Alliances and networks. *Strategic Management Journal, 19*(4), 293–317.

Gulati, R., Wohlgezogen, F., & Zhelyazkov, P. (2012). The two facets of collaboration: Cooperation and coordination in strategic alliances. *The Academy of Management Annals, 6*(1), 531–583.

Gundlach, G. T., Achrol, R. S., & Mentzer, J. T. (1995). The structure of commitment in exchange. *Journal of Marketing 59*(1), 78–92.

Hagedoorn, J. (1993). Understanding the rationale of strategic technology partnering: Interorganizational modes of cooperation and sectoral differences. *Strategic Management Journal, 14*(5), 371–385.

Hamel, G. (1991). Competition for competence and interpartner learning within international strategic alliances. *Strategic Management Journal, 12*(S1), 83–103.

Hanson, D., & Lackman, C. (1998). Managing through cultural differences. *Competitiveness Review 8*(2), 46–54.

Haselhuhn M. P., Wong, E. M., & Ormiston, M. E. (2013). Self-fulfilling prophecies as a link between men's facial width-to-height ratio and behavior. *PLoS ONE, 8*(8), e72259.

Hinds, P. J., Carley, K. M., Krackhardt, D., & Wholey, D. (2000). Choosing work group members: Balancing similarity, competence, and familiarity. *Organizational Behavior and Human Decision Processes, 81*(2), 226–251.

Hogan, R. (1983). A socioanalytic theory of personality. In M. Page (Ed.), *Nebraska symposium on motivation* (pp. 336–355). Lincoln: University of Nebraska Press.

Holmberg, S. R., & Cummings, J. L. (2009). Building successful strategic alliances: Strategic process and analytical tool for selecting partner industries and firms. *Long Range Planning, 42*(2), 164–193.

Howe, L. C., Leibowitz, K. A., & Crum, A. J. (2019). When your doctor "gets it" and "gets you": The critical role of competence and warmth in the patient-provider interaction. *Frontiers in Psychiatry, 10*, 475.

Jonason, P. K., & Fletcher, S. A. (2018). Agentic and communal behavioral biases in the dark triad traits. *Personality and Individual Differences, 130*, 76–82.

Judd, C. M., James-Hawkins, L., Yzerbyt, V., & Kashima, Y. (2005). Fundamental dimensions of social judgment: Understanding the relations between judgments of competence and warmth. *Journal of Personality and Social Psychology, 89*(6), 899–913.

Kale, P., & Singh, H. (2009). Managing strategic alliances: What do we know and where do we go from here? *Academy of Management Journal, 23*(3), 45–62.

Kale, P., Dyer, J., & Singh, H. (2002). Alliance capability, stock market response and long-term alliance success: The role of the alliance function. *Strategic Management Journal, 23*(8), 747–767.

Kenworthy, J. B., & Tausch, N. (2008). Expectations about the accuracy and stability of warmth versus competence traits: An intergroup analysis. *European Journal of Social Psychology, 38*(7), 1121–1129.

Kervyn, N., Bergsieker, H. B., & Fiske, S. T. (2012). The innuendo effect: Hearing the positive but inferring the negative. *Journal of Experimental Social Psychology, 48*(1), 77–85.

Kraft-Todd, G. T., Reinero, D. A., Kelley, J. M., Heberlein, A. S., Baer, L., & Riess, H. (2017). Empathic nonverbal behavior increases ratings of both warmth and competence in a medical context. *PLoS ONE, 12*(5), e0177758.

Küfner, A. C., Nestler, S., & Back, M. D. (2013). The two pathways to being an (un-) popular narcissist. *Journal of Personality, 81*(2), 184–195.

Kumar, R., van Kleef, G. A., & Higgins, E. T. (2019). How emotions influence alliance relationships: The potential functionality of negative emotions. *Organizational Psychology Review, 9*(2/3), 157–183.

Lambe, C. J., Spekman, R. E., & Hunt, S. D. (2002). Alliance competence, resources, and alliance success: Conceptualization, measurement, and initial test. *Journal of the Academy of Marketing Science, 30*(2), 141–158.

Lewicki, R. J., Tomlinson, E. C., & Gillespie, N. (2006). Models of interpersonal trust development: Theoretical approaches, empirical evidence, and future directions. *Journal of Management, 32*(6), 991–1022.

Liu, Y., Sarala, R. M., Xing, Y., & Cooper, S. C. L. (2017). Human side of collaborative relationships: A microfoundational perspective. *Group and Organization Management, 42(2)*, 151–162.

Lumineau, F., & Quélin, B. V. (2012). An empirical investigation of interorganizational opportunism and contracting mechanisms. *Strategic Organization, 10*(1), 55–84.

Luvison, D., & Cummings, J. L. (2017). Decisions at the boundary: Role choice and alliance manager behaviors. *Group and Organization Management, 42(2)*, 279–309.

Marchington, M., & Vincent, S. (2004). Analyzing the influence of institutional, organizational and interpersonal forces in shaping inter-organizational relations. *Journal of Management Studies, 41*(6), 1029–1056.

Montepare, J. M., & Dobish, H. (2003). The contribution of emotion perceptions and their overgeneralizations to trait impressions. *Journal of Nonverbal Behavior, 27*(4), 237–254.

Ness, H. (2009). Governance, negotiations, and alliance dynamics: Explaining the evolution of relational practice. *Journal of Management Studies, 46*(3), 451–480.

Nickerson, R. S. (1998). Confirmation bias: A ubiquitous phenomenon in many guises. *Review of General Psychology, 2*(2), 175–220.

Nooteboom, B. (2002). *Trust: Forms, foundations, functions, failures and* figures. Cheltenham, England: Edward Elgar.

O'Boyle, E. H., Jr., Forsyth, D. R., Banks, G. C., & McDaniel, M. A. (2012). A meta-analysis of the dark triad and work behavior: A social exchange perspective. *Journal of Applied Psychology, 97*(3), 557–579.

Oyserman, D., Coon, H. M., & Kemmelmeier, M. (2002). Rethinking individualism and collectivism: Evaluation of theoretical assumptions and meta-analyses. *Psychological Bulletin, 128*(1), 3–72.

Pangarkar, N. (2003). Determinants of alliance duration in uncertain environments: The case of the biotechnology sector. *Long Range Planning, 36*(3), 269–284.

Paulhus, D. L., & Trapnell, P. D. (2008). Self-presentation of personality: An agency-communion framework. In O. P. John, R. W. Robins, & L. A. Pervin (Eds.), *Handbook of personality psychology: Theory and research* (pp. 492–517). New York, NY: Guilford Press.

Paulhus, D. L., & Williams, K. M., (2002). The dark triad of personality: Narcissism, machiavellianism, and psychopathy. *Journal of Research in Personality, 36*(6), 556–563.

Peeters, G., & Czapinski, J. (1990). Positive-negative asymmetry in evaluations: The distinction between affective and informational negative effects. In W. Stroebe, & M. Hewstone (Eds.), *European review of social psychology* (Vol. 1; pp. 33–60). London, England: Wiley.

Porter, C. M., & Rigby, J. R. (2019). Relationship context and personality shape people's preferences for network relationship partners. *Personal Relationships, 26*(2), 310–330.

Porter, C. M., & Woo, S. E. (2015). Untangling the networking phenomenon: A dynamic psychological perspective on how and why people network. *Journal of Management, 41*(5), 1477–1500.

Rosenberg, S., Nelson, C., & Vivekananthan, P. S. (1968). A multidimensional approach to the structure of personality impressions. *Journal of Personality and Social Psychology, 9*(4), 283–294.

Schilke, O., & Cook, K. S. (2013). A cross-level process theory of trust development in interorganizational relationships. *Strategic Organization, 11*(3), 281–303.

Schlenker, B. R. (2012). Self-presentation. In M. R. Leary, & J. P. Tangney (Eds.), *Handbook of self and identity* (pp. 542–570). New York, NY: Guilford Press.

Schreiner, M., Kale, P., & Corsten, D. (2009). What really is alliance management capability and how does it impact alliance outcomes and success? *Strategic Management Journal, 30*(13), 1395–1419.

Schweitzer, M. E., Hershey, J. C., & Bradlow, E. T. (2006). Promises and lies: Restoring violated trust. *Organizational Behavior and Human Decision Processes, 101*(1), 1–19.

Senge, P. M. (1990). *The fifth discipline: The art and practice of the learning organization.* New York, NY: Doubleday/Currency.

Shah, R. H., & Swaminathan, V. (2008). Factors influencing partner selection in strategic alliances: The moderating role of alliance context. *Strategic Management Journal, 29*(5), 471–494.

Sivadas, E., & Dwyer, F. R. (2000). An examination of organizational factors influencing new product success in internal and alliance-based processes. *Journal of Marketing, 64*(1), 31–49.

Skowronski, J. J., & Carlston, D. E. (1989). Negativity and extremity biases in impression formation: A review of explanations. *Psychological Bulletin, 105*(1), 131–142.

Spekman, R. E., Isabella, L. A., MacAvoy, T. C., & Forbes, T. I. (1996). Creating strategic alliances which endure. *Long Range Planning, 29*(3), 346–357.

Steinel, W., & De Dreu, C. K. W. (2004). Social motives and strategic misrepresentation in social decision making. *Journal of Personality and Social Psychology, 86*(3), 419–434.

Steinmetz, J. (2018). Impression (mis)management when communicating success. *Basic and Applied Social Psychology, 40*(5), 320–328.

Tse, D. K., Francis, J., & Walls, J. (1994). Cultural differences in conducting intra- and inter-cultural negotiations: A Sino- Canadian comparison. *Journal of International Business Studies 25*(3), 537–555.

Uleman, J. S., Adil Saribay, S., & Gonzalez, C. M. (2008). Spontaneous inferences, implicit impressions, and implicit theories. *Annual Review of Psychology, 59*, 329–360.

Van Lange, P. A. M., & Kuhlman, D. M. (1994). Social value orientations and impressions of partner's honesty and intelligence: A test of the might versus morality effect. *Journal of Personality and Social Psychology, 67*(1), 126–141.

Van't Wout, M., & Sanfey, A. G. (2008). Friend or foe: The effect of implicit trustworthiness judgments in social decision-making. *Cognition, 108*(3), 796–803.

Williams, L. A., & Bartlett, M. Y. (2015). Warm thanks: Gratitude expression facilitates social affiliation in new relationships via perceived warmth. *Emotion, 15*(1), 1–5.

Willis, J., & Todorov, A. (2006). First impressions: Making up your mind after a 100-ms exposure to a face. *Psychological Science, 17*(7), 592–598.

Wojciszke, B. (2005). Morality and competence in person- and self-perception. *European Review of Social Psychology, 16*(1), 155–188.

Wojciszke, B., Abele, A. E., & Baryla, W. (2009). Two dimensions of interpersonal attitudes: Liking depends on communion, respect depends on agency. *European Journal of Social Psychology, 39*(6), 973–990.

Zaheer, A., McEvily, B., & Perrone, V. (1998). Does trust matter? Exploring the effects of interorganizational and interpersonal trust on performance. *Organization Science 9*(2), 141–159.

Zebrowitz, L. A. (2017). First impressions from faces. *Current Directions in Psychological Science, 26*(3), 237–242.

Zebrowitz, L. A., Fellous, J. M., Mignault, A., & Andreoletti, C. (2003). Trait impressions as overgeneralized responses to adaptively significant facial qualities: Evidence from connectionist modeling. *Personality and Social Psychology Review, 7*(3), 194–215.

CHAPTER 3

MANAGING INTERPARTNER HARMONY IN STRATEGIC ALLIANCES

T. K. Das
Rajesh Kumar

ABSTRACT

We propose a framework to understand interpartner harmony in strategic alliances. Interpartner harmony in strategic alliances denotes the mutual understanding that alliance members accomplish by managing commitment and forbearance in the context of their interdependence. We proceed from the notion that the pervasive conflict-based view of alliances has clouded the consideration of the quest for harmony as a significant factor in alliance dynamics. We believe that alliances have an inbuilt resilience that makes the emergence of harmony a natural outcome, through the joint exercise of commitment and forbearance, even as conflict and opportunism persist as inevitable challenges. We describe the four kinds of interpartner harmony in alliances—superficial, specious, constrained, and communal—based on the degrees of commitment and forbearance. We also discuss the salience of each of these interpartner harmony types in the three principal types of alliances (equity joint ventures, minority equity alliances, and nonequity alli-

Managing the Partners in Strategic Alliances, pages 51–84

ances). Implications of the analysis are discussed for further research as well as managerial practice.

INTRODUCTION

The globalization of markets and technological advances have combined to heighten the interdependence among business firms. This interdependence is prominently reflected in the rapidly growing number of strategic alliances, which can range from joint R&D to equity-based joint ventures. Inevitably, partner firms in alliances need to effectively control the ever-present potential for interpartner conflict and decide upon the level of their own commitment in the alliances. The management of interdependence also necessitates negotiations, whereby alliance partners seek to resolve the incompatibility of their goals. The backdrop to such negotiations may be contentious or harmonious, depending on the motivations of the alliance partners and the strategies they employ to manage conflict. Scholars note that failure rates in strategic alliances, excluding pre-determined terminations, are as high as 50% or more (Das & Teng, 2000). It has also been argued that conflicts in alliances are a result of the inherent opportunistic tendencies of partner firms.

We contend that the same motivation that prompts the formation of alliances among firms engenders the quest for interpartner harmony. Whereas alliances are fraught with potential and actual conflict between the partners, it nevertheless remains true that the foundation of the relationship is one of cooperation and harmony. In other words, although conflicts do happen in the warp and woof of interactions between partners in the normal course of alliance functioning, the original motivation to cooperate in conditions of harmony remains pervasive. How else is it that strategic alliances survive despite the acknowledged endemic conflicts among alliance partners? Our thesis is that alliances persist despite conflicts because there is the foundational attribute of interpartner harmony. The fact that such conflicts lead to alliance failures—in substantial numbers too—does not negate the existence and potency of the quest for interpartner harmony.

Although it would be simplistic to deny the presence of opportunism among alliance partners (Das & Rahman, 2009), it needs to be acknowledged that opportunistic inclinations are neither always present in interorganizational interactions nor always a contributor to conflicts among alliance partners (e.g., Chen, Peng, & Saparito, 2002; Park & Ungson, 2001; Zajac & Olsen, 1993). Furthermore, even if opportunistic inclinations are present, scholars note that their impact is often mitigated by the presence of control systems (Das, 2005; Das & Rahman, 2001, 2002). For instance, Coletti, Sedatole, and Towry (2005) demonstrate, through experimental simulations, that control systems can facilitate collaboration provided that the participants are able to witness the cooperative benefits of control systems. Hence, whereas one cannot deny the potential for opportunism, it would be equally unrealistic to suggest that alliance dynamics necessarily and always involve the presence of opportunism. This suggests that conflict may be less prevalent than is generally assumed, given that the disposition of alliance members is ordinarily one of seeking harmony through reciprocal commitment. In related research, scholars have also drawn a distinction between weak and strong reciprocity (e.g., Kahan, 2003). Weak reciprocators are concerned only with maximizing their own gain whereas strong reciprocators demonstrate a much higher level of commitment. As Kahan (2003) notes, strong reciprocators "will condition their contribution to collective goods on the contributions of others even in fleeting transactions with multiple actors whose behavior they cannot keep track of and whose identities they can't even discern" (p. 73).

We divide the remainder of the chapter into several parts. We begin by noting that harmony in alliances is often given less attention than conflict in the literature. Second, we discuss the conflict-based view that pervades a good part of the alliance literature. Third, we briefly assess the interdisciplinary literature on harmony. Fourth, we put forward the concept of interpartner harmony in strategic alliances and suggest a definition. We next propose that interpartner harmony comprise both commitment and forbearance, and follow up with a four-part typology of interpartner harmony in strategic alliances. We also comment on the nature of interpartner harmony in different types of alliances. We conclude with suggestions for further research and discuss the implications of our analysis here for practice, suggesting ways to foster and manage greater interpartner harmony in alliances.

Conflict and Harmony

The idea that harmony may be more prevalent in alliances than is traditionally assumed is supported by both qualitative studies of alliances (e.g., Frey & Schlosser, 1993; Korine, Asakawa, & Gomez, 2002; Yoshino & Fagan, 2003) and a few theoretical contributions to the literature (e.g., Zajac & Olsen, 1993). Yoshino and Fagan (2003) provide an illuminating case study of the alliance between Renault and Nissan that by all accounts is doing fairly well. The success of the alliance is well captured in a quote by Carlos Ghosn, the president and CEO of Nissan Motors:

> In the alliance our principle is not to impose things. You have to create the eagerness in each company to boost their performance. And when this ea-

> gerness is strong enough, then Nissan people will go by themselves to see what Renault is doing, and vice-versa. Everything which is imposed has limits. Everything which comes from eagerness and motivation from people, has no limits. (Yoshino & Fagan, 2003, p. 15)

Although case studies may not capture the full range of characteristics of alliances in general, they provide us with a reasonable basis to raise some issues. First, if conflict is assumed to be such a major aspect of alliances, why is it the case that the companies continue to form these alliances? Ireland, Hitt, and Vaidyanath (2002) note that "more than 80% of surveyed top level managers view strategic alliances as a primary growth vehicle" (p. 439). Consistent with this, an experimental study involving MBA students by Dollinger, Golden, and Saxton (1997) demonstrated that decision makers are not averse to forming alliances with competitors even though this may potentially lead to loss of confidential and sensitive information.

Secondly, the level of conflict in alliances may not necessarily be higher than what one might encounter in other intraorganizational or interorganizational interactions. Finally, conflicts in alliances, as and when they occur, are not necessarily intractable. A shadow of the future, the presence of an intermediary, and competitive pressures, may all induce the alliance firms to contain conflicts. The firms are likely to be concerned about their reputation and the economic value that may be at stake in the alliance, creating pressures for maintaining harmony through judicious commitment and overlooking their partners' indiscretions. For example, evidence from buyer–seller relationships suggests that not all contractual violations are necessarily detrimental to the relationship (Kingshott, 2006).

Furthermore, not all such conflicts are rooted in self-interested partner behavior, because some may spring from elements of national and organizational cultures, different goals, and, more broadly, in the inherent complexities of managing an alliance (Das & Teng, 2000). The view that we wish to advance in this chapter is that while conflict may very well be an inevitable by-product of interdependence among alliance members, and while interdependence clearly has the potential for creating dissatisfaction and resentment toward one's partner, such conflict is not necessarily overwhelming, or always predominant, in strategic alliances.

Scholars point out that interdependence has consequences not only for immediate behavior and outcomes but also for future behavior and outcomes, and this temporal linkage may also shape actors' behavior (Rusbult & Van Lange, 2003). We know that when partners enter into a relationship they exchange information, technologies, personnel, and so on. These exchanges may engender reciprocal behavior, strengthening the relationship among the partner firms (Cropanzano & Mitchell, 2005). Over time the ensuing relationship may influence the pattern of subsequent exchanges.

In other words, we would suggest that there are built-in mechanisms that fortify the alliance relationship. Alliances are thus also the arena where partners seek to foster conditions of harmony even though that endeavor is not always explicitly or publicly evident or always successful. It is this theme of seeking harmony, even if in silence or unacknowledged, that we wish to explore and develop here, considering interpartner harmony in terms of the mutual understanding that alliance members accomplish by managing commitment and forbearance in the context of their interdependence. It is also worth pointing out at the outset that from our perspective harmony is a state that emerges from the commitment and forbearance of the alliance partners and the manner in which conflict is managed. Harmony and conflict are therefore different constructs, with harmony representing a higher order construct vis-à-vis conflict.

The Conflict-Based Perspective of Alliances

A selective review of the vast literature on strategic alliances seems to suggest that most authors recognize the potential for conflict in alliances (see Table 3.1). While many do recognize that conflictful and harmonious dispositions may coexist, very few consider the fact that the desire for harmony may be a strong orientation. As Zajac and Olson (1993) put it,

> Firms involved in a joint venture, for example, while obviously interested in satisfying their own interests, are also interested in maintaining the co-operative arrangement to satisfy these interests—which requires some consideration of the satisfaction of their partner's valued interests. (p. 134)

The disposition to collaborate in harmony even in the presence of dissatisfaction is not simply motivated by the costs of terminating a relationship, even though that may be a factor. We would suggest that the threshold for

TABLE 3.1 The Conflict Perspective in Strategic Alliances

Authors	Illustrative Observations	Remarks
Das & Teng (1998)	"Scholars often cite a lack of cooperation and the opportunistic behavior of partners as causes for the relatively high rate of failure of alliances" (p. 491). "Firms in alliances tend to be more confident about partner cooperation when they feel they have an adequate level of control over their partners" (p. 493).	The perception of potential opportunistic behavior may be mitigated by confidence building measures like communication, risk taking, equity preservation and interfirm adaptation.

(continued)

TABLE 3.1 The Conflict Perspective in Strategic Alliances (Continued)

Authors	Illustrative Observations	Remarks
Das & Teng (2000)	"A balance between cooperation and competition is what importantly contributes to an enduring alliance" (p. 86). "All in all, the internal tensions perspective helps us understand that the inherent instabilities of strategic alliances spring from the difficult challenge of balancing many competing forces simultaneously" (p. 94).	There is a natural opposition between cooperation and competition in an alliance.
Gould et al. (1999)	"A potential exists therefore in all alliances that they may have destructive characteristics, as new relationships supplant and destroy cherished, well established, and familiar ones" (p. 701). "In sum we argue that the organizational configuration of the Design Group was a defensive structural enactment of the deep ambivalence the partners felt about the joint venture. Needing the relationship, but fearing it as well, they created a compromised and a flawed structure which sustained the illusion for each of them of having it both ways—that is, they could simultaneously have a partnership, but invest little in it, and thereby maintain the belief that they could easily go their separate ways if it came to that" (p. 719).	The initiation of new relationships is fraught with ambiguity and tension and the latent tension, if not appropriately managed, may exacerbate conflict among partners.
Gulati & Singh (1998)	"While appropriation concerns originating from contracting obstacles, coupled with behavioral uncertainty, can clearly be an important concern, once firms decide to enter an alliance there is another set of concerns that arise from anticipated coordination costs" (p. 782). "Firms choose governance structures both to manage anticipated coordination costs and to address appropriation concerns. This finding is consistent with our belief that hierarchical controls are more than mechanisms to control opportunism and provide incentive alignment across partners; they also provide an organizational context that determines the rules of the game and creates an administrative structure within which the partnership proceeds" (p. 811).	The concerns in an alliance may well shift over time but motivational disposition, be it one of conflict or harmony, remains critical during all stages of the alliance life cycle.

(continued)

TABLE 3.1 The Conflict Perspective in Strategic Alliances (Continued)

Authors	Illustrative Observations	Remarks
Kale et al. (2000)	"Conflict is inherent in alliances because of partner opportunism, goal divergence (Doz, 1996) and cross cultural differences, and using explicit mechanisms to manage conflict will help firms to deal with these difficulties" (p. 218). "Firms' concerns about opportunistic behavior by their partners are likely to lead to high transaction costs" (p. 220).	Relational capital among partners may help overcome the challenges inherent in competitive collaboration.
Khanna et al. (1998)	"A firm's propensity to engage in competitive racing behavior may be related to activities of the firms that are not within the scope of the alliance" (p. 201). "Our models suggest that if firms view their relationship with others in the alliance as either strictly competitive or strictly cooperative, this may give rise to suboptimal outcomes for one or more firms in the alliance" (p. 205).	The motivational disposition of conflict vs. harmony is crucially shaped by the ratio of private to common benefits in an alliance. The greater the ratio of common benefits to private benefits the greater the likelihood of harmonious disposition.
Kumar & Nti (1998)	"Evidently, if all the firms adopt a cooperative mode of behavior, then each partner is likely to have positive feelings of psychological attachment to the relationship, but a preponderance of non-cooperative behavior is likely to produce dissatisfaction with the alliance relationship" (p. 359). "Failure to attain a sustainable interorganizational equilibrium will impede the ability of the alliance to create economic value and knowledge, and may adversely affect the partners' feelings of psychological attachment to the relationship, especially the higher order attitudinal variables of commitment, trust, and social harmony that hold the alliance together" (p. 361).	The partners' dispositions are sensitive to the presence or the absence of psychological attachment among the partners.
Madhok (1995)	"Development of the relationship over time leads to lower costs of transacting, due both to a greater knowledge of the partner resulting in a lower scope for opportunism and greater trust over time leading to a lower proclivity to be opportunistic" (p. 61). "Given the dialectic, what is of critical importance is not just the process of collaborating but also of competing. With a need for flexibility in the conduct of a relationship, bargaining, problem solving, and conflict resolution become important activities" (p. 65).	The strategic predispositions of the partners may well shift over time, resulting perhaps in less opportunistic behavior and conflict.

(continued)

TABLE 3.1 The Conflict Perspective in Strategic Alliances (Continued)

Authors	Illustrative Observations	Remarks
Nti & Kumar (2000)	"When effort supplied is observable but knowledge appropriated is not, it may be difficult for the partners to renegotiate equitable revenue shares as disparities in effort contributions emerge" (p.128). "Competition among alliance partners appears to be engendered by the presence of learning opportunities. This learning motive is strong in alliances where the firms desire to discover new opportunities or to acquire new capabilities (Koza and Lewin, 1998)" (p. 119).	Ambiguity intensifies the fear that one's partner may act opportunistically.
Park & Ungson (2001)	"Opportunistic hazards are inevitable in strategic alliances because of this competitive rivalry among partners" (p. 43). "Collective benefits from an alliance are typically future oriented and uncertain, while opportunity costs from cheating are more immediate and often tangible, which further aggravates opportunistic tendencies in an alliance" (p. 42).	Interfirm rivalry is an impediment to the attainment of interpartner harmony, and its impact is further accentuated by differences in national and corporate cultures among alliance partners
Parkhe (1993)	"Indeed, the growing occurrence of potential opponents' nominal cooperation suggests greater emphasis on a subtler form of competition than the brazenly 'red in the fang and claw' variety: interfirm cooperation in the pursuit of individual competitive advantage" (p. 819).	Alliances are inherently unstable due to the hazards of opportunism with the structure of the game determining the significance of the threat from opportunistic behavior.
Ring & Van de Ven (1992)	"We argue that greater harmony (and an enhanced ability to preserve a relationship) flows from the increased production and transaction flexibility available to the parties through relational contracts" (p. 493).	Credible commitments may foster interpartner harmony.
Ring & Van de Ven (1994)	"Interaction processes among cooperating parties may cast a positive, neutral, or negative overtone to the relationship, influencing the degree to which parties settle disputes arising out of the IOR (Lowenstein, Thompson, & Bazerman, 1989; Pruitt & Rubin, 1986; Schmitt & Marwell, 1972)" (p. 91). "Reliance on trust developed at the interpersonal level may be conditioned by legal systems or organizational role responsibilities, mitigating the ability of the parties to rely on trust as a matter of first preference" (p. 93).	The disposition to be conflictful or harmonious is not entirely a matter of voluntary choice.

such drastic action could be very high, given the implicit social norms of trying to make the relationship work. Implicit in this line of reasoning is the recognition that alliance firms are generally disposed to collaborating in harmony rather than to unthinkingly slide into conflict and the termination of a relationship in the event of some dissatisfaction. The inclination to collaborate in harmony rather than enter into conflicts reflects the dominance of the associative and communal systems of exchange in these relationships as opposed to the more popular conception of a price-based exchange system.

At this point, one needs to appreciate the basis for the prevailing conflict-based view of alliances, a view that proceeds on the assumption that conflict is intrinsic to all forms of interorganizational interactions. Whether or not conflict is functional or dysfunctional in any specific situation depends on how the actors deal with the situation confronting them. Conflict has been defined as the "perceived divergence of interest, or a belief that the parties' current aspirations cannot be achieved simultaneously" (Rubin, Pruitt, & Kim., 1994, p. 5). Such perceived divergence of interests among actors can exist at the interpersonal as well as inter-group levels, and may involve issues of task and relationship. There is also a linkage between these two dimensions, so that unresolved task-related conflicts may generate relational conflicts and vice versa (Euwema, Van de Vliert, & Bakker, 2003).

It is worthwhile to note that in most cases the perceived divergence of interests among the actors is contextual. The contextual embeddedness of conflict has a number of implications. First, and perhaps most crucially, embeddedness creates its own logic for managing conflict. As McGinn and Keros (2002) note,

> Embedded transactions nearly always involved opening up, reflecting a logic of full mutual honesty. Unlike the distributive and integrative logics underlying haggling and working together, respectively, a logic of full mutual honesty is seldom mentioned in the negotiation literature or in game-theoretic models of bargaining. (p. 468)

Thus, while conflicts may be inevitable, dysfunctional conflicts may be precluded by the logic of exchange that emerges in embedded transactions. Perhaps even more significantly, Uzzi (1997), in a study of the women's apparel industry in New York, has demonstrated that social embeddedness leads to continuing cooperation, even if it may not be strictly rational for the firms to maintain cooperation. Consistent with this, Luo (2002) found that social embeddedness was important in enhancing the performance of international joint ventures in China, and noted that "IJV pay-offs can only be maximized when opportunism is controlled through the incentive structure and internal reciprocity is created through social norms" (p. 917).

A study of procurement practices of two major U.S. auto manufacturers (Ford & Chrysler) revealed that embeddedness is often associated with joint dependence that has proved beneficial for the manufacturers (Gulati & Sytch, 2007). Scholars studying interdependent relationships have mostly focused on the power imbalance between actors, often overlooking the notion of joint dependence. The distinction is important because the behavioral dynamics associated with joint dependence are at odds with the behavioral dynamics associated with power imbalance. Actors who are focused on deriving advantage from a power imbalance in their favor may be destroying value rather than creating value. As Gulati and Sytch (2007) note, "While automotive manufacturers may be getting the bigger share of the pie through coercion, the size of the pie can diminish at a faster rate, leaving them with a net loss" (p. 59). Actors who are focused on maximizing the benefits of joint dependence, by contrast, have their behavior circumscribed by the logic of social embeddedness. Joint dependence, as the authors note, enhances the interaction quality among the partners through greater mutual identification, increased empathetic responding, and lowered levels of conflict. In a similar vein, Poppo and Zenger (2002) make the argument that relational governance is an essential complement to contractual governance in exchange relationships, and conclude that "managers tend to employ greater levels of relational norms as their contracts become increasingly customized, and to employ greater contractual complexity as they develop greater levels of relational governance" (p. 721). The overall implication is that the higher the level of relational embeddedness the greater the probability that dysfunctional conflicts will be avoided.

All this suggests that social embeddedness transforms a price system of exchange into one that is more associative in character (Biggart & Delbridge, 2004), and we would also surmise that in some circumstances it may even evolve into a communal system of exchange. Biggart and Delbridge (2004) have drawn a distinction between four alternative types of exchange systems, namely the price system, associative system, moral system, and communal system. One of the key distinctions between these exchange systems revolves around the notion of the allocative principle. For example, in the price system the allocative principle is the spot price, in the associative system it is the long term price, in the moral system it is the fair price, while in the communal system it is the preferential, tiered pricing.

One way of resolving the divergence of interests of alliance partners is to employ the dual concern model, which highlights the different strategies that actors may use to resolve their conflict (Rubin et al., 1994). The model postulates that actors have two independent levels of concerns, namely, concern about one's own outcomes and concern about the other actor's outcomes. This leads to four alternative strategies for managing conflict. The strategies have been labeled as (a) contending, (b) yielding, (c) inaction, and (d) problem solving. Contending involves the strong concern of the actors for their own outcomes with little concern for the other party's outcomes. Yielding implies little concern for one's own outcomes but high concern for the other party's outcomes. Inaction involves little or no concern with either one's own or the other party's outcomes, whereas problem solving is a strategy involving high concern for both one's own outcomes and for the other party's outcomes.

A problem solving strategy is likely to facilitate the development of an integrative agreement because it encourages information flow among the parties. An integrative agreement is one in which the parties are able to either expand the total pie that is available to the parties or to redefine the negotiating situation in a manner that allows both parties to achieve their own goals (Walton & McKersie, 1965). Scholars note that much of the literature on negotiation has had a strong normative bias in favor of problem solving and cooperation (Lewicki, Weiss, & Lewin, 1992). This bias is understandable because, although the bargaining approach may prove to be more efficient in certain classes of transactions than the problem solving approach, the vast majority of negotiating situations do not lend themselves to the concession–convergence model implied in the bargaining approach (Hopmann, 1995).

In Search of Harmony

Much of the available work on harmony is informed by the conflict and cross-cultural management literature (see Table 3.2). Kozan (1997) draws a distinction between the harmony and the confrontational and the regulative approach of managing conflict, and notes that "conflicts are usually seen as part of the long term relations of the two parties and the network of others surrounding them" (pp. 344–345). In other words, within this framework, conflicts tend to be defined in their totality, and this perspective

TABLE 3.2 Harmony in the Interdisciplinary Literature

Authors	Conceptions of Harmony and Illustrative Observations	Remarks
Chen et al. (2002)	"When there is a conflict of interest between an ingroup and an outgroup, the collectivistic will have a greater opportunistic propensity on behalf of the ingroup than will the individualist." (p. 576)	The normative ideal of harmony is relativistic in character. Harmony is fluid depending in large part on the situational context.

(continued)

TABLE 3.2 Harmony in the Interdisciplinary Literature (Continued)

Authors	Conceptions of harmony and illustrative observations	Remarks
Kozan (1997)	"The harmony model stresses cooperative behavior in handling differences." (p. 345) "In the harmony model criteria for judging effectiveness of resolution include face saving concerns along with distributive justice." (p. 348) "The harmony model uses a long time frame for judging effectiveness of resolution." (p. 348) "Conflict management in this model essentially attempts, by various non-confrontational means, to maintain group harmony." (p. 344)	Harmony is about process as well as outcome with process playing an important role in maintaining and strengthening relationships among parties. Harmony represents desirable modes of behavior.
Leung et al. (2002)	"Our preceding analysis suggests that the notion of harmony is best conceptualized as dualistic, with the value perspective emphasizing the intrinsic importance of harmony, and the instrumental perspective emphasizing its behavioral importance." (p. 210) "In our model, instrumental and value harmony constitute the dualistic structure of harmony, while disintegration avoidance and harmony enhancement are the behavioral syndromes that manifest these two dimensions." (p. 216)	Harmony is all about process, but the process may have either an instrumental or a symbolic importance.
Nader (1991)	"Harmony and conflict are not as antithetical as previous theories of conflict have suggested." (p. 45) "Harmony may be used to suppress peoples by socializing them towards conformity in colonial contexts, or the idea of harmony may be used to resist external control." (p. 45) "Harmony ideology serves to control confrontational politics; it also controls or suppresses criticism." (p. 54)	Harmony is most fundamentally instrumental, although the instrumentality may not be apparent. Harmony is a mechanism for political and social control.
Tjosvold et al. (2001)	"Although East Asian collectivist values emphasize harmony, the reality is that in work relationships such as those between contractors and subcontractors there are many conflicts." (p. 308) "In contrast to the traditional argument in cross cultural research that interdependence induces conflict avoidance, findings indicate that to the extent that contractors and subcontractors were mutually dependent the subcontractor dealt openly with conflicts for mutual benefit." (p. 305)	Harmony does not necessarily imply avoidance or suppression of conflict by any means. Harmony as an "ideal" may not be reflected in the ground reality.

leads to strategies of avoidance and accommodation rather than compromise (Leung, Koch, & Lu, 2002).

The term "harmony" draws its meaning from a number of different sources. Among the connotations of harmony in *Webster's Third New International Dictionary* (1993) are "combination into a consistent whole" and "the arrangement of parts in pleasing relation to each other" (p. 1035). The concept of harmony has also drawn inspiration from the East Asian cultural tradition, where it forms one of Confucianism's core cultural values (Kirkbride, Tang, Westwood, 1991; but for a different view on this see Leung et al., 2002). Although the origin of this concept is varied, there is general agreement on one key component of harmony, namely, the notion of order and balance. The concept of harmony highlights most fundamentally the importance of maintaining order—be it social order, as in a society, or the maintenance of rhythm, as in a musical composition.

Integrative (win–win) agreements, alluded to in the preceding section, do have underlying it the concept of harmony, in that such agreements recognize the interests of the different actors and seek to maximize benefits for all the actors. This underpinning of harmony is reinforced by a strong normative emphasis on the desirability of integrative as opposed to distributive agreements. While the concept of harmony may well be implicit in negotiation theorizing, it is fundamentally conceived of as an end-state that is integrative in character.

While there are merits of conceiving harmony in this integrative fashion, there are also clear limitations. The implicit assumption in extant theorizing appears to be that if the parties interacted in the right way an integrative solution would be found. However, Watkins (1999) notes that most negotiating situations are neither purely integrative nor purely distributive. Wetlaufer (1990) also observes that even if opportunities for integrative bargaining were present, the expanded pie would have to be divided, which would lead to distributive bargaining. There is also no guarantee that the parties would see the situation in integrative terms, even though such may well be the perception by outsiders. As Tidwell (1998) notes: "For some conflict there is simply no way to create a mutual gain; one side may have to win while the other loses" (p. 26).

The fact that the literature has sought to portray the distinction between integrative and distributive bargaining in somewhat simplistic terms does not necessarily imply that harmony is not possible. To begin with, it is perhaps useful not to conceive of harmony as an absolute end state that either exists or does not exist. In other words, there may be varying degrees of harmony associated with varying levels of integrativeness in the negotiation outcomes. Whether integrativeness is high or low will depend in large part on whether the interests of the parties are congruent. The more congruent the interests, the greater the possibility of attaining an integrative outcome.

Second, while it is true that different actors may perceive negotiation outcomes in different ways, it is not always clear that these perceptions are always rigidly held. Here, a clear set of standards can help actors evaluate different negotiation outcomes.

Much of the experimental research on bargaining and negotiation assumes that people know what their goals are. If goals are known at the outset, it is relatively easy to conceive of what the parties might construe as integrative or distributive outcomes. But if, as Brett, Northcraft, and Pinkley (1999) observe, "The process of negotiation may lead negotiators to 'discover what to want'" (p. 437), the notions of integrative and distributive outcomes acquire a greater degree of ambiguity. Hence, in a dynamic environment, where actors' preferences are evolving, negotiation impasses may be less frequent than might otherwise be the case. Although the potential for negotiation impasses may be less, whether or not the alliance members are able to overcome these impasses depends on the negotiation strategies they employ. After all, the perception of what constitutes an integrative agreement is itself subject to some degree of variability. In other words, the basis for attaining harmony may be broader than what is generally assumed, although whether or not that harmony is attained depends critically on the negotiation strategies pursued by the parties.

Defining Interpartner Harmony in Strategic Alliances

When partner firms enter into an alliance, they do so with the objective of creating economic value, whether by creating new products, gaining entry into new markets, or developing new technology. In this joint endeavor, member firms face the task of coordinating their activities to achieve their desired goals. The process of coordination may or may not give rise to conflicts among member firms. If conflicts do emerge, the member firms may manage them using either the strategy of contending, problem solving, yielding, or avoiding (Rubin et al., 1994). In any event, the interactions among the member firms provide the context for the emergence of harmony.

We define *interpartner harmony in strategic alliances* as *the mutual understanding that alliance members accomplish by managing commitment and forbearance in the context of their interdependence.* The notion of mutual understanding highlights the fact that the concept of interpartner harmony is indicative of the relational patterns among the alliance members. Commitment is indicative of a desire among the alliance partners to ensure the success of the alliance (Gulati, Khanna, & Nohria 1994; Morgan & Hunt, 1994; Swailes, 2002). These relational patterns are emergent and inherently dynamic, changing their character in accordance with relative dominance of commitment and forbearance within the context of alliance member interdependencies. The role of forbearance among alliance partners may be task related or partner related. The management of forbearance refers to the way in which the alliance members manage the interactions with their partners, some involving conflicts of various kinds and intensities, and the way they deal with alliance outcomes. Alliance members can be open and transparent (within limits), be responsive to their partners' concerns, and be cautious in making judgments about their partners' motives and intentions. They can, of course, also behave in precisely the opposite way. Similarly, when the alliance fails to yield the expected results, the member firms could adopt a more deliberate approach in dealing with the performance shortfall, or alternatively, they could rush to curtail their commitment to the venture, fearing the worst.

The state of mutual understanding may take varying forms. It may exhibit an underlying stability, but it may also be quite fragile. The emergent understanding is the product of both deliberate as well as accidental actions undertaken by the members. It is also worth noting that the state of understanding that emerges is a product of the joint actions of all alliance members. In other words, one member firm, by itself, cannot fully control the evolution of the interaction. Finally, the alliance members may or may not be fully conscious of the emergent understanding, and the members may also differ in their perception of that understanding. That is to say, one alliance member may be satisfied with the nature of the understanding that emerges even as the other member remains dissatisfied.

It is worth mentioning that the concept of interpartner harmony is related to, but is distinct from, the concept of interpartner legitimacy (Kumar & Das, 2007). Interpartner legitimacy relates to the appropriateness of the alliancing firms' behaviors, whereas interpartner harmony relates to the alliancing firms' level of commitment and forbearance. When alliancing partners demonstrate a high level of commitment and forbearance, interpartner legitimacy of a communal sort will be a natural consequence. We can surmise from this that interpartner harmony (and especially of the communal type) may provide the foundation for the emergence of interpartner legitimacy. However, the converse proposition, that is, interpartner legitimacy resulting in communal harmony, may not necessarily be true.

The Dimensions of Alliance Harmony

We have defined interpartner harmony in strategic alliances as the state of mutual understanding in the interaction among the member firms that is accomplished through managed commitment and forbearance. In this section we argue that this emergent state of mutual understanding can take distinct forms, making for a typology of interpartner harmony in alliances.

The objective of this typology is to delineate the different forms of mutual understanding or harmony that arise in alliances. These forms of interpartner harmony can be characterized along two dimensions; namely, (a) the commitment dimension and (b) the forbearance dimension. The commitment dimension pertains to the degree to which the partners are dedicated to making the alliance a success. It may be the case that the alliance in question is of considerable importance for both the partners. In this scenario, the commitment will be high. By contrast, the alliance may be more important for one member vis-à-vis its partner, in which case the level of commitment will be low. The forbearance dimension highlights the one key theme inherent in interpartner harmony, that is, the theme of potential conflict among the alliance partners. Do the alliance partners seek to resolve their conflicts with restraint, tolerance, and constructiveness, as opposed to an acrimonious manner? Do they trust and respect each other? How much confidence do they have in their partner's willingness to cooperate with them?

The Commitment Dimension

Firms enter into strategic alliances to attain their mutual objectives. This they do because either of them alone would not have been able to attain desired objectives. New product development, gaining access to new markets, or new technologies are some of the major motivations for the formation of strategic alliances. The very basis for such formation implies the existence of interdependence among the partners. It is reasonable to surmise that the higher the level of interdependence among the alliance partners the greater would be their commitment to make the alliance succeed. *Webster's Third New International Dictionary* (1993) defines commitment as "the obligation or pledge to carry out some action or policy or to give support to some policy or person" or "the state of being obligated or bound (as by intellectual conviction or emotional ties)" (p. 457).

A strategic alliance may be said to have high commitment when all of the members are highly dependent on their counterparts to achieve goals. This dependence may be structural, psychological, or both. Structural dependence implies that both of the partners are dependent on the alliance specific investments that they have made. When these investments lead to a high degree of economic integration, that is, the specific investments made by the alliance partners are well blended, the alliance partners' relationship is likely to be qualitatively transformed. As Luo (2008b) observes, "Levels of commitment, forbearance, and reciprocity may increase with economic integration because of the increased convergence of interests and goals of the different parties" (p. 619). Psychological dependence implies that the partners feel reluctant to dissolve the relationship in the absence of a compelling strategic rationale. The two forms of dependence are inter-related as we suspect that high levels of structural dependence will also lead to high levels of psychological dependence. Commitment is a matter of degree—it can range from low to high, and it can be enhanced during the course of the relationship if the alliance partners make relation-specific investments, institute knowledge-sharing processes that maximize learning, establish mechanisms for combining complementary resources, and establish effective governance mechanisms (Das & Kumar, 2007; Dyer & Singh, 1998; Gundlach, Achrol, & Mentzer, 1995).

Without some form of commitment between the actors there would be no business relationship to speak of. An arm's-length relationship between the different actors represents a low level of commitment, whereas buyer–seller relationships where partners make relation-specific investments represent higher degrees of commitment. The greater the satisfaction of the alliance partners with a particular relationship, the greater would be their commitment to the relationship (Rusbult & Buunk, 1993). Scholars note that interdependence and satisfaction with a given relationship are orthogonal dimensions (e.g., Thibaut & Kelly, 1959). A member's satisfaction with a relationship is dependent on the outcomes obtained from that relationship vis-à-vis a comparison level, whereas the member's dependence on a relationship relies on other alternatives open to it. Thus, for example, an alliance member may be highly dependent on a relationship but may not be particularly satisfied with it. Alternatively, each member could be less dependent on the relationship, but may nevertheless be satisfied with it. Scholars note that interdependence leads parties to use non-coercive strategies (Gundlach & Cadotte, 1994) and to interact with each other in a predictable manner (Mastenbroek, 1999). In a study of manufacturer–distributor relationships, Gundlach and Cadotte (1994) found that "increasing magnitudes of interdependence are associated with more frequent use of noncoercive strategies, lower levels of residual conflict, and more favorable evaluations of partner performance" (pp. 524–525). A study of U.S.–Chinese joint ventures conducted by Yan and Gray (1994) also found that heightened interdependence was associated with less opportunistic behavior. The greater the satisfaction of the alliance partners with a particular relationship, the greater would be their commitment to the relationship (Rusbult & Buunk, 1993).

The Forbearance Dimension

Webster's Third New International Dictionary (1993) defines forbearance as "a delay in enforcing or a suspension of or a refraining from enforcing debts, rights of action, rights, privileges, claims, or obligations" or "the exercise of patience or restraint" or "indulgence toward offenders or enemies" (p. 886). The forbearance dimension in alliances relates to the ever-present need to be restrained, patient, and open-minded in circumstances involving actual or perceived incompatibility of the member firms' actions with expected norms of behavior. This dimension also refers to the level of patience exercised by the alliance partners in evaluating alliance performance. Measuring alliance performance is tricky (Das & Teng, 2003) and it gets further exacerbated by differences in the partners' strategic goals and their national and corporate cultures. More fundamentally, the concept of forbearance focuses on the notion of tolerance, be it in relation to the other partner's behavior or to alliance outcomes. Scholars have shown that high levels of competence trust leads managers to persist with an alliance that is performing below expectations (Patzelt & Shepherd, 2008). In other words, alliance partners often do show forbearance in endeavors characterized by a high level of ambiguity and uncertainty. Scholars have noted that the alliance must demonstrate flexibility in environments that are unstable (Palmatier, Dant, & Grewal, 2007) and we surmise that forbearance is essential to flexibility. This perceived incompatibility may center on the goals of the alliance, the evaluation of the alliance performance, or the managerial mechanisms in place in the alliance. The greater the perceived incompatibility of goals, the higher will be the potential for conflict among the alliance members. If the members are unable to resolve their goal incompatibilities, the conflict is likely to escalate, and may then move beyond the simple incompatibilities to a focus also on the process by which they seek to resolve such conflict. This forbearance dimension captures both task-related as well as relationship-related transgressions among the member firms (McCullough, Fincham, & Tsang., 2003), and varies on a continuum from low to high.

The relational conflicts among the partner firms may have their origins in task related conflicts or may be a function of differences in culture and personalities among the partner firms. Scholars now increasingly recognize that both task and relational conflicts are interdependent phenomena (e.g., Euwema et al., 2003), and that it is difficult to resolve one without resolving the other. Scholars maintain that in a business context the moral appropriateness of an outcome may be less meaningful than arriving at an agreement that may be acceptable to all (Dingwall, 2002). The implication here is not that moral concerns are inappropriate in resolving conflicts, only that they are not determinative in the final scheme of things. Thus, whereas conflict resolution may be difficult, even intractable at times, it does not represent the critical stumbling block that prevents the alliance partners from their quest for harmony.

Four Types of Interpartner Harmony

The typology of interpartner harmony that we propose relates levels of commitment to varying degrees of forbearance (see Figure 3.1). The four

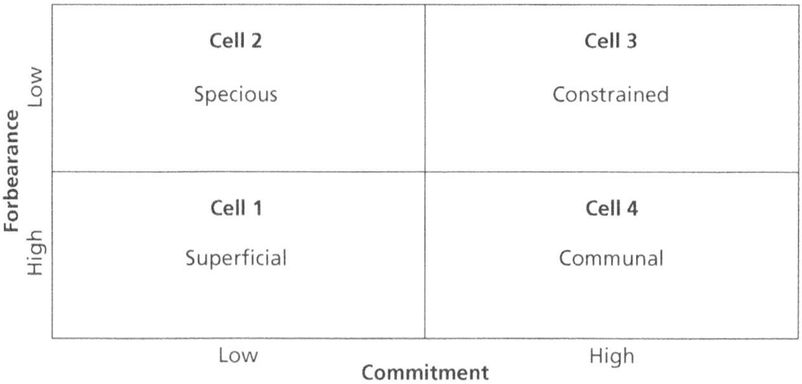

Figure 3.1 Typology of interpartner harmony in strategic alliances.

different kinds of interpartner harmony are each associated with a unique kind of mutual understanding: superficial, specious, constrained, and communal.

Superficial Interpartner Harmony

When commitment is at a low level and forbearance is at a high level, the condition in an alliance can be described as one of superficial harmony. This is a situation characterized by the absence of conflict. In this condition, while the alliance members do not have any grudges or resentment toward their partners for what they did or did not do, they are equally unlikely to have a strong degree of enthusiasm for collaboration. The relationship survives because of its strategic logic and managerial inertia and not because of a high degree of social embeddedness. Although the partners may be passively satisfied with the manner they interact with each other, the low level of commitment may militate against the longer-term stability of the alliance relationship. When the commitment level is low, partners may be reluctant to put in the effort necessary for the alliance to function beyond minimally acceptable levels. Problems may accumulate and may cause a longer-term restructuring of the relationship. It is also unlikely for the alliance to have developed the social embeddedness needed for generating social capital and thereby recasting the course of the venture. Although this lack of long-term stability is not likely to cause the alliance partners any great discomfort, it is conceivable that the potential upside of the relationship under changed circumstances may not be foreseen. Superficial harmony may be likened to an alliance state where the perception of alliance value (benefits vs. costs) is relatively low. White (2005) has argued that an alliance may either be brought to termination or be restructured if the cooperation costs are higher than the benefits. Cooperation costs are defined by White (2005) as costs that are "those incurred by a firm to establish and maintain an interorganizational interface and make adjustments in the process of undertaking a collaborative activity" (p. 1404).

In other words, while day-to-day conflicts may be rare, the level of psychological devotion to the relationship is likely to be low. A good example of this is the alliance that was established between Saab and Fairchild in the 1980s to develop and market a new commuter aircraft (Cauley de la Sierra, 1995). Although the partners had complementary capabilities, and sufficient forbearance on the part of both firms, the venture did not develop in the expected manner owing to the volatility of the external environment. Faced with a cash crunch, when it had to make a choice between two development projects, Fairchild withdrew from the venture in 1985 as its commitment to the venture was low.

Specious Interpartner Harmony

When the commitment and forbearance are both at low levels, we have what we euphemistically call specious harmony. Here, the harmony is at best illusory, and there is usually no alternative to eventual dissolution. A good example of this is the alliance between AT&T and Olivetti (see Das & Teng, 1999). The alliance was formed in 1983 with the hope that both the parties would be able to market each other's products. Given the differing cultures of the two companies, there were frequent clashes and no effective managerial mechanisms were established to govern the alliance based on an adequate degree of mutual forbearance. This was also a situation characterized by low commitment, in that neither of the companies possessed sufficient capabilities to effectively sell each other's products. The alliance was terminated in 1989. If such low commitment is coupled with low forbearance and unacceptable outcomes, a termination of the alliance is almost assured. Another example of an alliance of this type was the alliance between General Motors and Daewoo Corporation of Korea. This alliance failed because it did not turn out products of acceptable quality and the strategic objectives of the companies turned out to be divergent, a consequence perhaps of a low level of mutual commitment and forbearance (Das & Teng, 1999).

Constrained Interpartner Harmony

When commitment is at a high level and forbearance at a low level, we have constrained harmony. Whereas strong commitment exists, the low forbearance renders all interpartner interactions problematic. This situation may prevail because the process is perceived to be unfair or positive outcomes uncertain. This is evident in the alliance between Advanced Robotics, General Robotics, and Tech International that had been established to develop a new generation of advanced robotics devices. The alliance was initiated by the United States government with the objective of improving America's competitive position in manufacturing. General Robotics recognized the potential payoffs from this venture but was wary of cooperating with the other companies whom it viewed as potential competitors. This, coupled with the fact that the company was not given the lead role in managing the venture, created considerable tensions. As Gould, Ebers, and Clinchy (1999) note:

> These behaviors, in which staff from the three companies engaged, often led to intense and chronic squabbling, as each projected all of the difficulties onto others, and accused them of withholding, being uncooperative, wrong minded, obstinate, not up to the task and worse (p. 708).

With such lack of forbearance, the performance of the venture predictably suffered, and consultants had to be brought in to undo the damage. It is unclear as to how the venture evolved over time, as the consultants were not invited back for any follow-up work.

If high commitment is coupled with unacceptable outcomes, there may be sufficient motivation to restructure the relationship, with more forbearance, for better results. This is a difficult process, and it is not clear that the effort can be effective or sufficient. A good illustration of this is the Corning-Vitro alliance, established in 1992 with the objective of competing in the consumer housewares business (Cauley de la Sierra, 1995). Corning hoped to gain access to the Mexican market while Vitro wanted to establish a presence in North America. The shared rationale for the venture was strong and the companies merged their consumer housewares operations to realize potential synergies. The venture faced stiff competition from low-cost Asian imports and was unable to realize its objectives. As Cauley de la Sierra (1995) notes: "While market pressures mandated swift decision making, the complex organizational and ownership structure worked against them" (p. 29). The member firms were unable to revamp the structure in a timely fashion and the joint venture was dissolved. Owing to their high commitment, however, the companies continued to collaborate with each other via a cross-distribution agreement.

Communal Interpartner Harmony

When the level of both commitment and forbearance is high, we have communal type of harmony. The GE-Snecma alliance is an alliance that belongs to this type. This alliance was formed in 1969 to develop commercial jet engines. Although it initially experienced some difficulties, the alliance has withstood the test of time and is often cited in the literature for performing extremely well (Cauley de la Sierra, 1995). Another alliance that fits this pattern is the Renault-Nissan alliance mentioned earlier. The performance of this latter alliance is considered to be exemplary, with the revitalized venture emerging as a major player in the auto industry (Yoshino & Fagan, 2003). The economic performance of the alliance was mirrored by an equally strong social commitment that had developed among the partners. Yoshino and Fagan (2003) cite an executive who knew of the personal ties between Renault chairman Schweitzer and Nissan chairman Hanawa as saying: "Every time they get together, Schweitzer asks Hanawa how people at Nissan feel about the alliance, and wants to know the real feelings of the ranks and file. It is not just a perfunctory question, but he is truly interested" (p. 14).

It is fair to say that the emergence of communal interpartner harmony is reflective of a high degree of commitment of the partners to the alliance. High commitment means that the partners find it worthwhile to put in maximum effort in the alliance, while a high level of mutual forbearance means that the lack of fairness is not a source of contention among the alliance partners. The high level of commitment implies that the alliance partners are likely to be actively involved in alliance management. Golicic, Foggin, and Mentzer (2003) draw a distinction between active and passive forms of collaboration, which would seem to imply that high levels of commitment are associated with more active forms of collaboration.

We would like to note a few additional points about our proposed typology. First, we make the assumption that the perceptions of commitment and forbearance levels, rather than some "objective" measures of these variables, are more pertinent in determining the type of interpartner harmony. The perceptions that count are the perceptions of the top management team, no doubt influenced by the perceptions at other organizational levels. Secondly, the typology does not specify the temporal aspects of relationship evolution. For instance, while low commitment and low forbearance may well lead to relationship dissolution, the exact time period over which this may occur will vary from one alliance to another depending on their time perspective (Das, 2006). Finally, there may also be conflicting perceptions among the partners as to the state of the relationship. The not-unreasonable assumption we make here is that the alliance member with the stronger motive to manage the relationship will dominate the evolution of the relationship.

Interpartner Harmony in Different Alliance Types

Scholars have argued that alliances can be usefully examined in terms of three major types, namely, equity joint ventures, minority equity alliances, and nonequity alliances (e.g., Das & Teng 1998). The three types of alliances differ in their level of commitment of the alliance partners as also in the level of mutual forbearance that characterizes each alliance type. Our purpose in

TABLE 3.3 Interpartner Harmony in Different Alliance Types

Interpartner Harmony Types	Alliance Types		
	Equity Joint Ventures	Minority Equity Alliances	Nonequity Alliances
Superficial	Absent	Low commitment level High forbearance level	Low commitment level High forbearance level
Specious	Absent	Low commitment level Low forbearance level	Low commitment level Low forbearance level
Constrained	High commitment level Low forbearance level	Absent	Absent
Communal	High commitment level High forbearance level	Absent	Absent

this section is, therefore, to assess the nature of interpartner harmony that is likely to prevail in each of these types of alliances (see Table 3.3).

Interpartner Harmony in Equity Joint Ventures

Equity joint ventures denote the creation of an independent entity that is managed jointly by the partner firms in an alliance. This may entail a high level of financial and managerial commitment among the partners that cannot easily be reversed. Actions taken by one or all of the partners may decisively shape the evolution of the venture. High levels of commitment also imply frequent interactions among employees of the partner firms. As the joint venture evolves over time, increasing interaction may promote greater familiarity among the partner firms and in doing so cement the positive interdependencies through social embeddedness.

The forbearance level among the partners may be high or low depending on their prior experiences in managing joint ventures, their history, if any, in working together, the suitability of the governance mechanisms employed to manage the joint venture, and the negotiation strategies employed by the alliance members. For example, high levels of task related conflict among the joint venture partners could be accentuated or reduced by the level of relational conflicts that exist among the partners. The lower the level of relational conflict, the less the negative impact of task related conflict on venture performance. This would imply that interpartner harmony in this type of alliance is likely to be communal if there is sufficient mutual forbearance, such that task related conflicts are moderated by adequate forbearance to ensure low levels of relational conflict. By contrast, the interpartner harmony in this alliance will be constrained if a high level of task related conflict is accompanied by the lack of adequate forbearance to neutralize the effects of high levels of relational conflict. These are, to be sure, the extreme end points but the fundamental point is that whether forbearance is high or low critically impacts upon the two kinds of conflicts.

Interpartner Harmony in Minority Equity Alliances

Minority equity alliances involve one member firm taking an equity stake in its partner firm. If one member maintains a dominant control over the venture, it is not likely to be too dependent on its partner, so that the perceived level of interdependence would be low. These conditions would seem to guarantee some kind of stability in interactions among the partner firms, even as this stability, maintained at a lowered level of commitment, may not have much resilience. The forbearance level among the members may be high or low, depending on their familiarity with each other and their experience in managing these types of alliances. Given the low level of commitment among the partner firms, it is quite likely that the forbearance among the partner firms may not be that strong to effectively deal with any task related conflict that may arise. In other words, the social embeddedness is likely to be low, so that task related conflicts could undermine the venture. This would imply that the dominant type of interpartner harmony in this alliance type is likely to be superficial or specious.

Interpartner Harmony in Nonequity Alliances

Nonequity alliances are contractual arrangements without any form of equity sharing. The degree of financial and the managerial commitment will be lower here vis-à-vis joint ventures. The lower level of commitment among the partner firms leads to both lower expectations as well as a lower degree of social embeddedness among the alliance partners. We would also surmise that task related conflict may not become very salient here if some mutual forbearance is present. However, should such conflicts become an issue, they may not be easily resolved in view of the low level of social embeddedness. The commitment level would be low here, and when coupled with a high or a low level of forbearance, would result in either superficial or specious interpartner harmony.

In sum, from a theoretical perspective, our comments above show that there is a contingent relationship in the saliencies of four different types of interpartner harmony and the three major categories of alliances.

DISCUSSION

In examining the nature of interpartner relationships in strategic alliances, we have proposed that the traditional conflict-based view is a limited one because it ignores or at least under-appreciates the quest for a harmonious order. Harmony, in our analysis, may be more prevalent than is generally assumed. While conflicts are present in business relationships, we have argued for the existence of different types of harmony that member firms in alliances attempt to attain, even if this may appear to be a silent quest. The different types of harmony that emerge in alliance relationships are the joint products of the commitment and forbearance levels of the alliance partners. The motivation to attain and maintain harmony is on account of the socially embedded nature of alliance partnerships. The social embeddedness is reflected both in the levels of commitment among the partner firms and in their approaches to practicing forbearance in regard to partner activities that deviate from expectations. Although social embeddedness does not guarantee that all firms will be able to attain and maintain the same type of interpartner harmony, it does ensure that there are pressures during the alliance life cycle to maintain some form of interpartner harmony. This point of view, we believe, has not been sufficiently recognized in the existing literature on alliances, in which the governing assumption continues to be that dysfunctional conflicts pervade alliance functioning. Our thinking, by contrast, is that whereas conflict may indeed be salient in alliances, such conflict does not preclude the ability of the alliance partners to attain and maintain interpartner harmony through a judicious mixture of commitment and forbearance. The managerial challenge, in our view, is to leverage commitment and exercise reasonable forbearance to accomplish effective harmony in relationships among alliance members.

The analytical value of the concept of interpartner harmony in explaining the dynamics of alliances can be enhanced through a typology that enables us to capture the different scenarios that are likely to occur as an alliance evolves over time. We have accordingly proposed here a typology of interpartner harmony that captures the different kinds of interpartner relationships that can occur in an alliance. The typology is based on two dimensions, namely, the level of commitment by the partner firms and the level of forbearance among them. The level of commitment reflects the motivation of the partner firms to act in a manner that will maximize the success of an alliance while the level of forbearance reflects their capacity to productively manage their interactions in the alliance in the face of obvious or suspected deviation from expected partner behavior. From a theoretical perspective, this classification highlights the fact that different kinds of alliances are likely to exhibit different kinds of interpartner harmony. Thus, alliance partners in minority equity alliances and nonequity alliances are likely to continue functioning with superficial and specious interpartner harmony rather than trying to attain the ideal of communal interpartner harmony. In practical terms, not all types of alliances should be expected to attain the same type of interpartner harmony, nor should managerial effort be expended without regard to the type of alliance in which interpartner harmony is being sought.

The typology of interpartner harmony in alliances that we are proposing is important for several reasons. First, it provides a conceptual lens for assessing the state of the alliance at any given point in time and its likely evolution. The different states of interpartner harmony that we outline are surely subject to change over time, as a function of both internal and external factors. Second, the typology maps out in a convenient way the possible states of an alliance utilizing the variables of commitment and forbearance. Third, the typology is useful for understanding the factors that contribute significantly to alliance success and alliance failure.

The construct of interpartner harmony we have outlined here provides a unique perspective on alliances that has not been explored thus far in the literature. The construct captures not only the importance of the strategic interdependence of alliance partners in a socially embedded situation, but also the criticality of partners' ability to manage commitment and forbearance in such a context. To the best of our knowledge no study has analyzed the dynamics of interpartner harmony in alliances along the twin dimensions of commitment and forbearance among partners.

DIRECTIONS FOR FUTURE RESEARCH

The emergence of a particular type of harmonious order is dependent on the negotiation strategies used by the alliance members in managing their interdependence. Inter-member negotiation in the alliance context is an area deserving further research. Scholars recognize that, basically, interorganizational relationships "only emerge, evolve, grow, and dissolve over time as a consequence of individual activities" (Ring & Van de Ven, 1994, p. 95). However, these individual activities critically implicate negotiation, because social interaction is most fundamentally a process of negotiation. While the relevance of this paradigm for studying relationships is now increasingly acknowledged, empirical and theoretical contributions to the study of alliance evolution are still sparse. Although we have not explicitly developed this point of view here, we have provided a general framework within which specific studies may be conducted. One may study, for example, how different kinds of negotiation strategies may help the emergence of particular types of interpartner harmony in alliances, or how the emergence of interpartner harmony, in turn, affect the subsequent negotiation strategies used by partners in dealing with commitment and forbearance. Further, one may wish to examine the interactive effects of different negotiation strategies and the role played by contextual factors in shaping the interpartner harmony outcomes.

The negotiation paradigm can be useful for studying how a harmonious order is attained and maintained. Most pertinently, researchers can track the conflict management strategies used by alliance partners to manage their interactions in their quest for a harmonious order. Some of the questions deserving academic attention might be: "Is there a uniquely dominant negotiation strategy for attaining and maintaining interpartner harmony?"; If not, then "What set of factors determines the effectiveness of a particular negotiating strategy?"; "Is the effectiveness of a particular negotiation strategy dependent on the stage of alliance development?"; "Is it conceivable or likely that disharmony at a particular stage of alliance development may engender forces that ensures the emergence of harmony subsequently?"; "How cognizant are the alliance partners of this intriguing possibility, and what are the implications of differences in their recognition of this possibility?"

Another set of issues worth examining revolve around the evolution of the different interpartner harmony states we have identified in the chapter. "How stable or unstable are these different states, and what are some of the underlying dynamics that may explain how alliances move from one state to another?" This is an important question from the standpoint of gaining a better understanding of alliance dynamics and an enhanced understanding of factors over which managers may have greater control and others over which their control may be relatively less. Of particular importance here, we think, are issues of justice. "How does the attainment or non-attainment of any particular kind of justice—namely, procedural, distributive, and interactional—affect both the emergence of and the movement toward a new harmonious state?"

Another key element here is time perspective. How do different perspectives on time held by different partner firms (Das, 2004, 2006) condition their perception of interpartner harmony as well as their choice of strategies in dealing with unsatisfactory situations? Clearly, time pressure constrains available choices in negotiation strategies to manage interpartner relations for enhancing and maintaining different aspired kinds of interpartner harmony.

Lastly, there are the obvious research issues of how each type of interpartner harmony is related to the performance of alliances, and the need to develop suitable measures of interpartner harmony. The different kinds of harmony states that we have identified may also be influenced by industry and national cultural characteristics. For example, in highly turbulent and rapidly changing industries communal forms of interpartner harmony may very well be the desired norm but at the same time be very difficult to attain and maintain. In turbulent environments alliance partners must demonstrate a high level of forbearance as well as commitment to cope with the rapid changes in the environment, necessitating the pursuit of communal harmony. By contrast, in slow moving or placid industries, high levels of commitment and forbearance are not required and hence communal harmony may not necessarily be the desired state. However, it is a state that may be easier to attain, as the forbearance of alliance partners will be less tested. The different states of interpartner harmony may also be a function of the national cultural characteristics of the alliance partners. In collectivistic cultures relationships and commitment are more highly valued relative to individualistic cultures. This has the key implication that the state of communal interpartner harmony may be more easily attained and maintained in alliances involving partners from collectivistic cultures.

MANAGERIAL IMPLICATIONS FOR BUILDING AND MAINTAINING INTERPARTNER HARMONY

Scholars and practitioners alike have understandably focused considerable attention on developing managerial mechanisms that will make for alliance success (e.g., Das, 2005; Das & Teng, 2000; Doz, 1996). Zeng and Chen (2003) suggest that structural and motivational solutions can help alliance partners achieve alliance stability. Structural solutions focus on enhancing the pay-off from cooperation, while motivational solutions stress the importance of improving communication, developing strong alliance identification and cooperative norms, and the longer term. However, helpful as they are, most of these recommendations have as their premise the fear of every member firm of being exploited by its partner. As we have argued here, while such fears no doubt exist, they are unlikely to be overwhelming enough to impede alliance stability. It is in this context that we have highlighted the usefulness of interpartner harmony as a pertinent concept for understanding alliance functioning and performance.

Although interpartner harmony may not be an easily attainable goal, it is clearly a desirable one for the effective functioning of alliances. The critical issue thus is what steps member firms need to take to attain interpartner harmony. In building interpartner harmony, our focus is primarily on the normative ideal of trying to attain the communal type of interpartner harmony in our proposed typology. Superficial interpartner harmony and specious interpartner harmony are not likely to be the explicit goals of any alliance member, although they may well be the unintended consequence of an alliance firm's actions.

Communal interpartner harmony is reflective of a state where there is a high level of commitment by the partner firms coupled with a high level of mutual forbearance. A high level of commitment is not something that can be created simply if one or the other member firm wills it. Basically, a high or a low level of commitment is usually predicated on the degree of strategic compatibility of the goals of different alliance members. In other words, this would usually be a given condition, and especially so at the formation stage. Clearly also, the ability to attain communal interpartner harmony is critically dependent on member firms' ability to maintain forbearance and manage conflict.

In managing conflict, the alliance members must not be fazed by the appearance of conflict. Conflicts can be both positive and negative in their consequence; much depends on how the member firms deal with them. If members deal with conflicts constructively, against a background of forbearance, their relationships are likely to be strengthened, lessening also the likelihood of other conflicts emerging. Second, the earlier a conflict is dealt with, the greater will be the likelihood for it to be contained within tolerable limits. In particular, the firms are unlikely to become defensive at an early stage, and this would bode well for the development of increased mutual forbearance through their subsequent interactions. It is also important for the member firms not to over-react or under-react to any problems. The calibration of the response is particularly important, and may go a long way in avoiding conflict escalation.

It is also essential that the alliance partners try to build or establish managerial mechanisms to contain potential conflicts (Das, 2005). The managerial mechanisms refer critically to appropriate governance structures. Institutionalized mechanisms for dealing with conflict may prevent conflicts from escalating to catastrophic levels. They may also help to strengthen the perception among the alliance partners that resolution of conflicts will be managed in a procedurally fair manner. Perceptions of procedural fairness are of vital importance in strengthening the commitment of the alliance managers to the venture. As Luo (2008a) notes, "Alliances need procedural justice when formulating, governing, and managing interorganizational entities because this justice serves as a foundation for interparty cooperation, knowledge sharing, economic exchange, and ongoing commitment" (p. 40). Developing trust between alliance partners would probably enhance the commitment and forbearance of the partners which, in turn, could lead to greater communal interpartner harmony. Also, the management of conflict acquires a new sense of urgency in alliances that bring together firms from different cultural milieus. Cultures differ in the ways they deal with conflicts. For instance, face-saving is crucial in many Asian cultures, with the consequence that there is a distinct tendency toward conflict-avoidance in these cultures.

In sum, we suggest in this chapter that the construct of interpartner harmony in strategic alliances is worthy of our attention for a more thorough understanding of alliance dynamics, complementing the currently limited conflict-based comprehension of alliances. We hope the typology of interpartner harmony in alliances presented here will enhance both this harmony-oriented research enterprise and the further development of effective guidelines for management practice.

ACKNOWLEDGMENT

This chapter, save some minor changes and updating, was earlier published as Das, T. K., & Kumar, R. (2009). Interpartner harmony in alliances: Managing commitment and forbearance. *International Journal of Strategic Business Alliances, 1*(1), 24–52.

REFERENCES

Biggart, N. W., & Delbridge, R. (2004). Systems of exchange. *Academy of Management Review, 29*(1), 28–49.

Brett, J. F., Northcraft, G. B., & Pinkley, R. L. (1999). Stairways to heaven: An interlocking self- regulation model of negotiation. *Academy of Management Review, 24*(3), 435–451.

Cauley de la Sierra, M. (1995). *Managing global alliances: Key steps for successful collaboration.* Reading, MA: Addison Wesley.

Chen, C. C., Peng, M. W., & Saparito, P. A. (2002). Individualism, collectivism, and opportunism: A cultural perspective on transaction cost economics. *Journal of Management, 28*(4), 567–583.

Coletti, A. L., Sedatole, K. L., & Towry, K. L. (2005). The effect of control systems on trust and cooperation in collaborative environments. *Accounting Review, 80*(2), 477–500.

Cropanzano, R., & Mitchell, M. S. (2005). Social exchange theory: An interdisciplinary review. *Journal of Management, 31*(6), 874–900.

Das, T. K. (2004). Time-span and risk of partner opportunism in strategic alliances. *Journal of Managerial Psychology, 19*(8), 744–759.

Das, T. K. (2005). Deceitful behaviors of alliance partners: Potential and prevention. *Management Decision, 43*(5), 706–719.

Das, T. K. (2006). Strategic alliance temporalities and partner opportunism. *British Journal of Management, 17*(1), 1–21.

Das, T. K., & Kumar, R. (2007). Learning dynamics in the alliance development process. *Management Decision, 45*(4), 684–707.

Das, T. K., & Rahman, N. (2001). Partner misbehavior in strategic alliances: Guidelines for effective deterrence. *Journal of General Management, 27*(1), 43–70.

Das, T. K., & Rahman, N. (2002). Opportunism dynamics in strategic alliances. In F. J. Contractor & P. Lorange (Eds.), *Cooperative strategies and alliances* (pp. 89–118). Oxford, England: Elsevier Science.

Das, T. K., & Rahman, N. (2009). Determinants of partner opportunism in strategic alliances: A conceptual framework. *Journal of Business and Psychology, 25,* 55–74.

Das, T. K., & Teng, B. (1998). Between trust and control: Developing confidence in partner cooperation in alliances. *Academy of Management Review, 23*(3), 491–512.

Das, T. K., & Teng, B. (1999). Managing risks in strategic alliances. *Academy of Management Executive, 13*(4), 50–62.

Das, T. K., & Teng, B. (2000). Instabilities of strategic alliances: An internal tensions perspective. *Organization Science, 11,* 77–101.

Das, T. K., & Teng, B. (2003). Partner analysis and alliance performance. *Scandinavian Journal of Management, 19*, 279–308.

Dingwall, R. (2002). What makes conflict resolution possible? *Negotiation Journal, 18*(4), 321–26.

Dollinger, M. J., Golden, P. A., & Saxton, T. (1997). The effect of reputation on the decision to joint venture. *Strategic Management Journal, 18*(2), 127–140.

Doz, Y. (1996). The evolution of cooperation in strategic alliances: Initial conditions or learning processes? *Strategic Management Journal, 17*(7), 55–83.

Dyer, J. H., & Singh, H. (1998). The relational view: Cooperative strategy and sources of interorganizational competitive advantage. *Academy of Management Review, 23*(4), 660–679.

Euwema, M. C., Van de Vliert, E., & Bakker, A. B. (2003). Substantive and relational effectiveness of organizational conflict behavior. *International Journal of Conflict Management, 14*(2), 119–139.

Frey, S. C., Jr., & Schlosser, M. M. (1993) ABB and Ford: Creating value through cooperationl. *Sloan Management Review, 35*(1), 65–72.

Golicic, S. L., Foggin, J. H., & Mentzer, J. T. (2003). Relationship magnitude and its role in interorganizational relationship structure. *Journal of Business Logistics, 24*(1), 56–75.

Gould, L. J., Ebers, R., & Clinchy, R. M. (1999). The systems psychodynamics of a joint venture: Anxiety, social defenses, and the management of mutual dependence. *Human Relations, 52*(6), 697–722.

Gulati, R., Khanna, T., & Nohria, N. (1994). Unilateral commitments and the importance of process in alliances. *Sloan Management Review, 35*(3), 61–70.

Gulati, R., & Singh, H. (1998). The architecture of cooperation: Managing coordination costs and appropriation concerns in strategic alliances. *Administrative Science Quarterly, 43*(4), 781–814.

Gulati, R., & Sytch, M. (2007). Dependence asymmetry and joint dependence in interorganizational relationships: Effects of embeddedness on a manufacturer's performance in procurement relationships. *Administrative Science Quarterly, 52*(1), 32–69.

Gundlach, G. T., Achrol, R. S., & Mentzer, J. T. (1995). The structure of commitment in exchange. *Journal of Marketing, 59*(1), 78–92.

Gundlach, G. T., & Cadotte, E. R. (1994). Exchange interdependence and interfirm interaction: Research in a simulated channel setting. *Journal of Marketing Research, 31*(4), 516–532.

Hopmann, P. T. (1995). Two paradigms of negotiation: Bargaining and problem solving. *Annals of the American Academy of Political and Social Science, 542*(1), 24–47.

Ireland, R. D., Hitt, M. A., & Vaidyanath, D. (2002). Alliance management as a source of competitive advantage. *Journal of Management, 28*(3), 413–446.

Kahan, D. M. (2003). The logic of reciprocity: Trust, collective action, and law. *Michigan Law Review, 102*(1), 71–103.

Kale, P., Singh, H., & Perlmutter, H. (2000). Learning and protection of proprietary assets in strategic alliances: Building relational capital. *Strategic Management Journal, 21*(3), 217–237.

Khanna, T., Gulati, R., & Nohria, N. (1998). The dynamics of learning alliances: Competition, cooperation, and relative scope. *Strategic Management Journal, 19*(3), 193–210.

Kingshott, R. P. J. (2006). The impact of psychological contracts upon trust and commitment within supplier-buyer relationships: A social exchange view. *Industrial Marketing Management, 35*, 724–739.

Kirkbride, P., Tang, S., & Westwood, R. (1991). Chinese conflict preferences and negotiating behavior: Cultural and psychological influences. *Organization Studies, 12*(3), 365–386.

Korine, H., Asakawa, K., & Gomez, P.Y. (2002). Partnering with the unfamiliar: Lessons from the case of Renault and Nissan. *Business Strategy Review, 13*(2), 41–50.

Koza, M. P., & Lewin, A. Y. (1998). The coevolution of strategic alliances. *Organization Science, 9*(3), 255–264.

Kozan, M. K. (1997). Culture and conflict management: A theoretical framework. *International Journal of Conflict Management, 8*(4), 338–360.

Kumar, R., & Das, T. K. (2007). Interpartner legitimacy in the alliance development process. *Journal of Management Studies, 44*(8), 1425–1453.

Kumar, R., & Nti, K. O. (1998). Differential learning and interaction in alliance dynamics: A process and outcome discrepancy model. *Organization Science, 9*(3), 356–367.

Leung, K., Koch, P. T., & Lu, L. (2002). A dualistic model of harmony and its implications for conflict management in Asia. *Asia Pacific Journal of Management, 19*(2), 201–220.

Lewicki, R. J., Weiss, S. E., & Lewin, D. (1992). Models of conflict, third party intervention, and negotiation: An overview. *Journal of Organizational Behavior, 13*(3), 209–252.

Lowenstein, G. F., Thompson, L., & Bazerman, M. H. (1989). Social utility and decision making in interpersonal context. *Journal of Personality and Social Psychology, 57*(3), 426–441.

Luo, Y. (2002). Contract, cooperation, and performance in international joint ventures. *Strategic Management Journal, 23*(10), 903–919.

Luo, Y. (2008a). Procedural fairness and interfirm cooperation in strategic alliances. *Strategic Management Journal, 29*(1), 27–46.

Luo, Y. (2008b). Structuring interorganizational cooperation: The role of economic integration in strategic alliances. *Strategic Management Journal, 29*(6), 617–637.

Madhok, A. (1995). Opportunism and trust in joint venture relationships: An exploratory study and a model. *Scandinavian Journal of Management,* 11(1), 57–74.

Mastenbroek, W. (1999). Negotiating as emotion management. *Theory, Culture, and Society, 16*(4), 49–73.

McCullough, M. E., Fincham, F. D., & Tsang, J. (2003). Forgiveness, forbearance, and time: The temporal unfolding of transgression-related interpersonal motivations. *Journal of Personality and Social Psychology, 84*(3), 540–557.

McGinn, K. L., & Keros, A. T. (2002). Improvisation and the logic of exchange in socially embedded transactions. *Administrative Science Quarterly, 47*(3), 442–473.

Morgan, R. M., & Hunt, S. D. (1994). The commitment-trust theory of relationship marketing. *Journal of Marketing, 58*(3), 20–38.

Nader, L. (1991). Harmony models and the construction of law. In K. Avruch, P.W. Black, & J. A. Scimecca (Eds.), *Conflict resolution: Cross-cultural perspectives* (pp. 41–59). New York, NY: Greenwood.

Nti, K.O., & Kumar, R. (2000). Differential learning in alliances. In D. O. Faulkner & M. de Rond (Eds.), *Cooperative strategy: Economic, business, and organizational issues* (pp. 119–194). Oxford, England: Oxford University Press..

Palmatier, R. W., Dant, R. P., & Grewal, D. (2007). A comparative longitudinal analysis of theoretical perspectives of interorganizational relationship performance. *Journal of Marketing, 71*(4), 172–194.

Park, S. H., & Ungson, G. R. (2001). Interfirm rivalry and managerial complexity: A conceptual framework of alliance failure. *Organization Science, 12*(1), 37–53.

Parkhe, A. (1993). Strategic alliance structuring: A game theoretic and transaction cost examination of interfirm cooperation. *Academy of Management Journal, 36*(4), 794–829.

Patzelt, H., & Shepherd, D. A. (2008). The decision to persist with underperforming alliances: The role of trust and control. *Journal of Management Studies, 45*(7), 1217–1243.

Poppo, L., & Zenger, T. (2002). Do formal contracts and relational governance function as substitutes or complements? *Strategic Management Journal, 23*(8), 707–725.

Pruitt, D. G., & Rubin, J. Z. (1986). *Social conflict: Escalation, stalemate, and settlement.* New York, NY: Random House.

Ring, P. S., & Van de Ven, A. H. (1992). Structuring cooperative relationships between organizations. *Strategic Management Journal, 13*(7), 438–498.

Ring, P. S., & Van de Ven, A. H. (1994). Developmental processes of cooperative interorganizational relationships. *Academy of Management Review, 19*(1), 90–118.

Rubin, J. Z., Pruitt, D. G., & Kim, S. H. (1994). *Social conflict: Escalation, stalemate, and settlement.* New York, NY: McGraw-Hill.

Rusbult, C. E., & Buunk, C. P. (1993). Commitment processes in close relationships: An interdependence analysis. *Journal of Social and Personal Relationships, 10*(2), 175–204.

Rusbult, C. E., & Van Lange, P. A. M. (2003). Interdependence, interaction, and relationships. *Annual Review of Psychology, 54,* 351–375.

Schmitt, D. R., & Marwell, G. (1972). Withdrawal and reward reallocation in response to inequity. *Journal of Experimental Social Psychology, 8*(3), 207–221.

Swailes, S. (2002). Organizational commitment: A critique of the construct and measures. *International Journal of Management Reviews, 4*(2), 155–178.

Thibaut, J. W., & Kelley, H. H. (1959) *The social psychology of groups.* New York, NY: Wiley.

Tidwell, A. C. (1998). *Conflict resolved? A critical assessment of conflict resolution.* London, England: Pinter.

Tjosvold, D., Cho, Y.-H., Park, H.-H., Liu, C., Liu, W.-C., & Sasaki, S. (2001). Interdependence and managing conflict with sub-contractors in the construction industry in East Asia. *Asia Pacific Journal of Management, 18,* 295–313.

Uzzi, B. (1997). Social structure and competition in interfirm networks: The paradox of embeddedness. *Administrative Science Quarterly, 42*(1), 35–67.

Walton, R. E., & McKersie, R. B. (1991). *A behavioral theory of labor negotiations: An analysis of a social interaction system* (2nd ed.). Ithaca, NY: ILR Press.

Watkins, M. (1999). Negotiating in a complex world. *Negotiation Journal, 15*(3), 245–270.

Webster's Third New International Dictionary. (1971). Springfield, MA: Merriam-Webster.

Wetlaufer, G. B. (1996). The limits of integrative bargaining. *Georgetown Law Journal, 85*(2), 369–394.

White, S. (2005). Cooperation costs, governance choice and alliance evolution. *Journal of Management Studies, 42*(7), 1383–1412.

Yan, A., & Gray, B. (1994). Bargaining power, management control, and performance in United States–China joint ventures: A comparative case study. *Academy of Management Journal, 37*(6), 1478–1517.

Yoshino, M. Y., & Fagan, P. L. (2003) *The Renault-Nissan alliance* (Case No. 9-303-023). Boston, MA: Harvard Business School.

Zajac, E. J., & Olsen, C. P. (1993). From transaction cost to transactional value analysis: Implications for the study of interorganizational strategies. *Journal of Management Studies, 30*, 131–145.

Zeng, M., & Chen, X. P. (2003). Achieving cooperation in multiparty alliances: A social dilemma approach to partnership management. *Academy of Management Review, 28*(4), 587–605.

CHAPTER 4

COPING WITH VULNERABILITY IN STRATEGIC ALLIANCES

Reciprocity, Altruism, and Blurred Hospitality

Angelos Kostis
Alex Örtegren

ABSTRACT

Ensuring the continuation of strategic alliances is challenging particularly due to the inevitable presence of relational risks and interpartner uncertainty that may discourage firms to accept becoming vulnerable to their partners' actions. Rendering oneself vulnerable, however, is critical to establish and maintain the smooth functioning of an alliance as well as realizing the fruitfulness of exchanging strategically important resources with firms that may have partially conflicting objectives. While prior research has provided rich insights into the efforts of the focal firm to manage and control the partner (e.g., by relational and contractual means), less light has been shed on the "relationality" aspect of strategic alliances and vulnerability management as

Managing the Partners in Strategic Alliances, pages 85–111

an interactive accomplishment. This chapter aims to advance the understanding of how firms can cope with vulnerability in strategic alliances. From a social exchange perspective, we suggest that firms can cope with vulnerability by establishing and relying on social norms, such as reciprocity and altruism. Furthermore, building on the Derridean notion of conditional and unconditional hospitality, we suggest that the cornerstones of reciprocity and altruism could be associated with the firms' engagement in different forms of hospitality. Finally, we construct an integrative model proposing blurred hospitality as the synergy that emerges when firms simultaneously engage in conditional and unconditional hospitality and discuss how this synergy facilitates coping with vulnerability effectively.

INTRODUCTION

A fundamental difference between strategic alliances and firm-level strategies is that in strategic alliances a firm needs to rely on others and render oneself vulnerable to its partners' behavior in order to realize the sought-after benefits. As strategic alliances are purposive and voluntary cooperative relationships between independent firms (Kale & Singh, 2009), developing effective interpartner relations is key to success. As Das and Teng (1996) highlight, "while the success of other strategies completely depends on how well the firm itself deals with the environment, the success of inter-firm alliances depends on an additional premise: a good working relationship among the partners" (p. 830). Developing such relations is challenging, however, because partners need to cope with an inevitable component of strategic alliances, namely, *vulnerability*.

Vulnerability is inherent in strategic alliances that involve "exchange, sharing, or co-development of products, technologies or services" (Gulati, 1998, p. 293) because behavioral uncertainty (Krishnan, Martin, & Noorderhaven, 2006) and relational risks are always present (Das & Teng, 1996, 1999). In strategic alliances, firms need to rely on each other to pursue challenging strategic objectives yet this means that each firm needs to commit strategically important resources to the alliance and become vulnerable to the actions of partners, who can behave opportunistically and may have hidden agendas (Dussauge, Garrette, & Mitchell, 2000; Park & Russo, 1996). Whereas vulnerability is a key and inevitable feature of strategic alliances, it has received limited attention by strategic alliance scholars. In prior research, vulnerability has mainly been discussed as a component of trust (McEvily, Zaheer, & Perrone, 2004; Tsui-Auch & Möllering, 2010), with trust often being defined as the willingness to render oneself vulnerable (Mayer, Davis, & Schoorman, 1995; Rousseau, Sitkin, Burt, & Camerer, 1998). Nonetheless, "very limited conceptual or empirical work so far exists that is explicitly directed to understand vulnerability itself" (Nienaber,

Hofeditz, & Romeike, 2014, p. 568), especially in the extant literature devoted to inter-firm relationships (Svensson, 2002, 2004) and more specifically to strategic alliances. Vulnerability, behavioral uncertainty, and relational risks are inter-related adversities that are present in strategic alliances yet prior research has mainly focused on the latter two and paid limited attention to the first. While rich insights have been provided into the efforts of the focal firm to deal with interpartner uncertainty (Das & Teng, 1999; Krishnan, Geyskens, & Steenkamp, 2016; Latusek & Vlaar, 2018; Lumineau & Quélin, 2012), considerably less light has been shed on the "relationality" aspect of strategic alliances and vulnerability management as an interactive accomplishment. To this end, we argue that deeper insights are needed into how firms can cope with vulnerability in strategic alliances in an interactive manner.

From a social exchange perspective (Blau, 1964; Cropanzano & Mitchell, 2005), prior research suggests that firms can cope with adversities and relational difficulties, such as vulnerability, by relying on informal processes and relational mechanisms, such as social norms. Social norms are important because they provide guidelines that support the engaged parties to interact in an effective and fruitful manner. In other words, social norms "provide a general frame of reference, order, and standards against which to guide and assess appropriate behavior in uncertain and ambiguous situations" (Cannon, Achrol, & Gundlach, 2000, p. 184). Social norms involve shared expectations of desirable behavior, encourage firms to engage in self-restraint (Heide & John, 1992) and are particularly important in strategic alliances especially due to the inherent incompleteness of contracts (Das & Teng, 2001; Mayer & Nickerson, 2005) and the need for constant relationship-specific adaptations (Cannon et al., 2000). By relying on relational norms, firms develop effective interpartner relationships and ensure smooth functioning of strategic alliances as concerns about partner opportunism are decreased (Carson, Madhok, & Wu, 2006; Zhou, Zhang, Zhuang, & Zhou, 2015), sharing of resources is encouraged, and inter-firm learning is enhanced (Muthusamy & White, 2005). Drawing on this body of research, we argue that social norms play an important role in coping with vulnerability in strategic alliances.

Prior studies informed by social exchange theory (SET) have discussed several social norms that can influence the continuation of inter-firm exchanges in light of relational difficulties, such as vulnerability (for a review, see Cropanzano & Mitchell, 2005). However, main attention has been paid to the norm of reciprocity, defined as a social norm that "dictates that an action performed by one party requires a repayment by the other (Meeker, 1983, p. 227) and concerns both expectations and behavior" (Swärd, 2016, p. 1842). We adopt the view that reciprocity is important for coping with vulnerability in strategic alliances, but also build upon Meeker (1971) and suggest that altruism is another, complementary social norm that plays an important role in guiding inter-firm exchange in the relational context of strategic alliances. Following this notion, we address a call for paying attention to both reciprocity and altruism in inter-firm exchanges and the synergy that is created when these two norms are employed simultaneously (Cropanzano & Mitchell, 2005). In particular, this chapter takes a first step to answer the following research question: "How can the social norms of reciprocity and altruism be established in strategic alliances and how can their simultaneous employment influence the process of coping with vulnerability?"

To provide an answer to this question, we build upon the Derridean notion of conditional and unconditional hospitality and argue that whereas the former acts as a catalyst for reciprocity, the latter acts as a catalyst for altruism. Furthermore, we construct an integrative model proposing blurred hospitality as the synergy that emerges when firms simultaneously engage in conditional and unconditional hospitality and discuss how this synergy facilitates coping with vulnerability effectively. The chapter concludes with a presentation of our contributions to the literature on managing vulnerability in strategic alliances.

INTERPARTNER UNCERTAINTY IN STRATEGIC ALLIANCES: A KEY PRECURSOR TO VULNERABILITY

Whereas the bright side of engaging in strategic alliances has been widely acknowledged, such endeavors are also characterized by a dark side. In the extant literature, this dark side has often been discussed in terms of relational risks (Das & Teng, 1998), behavioral uncertainty (Krishnan et al., 2006), and potentially detrimental aspects that may emerge in the pursuit of interactions among the engaged parties. Prior research has underlined that strategic alliances are inherently risky, can deliver undesirable outcomes and can prove to be detrimental unless they are appropriately managed (Dussauge et al., 2000; Park & Russo, 1996). According to Anderson, Christ, Dekker, and Sedatole (2014, p. 10), misalignment of incentives, meaning "the risk that an alliance partner has incentives to take actions that negatively affect the firm," is a major issue which can cause problems in the smooth functioning and continuation of such relationships. To this end, as strategic alliances often involve firms that have at the same time partially conflicting interests and competing objectives, they represent an essentially uncertain endeavor. Thus, looking at the dark side of strategic alliances, prior research has identified a plethora of risks.

Risks in strategic alliances are often discussed in relation to partner opportunism. Partner opportunism refers to "behavior by a partner firm that is motivated to pursue its self-interest with deceit to achieve gains at the expense of the other alliance members" (Das & Rahman, 2010, p. 57). Partner opportunism is particularly acute in strategic alliances as these relationships involve interactions among direct competitors (Pellegrin-Boucher, Le Roy, & Gurău, 2013; Schmoltzi & Wallenburg, 2012), who may be tempted to engage in misbehavior. The simultaneous pursuit of cooperation and competition make all three determinants of partner opportunism (see Das & Rahman, 2010) to be in place: economic, relational, and temporal determinants. To this end, firms may be willing to prioritize self-interests at the expense of the alliance's interests (Park & Ungson, 2001), misbehave, and take part in learning races (Khanna, Gulati, & Nohria, 1998). Further, intentional use of loopholes in contracts and formalized agreements (Morgan, Kaleka, & Gooner, 2007) can also occur as the partner may have the willingness to "opportunistically exploit the dependence relationship" (Langfield-Smith, 2008, p. 345). In addition, intentional underperformance due to lack of commitment (Das & Teng, 1999) or due to misaligned alliance horizons preferences (Das, 2006) is a key concern for the engaged parties.

Moreover, as Lumineau and Oliveira (2018) note, "in a given IOR [interorganizational relationship], the dark side probably occurs as a 'bundle of manifestations' in the sense that a set of dark-side manifestations may be tied together" (p. 239). Following this notion, research highlights that concerns about potential opportunism are often combined with concerns about intentional knowledge leakage, that is, "the focal firm's loss of private knowledge to partners through opportunistic activities such as private learning and unauthorized imitation" (Jiang, Li, Gao, Bao, & Jiang, 2013, p. 984). Partner opportunism and the fear of intentional knowledge leakage can make alliance partners unwilling to provide one another with resources and knowledge required for joint activities and innovation-related processes (Cassiman, Guardo, & Valentini, 2009). Due to such withholding and concerns about the future behavior of the partner, research has suggested that there is always the possibility that dysfunctional conflicts could arise (Schmoltzi & Wallenburg, 2012) and for a hostile environment to be cultivated.

What is more, the potential for unwitting knowledge spillover has consistently been discussed as a major issue involved in strategic alliances (Dussauge et al., 2000) and has mostly been associated with the tension between knowledge sharing and knowledge protection. Knowledge leakage can stem from over-embeddedness, for example, and too tight cooperation and knowledge sharing among the partners, which also can have a negative influence on innovation performance (Wu, 2014a). Too close cooperation also can entail loss of flexibility, over-similarity, over dependency, and eventually, loss of competitive advantage (Afuah, 2000). On the other hand, in interactions taking place in the light of over-skepticism about the future conduct of the partner, not only coordination costs become high, but also the danger of overregulation, which prevails with significant consequences for the flexibility of the interactions and the emergence of a hostile environment. This is in line with the idea that similarity in partner characteristics and expertise is not always fruitful for the success of an alliance (Doz & Hamel, 1998; Kim & Parkhe, 2009). Finally, experiencing failure can entail negative reputational consequences for the engaged firms (Cygler, Sroka, Solesvik, & Debkowska, 2018).

All the dark potentialities of strategic alliances above can make firms perceive heightened vulnerability to the partners' behavior, which is an inevitable and defining component of this relational context. The presence of vulnerability, nonetheless, can be perceived as a barrier hindering the required sharing processes and commitment of strategically important resources. Thus, firms need to identify ways to cope with the perceived vulnerability as failing to do so in an effective manner can lead to poor alliance performance or even alliance unrest. Yet, prior research has discussed vulnerability in a tautological manner with the neighboring concept of interpartner uncertainty, which means that the focus has mainly been on the actions of the focal firm to manage interpartner uncertainty, that is, on one side of the alliance (Lumineau & Oliveira, 2018). However, the relational processes which take place in order for vulnerability to be managed have received limited attention. In this chapter, we suggest that vulnerability is shaped and managed in an interactive manner. We conceptualize vulnerability as a positive and energizing social element of the strategic alliance texture and therefore as an element that needs to be embraced and not mitigated. Below, we first discuss briefly the literature on management of interpartner uncertainty as interpartner uncertainty and vulnerability have often been used interchangeably. Building on this body of research, we highlight the importance of relational means to be able to cope with perceived vulnerability in strategic alliances.

Dealing With Interpartner Uncertainty in Strategic Alliances

Dealing with interpartner uncertainty in interorganizational relationships has mainly been studied in terms of alliance governance, which refers to "how an alliance is managed, how it is organized and regulated by agreements and processes, and how the partners control and influence its evolution and performance over time" (Doz & Hamel, 1998, p. 120).

Alliance governance is based on governance mechanisms that represent specific formal and informal rules of managing the interactions between the engaged parties (Poppo & Zenger, 2002) and reducing uncertainty-related exchange hazards (Cao & Lumineau, 2015). Specifically, such governance mechanisms serve the purposes of coordinating, monitoring, and incentivizing the partners' behavior (Albers, 2010) and can be of two main types: contractual (or formal) and relational (or informal; Li, Poppo, & Zhou, 2010). These two types of governance mechanisms have different theoretical foundations and entail different responses to uncertainty. While contractual governance mechanisms have mainly been informed by a structural perspective and neoclassical contract theories, such as transaction cost economics (TCE), the importance of relational governance mechanisms has been highlighted primarily by studies building upon a relational perspective and relational contracting theories, such as SET and social capital theory (Cao & Lumineau, 2015; Faems, Janssens, Madhok, & van Looy, 2008; Roehrich, Selviaridis, Kalra, Van der Valk, & Fang, 2019).

From a structural perspective, TCE-informed studies (Williamson, 1985) advocate that management of interpartner uncertainty is based on contractual governance defined as "the use of an extensive set of terms and clauses specifying mutual rights and obligations with legal and private sanctions for noncompliance" (Krishnan et al., 2016, p. 2522). TCE argues that by investing in formal monitoring procedures and relying on detailed legal contracts and binding agreements, firms can control and safeguard against partner opportunism and mitigate exchange hazards (Lumineau & Quélin, 2012). This occurs in particular because contracts are used to reduce partners' willingness to engage in resource misappropriation, opportunism or intentional underperformance (Parkhe, 1993), to impose penalties in case of partner misbehavior (Lumineau & Quélin, 2012; Ryall & Sampson, 2009), and to clarify partner roles and responsibilities (Lui & Ngo, 2004). In addition, as contracts have both controlling and coordinating dimensions (Lumineau, 2017), they also serve as a means to establish a common understanding among the partners regarding the objectives of the relationship and specify communication and reporting procedures (Ryall & Sampson, 2009). However, contracts are not sufficient to safeguard against all eventualities (Mayer & Nickerson, 2005) as they are always incomplete and individuals are characterized by bounded rationality (Cannon et al., 2000). Further, contracts tend to be inflexible and cannot be easily adjusted to ongoing changes (Carson et al., 2006). To this end, a body of related research has drawn upon organizational design and suggested the implementation of flexible structural arrangements (Albers, Wohlgezogen, & Zajac, 2016) while others have adopted a real options theory perspective and placed emphasis on the need for flexible contracts that enable modifications and adaptations in the light of changes and unforeseen contingencies in the exchange (Schepker, Martynov, & Poppo, 2014).

Whereas the stream of research focused on contractual governance contribute to our understanding of interpartner uncertainty based on more formal means and structures, the key critique towards it is that it has an under-socialized view of human action (Faems et al., 2008) and does not allow for relationship-specific adaptations, which refer to "investments made to modify processes, product technologies, or procedures to the specific needs and/or capabilities of an exchange partner" (Cannon et al., 2000, p. 181). These limitations are addressed by a relational perspective on interpartner uncertainty management.

A relational perspective (Dyer & Singh, 1998) maintains that interpartner uncertainty is managed through relational governance mechanisms defined as "more emergent governance mechanisms that are manifested in socially derived 'arrangements' and that are more informal in comparison to contractual governance" (Roehrich et al., 2019, p. 1). Studies associated with SET (Blau, 1964) emphasize the sociological dimension of relational governance and underline the importance of reciprocity and trust in addressing the issue of interpartner uncertainty in interorganizational relationships (Faems et al., 2008; Gulati, 1995). Such studies suggest that social norms and trust support the partners to accept and embrace interpartner uncertainty in a non-calculative way (Möllering, 2006). Relational norms "reflect expectations about attitudes and behaviors parties have in working cooperatively together to achieve mutual and individual goals" (Cannon et al., 2000, p. 183) and provide flexible guidelines about how the partners should interact within a relationship. Thus, reliance on relational norms limits concerns about and creates disincentives against partner opportunism (Carson et al., 2006; Zhou et al., 2015) while at the same time, flexibility and adaptation are facilitated. All in all, the relational perspective maintains that management of interpartner uncertainty is based on informal processes and relational mechanisms. Adopting a relational perspective on the management of the dark side of strategic alliances, we build on SET and discuss reciprocity as a particularly important means for coping with vulnerability. But what is vulnerability and how can it be defined?

CONCEPTUALIZING VULNERABILITY AS A STRENGTH

Vulnerability is a key issue in interorganizational relationships (Svensson, 2002) and it is often discussed either interchangeably with the concept of uncertainty or as a phenomenon essential to trust, which is defined as the willingness to render oneself vulnerable (Mayer et al., 1995; Rousseau et al., 1998). However, it is rather surprising that "very limited conceptual or empirical work so far exists that is explicitly directed to understand vulnerability itself" (Nienaber et al., 2014, p. 568). Drawing on this limited body of research devoted to vulnerability in management and organization studies (e.g., literature on trust [Tsui-Auch & Möllering, 2010], identity work

[Corlett, Mavin, & Beech, 2019], management education [Hay, 2014], and supply-chain relations [Svensson, 2004]), we broadly define vulnerability as *the process of being exposed to the potentiality of being harmed due to unexpected partner (mis)behavior.* This definition is in line with Mayer, Davis, and Schoorman (1995) who note that "being vulnerable implies that there is something of importance to be lost" (p. 712). Similarly, Tsui-Auch and Möllering (2010) define vulnerability in relation to fear and potential loss of company resources or firms' competitive advantage over others due to harmful partner behavior. Furthermore, in the context of supply-chain relations, vulnerability is often linked to dependency, perceptions of deviation from what is expected and negative consequences of such deviation. For instance, Svensson (2004) defines vulnerability as "a condition that affects a firm's goal accomplishment [and is] dependent upon the occurrence of negative consequences of disturbance" (p. 470). Therefore, we choose to use the term vulnerability in this chapter to denote the process of being exposed to potentialities of harm as a result of partner (mis)behavior.

Yet, we argue that vulnerability is not merely a negative, one-sided phenomenon associated with fear of loss and insecurity, but also a relational phenomenon that can be stimulating for a relationship and positively influence the future behavior of the partners as well. McEvily, Zaheer, and Perrone (2004) highlight that "making ourselves vulnerable credibly commits us to follow a course of action that would not harm the counterpart, lest the counterpart exploit our vulnerability in return" (p. 3). In other words, when we allow ourselves to become vulnerable not only do we "take a risk that a party we depend on may harm us" (McEvily et al., 2004, p. 3), but at the same time, we can guide the future behavior of our counterparts by rendering ourselves vulnerable in a way that can be perceived by the partners as a credible commitment, often coupled with the request for social support, too. Therefore, there is a bright side of vulnerability and we suggest that firms may approach vulnerability in a more constructive manner and avoid protecting themselves against vulnerability. In the context of identity work, for instance, Corlett et al. (2019) conceptualize vulnerability as a positive element of a relation that acts as a precursor to social support by others, which encourages the engaged parties to cope with vulnerability in a non-conventional, non-defensive way. To this end, we adopt Corlett's et al. (2019) more positive and relational conceptualization of vulnerability, which portrays "vulnerability as relational processes, involving recognizing and claiming vulnerability, developing social support to share vulnerability with trusted others and recognizing alternative ways of reconceptualizing and responding to vulnerability" (p. 573). After all, "vulnerability becomes wisdom through the recognition and acceptance of restrictions relating to self" (Clarke & Knights, 2018, p. 1416). Following this notion, we argue that vulnerability is not necessarily a negative phenomenon that needs to be mitigated but can be approached as an energizing relational aspect that can rally social support and facilitate the realization of the fruitfulness of strategic alliances. To experience the energizing nature of vulnerability requires firms to cope with it in an effective manner. Adopting a social exchange perspective can shed light on this process and highlight the importance of social norms in coping with vulnerability.

Coping With Vulnerability: A Social Exchange Perspective

From a social exchange perspective (for a review, see Cropanzano & Mitchell, 2005), any economic exchange involves social exchanges which are defined as "voluntary actions of individuals that are motivated by the returns they are expected to bring and typically in fact bring from others" (Blau, 1964, p. 91). We adopt this definition and enrich it by adding that social exchanges also involve voluntary actions that are motivated by the prioritization of the partners' interests and not necessarily by expected returns. Social exchanges cannot be explicitly contracted, governed, and specified by the use of formal means and predefined contractual solutions, but are based on social norms which play a critical role in managing partners in strategic alliances. Social norms involve "expectations rather than rigid requirements of behavior" (Cannon et al., 2000, p. 184) and provide a "general frame of reference, order, and standards for relations, which help promote the continuity of exchanges" (Zhou et al., 2015, p. 2). Social norms are related to "patterns of behavior that are self-enforcing within a group" (Young, 2015, p. 359) and are important for coping with vulnerability as "everyone wants to conform when they expect everyone else to conform" (Young, 2015, p. 359). Highlighting that social norms matter not only to interpersonal relations but also to the development of effective interorganizational relations, prior research has utilized SET in the context of strategic alliances (Bignoux, 2006; Muthusamy & White, 2005) and alliance constellations (Das & Teng, 2002). Social norms, such as reciprocity and mutuality, are particularly important when dealing with partner opportunism (Cannon et al., 2000; Heide & John, 1992; Zhou et al., 2015) and coping with the entailed perceived vulnerability. Social norms are important because they encourage firms to engage in self-regulation and self-restraint (Heide & John, 1992), to prioritize their partners' interests and needs, and to motivate their partners to behave in a certain manner, albeit without creating any obligations. Thus, relationship-specific adaptations can be achieved, which is particularly important given that in strategic alliances resources are exchanged between the engaged parties in the light of incomplete contracts (Das & Teng, 2001). In other words, social norms, such as reciprocity, provide guidance to the partners and encourage the engaged parties to interact and reciprocate one another's behavior on a voluntary basis.

Experiencing reciprocal exchanges of strategically important resources is critical for the continuation of strategic alliances and the management of vulnerability. Following Swärd (2016), we define reciprocity as a social norm that "dictates that an action performed by one party requires a repayment by the other (Meeker, 1983, p. 227) and concerns both expectations and behavior" (p. 1842). Although SET suggests that social behavior is "contingent on rewarding reactions from others" (Blau, 1964, p. 6), it also highlights that the rewarding reactions expected are not an "end-in-themselves" and that the presence of positive expectations for reciprocal treatment by the partners is not a rational process characterized by a cost-benefit analysis that leads to rigid requirements or obligations. As Swärd (2016) highlights, reciprocity can be based both on a calculation of benefits and on a sense of duty. We adopt the latter view and argue that reciprocity is a key means for coping with vulnerability and sustaining the exchange in the long-run because it provides the partners with a "norm that compels people to help others who have helped them" (Swärd, 2016, p. 1844). After all, reciprocity is the "morality of being obliged to do something, a morality of duty, a morality of being indebted" (Pessers, 2014, p. 152).

Reciprocity can be of different types based on two dimensions: the number of parties involved and the immediateness of the reciprocal action. First, depending on the number of partners, reciprocity can be either restricted or generalized. Restricted reciprocity takes place between two firms as in bilateral strategic alliances where Firm A reciprocates the behavior of Firm B and vice versa. Generalized reciprocity, on the other hand, occurs among multiple firms as in alliance constellations where Firm A does not reciprocate Firm B in a direct manner while another party (e.g., Firm C) or the entire group has a "moral" obligation to give back to Firm B (Das & Teng, 2002). Second, depending on the immediateness of the reciprocal action (i.e., time-horizon for payback), reciprocity can be specific or diffuse. While specific reciprocity requires partners to reciprocate their partner in the short-term immediately, diffuse reciprocity is more long-term oriented (Swärd, 2016) and based on the idea that the firm will perceive a moral duty or "debt" to its partners; a social debt that needs to be repaid in future exchanges (Bignoux, 2006).

Mutuality is another social norm suggested to be important when dealing with adversities in strategic alliances. Mutuality refers to the shared "attitude that each party's success is a function of everyone's success and that one cannot prosper at the expense of one's partner... [Mutuality] expresses the sentiment of joint responsibility" (Cannon et al., 2000, p. 183). As in reciprocity, mutuality supports coping with vulnerability because it emphasizes the common interests of the engaged parties. Yet, neither reciprocity nor mutuality focuses explicitly on the interests of the partners that are not aligned with the ones of the focal firm's. While reciprocity and mutuality are useful social norms are useful for managing the partners in strategic alliances, we argue that coping with vulnerability in an interactive manner necessitates firms to be keen on satisfying their partners' interests and supporting them to fulfill their objectives. Only in this way will the counterparties maintain the willingness to render themselves vulnerable and facilitate the continuation of the alliance. Compared to reciprocity (i.e., I provide a "gift" in order to receive another "gift" at a later point in time; see discussion on page 98 on the Derridean paradox of the gift), mutuality involves certain actions that are undertaken by the focal firm for the common good (i.e., I provide a "gift" because everyone—including myself—will receive a gift) and thus, the interests of the partners are to some extent emphasized. To this end, what makes mutuality unique and particularly interesting in the context of strategic alliances is the altruistic part underlying this norm; firms actively pay attention to the interests of their partners. Following this notion, we view mutuality as a social norm related not only to the "attitude that each party's success is a function of *everyone's success*" (Cannon et al., 2000, p. 183), but also, and more importantly, to the attitude that each party's success is a function of *everyone's effort*. For the sake of conceptual clarity, in the following sections below, and to emphasize the altruistic actions undertaken by the engaged parties, we discuss the component of mutuality as a distinct social norm, namely altruism. Prior research has also discussed altruism as an exchange rule (Batson, 1995; Meeker, 1971) which received limited attention by studies informed by SET as "the majority of the models of SET in the organizational sciences focus primarily on principles of reciprocity, rather than altruism" (Cropanzano & Mitchell, 2005, p. 880). "Altruism is a selfless concern for the welfare and wellbeing of others" (Siu, Shek, & Law, 2012, p. 2) and "serves as a rule whereby we seek to benefit another person even at an absolute cost to ourselves" (Cropanzano & Mitchell, 2005, p. 879).

To sum up, by drawing on SET, we view reciprocity and altruism as instrumental social norms for coping with vulnerability in strategic alliances. While the importance of reciprocity has been implicitly acknowledged in the extant literature on strategic alliances, it has not been linked to the notion of vulnerability. Additionally, the concept of altruism has received limited attention, although it is critical for signaling to the partners that their interests are prioritized by the focal firm and can serve as a social norm guiding an exchange in a less authoritative manner. Further, "little attention has been given to the possibility that multiple rules are employed simultaneously" (Cropanzano & Mitchell, 2005, p. 880), such as in simultaneous employment of reciprocity and altruism.

Based on the above, we suggest that effective interpartner relations in alliance constellations are developed when firms establish and simultaneously follow norms of reciprocity and altruism as the interplay between these social norms facilitates embracement of perceived vulnerability. But how can these social norms be established in strategic alliances and how does their interplay influence the process of coping with vulnerability? To provide an answer to this question, we build upon Derrida's notion of conditional and unconditional hospitality.

DERRIDA'S NOTION OF CONDITIONAL AND UNCONDITIONAL HOSPITALITY

The concept of conditional and unconditional hospitality is described in Jacques Derrida's large number of writings on justice and ethics (Doty, 2006). This concept has often been discussed in the context of migration, which for example is reflected in an introduction to unconditional hospitality: "The growing tension between human security and state responsibility may be resolved within the balance of the *right to conditional hospitality* and the *duty of unconditional hospitality*, between the legal and political (including moral) concept of Asylum" (Savíc, 2005, p. 1). Although Derrida too discussed the concept of conditional and unconditional hospitality in the context of migration, for instance in an interview with Le Monde (Derrida, 2005), in his writings Derrida seemed not solely focused on human migration and citizenship but hospitality in a broad sense whether it concerned humans, or nonhuman entities (Derrida & Dufourmantelle, 2000).

Conditional hospitality is a hospitality of the invitation (Doty, 2006) and host and guest are important terms in understanding Derrida's hospitality. Derrida claims that norms, rights, duties are imposed on the host and the guest (Derrida & Dufourmantelle, 2000); it is a "welcome" by which certain rights, duties, and obligations follow (Kakoliris, 2015). To exemplify this, imagine a refugee (i.e., the guest) seeking asylum in a country of arrival (i.e., the host). A "welcome" in this context entails certain rights for the refugee but also duties and requirements for reciprocity. The refugee is welcome but only under certain conditions without which hospitality would be abstract (Kakoliris, 2015). Because of the rights, duties, and obligations that follow the welcoming of the guest, hospitality is always conditioned (Derrida & Dufourmantelle, 2000), which could be viewed as expectations on the guest of direct reciprocity.

In contrast, unconditional hospitality is a hospitality of the visitation; the guest arrives uninvited, unexpectedly, and requires unconditional acceptance, an unqualified welcoming of the guest in the absolute sense (Doty, 2006; 2015). The host is expected to give all and oneself to the guest. It is not simply a "come" but "enter," unconditionally, and not an act out of debt or duty (Derrida & Dufourmantelle, 2000), which could be seen as a process of giving of all and oneself without considering that norms of reciprocity will rule their interaction. Often, unconditional hospitality is described in the context of migration as no questions asked of the refugee, not even the refugee's name. Unconditional hospitality is thus a "welcome" that starts from nothing, a real event of hospitality that exceeds the pragmatic demands of a certain context, and in order to be true hospitality it must not discriminate (Kakoliris, 2015); it must not take place due to expected returns. According to Derrida, unconditional hospitality is impossible if the search for it is restricted to "realms of policy, law, and sovereign state edicts… codifications of accepted courses of action created therein" (Doty, 2015, p. 46). If instead this limited scope is expanded, there is "the possibility of the impossible" and the possible localization of practices the alignment of which transforms unconditional hospitality into a *promise* rather than a rule (Doty, 2015, p. 46). It becomes clear that unconditional hospitality as a rule is both impossible and indeed possible at the same time, something that "still may happen"; it always remains a promise and an "ethical encounter" even if only for a brief moment (Doty, 2006, p. 55, 65). This paradox between the possible and the impossible may remind readers of another Derridean paradox, namely that of the gift. True gifts, Derrida claims, are not part of a rational economy of exchange similar to the way one is expected to return a favor, gift or offer a "thank you" upon being given something. On the contrary, true gifts are spontaneous and singular events "occurring within a… system or 'economy' which knows no self-other distinction… must be 'impossible' [as] it stands *outside of*… this economy of exchange" (Wu, 2014b, pp. 1440, 1445). In other words, both hospitality and the gift are examples of *aporia* in Derrida's writings: paradoxes or seemingly impossible concepts.

What has been shown above is that conditional hospitality concerns rights, duties, and obligations following the "welcome" between host and guest, which could be interpreted as reciprocity: reciprocity is expected. Unconditional hospitality, on the other hand requires unconditional and absolute acceptance of the guest; giving all and oneself to the guest could be seen as a manifestation of altruism.

Conditional and unconditional hospitality might seem to be two distinct approaches *prima facie* but are not, so how are they related? Unconditional hospitality, Wu states, "underlies and determines all forms of conditional hospitality, which are based on conventional laws located within an economy of exchange… is prior to and 'conditions'… any conventional, public, official or legal conception of hospitality or of 'hosting' a 'guest'" (2014b, pp. 1439, 1445). In other words, unconditional hospitality inspires the plural laws of conditional hospitality. There would be no laws of hospitality, that is, conditions imposed, unless there was unconditional hospitality in the first place (Derrida & Dufourmantelle, 2000). This is not simply an opposition between two concepts. *It is between conditional and unconditional hospitality that responsibilities are formed and decisions made* (Derrida, 2005). In fact, "the very foundation of Derrida's teachings about the duties of an unconditional friendship, is a request for the establishment of a unique political friendship, a friendship with the other, the distant, the unfamiliar—in short, with the *stranger* as such" (Savíc, 2005, p. 4). Derrida (2005, p. 6) calls for a pure hospitality, which he describes as "the least bad conditions," as effective as possible, the most just legislation, a "welcome" before imposing any conditions. Unconditional hospitality thus becomes an attempt to achieve the best conditions possible. Kakoliris (2015) highlights that unconditional hospitality could be risky, however. To whom will pure hospitality be offered? Who is the guest and who knows how the guest will behave? What are the potential consequences? Perhaps Derrida's answer would be that it is about calculating the risks while not closing the door on the incalculable (cf. Derrida, 2005), again balancing between the possible and the impossible. After all, analyzing practices that approach unconditional hospitality can be useful in imagining alternative perspectives on the world (Doty, 2015).

Thus, *responsible action* is to continuously negotiate *between* the requirements of conditional and unconditional hospitality (Kakoliris, 2015). In the call of responsibility, there is a type of puzzlement, an *aporia*, the space between the possible and the impossible, recognizing that there is no certainty but absolute uncertainty. Thus, the fulfilment of responsibility is always a promise. It is justice on the basis of a gift (Doty, 2006), and the conditions transform that gift into a contract between the host and the guest (Derrida, 2005). Essentially, hospitality always includes a certain amount of hostility although not necessarily in the negative sense. Even if host sovereignty is what yields hospitality, violence resides in every act of hospitality as manifestations of host sovereignty (Kakoliris, 2015). Derrida (2005) even maintains that the first violence made, again in the context of migration, is that the refugee needs to make claims in a language that he or she does not speak. There are even etymological links between host, hostility, and hospitality, which is why sometimes the terms *hostipitality* and *hostipi*table are used (cf. Bida, 2018; Claviez, 2013). This shows how sovereignty both enables the host to offer hospitality and potentially to do violence, that is, displaying acts of hostility. Consequently, Kakoliris (2015) states that an essential amount of self-restraint needs to be exercised.

Is there not a risk, then, that hospitality can be used as a weapon? A host might offer a certain hospitality to a guest or entity which could in fact be a confirmation of sovereignty, an act of power, or an expression of status to be reaffirmed (Kakoliris, 2015). This becomes particularly evident if hospitality is imagined as a right. If the guest enjoys certain rights, it follows that the host has certain duties to help realize or meet the guest's rights. This means that certain duties are expected of a host or entity, possibly creating a situation where asymmetrical patterns of power are emphasized between host and guest, for instance when it comes to ability and capacity. Imagined as a right, hospitality can thus become too strongly connected to power (Cheah, 2013). In this context, Derrida also seems open to the possibility of shifting positions; the inviting host could become a "hostage" while the guest becomes the host's host (Derrida & Dufourmantelle, 2000).

Perhaps rightfully, then, Claviez (2013) asks whether there can ever be a place where unconditional hospitality can exist or if this simply is a utopia, a nonplace where naturally nothing can take place similar to the grey area that separates Derrida's conditional and unconditional hospitality. Kakoliris (2015) also asks whether the host can ever be hospitable enough. The appeal to the guest to "feel like home" becomes absurd were the guest to stay and enjoy the facilities permanently and unconditionally as if it were the guest's own home. The scenario above might serve as an example of what Wu (2014b) sees as a risk in that "conditioned acts of hospitality that emerge from their ground in unconditional hospitality may... 'pervert' the latter" (p. 1439). Another problem is that Derrida's unconditional hospitality signals that the host must not ask any questions, which in itself could be perceived as an inhospitable act (Claviez, 2013). Nevertheless, one may engage in acts of conditional and unconditional hospitality at the same time; consequently what is perceived as a hospitable act is not a matter of whether responsibility is assigned to the guest by the host, but whether the responsibility is formed on the basis of a continuous negotiation between conditional and unconditional hospitality, which Kakoliris (2015) suggests.

EMBRACING VULNERABILITY BY ENGAGING IN BLURRED HOSPITALITY

Hitherto, we discussed vulnerability as an inherent aspect in strategic alliances that needs to be embraced for the fruitfulness of the alliance to be realized. From a social exchange perspective, we suggested that the social norms of reciprocity and altruism are instrumental for coping with vulnerability in an effective manner in this relational context. Then, to build a foundation for answering the question—"How can the social norms of reciprocity and altruism be established in strategic alliances and how does their simultaneous employment influence the process of coping with vulnerability?"—we draw upon the Derridean notion of conditional and unconditional hospitality. In this section, we present an integrative model (see Figure 4.1) and provide an answer to the abovementioned question.

As the model shows, interpartner uncertainty and perceptions of dark potentialities that characterize the interactions among firms engaged in

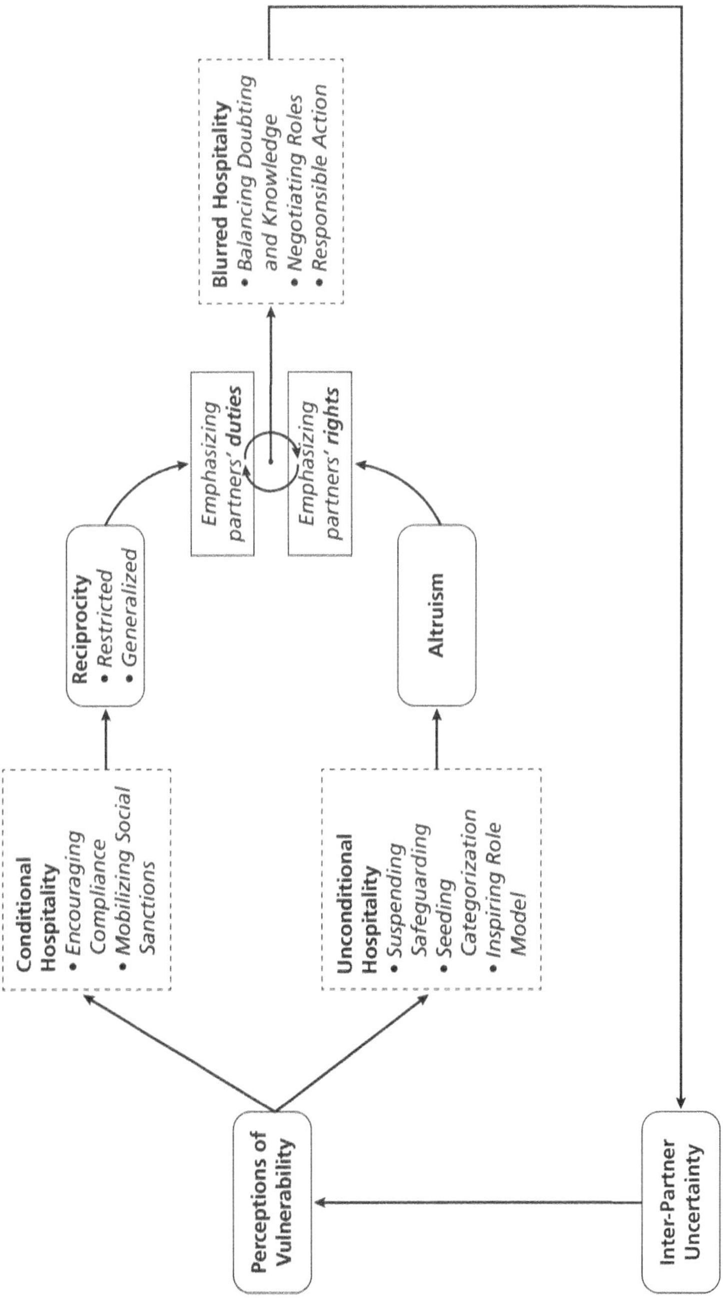

Figure 4.1 A model of coping with vulnerability in strategic alliances.

strategic alliances influence perceptions of vulnerability. To experience the benefits of strategic alliances, firms need to render themselves vulnerable to their partners and in Derridean terms become a host, the partners' host, by sharing strategically important resources (e.g., the sharing of knowledge). While sharing strategically important resources is an act of hospitality, such hospitality can be of different forms, meaning that firms engage with vulnerability in different ways.

The first mode of engaging with vulnerability is through conditional hospitality. In this way, vulnerability is viewed as positive and energizing yet the firms' willingness to be exposed to the potentiality of being harmed due to unexpected partner (mis)behavior relies on the presence of two key mechanisms. First, while the focal firm shares strategically important resources, the hospitality provided is conditioned as the sharing takes place in a manner that entails certain obligations, which enables the firm to perceive a certain degree of security. In the case of conditional hospitality, there are certain and explicit expectations regarding the partners' behavior that take the form of strict requirements or obligations which need to be fulfilled for the continuation of the exchange. Therefore, partners are encouraged to comply with the focal firm's expectations and recognize partner responsibility in supporting the focal firm to cope with the perceived vulnerability and achieve the sought-after benefits of the alliance. Second, engaging with vulnerability through conditional hospitality means that the focal firm not only specifies detailed conditions that need to be respected by the partners in order for the sharing of strategically important resources to be continued, but the focal firm also relies on the support of third parties in the monitoring and safeguarding of a partner's behavior. In that sense, acceptance of vulnerability by the focal firm is based on the expectations that social sanctions will be imposed by third parties, which are often associated with reputational consequences for the misbehaving partners. This is relevant to bilateral alliances as sharing information about opportunistic behavior by the partner can cause difficulty for the misbehaving partner in identifying partners in the future. It is also relevant to alliance constellations as social sanctions in this context means that "all member firms have the responsibility of observing the conduct of all other members," sharing these observations and influencing the reputation of a firm that behaves in an opportunistic manner (Das & Teng, 2002, p. 449). When the mechanisms presented above (i.e., encouraging compliance, mobilizing social sanctions) are set in motion and the welcoming act is accompanied by explicit requests for certain partner behavior, firms cultivate and operate on the basis of the social norm of reciprocity. This means that conditional hospitality enables firms to become vulnerable yet demand from partners to reciprocate one another's actions, either directly as in bilateral alliances or in a generalized manner, as in alliance constellations. To this end, obligations for reciprocal actions are explicitly established and in partner interactions the main emphasis is placed on the *partners' duties.*

An alternative mode of engaging with vulnerability is unconditional hospitality. By adopting the principles of unconditional hospitality, firms accept vulnerability in an unconditional manner which is supported by the presence of three key mechanisms. First, the focal firm shares strategically important resources yet suspends monitoring and safeguarding and relies on a self-fulfilling prophecy (Ghoshal & Moran, 1996) that no significant harm can occur although valuable resources are provided to partners holding partially conflicting objectives. Also, in unconditional hospitality, firms are more eager to cultivate "categorization," meaning "the self-classification of actors into particular groups" which is critical for the engaged firms to have a common understanding of their relationship and avoid conflicts (Weber & Mayer, 2014, p. 351). As categorization means firms view each other as partners, firms share resources in an unconditional manner and are not concerned about being exposed to the potentiality of being harmed due to unexpected partner (mis)behavior. Moreover, we argue that unconditional hospitality in strategic alliances means that firms behave based on a belief that moral obligations should not be made explicit and that the act of defining duties should be performed by the firms that receive the "gift" (i.e., strategically important resources) rather than the ones who provide it. What hosts can do, however, is to allow unintentional promotion of role models that can inspire partner behavior in an indirect and non-authoritative manner, which lessens the safeguarding against or even the mere consideration of partner misbehavior and enables firms to render themselves vulnerable in an unconditional manner. When the mechanisms presented above (i.e., suspending safeguarding, seeding categorization, and inspiring role model) are set in motion and the welcoming act is accompanied by unconditional social support, firms cultivate and operate on the basis of the social norm of altruism. This means that unconditional hospitality enables firms to become vulnerable and share strategically important resources in a voluntary manner which in turn may influence the future behavior of the partners, depending on whether the partners perceive a sense of categorization or an internal need to adopt the role model that is indirectly suggested by the focal firm. To this end, the focal firm influences the future behavior of their partners by supporting the partners unselfishly and emphasizing the *partners' rights.*

What we discussed so far is that whereas conditional hospitality acts as a catalyst for reciprocity, unconditional hospitality acts as a catalyst for altruism and that the two modes of engaging with vulnerability enable management of the partners either by emphasizing the partners' duties based on the norm of reciprocity or by emphasizing the partners' rights based on the norm of altruism. We suggest that adopting an either/or approach to the relationship between conditional and unconditional hospitality is problematic as these two can complement each other and their simultaneous enactment facilitates vulnerability embracement based on both reciprocity and altruism.

To illuminate the importance of this interplay between conditional and unconditional hospitality for the process of coping with vulnerability, we introduce the concept of *blurred hospitality*. Blurred hospitality emerges when firms pursue a balance between emphasizing the partners' duties and the partners' rights in the development of a strategic alliance. Doing so enables them to embrace vulnerability because of three main reasons.

First, the constant interplay between conditional and unconditional hospitality, that is, different approaches to vulnerability in strategic alliances, supports firms to cultivate collective organizational wisdom, which constitutes an active dialogue between partners that find themselves in a process of signaling and receiving signals of confidence and doubt about firms' duties and rights. Wisdom (Weick, 1998) is defined as "the capacity, in part, to simultaneously acknowledge and embrace opposing orientations, and thereby strive for a course of action that honors both" (Ashforth et al., 2014, p. 1465). Building on this, we propose that when firms engage with vulnerability through blurred hospitality, they interactively embrace vulnerability by acknowledging and accepting opposing orientations in a way that allows the continuation of the exchange even when unexpected alliance interruptions come into light. Thus, blurred hospitality suggests that firms calculate risks while not closing the door on the incalculable, to paraphrase Derrida.

Second, blurred hospitality encourages firms to adopt a very flexible interpretation of who is the host and who is the guest. The roles of host and guest are constantly negotiated as are positions, duties, and rights in the hospitality process. In other words, blurred hospitality is manifest in the grey zone between conditional and unconditional hospitality. In this context, firms do not simply place emphasis on rights or duties but criticize the very need of having the rights and duties of these roles defined. By prescribing constant relationship-specific adaptations, blurred hospitality enables role shifting and discourages persistent power asymmetries and partner opportunism.

Third, through blurred hospitality, the principles of *responsible action* emerge through a negotiation *between* the requirements of conditional and unconditional hospitality (cf. Kakoliris, 2015) and the collective puzzlement in which the partners identify themselves. As duties and rights are in constant flux, responsible action is an interactive accomplishment shaped by the negotiations among the partners who collectively navigate orientational difficulties. Responsible action is not guided by formal guidelines but by the interactions between the partners that form, enable, and constrain acts of conditional and unconditional hospitality. Duties and rights become blurred, hospitality couples with self-restraint, and more importantly, the gift and the *way* in which the gift is provided and received become the epicenter both of arriving at judgments about the partners' future behavior and of embracing vulnerability within interactions of "reciprocal altruism."

CONCLUDING REMARKS

In this chapter, we conceptualized vulnerability as a strength for firms engaged in strategic alliances and we built on SET and the Derridean notion of (un)conditional hospitality to answer the following question: "How can the social norms of reciprocity and altruism be established in strategic alliances and how does their simultaneous employment influence the process of coping with vulnerability?" Addressing this research question is important not only because becoming vulnerable to the partners' behavior is a prerequisite for the formation of alliances, but coping with vulnerability is particularly important also to manage strategic alliances effectively, facilitating smooth alliance functioning and preventing premature termination of the alliance. In the previous section, we provided an answer to this question and proposed an integrative model of embracing vulnerability in strategic alliances through blurred hospitality. In this section, we list a number of contributions that this chapter provides. This chapter contributes to existing literature on coping with vulnerability in strategic alliances and extends research on vulnerability in interorganizational relationships in four main ways (McEvily, Zaheer, & Perrone, 2004; Svensson, 2000, 2004; Tsui-Auch & Möllering, 2010).

First, while prior research has discussed vulnerability as a component of trust, we propose that vulnerability deserves closer scholarly attention as a separate social phenomenon that often emerges due to the presence of interpartner uncertainty. Importantly, we suggest that vulnerability is not a negative aspect that needs to be mitigated but a positive and energizing aspect that needs to be embraced for the alliance to provide the sought-after benefits. This is in line with an emerging stream of research approaching vulnerability as a strength rather than a problematic component of social relationships (Corlett et al., 2019; Hay, 2014).

Second, we answer a call for utilizing SET in management and organization studies (Cropanzano & Mitchell, 2005; Das & Teng, 2002) and we take a first step to shed light on how social exchange processes characterized by vulnerability are developed and sustained through the interplay between different social norms. In particular, the chapter strengthens arguments about the important role of the social norm of reciprocity in inter-firm relationships (Swärd, 2016), but also emphasizes the critical role of the social norm of altruism in the face of vulnerability. Whereas Meeker (1971) includes altruism as a fundamental exchange rule, this has not received adequate attention by strategic alliance scholars. By discussing altruism as a social norm that supports firms to cope with vulnerability in strategic alliances, we assist the literature in overcoming a major limitation in its approach to social norms as "the majority of the models of SET in the organizational sciences focus primarily on principles of reciprocity, rather than altruism" (Cropanzano & Mitchell, 2005, p. 880). We fill a part of this gap in the literature by suggesting that altruism is a social norm that places emphasis on vulnerability management as an interactive accomplishment. As we find this an interesting avenue for further research, we call for future studies on the role of altruism in strategic alliances. Additionally, another limitation of the literature is that "little attention has been given to the possibility that multiple rules are employed simultaneously" (Cropanzano & Mitchell, 2005, p. 880). We believe that our discussion on the simultaneous employment of reciprocity and altruism to cope with vulnerability in an interactive and effective way supports the literature to understand and pay closer attention to the synergies that can emerge when multiple social norms are employed simultaneously.

The third contribution of this chapter is related to the utilization of the notion of (un)conditional hospitality in the context of strategic alliances. By utilizing these Derridean concepts, we emphasize the relationality aspect of strategic alliances and we propose that depending on the form of hospitality chosen, different modes of engaging with vulnerability in strategic alliances are adopted and different social norms are employed. Following this notion, we suggest that conditional hospitality acts as a catalyst for reciprocity while unconditional hospitality acts as a catalyst for altruism. By doing so, mechanisms underlying the cultivation and sustaining of social norms in strategic alliances are discussed, which adds further insights into how social norms come into light, altered and maintained, such as through social sanctions, signaling membership in a group (Young, 2015) and role models (Legros & Cislaghi, 2020). Finally, a key contribution of this chapter is the introduction of the concept of blurred hospitality that emerges when firms engage in both conditional and unconditional hospitality and thereby, employ both reciprocity and altruism as social norms. Blurred hospitality holds promise for how social norms interrelate and produce synergy and for gaining deeper understanding of how the firms face and interactively cope with adversities and orientational difficulties in strategic alliances. Therefore, we call for empirical research on the role of blurred hospitality in strategic alliances and the pathways through which it emerges and shapes perceptions of vulnerability in this relational context.

REFERENCES

Afuah, A. (2000). How much do your co-opetitors' capabilities matter in the face of technological change? *Strategic Management Journal, 21*(3), 397–404.

Albers, S. (2010). Configurations of alliance governance systems. *Schmalenbach Business Review, 62*(3), 204–233.

Albers, S., Wohlgezogen, F., & Zajac, E. J. (2016). Strategic alliance structures: An organization design perspective. *Journal of Management, 42*(3), 582–614.

Anderson, S. W., Christ, M. H., Dekker, H. C., & Sedatole, K. L. (2014). The use of management controls to mitigate risk in strategic alliances: Field and survey evidence. *Journal of Management Accounting Research, 26*(1), 1–32.

Ashforth, B. E., Rogers, K. M., Pratt, M. G., & Pradies, C. (2014). Ambivalence in organizations: A multilevel approach. *Organization Science, 25*(5), 1453–1478.

Batson, C. D. (1995). Prosocial motivation: Why do we help others. In A. Tesser (Ed.), *Advanced social psychology* (pp. 333–381). New York, NY: McGraw-Hill.

Bida, A. (2018). *Mapping home in contemporary narratives.* New York, NY: Palgrave Macmillan.

Bignoux, S. (2006). Short-term strategic alliances: A social exchange perspective. *Management Decision, 44*(5), 615–627.

Blau, P. M. (1964). *Exchange and power in social life.* New York, NY: Wiley.

Cannon, J. P., Achrol, R. S., & Gundlach, G. T. (2000). Contracts, norms, and plural form governance. *Journal of the Academy of Marketing Science, 28*(2), 180–194.

Cao, Z., & Lumineau, F. (2015). Revisiting the interplay between contractual and relational governance: A qualitative and meta-analytic investigation. *Journal of Operations Management, 33–34*(1), 15–42.

Carson, S. J., Madhok, A., & Wu, T. (2006). Uncertainty, opportunism, and governance: The effects of volatility and ambiguity on formal and relational contracting. *Academy of Management Journal, 49*(5), 1058–1077.

Cassiman, B., Di Guardo, M. C., & Valentini, G. (2009). Organising R&D projects to profit from innovation: Insights from co-opetition. *Long Range Planning, 42*(2), 216–233.

Cheah, P. (2013). To open: Hospitality and alienation. In T. Claviez (Ed.), *The conditions of hospitality: Ethics, politics, and aesthetics on the threshold of the possible* (pp. 57–80). New York, NY: Fordham University Press.

Clarke, C. A., & Knights, D. (2018). Practice makes perfect? Skillful performances in veterinary work. *Human Relations, 71*(10), 1395–1421.

Claviez, T. (2013). Introduction: "Taking place": Conditional/unconditional hospitality. In T. Claviez (Ed.), *The conditions of hospitality: Ethics, politics, and aesthetics on the threshold of the possible* (pp. 1–9). New York, NY: Fordham University Press.

Corlett, S., Mavin, S., & Beech, N. (2019). Reconceptualising vulnerability and its value for managerial identity and learning. *Management Learning, 50*(5), 556–575.

Cropanzano, R., & Mitchell, M. S. (2005). Social exchange theory: An interdisciplinary review. *Journal of Management, 31*(6), 874–900.

Cygler, J., Sroka, W., Solesvik, M., & Dębkowska, K. (2018). Benefits and drawbacks of coopetition: The roles of scope and durability in coopetitive relationships. *Sustainability, 10*(8), 2688.

Das, T. K. (2006). Strategic alliance temporalities and partner opportunism. *British Journal of Management, 17*(1), 1–21.

Das, T. K., & Rahman, N. (2010). Determinants of partner opportunism in strategic alliances: A conceptual framework. *Journal of Business Psychology, 25*(1), 55–74.

Das, T. K., & Teng, B. (1996). Risk types and inter-firm alliance structures. *Journal of Management Studies, 33*(6), 827–843.

Das, T. K., & Teng, B. (1998). Between trust and control: Developing confidence in partner cooperation in alliances. *Academy of Management Review, 23*(3), 491–512.

Das, T. K., & Teng, B. (1999). Managing risks in strategic alliances. *Academy of Management Executive, 13*(4), 50–62.

Das, T. K., & Teng, B. (2001). Trust, control, and risk in strategic alliances: An integrated framework. *Organization Studies, 22*(2), 251–283.

Das, T. K., & Teng, B. (2002). Alliance constellations: A social exchange perspective. *Academy of Management Review, 27*(3), 445–456.

Derrida, J., & Dufourmantelle, A. (2000). *Of hospitality: Anne Dufourmantelle invites Jacques Derrida to respond.* Stanford, CA: Stanford University Press.

Derrida, J. (2005). The principle of hospitality. *Parallax, 11*(1), 6–9.

Doty, R. L. (2006). *Fronteras compasivas* and the ethics of unconditional hospitality. *Millenium: Journal of International Studies, 35*(1), 53–74.

Doty, R. L. (2015). Practices of hospitality in a sovereign world. *Theory in Action, 8*(2), 45–68.

Doz, Y. L., & Hamel, G. (1998). *Alliance advantage: The art of creating value through partnering.* Brighton, MA: Harvard Business Press.

Dussauge, P., Garrette, B., & Mitchell, W. (2000). Learning from competing partners: Outcomes and durations of scale and link alliances in Europe, North America and Asia. *Strategic Management Journal, 21*(2), 99–126.

Dyer, J. H., & Singh, H. (1998). The relational view: Cooperative strategy and sources of interorganizational competitive advantage. *Academy of Management Review, 23*(4), 660–679.

Faems, D., Janssens, M., Madhok, A., & Looy, B. V. (2008). Toward an integrative perspective on alliance governance: Connecting contract design, trust dynamics, and contract application. *Academy of Management Journal, 51*(6), 1053–1078.

Ghoshal, S., & Moran, P. (1996). Bad for practice: A critique of the transaction cost theory. *Academy of Management Review, 21*(1), 13–47.

Gulati, R. (1995). Social structure and alliance formation patterns: A longitudinal analysis. *Administrative Science Quarterly, 40*(4), 619–652.

Gulati, R. (1998). Alliances and networks. *Strategic Management Journal, 19*(4), 293–317.

Hay, A. (2014) "I don't know what I am doing!": Surfacing struggles of managerial identity work. *Management Learning, 45*(5), 509–524.

Heide, J. B., & John, G. (1992). Do norms matter in marketing relationships? *Journal of Marketing, 56*(2), 32–44.

Jiang, X., Li, M., Gao, S., Bao, Y., & Jiang, F. (2013). Managing knowledge leakage in strategic alliances: The effects of trust and formal contracts. *Industrial Marketing Management, 42*(6), 983–991.

Kakoliris, G. (2015). Jacques Derrida on the ethics of hospitality. In E. Imafidon (Ed.), *The ethics of subjectivity: Perspectives since the dawn of modernity* (pp. 144–156). New York, NY: Palgrave Macmillan.

Kale, P., & Singh, H. (2009). Managing strategic alliances: What do we know now, and where do we go from here. *Academy of Management Perspectives, 23*(3), 45–62.

Khanna, T., Gulati, R., & Nohria, N. (1998). The dynamics of learning alliances: Competition, cooperation, and relative scope. *Strategic Management Journal, 19*(3), 193–210.

Kim, J., & Parkhe, A. (2009). Competing and cooperating similarity in global strategic alliances: An exploratory examination. *British Journal of Management, 20*(3), 363–376.

Krishnan, R., Geyskens, I., & Steenkamp, J. B. E. (2016). The effectiveness of contractual and trust-based governance in strategic alliances under behavioral and environmental uncertainty. *Strategic Management Journal, 37*(12), 2521–2542.

Krishnan, R., Martin, X., & Noorderhaven, N. G. (2006). When does trust matter to alliance performance? *Academy of Management Journal, 49*(5), 894–917.

Langfield-Smith, K. (2008). The relations between transactional characteristics, trust and risk in the start-up phase of a collaborative alliance. *Management Accounting Research, 19*(4), 344–364.

Latusek, D., & Vlaar, P. W. (2018). Uncertainty in interorganizational collaboration and the dynamics of trust: A qualitative study. *European Management Journal, 36*(1), 12–27.

Legros, S., & Cislaghi, B. (2020). Mapping the social-norms literature: An overview of reviews. *Perspectives on Psychological Science, 15*(1), 62–80.

Li, J. J., Poppo, L., & Zhou, K. Z. (2010). Relational mechanisms, formal contracts, and local knowledge acquisition by international subsidiaries. *Strategic Management Journal, 31*(4), 349–370.

Lui, S. S., & Ngo, H. Y. (2004). The role of trust and contractual safeguards on cooperation in non-equity alliances. *Journal of Management, 30*(4), 471–485.

Lumineau, F. (2017). How contracts influence trust and distrust. *Journal of Management, 43*(5), 1553–1577.

Lumineau, F., & Oliveira, N. (2018). A pluralistic perspective to overcome major blind spots in research on interorganizational relationships. *Academy of Management Annals, 12*(1), 440–465.

Lumineau, F., & Quélin, B. V. (2012). An empirical investigation of interorganizational opportunism and contracting mechanisms. *Strategic Organization, 10*(1), 55–84.

Mayer, K. J., & Nickerson, J. A. (2005). Antecedents and performance implications of contracting for knowledge workers: Evidence from information technology services. *Organization Science, 16*(3), 225–242.

Mayer, R. C., Davis, J. H., & Schoorman, F. D. (1995). An integrative model of organizational trust. *Academy of Management Review, 20*(3), 709–734.

McEvily, B., Zaheer, A., & Perrone, V. (2004). *Vulnerability and the asymmetric nature of trust in interorganizational exchange* [Working Paper]. Carnegie Mellon University, Pittsburgh, PA.

Meeker, B. F. (1971). Decisions and exchange. *American Sociological Review, 36*(3) 485–495.

Meeker, B. F. (1983). Cooperative orientation, trust, and reciprocity. *Human Relations, 37*, 225–243.

Morgan, N. A., Kaleka, A., & Gooner, R. A. (2007). Focal supplier opportunism in supermarket retailer category management. *Journal of Operations Management, 25*(2), 512–527.

Muthusamy, S. K., & White, M. A. (2005). Learning and knowledge transfer in strategic alliances: A social exchange view. *Organization studies, 26*(3), 415–441.

Möllering, G. (2006). *Trust: Reason, routine, reflexivity*. Bingley, England: Emerald Group.

Nienaber, A.-M., Hofeditz, M., & Romeike, P. D. (2015). Vulnerability and trust in leader-follower relationships. *Personnel Review, 44*(4), 567–591.

Park, S. H., & Russo, M. V. (1996). When competition eclipses cooperation: An event history analysis of joint venture failure. *Management Science, 42*(6), 875–890.

Park, S. H., & Ungson, G. R. (2001). Interfirm rivalry and managerial complexity: A conceptual framework of alliance failure. *Organization science, 12*(1), 37–53.

Pellegrin-Boucher, E., Le Roy, F., & Gurău, C. (2013). Coopetitive strategies in the ICT sector: Typology and stability. *Technology Analysis & Strategic Management, 25*(1), 71–89.

Pessers, D. (2014). The normative foundation of legal orders: A balance between reciprocity and mutuality. *Netherlands Journal of Legal Philosophy, 43*(2), 150–157.

Poppo, L., & Zenger, T. (2002). Do formal contracts and relational governance function as substitutes or complements? *Strategic Management Journal, 23*(8), 707–725.

Roehrich, J. K., Selviaridis, K., Kalra, J., Van der Valk, W., & Fang, F. (2020). Interorganizational governance: A review, conceptualization and extension. *Production Planning & Control, 31*(6), 453–469.

Rousseau, D. M., Sitkin, S. B., Burt, R. S., & Camerer, C. (1998). Not so different after all: A cross-discipline view of trust. *Academy of Management Review, 23*(3), 393–404.

Ryall, M. D., & Sampson, R. C. (2009). Formal contracts in the presence of relational enforcement mechanisms: Evidence from technology development projects. *Management Science, 55*(6), 906–925.

Savíc, O. (2005). Introduction—Duty of unconditional hospitality. *Parallax, 11*(1), 1–5.

Schepker, D. J., Oh, W. Y., Martynov, A., & Poppo, L. (2014). The many futures of contracts: Moving beyond structure and safeguarding to coordination and adaptation. *Journal of Management, 40*(1), 193–225.

Schmoltzi, C., & Wallenburg, C. M. (2012). Operational governance in horizontal cooperations of logistics service providers: Performance effects and the moderating role of cooperation complexity. *Journal of Supply Chain Management, 48*(2), 53–74.

Siu, A. M., Shek, D. T., & Law, B. (2012). Prosocial norms as a positive youth development construct: A conceptual review. *Scientific World Journal, 2012*, Article ID 832026.

Svensson, G. (2000). A conceptual framework for the analysis of vulnerability in supply chains. *International Journal of Physical Distribution & Logistics Management, 30*(9), 731–750.

Svensson, G. (2002). Dyadic vulnerability in companies' inbound and outbound logistics flows. *International Journal of Logistics: Research and Applications, 5*(1), 1–31.

Svensson, G. (2004). Vulnerability in business relationships: The gap between dependence and trust. *Journal of Business & Industrial Marketing, 19*(7), 469–483.

Swärd, A. (2016). Trust, reciprocity, and actions: The development of trust in temporary interorganizational relations. *Organization Studies, 37*(12), 1841–1860.

Tsui-Auch, L. S., & Möllering, G. (2010). Wary managers: Unfavorable environments, perceived vulnerability, and the development of trust in foreign enterprises in China. *Journal of International Business Studies, 41*(6), 1016–1035.

Weber, L., & Mayer, K. (2014). Transaction cost economics and the cognitive perspective: Investigating the sources and governance of interpretive uncertainty. *Academy of Management Review, 39*(3), 344–363.

Weick, K. E. (1998). The attitude of wisdom: Ambivalence as the optimal compromise. In S. Srivastva & D. L. Cooperrider (Eds.), *Organizational wisdom and executive courage* (pp. 40–64). San Francisco, CA: New Lexington Press.

Williamson, O. E. (1985). *The economic institutions of capitalism: Firms, markets, relational contracting.* New York, NY: Free Press.

Wu, J. (2014a). Cooperation with competitors and product innovation: Moderating effects of technological capability and alliances with universities. *Industrial Marketing Management, 43*(2), 199–209.

Wu, M. (2014b). Hundun's hospitality: Daoist, Derridean and Levinasian readings of Zhuangzi's parable. *Educational Philosophy and Theory, 46*(13), 1435–1449.

Young, H. P. (2015). The evolution of social norms. *Economics, 7*(1), 359–387.

Zhou, Y., Zhang, X., Zhuang, G., & Zhou, N. (2015). Relational norms and collaborative activities: Roles in reducing opportunism in marketing channels. *Industrial Marketing Management, 46*, 147–159.

CHAPTER 5

MANAGING INTERPARTNER NEGOTIATIONS IN STRATEGIC ALLIANCES

T. K. Das
Rajesh Kumar

ABSTRACT

The purpose of this chapter is to propose a strategic framework for understanding interpartner negotiation dynamics in alliances. We define *interpartner negotiations* as *a process of reconciling and integrating the interests of the partners in an alliance*, and consider four types of interpartner negotiation strategies—problem solving, contending, yielding, and compromising—and then discuss the dynamics of these negotiation strategies in the formation, operation, and outcome stages of alliance development. The framework makes clear that the four types of interpartner negotiation strategies identified in the chapter need to be appreciated as having differential impact at each stage of alliance development. As interpartner negotiations occur at all stages of alliance evolution, future research may seek to empirically assess the impact of different interpartner negotiation strategies. We also discuss how alliance managers can deploy effective interpartner negotiation strategies for achieving alliance objectives at each of the three developmental stages. The chapter responds

Managing the Partners in Strategic Alliances, pages 113–140

to the need of managers with alliance responsibilities for a framework to help identify and exploit the most effective ways to conduct interpartner negotiations in alliances for productive interactions at different alliance development stages.

INTRODUCTION

Strategic alliances have become a prominent feature of the contemporary business landscape. Firms rely on alliances to facilitate market entry, initiate new product development, and share risks. However, as many studies have suggested, alliances are also notoriously unstable entities, and we need to recognize that alliance partners are in a state of interdependence that may be a precursor of potential conflicts in the alliance. The critical issue is how the partners manage the interdependence that exists between them. The management of interdependence necessitates negotiation, making salient the intriguing subject of the nature and dynamics of negotiation strategies that are pursued by the alliance partners. Might the failure of the alliances be attributed to the dynamics stemming from the use of inappropriate negotiation strategies? How flexible are the alliance partners in terms of the negotiation strategies that they employ as the alliance evolves over time? Are different types of negotiation strategies more appropriate at different developmental stages of the alliance? Can a troubled alliance be rescued by an alteration in the negotiation dynamics between the partner firms? These issues are surely relevant but have only received fragmented attention in the literature so far.

We first introduce the concept of interpartner negotiation dynamics, and then discuss in some detail the framework of interpartner negotiations covering four types of negotiation strategies—problem solving, contending, yielding, and compromising—in the three alliance development stages of formation, operation, and outcome. We conclude with a discussion of managerial implications of the framework.

THE CONCEPT OF NEGOTIATION

Negotiation refers to "the deliberate interaction of two or more complex social units which are attempting to define or redefine the terms of their interdependence" (Walton & McKersie, 1965, p. 3). This definition suggests that interdependence is a key element of all negotiations. If parties were not interdependent there would really be no need for negotiations. The management of interdependence is a process that is often fraught with ambiguity but also offers at once the potential for learning as the partners may get to know more about each other and from each other during the course of interaction (Das & Kumar, 2007). The partners in a negotiation have to calibrate their expectations, determine appropriate negotiation strategies, and respond to their counterpart's offers. Exaggerated expectations, for example, may prevent the partners from reaching an agreement but at the same time low expectations may allow the other party to benefit disproportionately from the negotiated agreement. Similarly, a small concession by one party may generate anger but a large concession may induce the other party to revise expectations.

Bartos (1977) proposes that negotiation is a process that pits the individual (competitive) motivation of an actor to maximize his/her utility against the collectivistic (cooperative) motivation to attain a fair solution. Cross (1977) posits negotiation as a learning process in which negotiators adjust their expectations based upon the results of their interactions. If the learning rate is high then the length of the negotiation process may be reduced. Zartman (1977) conceives of negotiation as a decision making process in which negotiators seek to develop a joint formula. Once such a formula is decided upon the parties begin to focus on issues concerning the details. As the parties negotiate, the partners are also required to deal with the different types of conflicts that may arise in an alliance, namely conflicts about interests, intellective problems, or evaluative problems (Harinck et al., 2000). Conflicts of interest center on the issue of resource scarcity, conflicts involving intellective problems deal with the question of conflicting positions regarding a particular issue, whereas conflicts involving evaluative problems represent conflicting positions on issues and are also referred to as "value conflicts."

The process of defining or redefining interdependence may be the immediate precursor for the emergence of conflict in an interorganizational context. As parties seek to define or redefine the terms of their interdependence they may be stating their demands, rebutting their partners' demands and expectations, and above all may be engaged in a negotiating game as they seek to diffuse conflicts and prevent conflicts from escalating. If, for example, in a dyadic alliance, one of the alliance firms seeks to impose new requirements on its partner, such as completing a particular task earlier than originally agreed upon, the partner is likely to resist and this may provide the basis for the emergence of conflict.

Thomas (1976) defines conflict as "the process which begins when one party perceives that another has frustrated, or is about to frustrate, some concern of his" (p. 891). Pondy (1967) in a discussion of organizational conflict suggests that conflict is a dynamic process whose roots may lie in resource scarcity, need for autonomy, and divergence in subunit goals. We would surmise that these factors are also germane to studying conflict in the alliance context. In a dyadic alliance, for example, the partners may quibble as to the amount of resources they are expected to contribute to the alliance. They may also be very protective of their independence and may differ in terms of the goals that they are hoping to realize from the alliance. Although the definitions may differ in terms of their various emphases, they all focus on the issues of interdependence, perceived incompatibility among the parties' interests, and interactional dynamics (Thomas, 1992). The negotiation strategies are mechanisms for the effective management of conflict. In managing conflicts, negotiators are confronted with the need to balance the competing motivations of value creation and value appropriation.

TYPES OF NEGOTIATION

A number of perspectives on how conflict can be managed have appeared in the literature. Pruitt's (1983) dual concern model suggests that negotiators have open to them four alternative strategies; namely, problem solving, contending, yielding, and inaction. These strategies are derived on the basis of two orthogonal dimensions—namely, concern for one's own outcomes versus concern for the other's outcomes. Contending as a negotiation strategy is likely to be chosen when concern for one's own outcomes is high and the concern for the other's outcomes is low. Problem solving strategy, by contrast, is likely to be chosen when both of these concerns are high. The problem solving approach is akin to Follet's (1941) notion of integration, as the aim is to construct a new alternative that may appeal to all parties. The strategy of contending has one actor imposing his/her will on the other. Yielding means that the negotiators reduce their aspiration levels while inaction implies doing very little of anything in the negotiation process.

Follett (1941) held that conflict can be managed either through domination, compromise, or integration. The dominating strategy suggests victory for one party over another. Compromise involves mutual give and take in which each party gives a little to secure an agreement. Integration represents the construction of a new alternative in which the interests of the parties are reconciled in ways that may be beneficial to both.

Thomas (1976) proposed a typology of five conflict modes (competition, accommodative, sharing, collaborative, and avoidance) based on the dimensions of cooperativeness and assertiveness. Cooperativeness refers to the desire to satisfy the other party's concern while assertiveness refers to attempts to satisfy one's own concern. Competition means satisfying one's own concerns even if it involves imposing a cost on the partner. An accommodative stance implies satisfying the partner's concerns without concentrating on one's own needs. Sharing gives rise to a moderate but not complete satisfaction for the parties involved. Collaboration is integration in that it is associated with fully satisfying the concerns of both of the parties. Finally, an avoidant orientation implies an indifference to either party's concerns.

Putnam and Wilson (1982) proposed a typology of nonconfrontation, solution orientation, and control. Non-confrontation represents an indirect way of managing conflict whether through withdrawal or minimizing differences. Solution orientation represents a problem solving approach to manage conflict in which an attempt is made to integrate the interests of the parties. A control strategy involves an open and direct defense of one's position.

Gelfand et al. (2008) developed a theory of organizational conflict cultures. They propose four alternative conflict cultures: dominating, collaborative, avoidant cultures, and passive-aggressive. The typology was derived on the basis of active vs. passive conflict management norms and agreeable vs. disagreeable conflict management norms. A dominating conflict culture is characterized by norms that are both active and disagreeable. A collaborative conflict culture possesses norms that are agreeable and active. A conflict avoidant culture has norms that are both agreeable and passive. Finally, in a passive-aggressive conflict culture the norms are both disagreeable as well as passive. Harinck et al. (2000) note that different types of conflict are often associated with different types of negotiation strategies. In particular, they found that conflicts rooted in interests lead negotiators to pursue integrative strategies whereas conflicts rooted in intellectual or evaluative problems are not amenable to such a resolution.

Lastly, Pinkley and Northcraft (1994) tested the impact of conflict frames on both the processes and outcomes of conflict. Three alternative frames have been identified in the literature; namely, relationship vs. task, emotional vs. intellectual, and cooperate vs. win (Pinkley, 1990). It was found that individuals achieved a high pay-off solution when the dominant frame that characterized them and their partner was a task-oriented frame.

The dual concern model (Pruitt, 1983) mentioned earlier has received strong empirical support both in the laboratory as well as in field studies and is now prominent in the field of conflict management (De Dreu et al., 2001). Negotiation scholars have also drawn a distinction between integrative (win–win) and distributive (win–lose) bargaining (Walton & McKersie, 1965). The distinction between integrative and distributive bargaining can easily be mapped onto the strategies of problem solving and contending in the dual concern model. We will use the dual concern model as our organizing framework for discussing interpartner negotiation strategies for several reasons. First, this is a framework, as De Dreu et al. (2001) suggest, that has received substantial support in the literature. Second, the dual concern framework is useful in highlighting the mixed motive character of the alliance context in that negotiators have to find the optimal balance between concern for one's own outcomes and concern for the partner's outcomes. And third, the dual concern model suggests that alliancing firms may find all of the strategies attractive depending upon the circumstances (Pruitt & Kim, 2004). We should note, however, that Pruitt's (1983) framework does not discuss compromising as a strategy but other theorists such as De Dreu et al. (2001) consider this to be a viable option. If the alliancing firms are willing to compromise, an agreement may well be at hand although it may not be a truly integrative agreement. Our discussion of interpartner negotiation, thus, will comprise of the following four strategies—problem solving, contending, yielding, and compromising.

A few caveats are also in order. First, it should be noted that in practice alliance managers may choose to use a number of strategies simultaneously (Euwema et al., 2003) and may use different strategies at different stages of alliance development. Euwema and colleagues develop the notion of conglomerated conflict behavior in which actors utilize multiple conflict strategies in a negotiation process. This no doubt makes the analysis more complex, but it does not detract from the fact that different strategies are in principle associated with different substantive and relational outcomes. Secondly, and assuming a dyadic alliance context, the outcome of the negotiation process is dependent on whether the negotiation strategies adopted by the alliance partners lead towards convergence or whether they enhance the distance between the parties. That said, the principle objective of this chapter is to map out the consequences of alternative negotiation strategies.

INTERPARTNER NEGOTIATIONS IN ALLIANCES

As they weigh the prospects of entering into an alliance, or alternatively seek to restructure their relationship if already in an alliance, the alliance firms are confronted with the necessity to effectively manage their interdependence. This requires the partners to choose negotiation strategies that are well calibrated to suit their situation. Consider, for example, the alliance between Renault and Nissan. When the parties explored the possibility of forming an alliance, both companies faced severe challenges. Nissan was facing a loss of market share and financial strain while Renault was just emerging from a failed alliance with Volvo (Korine et al., 2002). The companies were also embedded in different societal cultures, with Renault (French) an embodiment of individualistic societal values whereas Nissan (Japan) represented collectivistic societal values. The partners had to engage in extensive sensemaking and while this was no doubt a tricky and a time-consuming affair it paid good dividends for both companies over the long term. The companies had to grapple with both task and relational issues. As the cultural distance was substantial, relational issues were quite important at the outset. As the partners initiated their relationship and built it over a period of time, they were careful to choose negotiation strategies that avoided any longer term harm. As Korine and colleagues (2002, p. 42) note, "First, they took a long term, encompassing view at critical junctures in the process, rather than a short term bargaining perspective." A good illustration of this is the strategic decision on the part of Renault not to put more pressure on Nissan when DaimlerChrysler backed out of bidding for Nissan. Interpartner negotiations not only involve finding the right balance between the task and relational demands, but it also means calibrating the strategies that might build upon each other. The Renault–Nissan negotiations may be unique in many aspects but they clearly highlight some of the key issues in managing interdependence among partners.

We define *interpartner negotiations* as a process of reconciling and integrating the interests of the partners in an alliance. These negotiations may or may not be successful. In addition, they may vary in the level of integrativeness that they exhibit. It needs to be noted that this is not a one-off process. The process of reconciliation and integration must be carried out over the alliance life cycle, and different alliance partners may employ different strategies depending on the level of concern that they have for their own outcomes versus the other's outcomes. Third, there are different types of negotiation outcomes, namely, economic and relational outcomes (Gelfand et al., 2006), and we would suppose that different negotiating strategies may be associated with different kinds of outcomes. Curhan et al. (2006) note that negotiators may often be as much concerned about subjective outcomes as they are about objective outcomes. Subjective outcomes included feelings pertaining to (a) instrumental outcomes; (b) feelings pertaining to self; (c) feelings relating to the negotiation process; and (d) feelings pertaining to relationships. In terms of the dual concern model, the process of reconciliation and integration may range from problem solving at one extreme to contending at the other. In a problem solving approach the reconciliation and integration involve a genuine concern for understanding the other party's perspective. In a contending strategy, reconciliation and integration, for example, simply mean that the dominant partner's perspective usually prevails. A problem solving approach is likely to lead to positive economic and relational outcomes, while a contending strategy may lead to negative economic and relational outcomes.

The literature on interpartner negotiations in strategic alliances is rather limited but we could identify a few studies that discussed such negotiations to a certain extent. These studies variously suggest that negotiation can be a difficult process (e.g., Arino & Reuer, 2004; Reuer, Zollo, & Singh, 2002), that effective negotiation is critical in enhancing alliance performance (e.g., Lin & Germain, 1998), that the use of distributive strategies is often context dependent (Luo, 1999), and that structural conditions are often highly important in shaping negotiation outcomes. In Table 5.1 we have listed some of these studies. Limited in number though these studies might

TABLE 5.1 Selected Studies of Negotiation in Alliances

Authors	Illustrative Observations
Arino & Reuer (2004)	"Executives need to balance the costs of negotiating, monitoring and enforcing complex contracts against the threat of opportunistic behavior" (p. 38).
Lin & Germain (1998)	"Conflict resolution strategy is expected to affect JV performance" (p. 183).
Luo (1999)	"Distributive strategies are less likely in IJV negotiations, however, when such ventures involve interpartner learning and future interdependence" (p. 144).
Parry, Song, & Spekman (2008)	"We hypothesized that integrative potential was higher (or perceived to be higher) in decisions involving R&D task conflict than in decisions involving marketing task conflict" (pp. 211–212).
Rao & Schmidt (1998)	"Negotiators who believed that their firms would cooperate in the future used more rational tactics in negotiations. They focused on the exchange of information and provided strongly data driven reasons for their demands" (p. 681).
Reuer, Zollo, & Singh (2002)	"We also suggested that changes in the alliance's governance structure can be costly and risky due to the need for renegotiation after collaborators have made resource commitments, which implies that firms will be selective when undertaking governance changes and incurring these costs and risks" (p. 148).
Yan & Gray (1994)	"The findings of this comparative case study provide confirmative evidence that the relative levels of joint venture partners' bargaining power has a significant impact on the pattern of parent control in the venture's management" (p. 1511).

be, they do serve to highlight the relevance of studying interpartner negotiation in alliances.

INTERPARTNER NEGOTIATIONS IN ALLIANCE DEVELOPMENT STAGES

Interpartner negotiations are vital for successful cooperation between alliance partners. The negotiation process is intrinsically not simple; its complexity is clearly magnified in the alliance context because alliances involve partners that are potential competitors. Partners may therefore be reluctant to share information lest such information be used to gain advantage. They may also be sensitive to potential partner opportunism in the alliance context and this may deter them from being fully committed to the venture. But at the same time the partners recognize that they must cooperate, for otherwise there would be no point in entering into an alliance. It is finding the right balance between cooperation and competition that may and often does prove tricky for the partners. The balance between cooperation and competition is reflected in the type of negotiation strategies that are chosen by the partners. Within the framework of the dual concern model a problem solving strategy would signify cooperation while a contending strategy would be indicative of a competitive intent.

We have noted that alliances evolve through the stages of formation, operation, and outcome (Das & Teng, 2002a). Each of these stages has its own unique challenges. In the remainder of this section we discuss the relevance and implications of the different negotiation strategies at different stages of alliance development. We also summarize in Table 5.2 the likely outcomes of the different negotiation strategies at each of the developmental stages, and

TABLE 5.2 Negotiation Strategies and Their Impact at Different Stages of Alliance Development

Negotiation Strategy	Alliance Development Stage		
	Formation	**Operation**	**Outcome**
Problem solving (likely to be pursued by member firms that are cooperative, flexible, and long-term oriented)	will develop mutual trust or strengthen their pre-existing relationship	will be successful in preventing the escalation of mutual conflict	will strengthen their relationship; will deal with negative developments in a calm and a dispassionate manner
Contending (likely to be pursued by member firms that are competitive, rigid, and short-term oriented)	will not be successful	will result in distrust and make success less likely	will weaken their relationship; will find it costly and time-consuming
Yielding (likely to be pursued by member firms that are cooperative, flexible, and long-term oriented)	will not achieve an integrative outcome	will be successful in preventing the escalation of mutual conflict but whether it adequately deals with the issues confronting the alliance may not be immediately clear	will find it economical and time-efficient; will not affect their relationship
Compromising (likely to be pursued by member firms that are moderately cooperative, moderately flexible, and short-term oriented)	will not achieve an integrative outcome	will be successful in preventing an immediate alliance failure, but fundamental problems may still persist; will be only moderately successful	will not achieve an integrative outcome; will not adversely affect their relationship

also provide a few illustrative alliance cases that may help in appreciating the different interpartner negotiation strategies that we discuss in this chapter.

Interpartner Negotiations in the Formation Stage

The negotiation of an agreement between the potential partners is the central issue at this stage. The alliance partners will have to negotiate a wide range of issues ranging from the type of the proposed venture (equity vs. nonequity), to the level of resources that each partner will commit to the venture, and the mechanisms for managing the venture (shared vs. dominant control). The issue of the optimum level of control may itself be a tricky one, because on the one hand a dominant control may minimize the possibility of opportunistic behavior while also being detrimental to trust (Li et al., 2009). Another key issue may be the level of contractual complexity (Reuer & Ariño, 2007). This refers to the stringency of the contractual provisions pertaining to issues of both enforcement and coordination. Some have suggested that trust and contracts may be substitutes (Ghoshal & Moran, 1996) but others have argued that the two work in tandem (Poppo & Zenger, 2002). Although contracts may well be essential to all alliances the relative emphasis that alliance partners give to one or the other may itself be a product of the effectiveness of interpartner negotiations.

This is not an exhaustive list of issues but is only suggestive of some of the key elements critical to negotiation. As the partners begin the process of negotiations, the negotiating dynamics that come into play may be influenced by a wide variety of factors (alluded to earlier) ranging from perceptions of trust, to relative power and cultural differences. A related factor, but by no means less important, is the need for building a relationship with one's partner with the objective of fostering trust. Trust is often deemed vital in collaborative arrangements because it may help to mitigate opportunistic behavior (Das & Teng, 1998). It has also been maintained that the link between trust and performance "is stronger when market uncertainty is higher, resource interdependency is stronger, risk sharing is more commensurate, or reciprocal commitment is greater (Luo, 2002, p. 689). At the same time, trust permits the alliance partners to deepen their collaboration, knowing that their partner may not take advantage of them. The relevance of trust is closely linked with the importance of relational outcomes that negotiators seem to value (Curhan et al., 2006; Gelfand et al., 2006). We will now explore the implications of the different negotiation strategies that the partners may employ using the dual concern framework.

Problem Solving Strategy

The problem solving strategy is associated with a concern for a member firm's own outcomes and an equally salient concern for its partner's outcomes. In this scenario, the focal firms are likely to freely share information, be responsive to their partner's concerns, and be in a good position to not only negotiate successfully but also to be able to develop a truly integrative solution. As Pruitt (1983) notes, "In joint problem solving, the parties exchange accurate information about their underlying interests, collectively identify new issues in light of this information, brainstorm to locate alternate ways of dealing with these issues, and (sometimes) work together to evaluate these alternatives" (p. 168). Scholars note that a problem solving strategy, if employed by all partners in an alliance, will not only guarantee successful negotiations but also result in a negotiated outcome that will be associated with trust building (Euwema et al., 2003).

For a real-world example of a problem solving strategy in the formation stage of strategic alliances, consider the joint venture between Fiat of Italy and Tata of India. The case of Fiat and Tata illustrates how a problem solving strategy may be pursued at the alliance formation stage (Mitchell & Hohl, 2008). Fiat was Italy's biggest car manufacturer and was also one of the major industrial groups in the country. In recent years, the company had experienced severe economic difficulties. It lost about US$12 billion during the period 2001–2004. As Mitchell and Hohl (2008) note, "Several reasons were seen to contribute to Fiat's difficulties including its low- margin mix of smaller cars, languid new product introductions and the onslaught of more Japanese cars in Italy due to the abolition of quotas on foreign imports" (p. 6). Fiat had established a joint venture initially with Premier Automobiles to manufacture Uno at Premier's plant in Kurla, Mumbai. Over time Fiat took total control of this venture. The plant had difficulty in achieving profitability and in 2006 it initiated steps to close the Kurla plant and to consolidate all of production at a new facility. The company was also faced with the strategic decision at this time to either close down the Indian operation or look for a new partner. They decided on the latter and in Tata Motors they found one of India's most respected industrial groups. Tata Motors remained India's biggest automotive manufacturer (taking all types of vehicles into account) and had sales of 4.5 billion Euros at that time (Mitchell & Hohl, 2008). Tata Motors had first initiated the manufacture of passenger vehicles in 1991 with the production of Sierra and had more recently developed Indica, "a compact economy car" that was seen as representing new technological advances for the Indian industry.

The two companies were quick in finding common ground as regards to the new venture. As De Filippis noted,

> We started with a blank white board and talked about where we saw potential opportunities. As more meetings took place, we saw that we shared a common set of values. Even if two companies have common values, they may not cooperate. However, we were very fast in finding common ground. (Mitchell & Hohl, 2008, p. 12)

Similarly, as Lombardi noted, "From the meetings, we saw that they really had a great commitment to the long term. We concluded that their management has a similar spirit to ours" (Mitchell & Hohl, 2008, p. 12). The parties met once every month from Autumn 2006 to Autumn 2007 to negotiate the venture. No major obstacles emerged in this process. As Graziolli noted, "Since I've been involved with the negotiations, there has not been a roadblock or one big issue to face. The overriding issue was getting through the volume of work in the specified time period" (Mitchell & Hohl, 2008, p. 15). The commitment to a problem solving strategy was further evidenced by the fact that often enough the parties had discussions with each other in the absence of legal advisors. In other words, there seemed to be a high degree of trust among the partners to have been able to adopt this strategy. This is a good example of how a problem solving strategy yielded positive outcomes for the parties.

Contending Strategy

The contending strategy implies a high concern for one's own outcomes accompanied by a low concern for the partner's outcomes. This is a strategy in which one party tries to impose its own wishes and demands on the other without any concern for the other's interests. Firms pursuing this strategy often resort to threats, non-disclosure of information, or putting the partner under pressure. It has often been maintained that when parties adopt a contending strategy the likelihood of a successful agreement is relatively low. There is no doubt that conflicts will escalate under such conditions, but Pruitt notes that this may not always be the case because "contending is often a necessary precursor to successful problem solving" (1983, p. 170). While we agree that contending may not always lead to a negative outcome, the alliancing context is somewhat different. The partners are, to begin with, wary of each other, given the fact that they are often competing with the potential collaborators. Secondly, in an alliancing context, and especially at the formation stage of the alliance, the partners always have options, in the sense that they can always decide not to proceed with the alliance. The conflict spiral model, for example, suggests that when one party pursues a contending strategy, the other party will likely reciprocate this, thus leading to an escalation of the conflict (Pruitt & Kim, 2004). The motivation for each party is to punish the other for the costs that it has imposed on the other. It is often difficult to stop these spirals because an absence of a retaliatory action may often be viewed as a sign of weakness. These spirals often tend to increase in intensity as one party's defensive actions are viewed as escalatory by the other party. Finally, a contending strategy may lead to low levels of interpersonal trust as this strategy would have communicated to the other partner that its counterpart is solely concerned with obtaining maximal outcomes for itself (Beersma & De Dreu, 1999).

This is a strategy likely to be adopted by firms that have a strongly competitive, rigid, and short-term orientation. Firms that are competitive are likely to insist on an agreement on their own terms. They are less likely to respond to their partner's concerns and may propose a take-or-leave offer. They may also be inclined to use aggressive tactics and this may not endear them to their partner. Firms which are rigid are unlikely to make concessions and the absence of concessions in a negotiation process may in itself be viewed as a hostile or an escalatory act. Finally, firms with a short-term orientation, will not be minded to consider the longer-term implications of their actions; namely, that an escalatory action may invite retaliatory actions.

We illustrate the application of a contending strategy in the formation stage of strategic alliances with the negotiation between Nora, a Malaysian supplier of telecom equipment, and Sakari, a Finnish manufacturer of cellular phone sets and switching systems. Nora was a leading supplier of telecom equipment in Malaysia while Sakari was a major player in the manufacture of cellular phone sets and switching systems (Ainuddin, 2006). Peter Mattson, who headed Sakari's regional office in Singapore, had approached Nora with the possibility of setting up such a venture. Nora had obtained a contract from Telekom Malaysia (Bhd) for the installation of digital switching installations in the country. The Malaysians were finding it difficult to negotiate with the Finns because the Finns were rather reserved and cold. The negotiations were also made difficult by the fact that Sakari was not unified in its decision to pursue projects in Malaysia, with one group within Sakari suggesting that the company should pursue projects in the United Kingdom. As Ainuddin (2006) notes, "Some of the issues which they complained were difficult to resolve had often led to heated arguments between the two negotiating teams" (p. 13). The parties experienced difficulties over the issues of equity ownership, technology transfer, royalty payment, expatriates' salaries and perks, and arbitration. This was a negotiation in which both parties adopted a contending strategy. Perhaps this explains why even after 5 days of negotiations many issues could not be resolved.

Yielding Strategy

In a yielding strategy the partner firms reduce their demands or concede to what the opponent is expecting of them. Concern for others' outcomes is high and concern for one's own outcomes low. Yielding may allow the partners to conclude their negotiations expeditiously, but on the other hand there is the possibility that by yielding one of the parties allows the other to take the major share of the benefits. Yielding also lessens the possibility that the partners will be able to find an integrative agreement. As Pruitt (1983) notes, "Out of a fear of conflict or of failure to reach agreement, they may both yield so far that they are not challenged to be creative" (p. 171). Euwema et al. (2003) note that a strategy of accommodating the other party's wishes will have no significant impact on relational outcomes. Although yielding is a possible option for alliancing firms, and they may use it from time to time, we do not think that this option will be exercised frequently by alliancing firms as yielding connotes surrender and this may be unlikely in a mixed motive context such as strategic alliances. Alliancing firms that have a cooperative, flexible, and short-term orientation are likely to pursue such a strategy. Firms that have a cooperative orientation are more likely to be concerned about their counterpart's interests and insofar as that is the case may lower their demands to satisfy their counterpart. Flexibility also implies that the firms are not dead set in terms of what they want and this may allow yielding. Finally, those with a short-term orientation may be less concerned about the longer-term consequences of their actions in that a reputation for yielding may lead other potential partners to make a similar demand of them.

Compromising Strategy

Compromising implies a moderate amount of concern for one's own outcomes as well as for the other party's outcomes. A compromise leaves gains on the table and insofar as that is the case it would be associated with the emergence of conflicts. Compromising might have been expected to enhance relational satisfaction (Euwema et al., 2003), but their empirical study involving Dutch nurses does not validate this promise. We would surmise that firms that are moderately cooperative, moderately flexible, and short-term oriented will pursue this strategy. Firms that are moderately cooperative will tend to make concessions but perhaps not on all of the issues or not on those issues that are most salient to them. The moderately flexible firm will also be prepared to make concessions, but, once again, will resist doing the same on issues that might be deemed as most important to them. Finally, the short-term nature of the orientation implies that the firms may not be willing to put in the necessary effort to truly obtain an integrative solution.

Interpartner Negotiations in the Operation Stage

The operation stage tests the partner's commitment to the venture. At this stage the negotiated agreement has to be put into practice. The partners must deploy their resource contributions, develop a mechanism for coordinating with their partner, select employees, and begin with the agreed task of the alliance, be it the development of a new technology or the establishment of a new production facility. The operation stage may, once again, expose the alliance partners to ambiguity and uncertainty, and especially so if the alliance partners have been unable to develop a set of cooperative exchange norms. Bercovitz et al. (2006) suggest that if the partners have made transaction specific investments and there is a high degree of transparency then cooperative exchange norms might emerge. While this is no doubt a possibility, the known inherent instabilities of alliances seem to suggest that this may not be very common.

Interpartner negotiations at the operation stage have the central goal of resolving the conflicts that arise in the normal course of partner interactions. These negotiations may be difficult because they will test both the relationship and the commitment of the partners to the venture. The negotiations may also be delicate because in the midst of ambiguity and uncertainty it may be easy to misinterpret the actions of one's partner. Accusations may be made or alleged that do not stand the test of time. The different negotiation strategies employed by the alliance partners have divergent implications both for the relationship among alliance partners as well as for the overall success of the alliance.

Problem Solving Strategy

The problem solving strategy is associated with a concern both for the focal firm's own outcomes as well as the outcomes of its partner. In the face of conflicts alliance managers who use a problem solving strategy will be tactful and patient in dealing with the problem at hand. The problem solving strategy can vary from being overt to being covert (Pruitt & Kim, 2004). In an overt strategy the partners are likely to openly discuss as to how best to deal with the conflicts. By contrast, in a covert strategy, the alliancing partners may rely on informal problem solving using back channel contacts, track-two diplomacy, reliance on intermediaries, or sending conciliatory signals (Pruitt & Kim, 2004). They will be hesitant in making accusations on the basis of inconclusive evidence and will seek to unearth more information before proceeding further. Perhaps even more importantly, when firms pursue a problem solving strategy, they may demonstrate greater flexibility in the use of the contract that governs their relationship. Scholars have demonstrated that flexibility in contract application may generate positive goodwill trust dynamics at both the operational and managerial levels and may further strengthen parties' perceptions about the success of the project (Faems et al., 2008). Such a strategy may have the potential of creating a virtuous cycle among the alliance partners. In particular, this strategy will also avoid the danger of escalation because problems will not lead to direct accusations or confrontational exchanges. Finally, a problem solving strategy will pay as much attention to the relationship between parties as to the underlying problems they are dealing with. A potential downside to this strategy may arise if the other partner does not reciprocate the problem solving strategy. If so, then the firm that initiates this strategy may run the risk of suffering either an image loss, position loss, or an information loss (Pruitt & Kim, 2004).

An example of a problem solving strategy can be observed in the alliance between General Electric and Snecma to manufacture jet engines (Cauley de la Sierra, 1995). The alliance was first established in 1969 but, interestingly, the company got no orders for the first 8 years. This might have been construed as a crisis but, as it turns out, neither partner was overly concerned about the delay as they both recognized that it would take some time to generate revenue. In 1991, the company had annual revenues of US$31.1 billion—an eloquent testimony to their success. Problem solving in this context meant modifying expectations, being patient, and working with and not against the partner.

Contending Strategy

The strategy of contending focuses only on one's own outcomes. This is an aggressive and a contentious strategy in which the partners may easily accuse each other of violating the terms of the deal. Accusations of opportunism may fly thick and fast. The goal of the parties is to compel the other to change its behavior in accordance with one's own wishes. Threats to walk away from the alliance or to take the other party to the court may occur. Crisis escalation makes the successful resolution of a conflict even less likely.

We give an example of a contending strategy that relates to the interactions between Deepak Singhania, Managing Director of LML Ltd., and the Piaggio Group (Sirisha, 2002). LML Machinery had been established in 1975 and was engaged in manufacturing textile machinery. Over time the company entered into the manufacture of scooters and subsequent to that entered the motorcycle segment of the industry. The LML–Piaggio relationship began in 1984 when the partners entered into a licensing agreement. This was subsequently restructured as a joint venture with Piaggio taking a 23.6% stake in the company. The Singhanias were responsible for the operational aspects of the joint venture while Piaggio had control over technology and quality control. In the early years the venture progressed well with the market share of the joint venture increasing from 19.8% to 27.6% in April–June 1998. The problems began to emerge when Giovanni, who was the heir to the Agnelli family, died. This made the Singhanias apprehensive because their relationship with the rest of the Agnelli family, save Giovanni, was not very good. For instance, the rest of the family had wanted to form a joint venture with Bajaj Auto instead of the Singhanias. This apprehension about the intentions of the Agnelli family led the Singhanias to initiate a process by which they could buy out Piaggio's stake. This was clearly an example of a contending strategy and, as we might expect, Piaggio responded aggressively by challenging Singhania's actions.

Yielding Strategy

The strategy of yielding means lowering one's expectations and conceding to the demands of the other. Whether alliancing firms choose to adopt this strategy depends on the nature of the demands that are imposed upon them. Allegations and accusations of opportunism are unlikely to be accepted by the partners even if they recognize their own contribution to the problem. If, however, the partners are agreed that the alliance cannot continue as it is and that structural and behavioral changes need to be made to resurrect the alliance, and they find their counterpart's suggestions appealing, they may well decide to yield. Yielding also presupposes a certain level of trust in the other. It may also, however, be associated with a lack of bargaining power. It is also the case that yielding will prevent any conflict escalation.

An illustration of a yielding strategy can be found in the case of the joint venture between the French company Essilor and its Korean distributor Samyung Trading. Essilor was a major player in the optical market in France. The company specialized in "value-added, technology-intensive corrective lenses." The company was adept in expediting delivery of customized lenses to customers with a turnaround time of 24–36 hours. In 2003, Essilor re-entered Korea and it did so with a 50–50 joint venture with its trading partner Samyung Trading. Essilor wanted a partner who could both provide the manufacturing base as well as access to the local market. As Pant (2009), states:

> In the partnership, known as Essilor Korea, Essilor agreed to provide both the Essilor and Nikon brands as well as various corrective lens technologies. This would enable Samyung Trading to establish itself in the value added, branded segment of the Korean eyewear market. Samyung Trading, in turn, would give Essilor access to the Korean market and a manufacturing facility for commodity finished lenses and blanks, not only for the Korean market, but also for Essilor's worldwide operations. (pp. 3–4)

Under the original agreement the company would be led by two co-CEO's, one from Essilor and the other from Samyung Trading. The latter would also be the President of the joint venture. Essilor's representative was Steven Shawler, a U.S. citizen who had previously worked with Johnson & Johnson in Asia before being recruited by Essilor. The case study suggests that, on arrival in Korea, Shawler developed good relations with the Lee family, who had controlling interest in Samyung Trading, and who invited him to their home for dinner. Notwithstanding this relationship Shawler encountered numerous challenges in managing the joint venture. He did not or could not develop a relationship with the president of the joint venture, Mr.

S. J. Lee (unrelated to the Korean owners), who never invited him to any of his meetings even though Shawler invited him to his. His management style, in which he would invite members of his team to make a contribution, went unreciprocated. The team also, and much to Stephen's frustration, never entertained the possibility that Samyung might overtake the current market leader. He hired a few other people to assist him but they soon left, feeling that nobody seemed to trust them. As of October 2003, the company was lagging behind in meeting its targets. Subsequently, and to his surprise, Shawler was appointed president of the joint venture, and soon realized that his budget forecasts were not going to be met. He also had to deal with manufacturing problems that began to plague the venture. He made a number of changes in the process, including relocating the factory from Korea to China, to cut costs. To turn around the operations, he wanted to upgrade the laboratory and hire some key people from outside. Regrettably for him, the Lee family refused to fund any of these initiatives. But changes were being made gradually, and when he was able to hire J. G. Chung, whom he knew from his earlier stint in Johnson & Johnson, the orders started flowing much more easily. Even as things were improving, S. Y. Lee, who led Samyung Trading, called the regional CFO of Essilor to ask him to have Shawler replaced. The main criticism was that he was not running the company in the spirit of partnership and, also, that he favored the more Westernized staff in his company. Essilor were quite happy with the way that Shawler had performed but at the same time they were concerned that they not unnecessarily antagonize their partner. They finally decided to accede to Mr. Lee's request to replace Shawler. As is clear from the case the main reason why Essilor acceded to this was that they did not want the conflict to escalate.

Compromising Strategy

The strategy of compromising involves a moderate concern for one's own outcomes and also a moderate concern for the partner's outcomes. This strategy may well help to curb some of the dysfunctional effects of conflicting aims but it remains unclear as to how effectively this will help the partners deal with the problems in the alliance. Compromising means that both parties retreat from their original positions, and while this may be feasible in some cases it is unclear as to how relevant this strategy might be if one of the partners is primarily responsible for the problems confronting the alliance. Negotiation theorists often consider compromising to be a second best solution as it leaves gains on the table. On the positive side, though, a strategy of compromising might prevent the relationship from deteriorating further. It might also generate a space within which the partners can search for better solutions over time. An example of a compromising strategy involves the alliance between the Japanese automaker Honda and the Kinetic Group of

India (Mukund, 2002). Kinetic and Honda entered into a joint venture with the objective of manufacturing scooters and mopeds. As Honda had another joint venture with Hero to produce motorcycles the joint venture between Kinetic and Honda was confined to mopeds and scooters. During the operational phase of the joint venture, several sources of disagreements emerged among the partners. Kinetic felt that Honda was not sufficiently committed to the venture. For example, Kinetic wanted the company to spend more on advertising but Honda was reluctant to do so. They also felt that Honda was more focused on markets such as Indonesia and Thailand, which were growing rather rapidly. Honda, by contrast, claimed that the Kinetic group lacked the marketing acumen that their partner in the other joint venture, Hero, had demonstrated. The continuing difficulties led Honda to make an offer to Arun Firodia of Kinetic; namely, that either Firodia purchase 51% of their stake or alternatively Honda would buy out his 19% stake. A compromise meant that Firodia would buy out Honda's stake at Rs. 45 per share when the market price was close to double of that. This compromise agreement also dictated that the Kinetic Group would both manufacture and sell the Kinetic-Honda models. In return, Honda would continue to provide technical support in lieu of a royalty fee.

Interpartner Negotiations in the Outcome Stage

The outcome stage marks the point where the alliance partners come to evaluate the progress of the alliance. Has the alliance achieved its objectives? Has it gone from strength to strength? Alternatively, why has the alliance failed to perform according to expectations? Has the partner put in the necessary effort and commitment? If not, why not? If the alliance is underperforming, is it due to internal or external factors? Is it necessary to reinvigorate the alliance by deploying more resources, altering its strategic objectives, reinvigorating the relationship with one's partner? Or is it the time to throw in the towel and exit the alliance amidst growing acrimony with one's partner and an external environment not conducive to alliance success? These are critical decisions that need to be made by the partner firms for they are likely to have fateful consequences for how the alliance develops over time. It is pertinent to make the point that these negotiations are likely to be most critical when the alliance has experienced or is experiencing unfavorable outcomes. The different negotiation strategies have different implications for how best the alliance partners deal with such unfavorable outcomes.

Problem Solving Strategy

A problem solving strategy with its emphasis on an equal concern for one's own and the partner's outcomes, will seek to deal with the negative outcomes in a calm and focused manner. Alliance firms will refrain from blaming their partners and will not confront their counterparts unless they have clear-cut evidence that their partner has been at fault. Likewise, the firm will accept responsibility for any shortcomings if it realizes that errors have been committed and maybe things could have been handled differently. This will prevent any conflict escalation and will ensure that the partner firms remain focused on the task at hand. The partners will also debate alternatives calmly and reasonably. They may or may not decide to continue with the alliance but whatever is their decision their relationship is likely to be unaffected by negative outcomes.

Contending Strategy

A strategy of contending focuses solely on concerns with one's own outcomes. This is also a short-term strategy where the partner firms are trying to extract the maximal advantage in an unfavorable situation. The partners will engage in a blame game and deny any responsibility for the emergence of negative outcomes in the alliance. They will attribute the negative outcomes to their counterpart. If the alliance is to be dissolved, the partners may squabble about the termination process. How will the costs be shared? Threats of legal action and inflammatory actions may very well follow. The relationship is likely to deteriorate and it is more than likely that these partners will never again enter into another alliance. They may also seek to reevaluate the viability of alliances for their company as a whole.

A good example of a contending strategy is the alliance between Meiji Milk and Borden products (Cauley de la Sierra, 1995). The alliance had been in existence for some 20 years when problems erupted. The sales of Borden's products in Japan began to slow down and Borden felt that Meiji was doing this purposefully. Borden made the public statement that Meiji Milk had set out to destroy the relationship as it was seeking to develop its own products. Shortly thereafter, Borden exited from the alliance.

Yielding Strategy

The strategy of yielding implies lowering one's own expectations and acceding to the demand or the requests of one's partner. In a negative outcome context yielding could mean either agreeing with the partner to exit the alliance if requested it or alternatively to persist with the alliance if it would prefer that option. Yielding presupposes a lack of leverage or low bargaining power. However, it could also connote a good relationship with one's partner, as this may be a compelling reason to accede to its requests. We would suppose that a strategy of yielding would be neutral in terms of strengthening or weakening the relationship with one's partner. It is also the case that when a partner yields the interpartner negotiation process will be much less costly and time consuming.

Compromising Strategy

The strategy of compromising means a moderate concern for one's own outcomes and a moderate concern for the partner's outcomes. In this scenario the alliance partners will be willing to settle their differences through a process of give-and-take that meets each party's concern to a moderate degree. The parties' overall objective at this point is to try to resolve the situation confronting them as expeditiously as possible. They will be cognizant of the cost of delay and, in order to avert it, will be willing to make compromises. This is a strategy that is likely to be less than integrative, but on the other hand the partners will have achieved an agreement.

A good example of a compromising strategy can be found in the negotiations between Fiat and General Motors regarding their alliance. The alliance was entered into in 2000, and under the conditions of the negotiated agreement, GM got a 20% stake in Fiat Holdings B.V. while Fiat got a 5.1% stake in GM. The terms of the agreement also had a put option under which Fiat could sell the balance of its shareholdings (80%) to GM (Umashankar, 2005). Fiat found the alliance attractive because it could potentially help the company's auto division that had been experiencing losses since the 1990s. GM, for its part, found the alliance attractive to enhance the effectiveness of its operations both in Europe and Latin America. Unfortunately for the alliance, Fiat's operations continued to nosedive. The company sought recapitalization but when GM dropped out of it, its stake in Fiat Auto declined from 20% to 10%. In 2004, Fiat Auto therefore decided to exercise its option of selling the balance of the company (90%) to GM. In turn, GM made the counterclaim that the put option was no longer valid both due to the recapitalization of the company and the sale of Fiat's financing arm "Fidis." Given the conflicting, and the seemingly irreconcilable positions of the parties, GM sought to initiate the mediation process. Fiat now demanded $US 3 billion from the automaker in lieu of the put option. GM, by contrast, offered to pay Fiat only US$500 million which was the book value of GM's stake in Fiat Auto. Continuing negotiations ended in an agreement when GM agreed to pay Fiat $US 2 billion in lieu of dissolving the joint venture (Umashankar, 2005). One could view this as a kind of a compromise in that neither party quite got what they initially hoped for but were nevertheless able to arrive at an agreement.

CONCLUDING REMARKS

Contributions, Limitations, and Future Development of the Framework

The chapter has highlighted the relevance of negotiating strategies in the study of partner management in alliances. Our chapter discusses four alternative negotiation strategies and suggests that firms possessing certain characteristics are likely to pursue specific types of negotiation strategies. The issue of negotiations has only infrequently been studied in the alliance literature and our chapter goes some way in rectifying the limitations of the existing work on alliance management.

Another contribution of the chapter is in demonstrating the implications of different types of negotiation strategies at different stages of alliance evolution. For example, at the formation stage of the alliancing firms pursuing a problem solving strategy is likely to be more successful in forging a partnership than pursuing a contending strategy. At the operation stage the use of a contending strategy, for example, may amplify conflicts, while the use of a problem solving strategy may help to contain them. At the outcome stage, a problem solving strategy may strengthen the relationship between the partner firms while a contending strategy may weaken them.

The alliance literature has consistently stressed the importance of trust and trust building in influencing alliance evolution (Das & Teng, 1998). The literature remains unclear, however, as to the managerial processes that may facilitate trust building. Although the intuitive insight that interdependency may foster trust has been empirically demonstrated (Luo, 2002), the managerial processes that allow interdependence to foster trust have not been systematically discussed in the literature. Our chapter contributes to this literature by suggesting that the negotiation strategies employed by the alliance partners may play a crucial role in this. Problem solving strategies may facilitate trust while contending strategies may foster distrust.

That said, this chapter does not address some key issues that may well be worth exploring from the standpoint of partner management in alliances. First, implicit in our proposed framework is a model of a dyadic alliance. Many alliances, however, involve more than two partners (Das & Teng, 2002b). This makes the negotiation process more complex and hence more unpredictable. It would be interesting to explore the dynamics of partner management in multiparty alliances. Second, many alliances cross national boundaries. This inevitably brings national culture into play and scholars have begun to suggest that national cultural differences affect alliance evolution (Kumar & Das, 2010). This would inevitably have implications for partner management in such cross-national alliances. Third, the inter-linkages between negotiation strategies and the formation and sustenance of trust have not been empirically explored to date and this might be a worthwhile avenue of research. Fourth, it has been suggested that strategies such as contending may generate emotions and result in conflict escalation. Emotions are likely to be present in such negotiation situations (Kumar, 1997, 2008). Scholars have also drawn a distinction between dejection and agitation related emotions (Higgins, 1987), and it might be interesting to assess the role that these emotions play in strengthening or weakening the relationship between alliance partners. Dejection-related emotions represent the absence of a positive outcome, while agitation-related emotions represent the potential for the emergence of a negative outcome. Dejection-related emotions may lead negotiators to pursue a contending strategy while agitation-related emotions may lead negotiators to seek a compromise. In other words, it is conceivable that negotiators begin with one set of strategies, but depending on the presence or absence of particular emotions, transition to adopting a new set of strategies.

Managerial Implications of the Strategic Framework of Interpartner Negotiations

Alliances may be governed by contracts and by the commitments that the partners may have made in the new venture. The structural constraints as embodied in contracts or commitments may no doubt influence some aspects of a partner's behavior, but it is not determinative of it. As alliance firms interact with each other they are engaged at once in influencing their partner and in being influenced by them. Alliance managers must therefore become cognizant of their own negotiation style and the potential impact that it might have on their partner and on the success of the alliance. In a similar vein, they must be equally mindful of the negotiation style of their partner. Additionally, there must be a recognition that, notwithstanding the formal contract, the success of an alliance will be largely determined by how well the partners are able to manage their relationship. The realization that negotiation processes may have relationship implications is of great practical importance. It is also an issue that has been given less attention than it deserves.

Alliance managers must also be cognizant of the fact that different types of alliances may require the use of different types of negotiating strategies. The strategies of problem solving and contending may be appropriate for a joint venture but not so for a non-equity alliance. Negotiating is not a costless activity and the alliance managers must tailor their negotiating strategy to the type of alliance they are dealing with.

We have highlighted the different types of negotiation strategies that are potentially available to alliance partners. We have also shown the impact of these strategies at different phases of alliance development. It is important to note, however, that not all alliances share similar characteristics in terms of the level of commitment that is required or the amount of risk that the partners have to bear. Das and Teng (1998) note that different types of alliances differ in terms of alliance related investments, the pattern of interdependence among the partner firms, and the potential for opportunism. Scholars have drawn a distinction between equity, minority equity, and non-equity alliances. It follows then that the negotiation strategies adopted by the alliance partners will also vary as a function of the alliance type.

A major feature of joint ventures is high potential for gain accompanied by a high potential for loss. This would seem to imply that the alliance partners are likely to pursue a negotiation strategy that entails both problem solving and contending. Problem solving is essential for realizing potential gains but contending is essential to defending one's own interests in the event of opportunistic behavior by one's counterparts. Although both of these strategies may be potentially useful, alliance managers must learn to calibrate the use of these strategies effectively. In the formation stage of a joint venture, problem solving is essential to craft an integrative agreement but contending is essential to safeguard one's interests. Perhaps this may explain that even in the presence of a good relationship firms do not dispense with contracts as the latter provide a source of bargaining power. Contracts may not cover all of the possible contingencies but they are psychologically reassuring. The strategies yielding or compromising are unlikely to be deployed at the formation stage given the high stakes involved. During the operation stage of the alliance, critical negotiations will occur only if the alliance is experiencing unfavorable outcomes. Under these conditions the alliance partners will choose a contending strategy in the absence of trust or the presence of distrust, but will choose a problem solving or a compromising strategy if the relationship is relatively good. A strategy of yielding is unlikely given the stakes involved and so is the case with inaction. At the outcome stage, the alliance partners, in the face of unfavorable outcomes, may enhance the vigor with which they pursue a contending strategy.

In minority equity alliances the stakes for the partners are not equal. The partner with the lower equity stake may defer to the partner with a higher stake, and this deference may occur at all stages of alliance development (formation, operation, and outcome). We would therefore surmise that the firm with the lower stake may adopt a strategy of yielding to accommodate the wishes of its partner. This may occur even if the alliance is experiencing unfavorable outcomes. The firm with the lower equity stake may not consider it worthwhile to expend resources to resolve the underlying conflicts. This is also a less costly strategy and may be appropriate because the stakes are not too high. It would thus seem that firms in a minority equity alliance will generally pursue a yielding strategy in interpartner negotiations.

Non-equity alliances pose a minimal degree of risk for the partnering firms. Such alliances possess flexibility, and are characterized by a much lower level of commitment. Flexibility and lack of full commitment mean that the partners are not invested sufficiently to utilize a problem solving strategy. Although this negotiation strategy may yield integrative agreements it is a costly strategy. The contending strategy may also be inappropriate as the costs associated with it may not justify the additional benefits.

Hence a strategy of yielding or compromising may be the most beneficial for the partner firms. The strategy of compromising allows the firm to meet its goals halfway, whereas, a strategy of yielding defers to the partner but at an even lower cost than entailed in a compromise. This suggests that firms in a non-equity alliance will generally pursue a yielding or compromising strategy in interpartner negotiations.

In conclusion, interpartner negotiations may not be easy or costless but, as we have argued, essential for partner management. Alliance firms must develop and institutionalize the capability for interpartner negotiations so that the alliance managers involved can effectively interact and manage their counterparts in the partner firms.

ACKNOWLEDGMENT

This chapter, save some minor changes, was earlier published as Das, T. K., & Kumar, R. (2011). Interpartner negotiations in alliances: A strategic framework. *Management Decision, 49*(8), 1235–1256.

REFERENCES

Ainuddin, R. A. (2006). *Nora-Sakari: A proposed JV in Malaysia (Revised; Case # 906M06).* Ontario, Canada: Richard Ivey school of Business, University of Western Ontario.

Arino, A., & Reuer, J. J. (2004). Designing and renegotiating strategic alliance contracts. *Academy of Management Executive, 18*(3), 37–48.

Bartos, O. J. (1977). Simple model of negotiation: A sociological point of view. *Journal of Conflict Resolution, 21*(4), 565–579.

Beersma, B., & De Dreu, C. K. W. (1999). Negotiation processes and outcomes in prosocially and egoistically motivated groups. *International Journal of Conflict Management, 10*(4), 385–402.

Bercovitz, J., Jap, S. D., & Nickerson, J. A. (2006). The antecedents and performance implications of cooperative exchange norms. *Organization Science, 17*(6), 724–740.

Cauley de la Sierra, M. (1995). *Managing global alliances: Key steps for successful collaboration.* Reading, MA: Addison Wesley.

Cross, J. G. (1977). Negotiation as a learning process. *Journal of Conflict Resolution, 21*(4), 581–605.

Curhan, J. R., Elfenbein, H. A., & Xu, H. (2006). What do people value when they negotiate? Mapping the domain of subjective value in negotiation, *Journal of Personality and Social Psychology, 91*(3), 493–512.

Das, T. K., & Kumar, R. (2007). Learning dynamics in the alliance development process. *Management Decision, 45*(4), 684–707.

Das, T. K., & Teng, B. (1998). Between trust and control: Developing confidence in partner cooperation in alliances. *Academy of Management Review, 23*(3), 491–512.

Das, T. K., & Teng, B. (2002a). The dynamics of alliance conditions in the alliance development process. *Journal of Management Studies, 39*(5), 725–746.

Das, T. K., & Teng, B. (2002b). Alliance constellations: A social exchange perspective. *Academy of Management Review, 27*(3), 445–456.

De Dreu, C. K. W., Evers, A., Beersma, B., Kluwer, E. S., & Nauta, A. (2001). A theory based measure of conflict management strategies in the workplace. *Journal of Organizational Behavior, 22,* 645–668.

Euwema, M. C., Vliert, E. V., & Bakker, A. B. (2003). Substantive and relational effectiveness of organizational conflict behavior. *International Journal of Conflict Management, 14*(2), 119–139.

Faems, D., Janssens, M., Madhok, A., & Van Looy, B. (2008). Toward an integrative perspective on alliance governance: Connecting contract design, trust dynamics, and contract application. *Academy of Management Journal, 51*(6), 1053–1076.

Follett, M. P. (1941). Constructive conflict. In H. C. Metcalf & L. Urwick (Eds), *Dynamic administration: The collected papers of Mary Parker Follett* (pp. 30–49). London, England: Pitman.

Gelfand, M. J., Leslie, L. M., & Keller, K. M. (2008). On the etiology of conflict cultures. *Research in Organizational Behavior, 28,* 137–166.

Ghoshal, S., & Moran, P. (1996). Bad for practice: A critique of transaction cost theory. *Academy of Management Review, 23*(8), 707–725.

Harinck, F., De Dreu, C. K. W., & Van Vianen, A. E. M. (2000). The impact of conflict issues on fixed-pie perceptions, problem solving, and integrative outcomes in negotiation. *Organizational Behavior and Human Decision Processes, 81*(2), 329–358.

Higgins, E. T. (1987). Self-discrepancy: A theory relating self and affect. *Psychological Review, 94*(3), 319–340.

Korine, H., Asakawa, K., & Gomez, P-Y. (2002). Partnering with the unfamiliar: Lessons from the case of Renault and Nissan. *Business Strategy Review, 13*(2), 41–50.

Kumar, R. (1997). The role of affect in negotiations: An integrative overview. *Journal of Applied Behavioral Science, 33*(1), 84–100.

Kumar, R. (2008). Contested meanings and emotional dynamics in strategic alliances. In N. M. Ashkanasy & C. L. Cooper (Eds.), *Research companion to emotion in organizations* (pp. 561–574). Cheltenham, England: Edward Elgar.

Kumar, R., & Das, T. K. (2010). Strategic alliances and culture in a globalizing world. In J. Ulijn, G. Duysters, & E. Meijer (Eds), *Strategic alliances, mergers and acquisitions: The influence of culture on successful cooperation* (pp. 13–29). Cheltenham, England: Edward Elgar.

Li, J., Zhou, C., & Zajac, E. J. (2009). Control, collaboration, and productivity in international joint ventures: Theory and evidence. *Strategic Management Journal, 30*(8), 865–884.

Lin, X., & Germain, R. (1998). Sustaining satisfactory joint venture relationships: The role of conflict resolution strategy. *Journal of International Business Studies, 29,* 179–196.

Luo, Y. (1999). Toward a conceptual framework of international joint venture negotiations. *Journal of International Management, 5*, 141–165.

Luo, Y. (2002). Building trust in cross cultural collaborations: Toward a contingency perspective. *Journal of Management, 28*(5), 669–694.

Mitchell, J., & Hohl, B. (2008). *Fiat's strategic alliance with Tata (Case # SM-1528-E).* Barcelona, Spain: Center for Globalization and Strategy, IESE Business School, University of Navarra.

Mukund, A. (2002). *Kinetic Honda—The break-up (Case # 302-048-1).* Hyderabad, India: ICMR Center for Management Research.

Pant, I. (2009). *Essilor Korea (A), (B), (C), and (D) (Case # 409-037/040-1).* Fontainebleau, France: INSEAD.

Parry, M. E., Song, M., & Spekman, R. E. (2008). Task conflict, integrative potential, and conflict management strategies in joint ventures. *IEEE Transactions in Engineering Management, 55*(2), 201–218.

Pinkley, R. L. (1990). Dimensions of conflict frame: Disputant interpretations of conflict. *Journal of Applied Psychology, 75*, 117–126.

Pinkley, R. L., & Northcraft, G. B. (1994). Conflict frames of reference: Implications for dispute processes and outcomes. *Academy of Management Journal, 37*, 193–205.

Pondy, L. R. (1967). Organizational conflict: Concepts and models. *Administrative Science Quarterly, 12*(2), 296–320.

Poppo, L., & Zenger, T. (2002). Do formal contracts and relational governance function as substitutes or complements? *Strategic Management Journal, 23*(8), 707–725.

Pruitt, D. G. (1983). Strategic choice in negotiation. *American Behavioral Scientist, 27*(2), 167–194.

Pruitt, D. G., & Kim, S. H. (2004). *Social conflict: Escalation, stalemate, and settlement* (3rd ed.). New York, NY: McGraw Hill.

Putnam, L. L., & Wilson, C. E. (1982). Communicative strategies in organizational conflicts: Reliability and validity of a measurement scale. In M. Burgoon (Ed), *Communication Yearbook 6* (pp. 629–652). London, England: Sage.

Rao, A., & Schmidt, S. M. (1998). A behavioral perspective on negotiating international alliances. *Journal of International Business Studies, 29*(4), 665–694.

Reuer, J. J., & Arino, A. (2007). Strategic alliance contracts: Dimensions and determinants of contractual complexity. *Strategic Management Journal, 28*(3), 313–330.

Reuer, J. J., Zollo, M., & Singh, H. (2002). Post-formation dynamics in strategic alliances. *Strategic Management Journal, 28*(3), 313–330.

Sirisha, D. (2002). *The LML-Piaggio break-up (Case # 202-015-1).* Hyderabad, India: ICMR Center for Management Research.

Thomas, K. W. (1976). Conflict and conflict management. In M. Dunnette (Ed.), *Handbook of industrial and organizational psychology* (pp. 889–935). Chicago, IL: Rand McNally.

Thomas, K. W. (1992). Conflict and conflict management: Reflections and update. *Journal of Organizational Behavior, 13*(3), 265–274.

Umashankar, R. (2005). *Fiat and GM: The troubled alliance (Case # 305-032-1).* Retrieved from http://www.ibscdc.org/Case_Studies/Strategy/Strategic%20Alliances,%20Collaboration%20and%20Joint%20Ventures/SCJ0005.htm

Walton, R. E., & McKersie, R. B. (1965). *A behavioral theory of labor negotiations: An analysis of a social interaction system.* Ithaca, NY: ILR Press.

Yan, A., & Gray, B. (1994). Bargaining power, management control, and performance in United States- China joint ventures: A comparative case study. *Academy of Management Journal, 37*(6), 1478–1517.

Zartman, I. W. (1977). Negotiation as a joint decision making process. *Journal of Conflict Resolution, 21*(4), 619–638.

CHAPTER 6

ALLIANCE DECISION MAKERS AND HOW THEY SHAPE ALLIANCE PERFORMANCE

Jeffrey L. Cummings
Dave Luvison
Timothy B. Steele

ABSTRACT

In trying to understand how to improve alliance performance, executives and scholars have neglected to consider the role of *alliance decision makers* (ADMs) and the profound influence they can have in how partners are managed and subsequently on alliance performance. Alliances can only add value if put into operation in a manner that proves effective. In most firms, one or more key executives have several formative and ongoing roles affecting almost all aspects of how alliance outcomes are managed. Such ADMs matter because, in addition to being involved in defining their firm's initial alliance choice policies and partner selection processes, they also are often involved in setting the objectives to be achieved with the partner, defining the way in which the relationship with the partner will be governed, nurturing and supporting the organization's partner management cultures and capabilities-development processes, and designating who on their staff will directly interact with the partner. In addi-

Managing the Partners in Strategic Alliances, pages 141–164

tion, they also shape how handoffs might occur from one decision maker to the next throughout the alliance life cycle. Surprisingly, unlike with other senior leaders, scholars have paid little attention to either these ADMs or how their orientations and biases affect their decision making. We remedy this situation by tracing and analyzing how ADMs' attributes affect how alliance process will be managed at various stages of the alliance life cycle.

INTRODUCTION

Alliances provide a dilemma for executives. On the one hand, they have become common in most industries as they provide firms with a speedier, real options approach through which to enter new markets, achieve scale and scope, or accomplish some other joint or complementary objectives (Das & Teng, 1996, 2000; Eisenhardt & Schoonhoven, 1996; Gulati, 1998; Hamel & Prahalad, 1989; Kogut, 1991; Porter & Fuller, 1986; Spekman, Forbes, Isabella, & MacAvoy, 1998; Young-Ybarra & Wiersma, 1999). Some 25–50% of the top 1,000 firms' revenues have been estimated to be alliance based, and more than 70% of CEOs see their increasing use across both public and private enterprises (Anonymous, 2012). The impact can be even greater on a firm level; for example, software maker SAS and telecommunications equipment leader Cisco generate nearly all of their revenues through partnerships. On the other hand, executives have been somewhat flummoxed in their attempts to solve the widely reported underperformance problems that seem to accompany a majority of alliances, seemingly regardless of how performance is measured (Ariño, 2003; Christoffersen, 2013; Nielsen, 2007).

In trying to understand how to improve alliance performance, executives and scholars have neglected to consider the role of *alliance decision makers* (ADMs) and the profound influence they can have in how partners are managed and subsequently on alliance performance. Alliances can only add value if put into operation in a manner that proves effective. In most firms, one or more key players, whether chief executive officers, chief financial officers, chief technical officers, chief revenue/sales officers or heads of strategic alliances or business development, have several formative and ongoing roles affecting almost all aspects of how alliance partners and outcomes are managed. Such ADMs matter because, in addition to being involved in defining their firm's initial alliance choice policies and partner selection processes, they also are often involved in setting the objectives to be achieved with the partner, defining the way in which the relationship with the partner will be governed, nurturing and supporting the organization's partner management cultures and capabilities-development processes, and designating who on their staff will directly interact with the partner. In addition, they also shape how handoffs might occur from one decision maker to the next throughout the alliance life cycle. Lastly, because both the focal and partner firm would have ADMs, any mis-congruence between them in terms of their styles, approaches, or what we explore more fully below as goal orientations, can have a profound impact on the partnering relationship as well as performance. Surprisingly, scholars have paid little attention to either these ADMs or how their orientations affect their decision making.

We remedy this situation by tracing and analyzing how ADMs' attributes affect how alliance processes will be managed at several stages of the alliance life cycle. We begin by exploring and analyzing how ADMs' orientations could affect their alliances' ultimate management and performance. We know from prior research that introducing new ADMs has changed the tenor and direction of alliances, but there is a gap in our understanding of how ADMs' own psychologies can influence their decisions.

ALLIANCE DECISION MAKERS

ADMs are a multi-level concept; there can be several and at different levels in an organization. At the corporate executive (CXO) level, ADMs are the individuals who substantively shape alliance success by defining and/or interpreting the firm's written or unwritten policies at each stage of the alliance life cycle. Beginning with their determination as to who is involved in and how to conduct the alliance choice decision, in the subsequent alliance life cycle stages these executive ADMs in similar ways influence partner selection and due diligence activities; shape governance structures to guide the alliance's later operations; affect ramp-up and roll-out activities involved in the alliance's launch; shape management of the ongoing operation of the alliance; and finally, define acceptable reconfiguration paths for the alliance once it has achieved some level of ADM-defined performance or underperformance. In each of these activities ADMs can affect how the partnership develops and evolves as the activities involve engagements between the alliance partners.

At the functional level, where they hold titles such as head of business development, alliance executive or channel executive, ADMs are in the functional roles that mobilize internal resources to drive coordination with their partners in joint pursuit of performance objectives (Kale, Dyer, & Singh, 2001). Business development ADMs, for example, help shape who makes it into and through the partner selection and negotiation processes, alliance executive ADMs find ways to live with these partner selection decisions and to manage partner relations with respect to any positive or negative spillovers from tough negotiations (Cummings, 2011).[1]

To the extent that one ADM is involved throughout the alliance lifecycle, these ADMs will be subject primarily only to their own prior and ongoing decisions related to partner selections, positive or negative spillovers from tough negotiations or other ways in which their prior decisions later affect the alliance's performance. At a large division of Siemens, AG, one senior vice president oversees the full alliance life cycle, which the firm has defined as comprising alliance partner selection through development, operations and, if required, reconfiguration aligned to support the company's business units consistent with its centralized, global mandate. At the same time, it is not uncommon to find a CXO acting as an ADM in initial alliance choice and partner selection efforts, with another executive taking over subsequent decisions for the duration of the alliance life cycle. At AstraZeneca, for example, partnering decisions are taken by the chief medical officer supported by an organizationally aligned business development team, and ongoing governance and operations are handled by a cross- business alliance management function. At Cisco, where it has a deep commitment to a channel and alliance model, ADMs include the general managers of each business unit who are supported by a global alliance ADM, who are in turn supported by business and goal-aligned executive sponsors (i.e., CXOs). Thus, not only do firms involve different ADMs, they do so at different stages of the alliance life cycle, meaning that one or more ADMs, following one or more patterns of involvement, can have differential effects on partner relations and therefore alliance outcomes.

Further, the processes that ADMs follow often vary by firm and can range from being *ad hoc* in nature to being carefully codified in formal guidelines and procedures depending on the maturity of their alliance efforts. In the case of the former, it is clear that each ADM involved at each stage of the alliance life cycle could have a differential effect on alliance performance, since how they go about the related decisions and tasks could vary greatly. When one of the authors was initially hired into Siemens as a senior executive, for example, the company had been successful to date by following a "direct and/or reseller" sales model that targeted larger Telco's by individual countries or regions. However, in recognition of the changing nature of what it would take to dramatically expand the business' leverage with one major Telco, British Telecom, the author initiated a new globally oriented strategic alliance that took advantage of new partnership models outside of BT's home market in the United Kingdom, thereby greatly impacting the initial alliance's performance by allowing the platform to extend to relationships with other major Telco's such as AT&T and Verizon. In the case of the latter—where there are formally prescribed guidelines and procedures reflecting a more mature alliance culture—an ADM's actions would be constrained to within defined boundaries, thereby limiting their effects on alliance performance. Indeed, Siemens today has a mature collaboration culture and someone like the author would have a much less idiosyncratic impact on alliance performance.

Regardless of whether only one or several ADMs are involved, or if they operate within formal or informal boundaries, in this chapter we seek to understand how these ADMs can affect partner relations and alliance performance. As with any leaders, because ADMs can have different psychological and professional orientations and backgrounds, we should expect that no two ADMs will evaluate the critical decisions for an alliance in the same manner. For example, while ADMs with a longer-term perspective and who are very experienced with collaborations might define performance objectives for the alliance to be more learning- than risk-reduction- oriented, other ADMs might look for short-term, clearly defined gains. In either case, it is clear that an ADM's orientation could have effects across the entire life cycle, especially when their decision making orientations are hidden or unknown.

OUR APPROACH

An initial review of the literature suggested a gap related to the role of ADMs and their influence of alliance performance. Based on our own prior research and professional experience with the effects of leader personalities on decision making, we sought to investigate such effects on ADMs following a grounded theory approach. We conducted semi-structured interviews with several professionals who fit the profile of ADMs, or who are consultants to ADMs and alliance managers. These professionals were identified through contacts with the Association of Strategic Alliance Professionals (ASAP), a 3,000 member organization with which two authors are affiliated as academic members, and through professional contacts of the third author, who has been an ADM for over 2 decades at several Fortune 500 companies. In the following sections we explore our findings as to why it is important for a firm to trace the decision making influence of ADMs throughout the alliance life cycle.

HOW GOAL ORIENTATION INFLUENCES LEADERS' ACTIONS

Given ADMs' many decision-making roles, ranging from choosing to form an alliance to who to partner with to how to govern the alliance, among others, the question of how their decisions might be influenced by their orientations could prove important to understanding their alliances' ultimate performance and how they interact with their partners. We know from prior research that introducing new ADMs has changed the tenor and direction of alliances, but there is a gap in our understanding of how ADMs' own psychologies can influence their decisions (Ariño & de la Torre, 1998; Doz, 1996).

Over the past 3 decades, scholars have vastly expanded our understanding of how leaders' backgrounds, biases, values, and experiences can influence decision-making processes and preordain firms' strategy and structure. Beginning with a stream of work related to top management teams, Hambrick, Mason, and Finkelstein stressed the influence of leader characteristics, such as age, tenure and educational backgrounds on a firm's behaviors and performance. In what came to be known as "upper echelons theory," other observable leader characteristics, such as national culture and cooperative behaviors, were also shown to have strong effects on strategic behaviors (Crossland & Hambrick, 2011; Espedal, Kvitastein, & Grønhaug, 2012; Geletkanycz & Hambrick, 1997; Hambrick, 2007; Hambrick, Finkelstein, & Mooney, 2005; Hambrick & Mason, 1984).

Whereas the study of upper echelons theory tended to focus on the effect of observable leader characteristics (e.g., age, education, tenure) on decision-making, goal orientation theory has been applied with similar aims but with a focus on more cognitive characteristics of leaders. According to goal orientation theory, individuals are either performance or learning oriented with respect to how they view defining objectives and achieving related outcomes. Performance goal oriented individuals tend to see one's ability as fixed and therefore set objectives with a short-term temporal perspective and shun tasks that require new learning. Further, they also seek either to achieve positive or avoid negative comparisons to others depending on if they are performance prove or performance avoid oriented. In contrast, learning goal orientated individuals, because they believe that learning efforts and experience can lead to emergence of latent capabilities as a well as foster development of new ones, are more likely to pursue longer- term objectives and embrace difficult challenges (Brett & VandeWalle, 1999; Dragoni & Kuenzi, 2012; Geletkanycz & Hambrick, 1997; VandeWalle, Brown, Cron, & Slocum, Jr, 1999; VandeWalle & Cummings, 1997).

Given that different ADMs can have different psychological and professional orientations and backgrounds, we should expect that no two ADMs will evaluate the critical decisions for an alliance in the same manner. Indeed, while seeking to achieve positive comparison to others or to at least avoid negative comparisons may be appropriate in some circumstances, such as in a go-to-market alliance seeking near-term financial outcomes, in others, such as one focused on co-innovation efforts, a longer-term perspective fostering development of new abilities would likely be more appropriate. Similarly, if the firm cannot undertake significant risks, it might be more appropriate for a performance-oriented ADM, who will adopt a primarily risk-avoidance approach, to be the decision maker. Finally, it is often the case that an ADM, if senior enough, is the one responsible for defining the firm's entire alliance life cycle. In such cases, an ADM's orientation could have effects that ripple across the entire life cycle, not only for a given alliance but also for processes that will be followed in all of the firm's alliances. Nonetheless, ADMs—especially when their decision making orientation are hidden or unknown—remain an ignored player affecting nearly all aspects of partner relations and alliance performance.

ADMS AND THE ALLIANCE LIFE CYCLE

Five stages of the alliance life cycle, as shown in Figure 6.1, where ADMs can significantly affect alliance performance, and that senior managers should attend to as they evaluate the effects of ADMs, are (a) alliance choice, (b) partner selection and due diligence, (c) shaping of governance structures, (d) operation, and (e) reconfiguration. By understanding how ADMs, with their attendant influences, can help shape alliance performance throughout these stages, executives will be in a better position to control one more of the variables that contribute to alliance performance, namely, who will act as ADMs. In the following sections we discuss each of these five stages and examine the effects of AMDs' performance and learning goal orientations during the pre- and post-launch stages.

Pre-Launch Stage 1: Alliance Choice

The first way that ADMs affect alliance outcomes involves their role in the choice to pursue an alliance. In theory, ADMs engage in a rational build–buy–ally decision process to determine the best way from a transaction-cost

	Choice	ADM decides to pursue alliance vs. build, JV, or acquisition
Pre-Launch	**Partner Selection**	ADM seeks partner, sets alliance objectives, evaluates due dilligence
	Governance	ADM defines within-firm and with-partner structures, sets expectations, manages negotiations
Post-Launch	**Operations**	ADM staffs alliance management, develops alliance capabilities, fosters alliance culture
	Reset	ADM defines when partner's contributions or changes in external conditions merit reconfiguration and how to proceed

Figure 6.1 ADM decisions across alliance lifecycle.

or resource-dependency perspective to fill organizational gaps exposed by external challenges or internal issues (Faulkner, 1995; Harrigan, 1988). Often, when organizational gaps include the need to obtain tacit knowledge, resources or capabilities, alliances are preferred since they can be less costly, risky, or time consuming than the build or buy approaches especially when entering new international markets. In practice, the alliance choice "is not strictly economic, but also a social, psychological and emotional" (Tallman & Shenkar, 1994, p. 92) decision of the ADM (Contractor & Lorange, 1988; Lane, Salk, & Lyles, 2001). As such, how the business context is interpreted by the ADM in the alliance choice decision process is clearly of importance. While some research has examined ADM decision making orientations and personality characteristics such as cooperativeness and leadership styles, and other research has found that certain leader characteristics (e.g., education, concern for self-development) or prior positive alliance experiences are associated with the extent to which they pursue alliances, there have been no studies expressly linking ADM personality characteristics to alliance choice decisions. For example, Chao (2011) examines ADM decision making biases; Espedal, Kvitastein, and Grønhaug (2012) focuses on cooperativeness; and Osborn and Marion (2009) and Trim and Lee (2008) considered leadership styles. Nonetheless, because leader behaviors are subject to values, there is no reason not to believe that personality characteristics also influence how ADMs—the alliance leaders within their organizations—make alliance choice and other decisions.

Pre-Launch Stage 2: Partner Selection and Due Diligence

Once a decision to fill any gaps through an alliance has been taken, ADMs then lead their firm's partner selection process. In theory, ADMs select partners whose alliance objectives are in sync with those of their firm according to whatever forms of due diligence they conduct. Often, however, potential partners are

> presented for selection consideration more due to their cultural fit, since senior managers often know and trust those in other firms, than due to a more systematic assessment, [highlighting] the importance that managers place on being able to get along with and count on the behaviors and actions of partners (Cummings, Holmberg, & Yang, 2013, p. 26).

Nonetheless, research and practice have shown that a good partnering fit is about more than having partners who can help each other overcome relationship issues. While getting along is certainly important, it is equally important that the partners be able to accomplish certain tasks together, address specific and emerging risks and facilitate the learning necessary to achieve success against performance objectives. Geringer (1991) provided an initial set of task and partnering factors to be considered by ADMs in selecting partners; Cummings and Holmberg (2012) extended these factors to address risks and learning. Where any of these four fit aspects have been omitted from analysis during initial partner selection, alliances have faced a litany of issues, challenges, and failures to deal with, many of which might have been avoided altogether with greater due diligence up front. Surveys of alliance professionals have found that poor selection decisions are among the top complaints of alliance professionals (Cummings, 2011). It makes sense, then, that one of the culprits of poor alliance performance is seen as the quality of the alliance partners selected. Not surprisingly, partner selection processes, and a movement away from ad hoc, get-the-deal-done approaches, have received increasing attention in both the academy and the alliance management profession.

Pre-Launch Stage 3: Shaping of Governance Structures

Once an alliance partner has been selected, ADMs next shift to establishing the structural elements of the alliance. While alliance partners seek to cooperate to obtain common benefits through joint value creating activities, they also put in place policies, procedures, and administrative controls to prevent their firm from being exploited by their partners and to coordinate activities, allocate resources, and implement tasks as efficiently and effectively as possible. Such organizational elements make up the alliance governance model, which refers to the structures and mechanisms under which an alliance is managed, organized, and regulated (Albers, 2010; Anderson & Gatignon, 1986; Geringer & Hebert, 1991; Khanna, Gulati, & Nohria, 1998; Killing, 1982; Malhotra & Lumineau, 2011; Zhang, Shu, Jiang, & Malter, 2010).

Post-Launch Stage 4: Operation

In turn, during the alliance's launch and operations, ADMs allocate headcount to and supervise the alliance management function, and nurture and support different capabilities-development processes and partnering cultures. It is the alliance managers—the boots-on-the-ground—who run the alliance within the confines of the negotiated governance agreement, against performance objectives established by their ADMs, and in an environment whose alliance capabilities and cultural sensitivities are shaped by their ADMs. Given the central function of alliance managers in carrying out alliance operations, it is not surprising that there is a substantial amount of literature about their effects on performance nor that they are often held out as yet another of the culprits in poor alliance performance (Gerwin, 2004; Hoffmann & Schlosser, 2001; Shamdasani & Sheth, 1995; Spekman, Isabella, MacAvoy, & Forbes, 1996; Taylor, 2005). What is surprising, however, is the meager attention that has been paid to the ADMs who—just like other leaders who are influenced in part by their orientations—so substantially shape these launch environments, including by selecting and overseeing the alliance managers charged with operating the alliance.

Post-Launch Stage 5: Alliance Reconfiguration

The final way that ADMs affect alliance outcomes is by the role they play in defining when and how an alliance is reconfigured once relative contributions of the partners have become no longer acceptable. In theory, three paths are available to ADMs, including termination, acquisition, and re-evaluation/adjustment. The key is to exit the alliance in a manner that allows the firm to achieve its original objectives without compromising other competitive aspects of its operations (Serapio & Cascio, 1996; Tallman & Phene, 2006). As in the prior stages of the alliance life cycle, ADMs are by definition the decision makers with respect to when and how their firm will proceed in this final stage. In practice, ADMs have tendencies that affect the degree to which they learn to identify and avoid competency traps (Levitt & March, 1988), or view their alliances as real options (Bowman & Hurry, 1993; Haspeslagh & Jemison, 1991; Kogut, 1991) or as "a repetitive sequence of negotiation, commitment, and execution stages, each of which is assessed in terms of efficiency and equity" (Ring & Van de Ven, 1994, p. 97). Again, surprisingly, how ADM orientations can affect how they make such reconfiguration decisions is in need of further investigation.

In the following sections, we discuss the effects of ADMs' goal orientations on these alliance life-cycle stages, organized into pre-launch and post-launch phases.

EFFECTS OF ADMS' GOAL ORIENTATIONS PRE-LAUNCH

Performance Goal Oriented ADMs

The role of ADM personality characteristics in each of the pre-launch processes—and the fact that they can influence ADMs to delimit or preordain alliance choice, partner selection or governance criteria—could prove instrumental to understanding partner relations and alliance performance. The first aspect of partnering fit criteria affected by an ADM relates to alliance choice and the specific tasks that the alliance is formed to accomplish, whether they be to enhance offering scope by combining products, accelerate R&D by sharing knowledge, or provide some other mutually beneficial sharing of resources and capabilities. An ADM with a performance orientation will determine tasks that are readily measurable and within easy reach, thereby delimiting the universe of choice options and potential partners to those that possess attributes that suggest congruence with this profile. While appropriate in some circumstances, such as in a go-to-market situation where there are well-worn paths to follow, in others, such as in innovation-focused settings where constant adaptation and change are required, such an ADM may limit the choice options to building or buying rather than partnering, and then further limit any buying or partner-selection choices to inappropriate targets. In addition, such ADMs will carry over this orientation with respect to how they set criteria related to the other key criteria as well. Thus, they will seek only choices and/or partners with which they believe they can find easy relationships, use tightly-defined work plans to drive efforts toward predetermined outcomes, and readily adopt administrative controls to minimize risks.

Indeed, in our interviews we heard repeatedly about how certain ADMs seemed predisposed to go-to-market sales partnering "because it's less difficult and less risky" while others were willing to develop broader strategic partnerships that would leverage the full continuum of alliance integration points including in joint development, supply chain, marketing, or OEM activities. In some cases, the alliance organization only has the charter to form and execute go-to-market sales partnerships reflecting a likely "performance goal" orientation of the CXO team and or the ADM.

But administrative structures and work plans affect only a subset of firm behaviors in an alliance. Although experts call for partners to exhibit both forbearance and commitment if they are to be successful (Das & Kumar, 2009), the reality is that ADMs adopt different governance postures in alliances depending upon a number of factors, the foremost of which may be their goal orientations. For instance, when ADMs have a short-term, performance goal orientation they are more likely to expect partner opportunism and behave accordingly, regardless of any overarching governance arrangement, and this can have negative spillovers on partner relations. Similarly, whether ADMs approach the relationship with a prevention or promotion frame can not only affect the nature of the contractual agreement but also the resulting behaviors their firms are likely to carry into the alliance.[2] As a result, alliances are in practice governed through a combination of control and trust, suggesting that relational governance and firm adaptation may have a significant influence on ADM behaviors with their partners regardless of whether strong formal governance conditions are in place (Albers,

2010; Das, 2006; Das & Teng, 1998; de Man & Roijakkers, 2009; Reuer & Ariño, 2007; Weber & Mayer, 2011).

Just as temporal orientation and biases such as overconfidence, single outcome calculation and adjustment, and anchoring can affect decision making in the formulation and management of an alliance (Chao, 2011; Das, 2006), ADMs' goal orientations can have a similar effect. Because individuals with a performance goal orientation are less likely to take on difficult goals and will shun relationships that require them to develop new abilities, goal orientation theory indicates that their risk aversion will be more salient than for leaders with a learning goal orientation. Similarly, given the tendency of individuals to seek to avoid dissonance, performance goal oriented individuals will be more likely to anticipate similar orientations in others, which not only suggests that others would act in an opportunistic manner but that they would also be inclined to shirk alliance agreements that do not impose strong formal constraints. Thus, as a way to minimize the risk of failure from such situations, performance goal oriented ADMs would favor less difficult outcomes and more formalized governance arrangements to tie down partner commitments, thereby constraining how partner relations unfold (Festinger, 1957; Gulati, Sytch, & Mehrotra, 2008).

Not only do ADMs define the governance model through which to monitor and control an alliance and that substantially affects partner relations, they also set the performance goals for the alliance. As has been explained by both upper echelons and goal orientation theories, organizational performance expectations can be influenced by the orientation of the firm's leader. As such, an ADMs' goal orientation will determine their own, and therefore their alliance's performance expectations and, hence, influence how both the partner and those within the firm responsible for implementing the alliance prioritize their behaviors.

Because leaders with a performance goal orientation are likely to view ability as fixed, they will tend to shun tasks that require new learning and, instead, set short-term objectives that seek to avoid negative consequences. Thus, ADMs with a performance goal orientation will deemphasize the importance of adaptive learning requirements in the alliance and, instead, prioritize the achievement of tangible outcomes. As a result, they would seek to assess responsible individuals, including partners, on how effectively they execute functional tasks, such as achieving sales objectives in a go-to-market alliance or meeting project development milestones in a discovery-focused innovation alliance. ADMs with a performance goal orientation would view this focus as appropriate because they expect members of the alliance to employ routines that minimize risk. Depending on the goal orientation of their partner, this could lead to smooth or rough relations, as if the partner is similarly oriented they would adopt a similar focus, but if learning goal oriented might chafe at such a focus, which in turn could result in more challenging partner relations.

Learning Goal Oriented Alliance Decision Makers

The second type of ADM, those who have a learning goal orientation, are inclined to pursue and therefore define long-term "stretch" objectives and related tasks. As a consequence, they seek choices, partners, and governance structures which will allow them to accomplish defined tasks while engaging in constant relationship building and feedback and adaptation processes. Risks, while still important, are to be addressed through these same relationship and learning processes. Further, since learning goal oriented ADMs believe that ability can be developed—unlike performance goal oriented individuals who see it as fixed—they are therefore more open to experience. As a result, they are more likely to be adaptive and undertake challenging tasks. Further, despite the fact that they ultimately seek to achieve performance objectives, such ADMs are more willing to accept difficult challenges and embrace long-term initiatives. This suggests that ADMs with a learning goal orientation would, in the case of the alliance choice (Prelaunch Stage 1) condition mentioned above, opt toward a build or ally decision over a buy decision. In other words, to the extent that they are at the CXO level and could make such decisions, they would be less oriented toward the certainty of buying an existing solution than they would be intrigued by the greater potential that self-development or an alliance could offer. Even if the build, buy, or ally decision rests with the CEO, or head of business development, strategy or M&A, learning goal oriented ADMs would nonetheless seek to influence such decisions in favor of build or ally.

In addition, learning goal oriented ADMs would also set objectives for their alliance that anticipate the need for adaptation and adjustment, suggesting that they should be more likely to set difficult goals and accept feedback to help them achieve those goals. Moreover, seeing such a pattern in others would make them more open to collaborative behaviors, affecting choice, and a relational governance model that supported that, because they believe they would have greater ability to manage without strict contractual constraints (Macaulay, 1963). As such, the roles of those operating the alliance in these situations will be defined less in terms of how well they execute functional tasks, such as selling or project management, and more in terms of how they are able to enable the partnering firms to adapt to one another's differences. In essence, congruent with the structure a learning goal oriented ADM anticipates, namely an emphasis on relational governance and the presence of routines that encourage knowledge exchange and opportunity identification, those responsible for the alliance, including the partner, would be assessed on the basis of how well they facilitate the collaboration. As above, depending on the goal orientation of their partner, this could lead to smooth or rough relations, as if the partner is similarly oriented they would adopt a similar focus, but if performance goal oriented might find it difficult to deal with the attendant ambiguity and looseness, thereby affecting partner relations.

In one of our interviews with a large global technology company, the ADM shared the importance of having both alliance leadership and the business development personnel typically focused on prelaunch activities involved in framing strategic partnerships. By taking such a "clear canvas" view in framing its strategic partnerships, this company was able to undertake an alliance that required joint development investments, leveraged the supply chain of the target partner and created a highly innovative new model to bundle both entities' products and services. This type of clear canvas partnership design would only work through a learning goal orientated ADM given the level of unknowns, long timelines, and risks involved.

EFFECTS OF ADMS' GOAL ORIENTATIONS POST-LAUNCH

Performance Goal Oriented ADMs

The role of ADM personality characteristics in each of the post-launch processes—operation and reconfiguration—could also prove instrumental to understanding partner relations and alliance performance, especially since studies have shown that how firms oversee their alliance operations is related to overall alliance performance (Heimeriks & Duysters, 2007; Kale, Dyer, & Singh, 2002; Schreiner, Kale, & Corsten, 2009). In operations, an alliance is significantly impacted by the alliance manager(s) "charged with carrying the alliance forward" (Spekman et al., 1998, p. 352). Since it is the ADMs who select and oversee the alliance manager(s), the individual ADM's goal orientation can have an outsized influence on the extent to which the alliance manager(s) work inside or outside of prescribed routines (Spekman et al., 1998), and are concerned with managing the various risks inherent in alliances (Das & Teng, 1999) and fostering performance- vs. trust-based relationships (Parkhe, 1998) in order to ensure ongoing fit (Das & Teng, 1999; Douma, Bilderbeek, Idenburg, & Looise, 2000).

ADMs with a performance goal orientation are known to promote the creation of organizational routines that focus intently on ensuring desired outcomes, whether in the form of specific task delineations, use of project management tools or other means. Due to a reliance on planning and control processes (Mehta, Feild, Armenakis, & Mehta, 2009; VandeWalle et al., 1999), "they are likely to see the role of tools, processes and the alliance management function being to limit non-productive actions of partners" (Luvison & Cummings, 2015, p. 101). Further, they would see these capabilities, which include tools and processes such as business planning protocols, codified best practices, and specialized alliance training (Heimeriks & Duysters, 2007; Heimeriks, Klijn, & Reuer, 2009) as relatively fixed and unchangeable. As a result, they would seek to apply alliance capabilities only that minimize risks, for example by focusing on policies on information confidentiality, conflict escalation processes, and reward systems that emphasize tangible and narrow financial objectives. Similarly, because these ADMs focus on tangible outcomes and objectives (Dragoni & Kuenzi, 2012), they are likely to keep operations focused on activities that directly contribute to the achievement of such objectives, whether they be revenue generation in a go-to-market alliance (Smith, 1997; Smith & Barclay, 1999) or project development milestones in an innovation alliance (Gerwin, 2004). Lastly, they would see their and their alliance managers' roles more as functionally based (e.g., sales, business development, project management) rather than focused on pursuing collaborative outcomes.

Taken together, these attributes of performance goal oriented ADMs portend situations where operations are managed more like in a project management environment than in a collaborative one, and where the relationships are seen as calculative (Williamson & Craswell, 1993), there is great concern regarding appropriation risks (Dyer, Singh, & Kale, 2008) and values guarding against opportunism are emphasized (Das, 2005, 2006). Further, since ADMs with a performance goal orientation see ability as fixed and avoid feedback, they are ill-suited to situations that are subject to trial and error. As a result, when it comes to reconfiguration options, ADMs with performance goal orientations would pursue only the most readily identifiable and directly controllable options. Depending on the goal orientation of their partner ADM, these attributes would be seen as favorable and allow easy interaction and decision making, or unfavorable, and a cause of challenging partner relations.

Learning Goal Oriented ADMs

ADMs with a learning goal orientation are likely to see operations and reconfigurations as requiring constant modifications. Given that learning goal oriented ADMs "see effort as necessary to expand abilities, they likely have a greater willingness to 'try and try again' than those with a performance goal orientation" (Luvison & Cummings, 2015, pp. 101–102). The types of capabilities these ADMs value would include those that foster open communication, easy knowledge transfer, sharing of best practices, and use of broad rather than specific objectives to allow for experimentation, small failures, and flexibility in performance (Luvison & Cummings, 2015). Thus, these ADMs would seek to enhance rather than take as a given, the various business planning protocols, codified best practices, and specialized alliance training and other tools and processes the firm has in place. Kale et al. (2001) suggest that the alliance management function facilitates sharing of learning and best practices, building support for alliances, coordinating resources and measuring/monitoring performance. Such activities correspond to a learning goal orientation and could be contrasted with a more functionally defined model (e.g., driving sales, managing project milestones). As a result, learning goal oriented ADMs will be more likely to create an alliance management function that promotes cooperatively oriented roles, and they will be more open to evaluating options in reconfiguration, whereas performance goal oriented ADMs will lean toward functionally defined roles and be strictly confined to following pre-determined paths in reconfigurations.

Lastly, because alliances by virtue of bringing companies together face potential cultural differences, ADMs can have an outsized influence on the extent to which partners' motives are correctly interpreted. As cited in Luvison and Cummings (2015), learning goal oriented ADMs

> are likely to foster more open pathways for their firm to interact internally and externally (Ibarra & Hansen, 2011) and to promote learning exchange (Lopez et al., 2004; Ng et al., 2009). Further, such organizations [as influenced by learning goal oriented ADMs] are more likely to delegate responsibilities, tolerate creative mistakes, provide slack time to work on new ideas (Davenport & Prusak, 1998), and be willing to accept their partners' ideas (Hayes & Clark, 1985; Katz & Allen, 1982). (p. 104)

Thus, contrary to the performance goal oriented ADMs, learning goal oriented ADMs are more likely to help foster the kinds of openness, mutuality, trustworthiness, and a learning orientation in operations and reconfigurations that experts indicate allow for greater alliance success (Barney & Hansen, 1994; Sambasivan & Yen, 2010; Yeung, Ulrich, Nason, & von Glinow, 1999).

CONCLUSION

The alliance literature holds that the alliance formation process is driven by the need to fulfill strategic organizational objectives, such as efficiency, enhanced competitive position or organizational learning (Inkpen & Ross, 2001; Kogut, 1988). In this chapter we show that ADMs' goal orientations play an important role in how they interpret those objectives and affect decisions during each of the stages of the alliance life cycle. Indeed, just as studies have shown that the goal orientation of decision makers determines the objectives by which performance is evaluated (Brett & Vande-Walle, 1999; VandeWalle et al., 1999; VandeWalle, Cron, & Slocum, 2001), we suggest that an ADM's goal orientation will play a significant role in determining the firm's performance expectations for the alliance. Similarly, consistent with how upper echelons theory suggests that a firm's strategy and structural makeup derive from the priorities of the leaders (Hambrick et al., 2005; Hambrick & Mason, 1984), we likewise propose that the make-up of the firm's partner selection processes, alliance governance models, alliance operations, and alliance reconfigurations derive from, or are at least significantly influenced by, ADMs. As a result, we argue that not only is it necessary to clearly assess the needs of each specific alliance across its alliance life cycle in order to set it up for success, it is also necessary to understand how ADMs' goal orientations properly construe the firm's alliance opportunities and demands.

While others have examined various behavioral influences on alliances, including as trust (Gulati, 1995; Lui & Ngo, 2004; Luo, 2002; Malhotra & Lumineau, 2011), cooperation (Gulati, Wohlgezogen, & Zhelyazkov, 2012; Schreiner et al., 2009), conflict handling (Kauser & Shaw, 2004; Mohr & Spekman, 1994), and ADM behaviors (Luvison & Cummings, 2015), this is the first contribution that traces the influence of ADMs' goal orientations across the alliance life cycle stages. This is important because it helps explicate how ADMs' goal orientations can affect specific decisions routinely taken during the different stages. In turn, this allows for a better understanding of not only how these ADMs might affect alliance performance, but also how firms might better develop and match ADMs to fit with the needs of each stage of an alliance.

Thus, not only is it necessary to clearly assess the needs of each specific alliance across its alliance life cycle in order to set it up for success, it is also necessary to select ADMs whose goal orientations properly construe its opportunity and demands. For instance, in the context of a go-to-market alliance where revenue growth would be a primary goal, it would seem natural for ADMs to establish short-term sales objectives, the very types of metrics that performance- oriented ADMs would tend to adopt. However, if the ADM is not performance goal oriented they may take very different decisions, for example by seeking longer-term results or choosing to work with an unproven partner, thereby changing the dynamics of the alliance and affecting its performance. Moreover, if the actors in the firm were unaccustomed to working with external partners, a focus on learning how to collaborate, which is more in line with the type of objectives a learning goal oriented ADM would anticipate (Geletkanycz & Hambrick, 1997), might be more appropriate. Similarly, in a discovery-focused innovation alliance, where a longer-term perspective and the ability to deal with failure may be useful, and where effective knowledge sharing has been found to be related to how readily a partner is able to make its knowledge accessible through various sharing mechanisms, a learning goal orientation would also seem more appropriate (Brett & VandeWalle, 1999; Cummings & Holmberg, 2012; Cummings & Teng, 2003). However, if the potential for failure is too high for the firm it might be more useful to adopt the risk-avoidance approach that is exhibited by performance goal oriented ADMs (VandeWalle et al., 2001).

Further, given that the focal firm and partner firm each have their own ADMs, it is important to note that non-congruence between them regarding their goal orientations may create partnering environments that generate relational issues. Alliances, after all, "represent socially constructed partnerships in which the various participants' interpretations and relationships shape the alliances' processes and outcomes. As a result, it is important to consider any factors that may have an effect on collaborative performance" (Cummings & Holmberg, 2012, p. 147). For example, where one ADM is performance goal oriented and the other is learning goal oriented, as discussed above there is a host of conflicts that can emerge with respect to, among others: the strictness or looseness of the objectives set by each partner to guide performance; the preferred form of governance to be adopted; the degree of openness and types of communications that are fostered within and between the partners; the types of tools and processes that are used to guide activities; and the manners in which issues, including those surrounding reconfiguration options, are decided. As a result, even if the parties seek to work together in a positive manner, as found by Anand et al. (2002) and Dahan et al. (2010), "difficulties often arise due to the challenges inherent in bridging differences in culture, experiences, trust, communication patterns, social systems and institutional structures as well as in implementing appropriate interaction processes and administrative systems" (Cummings & Holmberg, 2012, p. 147).

What each of these examples suggest is that it is necessary to clearly assess the needs of each specific alliance in order to set it up for success. However, if ADMs are inclined to interpret the needs of the alliance in terms of their goal orientation, they may misconstrue its opportunity and demands. Given that initial partner conditions can change (Majchrzak, Jarvenpaa, & Bagherzadeh, 2015), thereby requiring adjustment by the actors involved in the alliance (Das & Teng, 2000), any mismatch between ADMs could make such adjustments more challenging. We therefore argue that goal orientation informs an important aspect of the decision making logic employed by ADMs and should be added to the calculus regarding how to make appropriate decisions throughout the alliance life cycle.

NOTES

1. This author conducted a survey of over 100 members of the Association of Strategic Alliance Professionals, finding more than one-half of respondents indicating "a different partner should have been selected" when asked what was the most important change that could have been made to help a poor performing alliance improve. Follow up discussions revealed that part of the reason why new partners should have been selected is because of the negative spillovers from tense negotiations conducted by ADMs, and other ways that ADMs became over-involved in some instances due to their relationships with the partners they selected.
2. For brevity purposes we do not explore the slightly different effects of ADMs with performance avoid orientations. In essence, they would have an even greater concern with making a choice or decision or finding a partner who will not push their firm to have to adapt or take on more challenging tasks. As a result, such ADMs will define selection criteria in a way that limits acceptable choice or partners to those with which they can accomplish only readily codified and clearly defined tasks. They will also seek choices or partners who will not push the focal firm to undertake significant relationship-building activities or learning-related efforts. Similar to performance-prove ADMs, performance-avoid ADMs will also seek and therefore define partner-selection criteria that supports selection of partners with whom strong formal controls can be established to limit risks.

REFERENCES

Albers, S. (2010). Configurations of alliance governance systems. *Schmalenbach Business Review: ZFBF, 62*(July), 204–233.

Anand, V., Glick, W. H., & Manz, C. C. (2002). Thriving on the knowledge of outsiders: Tapping organizational social capital. *Academy of Management Executive, 16*(1), 87–101.

Anderson, E., & Gatignon, H. (1986). Modes of foreign entry: A transaction cost analysis and propositions. *Journal of International Business Studies, 17*(3), 1–26.

Anonymous. (2012). *Leading through connections: Insights from the global chief executive officer study.* Somers, NY: Institute for Business Value, IBM Global Business Services.

Ariño, A. (2003). Measures of strategic alliance performance: An analysis of construct validity. *Journal of International Business Studies, 34*(1), 66–79.

Ariño, A., & de la Torre, J. (1998). Learning from failure: Towards an evolutionary model of collaborative ventures. *Organization Science, 9*(3), 306–325.

Barney, J. B., & Hansen, M. H. (1994). Trustworthiness as a source of competitive advantage. *Strategic Management Journal, 15*(S1), 175–190.

Bowman, E., H., & Hurry, D. (1993). Strategy through the option lens: An integrated view of resource investments and the incremental-choice process. *The Academy of Management Review, 18*(4), 760–782.

Brett, J. F., & VandeWalle, D. (1999). Goal orientation and goal content as predictors of performance in a training program. *Journal of Applied Psychology, 84*(6), 863–873.

Chao, Y.-C. (2011). Decision-making biases in the alliance life cycle. *Management Decision, 49*(3), 350–364.

Christoffersen, J. (2013). A review of antecedents of international strategic alliance performance: Synthesized evidence and new directions for core constructs. *International Journal of Management Reviews, 15*(1), 66–85.

Contractor, F. J., & Lorange, P. (1988). Competition vs. cooperation: A benefit-cost framework for choosing between fully-owned investments and cooperative relationships. *Management International Review, 28,* 14–41.

Crossland, C., & Hambrick, D. C. (2011). Differences in managerial discretion across countries: How nation-level institutions affect the degree to which CEOs matter. *Strategic Management Journal, 32*(8), 797–819.

Cummings, J. L. (2011). Association of strategic alliance professionals [Unpublished manuscript]. Department of Management and International Business, Loyola University Maryland.

Cummings, J. L., & Holmberg, S. R. (2012). Best-fit alliance partners: The use of critical success factors in a comprehensive partner selection process. *Long Range Planning, 45*(2/3), 136–159.

Cummings, J. L., Holmberg, S. R., & Yang, Q. (2013). The role of partnering factors in international learning alliance success. *International Journal of Strategic Business Alliances, 3*(1), 23–49.

Cummings, J. L., & Teng, B.-S. (2003). Transferring R&D knowledge: The key factors affecting knowledge transfer success. *Journal of Engineering and Technology Management, 20*(1/2), 39–68.

Dahan, N. M., Doe, J. P., Oetzel, J., & Yaziji, M. (2010). Corporate-NGO collaboration: Co- creating new business models for developing markets. *Long Range Planning, 43*(2), 326–324.

Das, T. K. (2005). Deceitful behaviors of alliance partners: Potential and prevention. *Management Decision, 43*(5), 706–719.

Das, T. K. (2006). Strategic alliance temporalities and partner opportunism. *British Journal of Management, 17*(1), 1–21.

Das, T. K., & Kumar, R. (2009). Interpartner harmony in strategic alliances: Managing commitment and forbearance. *International Journal of Strategic Business Alliances, 1*(1), 24–52.

Das, T. K., & Teng, B. (1996). Risk types and inter-firm alliance structures. *The Journal of Management Studies, 33*(6), 827–843.

Das, T. K., & Teng, B. (1998). Resource and risk management in the strategic alliance making process. *Journal of Management, 24*(1), 21–42.

Das, T. K., & Teng, B. (1999). Managing risks in strategic alliances. *Academy of Management Executive, 13*(4), 50–62.

Das, T. K., & Teng, B. (2000). Instabilities of strategic alliances: An internal tensions perspective. *Organization Science, 11*(1), 77–101.

Davenport, T. H., & Prusak, L. (1998). *Working knowledge: How organizations manage what they know.* Boston, MA: Harvard Business School Press.

de Man, A.-P., & Roijakkers, N. (2009). Alliance governance: Balancing control and trust in dealing with risk. *Long Range Planning, 42*(1), 75–95.

Douma, M. U., Bilderbeek, J., Idenburg, P. J., & Looise, J. K. (2000). Strategic alliances: Managing the dynamics of fit. *Long Range Planning, 33*(4), 579–598.

Doz, Y. L. (1996). The evolution of cooperation in strategic alliances: Initial conditions or learning processes? *Strategic Management Journal, 17*(S1), 55–83.

Dragoni, L., & Kuenzi, M. (2012). Better understanding work unit goal orientation: Its emergence and impact under different types of work unit structure. *Journal of Applied Psychology, 97*(5), 1032–1048.

Dyer, J. H., Singh, H., & Kale, P. (2008). Splitting the pie: Rent distribution in alliances and networks. *Managerial and Decision Economics, 29*(2/3), 137–148.

Eisenhardt, K. M., & Schoonhoven, C. B. (1996). Resource-based view of strategic alliance formation: Strategic and social effects in entrepreneurial firms. *Organization Science, 7*(2), 136–150.

Espedal, B., Kvitastein, O., & Grønhaug, K. (2012). When cooperation is the norm of appropriateness: How does CEO cooperative behaviour affect organizational performance? *British Journal of Management, 23*(2), 257–271.

Faulkner, D. O. (1995). *International strategic alliances: Co-operating to compete.* Maidenhead, England: McGraw-Hill.

Festinger, L. (1957). *A theory of cognitive dissonance.* Evanston, IL: Row Peterson.

Geletkanycz, M. A., & Hambrick, D. C. (1997). The external ties of top executives: Implications for strategic choice and performance. *Administrative Science Quarterly, 42*(4), 654–681.

Geringer, J. M. (1991). Strategic determinants of partner selection criteria in international joint ventures. *Journal of International Business Studies, 22*(1), 41–62.

Geringer, J. M., & Hebert, L. (1991). Measuring performance of international joint ventures. *Journal of International Business Studies, 22*(2), 249–263.

Gerwin, D. (2004). Coordinating new product development in strategic alliances. *Academy of Management Review, 29*(2), 241–257.

Gulati, R. (1995). Social structure and alliance formation patterns: A longitudinal analysis. *Administrative Science Quarterly, 40*(4), 619–652.

Gulati, R. (1998). Alliances and networks. *Strategic Management Journal, 19*(4), 293–317.

Gulati, R., Sytch, M., & Mehrotra, P. (2008). Breaking up is never easy: Planning for exit in a strategic alliance. *California Management Review, 50*(4), 147–163.

Gulati, R., Wohlgezogen, F., & Zhelyazkov, P. (2012). The two facets of collaboration: Cooperation and coordination in strategic alliances. *Academy of Management Annals, 6*(1), 531–583.

Hambrick, D. C. (2007). Upper echelons theory: An update. *Academy of Management Review, 32*(2), 334–343.

Hambrick, D. C., Finkelstein, S., & Mooney, A. C. (2005). Executive job demands: New insights for explaining strategic decisions and leader behaviors. *Academy of Management Review, 30*(3), 472.

Hambrick, D. C., & Mason, P. A. (1984). Upper echelons: The organization as a reflection of its top managers. *Academy of Management Review, 9*(2), 193–206.

Hamel, G., & Prahalad, C. K. (1989). Strategic intent. *Harvard Business Review, 83*(7/8), 63–76.

Harrigan, K. R. (1988). Joint ventures and competitive strategy. *Strategic Management Journal, 9*(2), 141–158.

Haspeslagh, P., & Jemison, D. B. (1991). *Managing acquisitions: Creating value through corporate renewal.* New York, NY: Free Press.

Hayes, R. H., & Clark, K. B. (1985). *Exploring the sources of productivity differences at the factory level.* New York, NY: Wiley.

Heimeriks, K. H., & Duysters, G. (2007). Alliance capability as a mediator between experience and alliance performance: An empirical investigation into the alliance capability development process. *Journal of Management Studies, 44*(1), 25–49.

Heimeriks, K. H., Klijn, E., & Reuer, J. J. (2009). Building capabilities for alliance portfolios. *Long Range Planning, 42*(1), 96–114.

Hoffmann, W. H., & Schlosser, R. (2001). Success factors of strategic alliances in small and medium-sized enterprises–An empirical survey. *Long Range Planning, 34*(3), 357–381.

Ibarra, H., & Hansen, M. T. (2011). Are you a collaborative leader? *Harvard Business Review, 89*(7/8), 68–74.

Inkpen, A. C., & Ross, J. (2001). Why do some strategic alliances persist beyond their useful life? *California Management Review, 44*(1), 132–148.

Kale, P., Dyer, J. H., & Singh, H. (2001). Value creation and success in strategic alliances: Alliancing skills and the role of alliance structure and systems. *European Management Journal, 19*(5), 463–471.

Kale, P., Dyer, J. H., & Singh, H. (2002). Alliance capability, stock market response, and long- term alliance success: The role of the alliance function. *Strategic Management Journal, 23*(8), 747–767.

Katz, R., & Allen, T. J. (1982). Investigating the not invented here (NIH) syndrome: A look at the performance, tenure and communication patterns of 50 R&D project groups. *R&D Management, 12*(1), 7–19.

Kauser, S., & Shaw, V. (2004). The influence of behavioural and organisational characteristics on the success of international strategic alliances. *International Marketing Review, 21*(1), 17–52.

Khanna, T., Gulati, R., & Nohria, N. (1998). The dynamics of learning alliances: Competition, cooperation, and relative scope. *Strategic Management Journal, 19*(3), 193–210.

Killing, J. P. (1982). How to make a global joint venture work. *Harvard Business Review, 60*(3), 120–127.

Kogut, B. (1988). Joint ventures: Theoretical and empirical perspectives. *Strategic Management Journal, 9*(4), 319–332.

Kogut, B. (1991). Joint ventures and the option to expand and acquire. *Management Science, 37*(1), 19–33.

Lane, P., Salk, J. E., & Lyles, M. A. (2001). Absorptive capacity, learning, and performance in international joint ventures. *Strategic Management Journal, 22*(12), 1139–1161.

Levitt, B., & March, J. G. (1988). Organizational learning. *Annual Review of Sociology, 14*(1), 319–340.

Lopez, S. P., Peon, J. M. M., & Ordas, C. J. V. (2004). Managing knowledge: The link between culture and organizational learning. *Journal of Knowledge Management, 8*(6), 93–104.

Lui, S. S., & Ngo, H.-y. (2004). The role of trust and contractual safeguards on cooperation in non-equity alliances. *Journal of Management, 30*(4), 471–485.

Luo, Y. (2002). Contract, cooperation, and performance in international joint ventures. *Strategic Management Journal, 23*(10), 903–919.

Luvison, D., & Cummings, J. L. (2015). Assessing the impact of psychological processes on leader alliance performance expectations and alliance structuring. *International Journal of Strategic Business Alliances, 4*(2/3), 93–115.

Macaulay, S. (1963). Non-contractual relations in business: A preliminary study. *American Sociological Review, 28*(1), 55–67.

Majchrzak, A., Jarvenpaa, S. L., & Bagherzadeh, M. (2015). A review of interorganizational collaboration dynamics. *Journal of Management, 41*(5), 1338–1360.

Malhotra, D., & Lumineau, F. (2011). Trust and collaboration in the aftermath of conflict: The effects of contract structure. *Academy of Management Journal, 54*(5), 981–998.

Mehta, A., Feild, H., Armenakis, A., & Mehta, N. (2009). Team goal orientation and team performance: The mediating role of team planning. *Journal of Management, 35*(4), 1026–1046.

Mohr, J. J., & Spekman, R. E. (1994). Characteristics of partnership success: Partnership attributes, communication behavior, and conflict resolution techniques. *Strategic Management Journal, 15*(2), 135–152.

Ng, K. Y., Van Dyne, L., & Ang, S. (2009). From experience to experiential learning: Cultural intelligence as a learning capability for global leader development. *Academy of Management Learning & Education, 8*(4), 511–526.

Nielsen, B. B. (2007). Determining international strategic alliance performance: A multidimensional approach. *International Business Review, 16*(3), 337–361.

Osborn, R. N., & Marion, R. (2009). Contextual leadership, transformational leadership and the performance of international innovation seeking alliances. *Leadership Quarterly, 20*(2), 191–206.

Parkhe, A. (1998). Understanding trust in international alliances. *Journal of World Business, 33*(3), 219–240.

Porter, M. E., & Fuller, M. B. (1986). Coalitions and global strategy. In M. E. Porter (Ed.), *Global Industries* (pp. 315–343). Boston, MA: Harvard Business School Press.

Reuer, J. J., & Ariño, A. (2007). Strategic alliance contracts: Dimensions and determinants of contractual complexity. *Strategic Management Journal, 28*(3), 313–330.

Ring, P. S., & Van de Ven, A. H. (1994). Developmental processes of cooperative interorganizational relationships. *Academy of Management Review, 19*(1), 90–118.

Sambasivan, M., & Yen, C. N. (2010). Strategic alliances in a manufacturing supply chain: Influence of organizational culture from the manufacturer's perspective. *International Journal of Physical Distribution & Logistics Management, 40*(6), 456–474.

Schreiner, M., Kale, P., & Corsten, D. (2009). What really is alliance management capability and how does it impact alliance outcomes and success? *Strategic Management Journal, 30*(13), 1395–1419.

Serapio, M. G., & Cascio, W. F. (1996). End-games in international alliances. *Academy of Management Perspectives, 10*(1), 62–73.

Shamdasani, P. N., & Sheth, J. N. (1995). An experimental approach to investigating satisfaction and continuity in marketing alliances. *European Journal of Marketing, 29*(4), 6–23.

Smith, J. B. (1997). Selling alliances: Issues and insights. *Industrial Marketing Management, 26*(2), 149–161.

Smith, J. B., & Barclay, D. W. (1999). Selling partner relationships: The role of interdependence and relative influence. *The Journal of Personal Selling & Sales Management, 19*(4), 21–40.

Spekman, R. E., Forbes, T. M., III, Isabella, L. A., & MacAvoy, T. C. (1998). Alliance management: A view from the past and a look to the future. *Journal of Management Studies, 35*(6), 747–772.

Spekman, R. E., Isabella, L. A., MacAvoy, T. C., & Forbes, T., III. (1996). Creating strategic alliances which endure. *Long Range Planning, 29*(3), 346–357.

Tallman, S., & Phene, A. (2006). Structuring and restructuring alliances: A theory based process model. In O. Shenkar & J. J. Reuer (Eds.), *Handbook of strategic alliances* (pp. 133–148). Thousand Oaks, CA: Sage.

Tallman, S. B., & Shenkar, O. (1994). A managerial decision model of international cooperative venture formation. *Journal of International Business Studies, 25*(1), 91–113.

Taylor, A. (2005). An operations perspective on strategic alliance success factors: An exploratory study of alliance managers in the software industry. *International Journal of Operations & Production Management, 25*(5), 469–490.

Trim, P. R. J., & Lee, Y.-I. (2008). A strategic approach to sustainable partnership development. *European Business Review, 20*(3), 222–238.

VandeWalle, D., Brown, S. P., Cron, W. L., & Slocum, J. W., Jr. (1999). The influence of goal orientation and self-regulation tactics on sales performance: A longitudinal field test. *Journal of Applied Psychology, 84*(2), 249–259.

VandeWalle, D., Cron, W. L., & Slocum, J. W., Jr. (2001). The role of goal orientation following performance feedback. *Journal of Applied Psychology, 86*(4), 629–640.

VandeWalle, D., & Cummings, L. L. (1997). A test of the influence of goal orientation on the feedback-seeking process. *Journal of Applied Psychology, 82*(3), 390–400.

Weber, L., & Mayer, K. J. (2011). Designing effective contracts: Exploring the influence of framing and expectations. *Academy of Management Review, 36*(1), 53–75.

Williamson, O. E., & Craswell, R. (1993). Calculativeness, trust, and economic organization. *Journal of Law and Economics, 36*(1), 453–478.

Yeung, A. K., Ulrich, D., Nason, S. W., & von Glinow, M. A. (1999). *Organizational learning capability*. New York, NY: Oxford University Press.

Young-Ybarra, C., & Wiersma, M. (1999). Strategic flexibility in information technology alliances: The influence of transaction cost economics and social exchange theory. *Organization Science, 10*(4), 439–459.

Zhang, H., Shu, C., Jiang, X., & Malter, A. J. (2010). Managing knowledge for innovation: The role of cooperation, competition, and alliance nationality. *Journal of International Marketing, 18*(4), 74–94.

CHAPTER 7

MANAGING INTERPARTNER LEARNING IN STRATEGIC ALLIANCES

T. K. Das
Rajesh Kumar

ABSTRACT

In this chapter we propose a framework for examining the dynamics of learning in the various stages of alliance development. We describe three kinds of learning in alliances—namely, content, partner specific, and alliance management—and discuss the saliencies and implications of particular types of learning in different alliance stages. The framework makes clear that alliance learning varies according to the stages of the alliance developmental process (formation, operation, outcome), and that different types of learning have different strategic implications. Briefly, content learning augments the collective strengths of the alliance, partner-specific learning (i.e., learning about a partner as opposed to learning from a partner) is crucial in determining whether or not an alliance gets formed, and alliance management learning helps build the confidence of the alliance partners in managing alliances. The chapter responds to the need of managers with alliance responsibilities for a framework to help identify and exploit the most effective types of learn-

Managing the Partners in Strategic Alliances, pages 165–194

ing opportunities, vis-à-vis partners and the alliance as a whole, during the specific alliance development stages of formation, operation, and outcome.

INTRODUCTION

Inter-firm alliances have become increasingly common due to globalization, deregulation, and the accelerating pace of technological change. These cooperative arrangements take many forms, ranging from joint marketing to equity-based joint ventures. Alliances allow the firms to share the costs of R&D development, expedite the introduction of new products in the global marketplace, minimize costs, gain access to resources, and provide a means for accessing new technologies of partner firms. In particular, the idea that alliances are an important vehicle for learning has considerable intuitive appeal and perhaps, for this reason, continues to dominate the academic as well as the practitioner literature on alliances (e.g., Anand & Khanna, 2000; Hamel, 1991; Kumar & Nti, 1998). However, the focus of much of the existing research is on how alliances may be useful for learning purposes in the competitive business arena, and not sufficiently on the internal learning dynamics of alliances. While the topic of learning by and through alliances is no doubt of relevance, the need for an adequate understanding of the learning dynamics within alliances is also clearly an important subject for examination for the effective management of alliances.

Furthermore, although there is by now a considerable amount of literature detailing the potential benefits and costs associated with learning in alliances, much remains to be investigated about the dynamics of learning in the alliance development process. As Das and Teng (2002) argue, the processual dynamics underlying the evolution of alliances are still a relatively unexplored phenomenon. In this paper we develop a framework for analyzing the learning dynamics in the various stages of strategic alliance development.

We divide the article into four parts. First, we discuss the different types of learning that are likely to occur when firms enter into alliances. Second, we review the literature for linkages between alliance process models and learning. We then elaborate on our framework for understanding the nature and dynamics of alliance learning in the different alliance stages. We conclude by noting the implications of this framework for studying and managing alliance learning.

THREE TYPES OF LEARNING IN ALLIANCES

We will attempt to identify here the basic themes in the vast literature on organizational learning that may have a bearing on our discussion of learning in alliances. Although learning is implicit in all social systems, the current emphasis on learning in the organizational literature has its roots in the intensification of the global competition in the late '70s. Scholars have focused their attention on three central issues in the literature. The first issue is a definitional one, namely, the nature of organizational learning. The second focuses on the processes of learning; namely, "How does learning occur?" The third deals with the fundamental question of learning to learn effectively, that is, the factors that impede the reliability and validity of the learning.

Definitions of organizational learning abound in the literature. An influential one is that by Huber (1991), who notes: "*An entity learns if, through its processing of information, the range of its potential behaviors is changed*" (p. 89, emphasis in original). Levitt and March (1996) view organizational learning as reflecting a change in organizational routines. Changes in routine are products of experiential learning and get embedded in the organization's memory. Crossan, Lane, and White (1999) take a somewhat broader perspective on organizational learning, viewing it as a mechanism that is critical for an organization's strategic renewal. Although the specific foci of the different definitions vary, the underlying commonality is the recognition that organizational learning entails a change in the knowledge structures of the organization. These knowledge structures are embodied in an organization's routines and are stored in an organization's memory. When firms enter into alliances the changes in knowledge structures may occur at different levels, and in varying degrees. First, by gaining knowledge from the alliance, the partners may reshape their strategy and the means of implementation. Alternatively, they may create a new knowledge structure in the alliance that they may help their performance. Finally, they may also develop skills for managing alliances effectively.

How does learning occur? It is important to note, first, that organizational learning is both intraorganizational as well as interorganizational, and that an adequate framework of learning dynamics would need to encompass the inter-relationships between these different levels (Argote, McEvily, & Reagans, 2003; Holmqvist, 2003). Intraorganizational learning, by itself, is a multilevel process that simultaneously and collectively involves the individual, the group, and the organization. Interorganizational learning is dependent on the learning strategies pursued by the different organizations. Integrative learning strategies will lead to collective knowledge development whereas distributive learning strategies may prevent that from occurring. Second, learning intent does not imply that valid learning will occur. Third, learning is a costly process because, in order to be effective, it involves a degree of institutionalization—a multilevel process necessitating the integration of individual, group, and organizational level perspectives. While the managerial school seems to suggest that this learning process can be managed (Bell, Whitwell, & Lukas, 1982), it would still be one that is unlikely to bear fruit overnight.

When learning is the primary motive for alliance formation it is easier to gauge the strategic intentions of one's partner and to put in place safeguards to minimize the potential risks of opportunistic behavior of the partner (Das, 2005). However, it is important to remember that even when learning is not the primary objective, it is possible that learning-related goals may subsequently displace the original intentions as the alliance evolves over time.

It is also important to note that even in those alliances where learning is the primary motive, there may well be very different kinds of learning that are involved. Lubatkin, Florin, and Lane (2001) draw a distinction between inter-firm collaborations that involve vicarious learning, knowledge absorption learning, knowledge grafting learning, and reciprocal learning. Vicarious learning alliances are alliances in which the knowledge to be transferred is easily accessible. Knowledge absorption alliances pose a slightly higher degree of difficulty, in that the ability to gain knowledge from one's partner is critically dependent on the focal firm's absorptive capacity. Knowledge grafting alliances are in the nature of mergers and acquisitions, whereas reciprocal learning alliances bring together partners working in different knowledge domains who are non-competitors in the core businesses. The key implication of these distinctions is that the focal firm has to discern and counter the strategic intentions of its partner according as these intentions vary across different forms of learning alliances.

Generally speaking, scholars have identified three different kinds of learning that occur in strategic alliances; namely, (a) content learning, (b) partner-specific learning, and (c) alliance management learning (Kale, Singh, & Perlmutter, 2000; Parise & Hendersen, 2001). We list in Table 7.1 some illustrative observations from the literature on these three kinds of learning in alliances. The purpose of this table is to provide the reader with an overview of the way in which scholars have looked at learning in alliances.

Content learning refers to the ability of an alliance firm to acquire and internalize knowledge from its partner. This type of learning may alter the bargaining power among the member firms if one of the partners outlearns the other (e.g., Hamel, 1991; Inkpen & Beamish, 1997; Reich & Mankin, 1986). The firm that outlearns its partner may apply the knowledge it has gained to other product domains, leading to superior economic performance. This will also afford the opportunity to either abandon its alliance partner or renegotiate for more favorable terms of collaboration. All this will have major strategic implications for the member firms as well as alliance evolution.

Partner-specific learning has two components; namely, (a) learning from a partner and (b) learning about a partner. While learning from a partner is undoubtedly a significant issue in alliances, learning about a partner is no less important. Learning about one's partner is crucial because the motivation and ability of a member firm to act in ways that will maximize joint value creation are clearly of some importance in sustaining and deepening commitment in the alliance. Partner-specific learning entails the use of the alliance as a mechanism for learning about the motivation and capability of

TABLE 7.1 Learning Types in Alliances

Authors	Learning Type	Illustrative Observations	Remarks
Alvarez Gil & Gonzalez de la Fe (1999)	Content	"Thus, while poor performance can lead to myopia that acts as a barrier to knowledge creation, the student partner may feel that the alliance does not yield satisfactory organizational performance because learning opportunities have been unexploited." (p. 403)	Content learning is limited both by the desire of the teacher to prevent the student from undertaking it as also by the performance of the alliance. Learning from a partner is very constraining inasmuch as opportunities for learning are constrained by the strategic motivations of the partner. Very much in contrast with the work of Dussauge, Garrette, & Mitchell (2000).
Anand & Khanna (2000)	Alliance Management	"Valuation of alliances cannot afford to ignore the dynamic, cross alliance benefits of entering into a particular relationship." (p. 313)	Study suggests that firms differ in their "alliance capabilities" with the implication that some firms are better than others in learning from alliances. As the authors themselves note, it is unclear if the enhanced learning capability reflects greater capability in either learning about a partner or learning from a partner. The ability to pick the right partner may avoid negative outcomes but it does not guarantee positive outcomes per se.
Ariño (2001)	Partner-specific	"Non cooperative behavior by omission has a lesser effect than cooperative behavior by commission on the firm's own non cooperative behavior." (p. 18)	Paper focuses on learning about a partner as opposed to learning from a partner. The fundamental idea is that learning about a partner entails attributions about intentionality with these attributions shaping subsequent behavior. Although attributions about intentionality shape behavior, partners may differ in their assessment as to what constitutes cooperative behavior by commission and what constitutes non-cooperative behavior by omission.

(continued)

TABLE 7.1 Learning Types in Alliances (Continued)

Authors	Learning Type	Illustrative Observations	Remarks
Ariño & de la Torre (1998)	Content	"The existence of procedural solutions for conflict resolution may be an important aspect of initial conditions." (p. 323)	An empirical study of a joint venture suggests that partner-specific learning is fostered by how partners deal with perceptions of equity/inequity in the relationship. A case study very consistent with Kale et al. (2000), in that it highlights the importance of relational capital in determining how partners deal with perceptions of equity/inequity in relationships.
Doz (1996)	Content Partner-specific	Content learning is more likely to occur in projects that are of moderate importance to alliance partners. "Early small events in an alliance have a disproportionate importance in establishing, or not, a self reinforcing cycle of heightened efficacy expectations, greater institutional trust and personal trust and commitment, joint sense making and learning, and greater flexibility and adaptability." (p. 77)	Partner-specific learning is based on the ability to develop cooperation at the onset of the relationship. This work is consistent with other work suggesting that partners seek to maintain control over their core competencies to prevent giving away the store. The implication of this is that collaboration processes are critically dependent on the emergence of relational capital among the partners.
Dussauge, Garrette, & Mitchell (2000)	Content	"Because firms set up link alliances in order to take advantage of the complementary skills of the partner firms, the fact that the firms reorganize many link alliances by changing the allocation of activities among the partners suggests that the complementarity between the allies tends to shift over time." (p. 120)	Learning is more likely to occur in link as opposed to scale alliances. The authors note that content learning is a function of complementary skills among partners. If partners are aware of this complementarity and recognize that they might lose out in the alliance then why do they enter these alliances?

(continued)

TABLE 7.1 Learning Types in Alliances (Continued)

Authors	Learning Type	Illustrative Observations	Remarks
Dyer & Singh (1998)	Content	"Alliances generate competitive advantage only as they move the relationship away from the attributes of market relationships." (p. 662)	Alliance partners can maximize learning by investing in relationship specific assets, knowledge sharing routines, complementary resource endowments, and "effective governance." The theoretical argument in this study seems to go against the empirical evidence that suggests that joint value creation is problematical.
Edmondson & Moingeon (1996)	Content Partner-specific	Content learning is fundamentally a question of learning "how." "Learning how is required for the many situations in which speed and quality matter; learning why is required for diagnosis and relationship building." (p. 34)	Partner-specific learning is based on learning "why." The only piece that seeks to draw an explicit distinction between different forms of content learning; namely, learning why and learning how. Learning how may foster a more competitive mode of interaction whereas learning why may induce a different dynamic.
Hamel (1991)	Content	"Outlearning a partner simply means 'winning' a series of micro bargains." (p. 101)	Content learning is dependent on learning intent, transparency, and receptivity. One of the first empirical papers that explicitly takes a strategic view of the learning process, arguing that the learning processes and outcomes are critically influenced by the learning orientation of the partners.
Kale, Dyer, & Singh (2000)	Content	"Relational capital is linked not only to alliance success in general, but also to very specific and important objectives such as learning and limiting partner opportunism." (p. 232)	Content learning is dependent on the relational capital among the partners as well as their ability to manage conflicts integratively. The paper does not explicitly address the issue as to how relational capital gets established in the first place with partners that may be competitors.

(continued)

TABLE 7.1 Learning Types in Alliances (Continued)

Authors	Learning Type	Illustrative Observations	Remarks
Khanna, Gulati, & Nohria (1998)	Content	"Our models suggest that if firms view their relationship with others in the alliance as either strictly competitive or strictly cooperative, this may give rise to suboptimal outcomes for one or more firms in the alliance." (p. 205)	Content learning is predicated on the ratio of private to common benefits in an alliance. The greater the ratio of private to common benefits, the more competitive the interaction and the less likelihood that one partner may learn from another. A conceptual paper highlighting the dynamic tension that exists between cooperation and competition in an alliance. Beyond the recognition that alliance partners may differ in their assessment of private and common benefits the subjective determinants of these perceptions are not explicitly outlined.
Kumar & Nti (1998)	Partner-specific	"Unfavorable discrepancies may affect the partners' feelings of psychological attachment to the relationship as well as the pattern of interaction." (p. 365)	A conceptual paper suggesting that partner-specific learning is crucially shaped by how partners deal with unfavorable process and outcome discrepancies. The idea that the attributions about the discrepancies made by the partners determines the strategy pursued by alliance partners is very similar to the arguments advanced by Ariño and de la Torre (1998) and Kale et al. (2000).
Lane & Lubatkin (1998)	Partner-specific	"Simply put, while imitating one's peers may not always be an effective course of action, the high level of relative absorptive capacity a firm will tend to have with its peers may make them the most easily understood teachers." (p. 474)	The ability of one partner to learn from another is dependent on (a) similarity of firms' knowledge bases; (b) organization structure and compensation policies; and (c) dominant logics.

(continued)

TABLE 7.1 Learning Types in Alliances (Continued)

Authors	Learning Type	Illustrative Observations	Remarks
Makhija & Ganesh (1997)	Content	"The model indicates that only when the bargaining power is perceived to be more or less balanced will the chances for a successful relationship improve. A balance in bargaining power will enable both partners to institute controls appropriate for their own objectives in the learning related joint venture." (p. 524)	Content learning is based on the kind of knowledge sought by each partner. Dissimilar learning needs lead to unequal learning rates, which affect the bargaining power among partners. Consistent with other works in highlighting the dynamic instability of alliances due to the possibility of differential learning. The paper has more of an economic as opposed to a sociological focus inasmuch as it does not explicitly deal with the relationship among partners and how such a relationship may moderate the dynamics of the relationship.
Mowery, Oxley, & Silverman (1996)	Content	"The presence of some alliances in our sample in which the firms display 'divergent development' i.e. declining technological overlap suggests that some alliances are vehicles accessing rather than 'acquiring capabilities'." (p. 89)	An empirical paper highlighting the potential limitations of "capabilities acquisitions" view of strategic alliances. An empirical piece suggesting that content-based learning may not be as prominent as has traditionally been suggested. The evidence offered here is in contrast to the work by Dussauge et al., suggesting that such learning does occur.
Nti & Kumar (2000)	Content	"Firms with extremely high or low absorptive capacities may have difficulty in finding compatible alliance partners and they may actually end up in unstable learning alliances because they are likely to link up with firms whose absorptive capacities are very different." (p. 130)	Content learning is dependent on similarities among partners' absorptive capacities. What impact does the instability of the alliance have on the reputation of the partners? In other words, is there any detrimental impact of alliances?

(continued)

TABLE 7.1 Learning Types in Alliances (Continued)

Authors	Learning Type	Illustrative Observations	Remarks
Parkhe (1991)	Content	Content learning is impeded by interfirm diversity. "[W]hen Type I diversity (mutual interdependency) is larger than Type II diversity [interfirm differences], ceteris paribus, longevity will be high.…But when Type II diversity is larger than Type I diversity, ceteris paribus, longevity will be low." (p. 596)	The paper highlights the interplay of differences at the strategic and the organizational levels and their consequences for learning. A broad framework is developed and outlined here.
Stuart (2000)	Partner-specific	"Particularly when one of the firms in an alliance is a young or a small organization, or more generally an organization of ambiguous quality, I believe that alliances convey endorsements." (p. 818)	An alliance with a reputable partner enhances the reputation of the focal firm. The effect is particularly strong when the focal firm is not that well known. It is a little unclear if the impact on the reputation of a younger partner is temporary or long lasting when the alliance is a failure.
Zajac & Olsen (1993)	Partner-specific	"A focus on interorganizational exchange processes suggests that exchanges in interorganizational strategies are influenced by dynamic developmental processes with the processes themselves often subject to change." (p. 142)	Partner-specific learning is dependent on how interorganizational strategies evolve over time. Very similar to other process models reviewed earlier in stressing the fact that the learning processes are dynamically shaped by the strategies enacted by the different actors.

the partner to maximize value creation. This type of learning is especially valuable as a prelude to acquiring or merging with another firm (e.g., Balakrishnan & Koza, 1993; Mody, 1993). In the short to medium term, this may well be the most important component of learning in alliances for several reasons. First, if a firm is learning from its partner, and second, if what it learns about its partner is positive, its motivation to continue with the alliance will be enhanced. Ahuja (2002) points out that if a partner firm has a high level of technical or commercial capital, its attractiveness as a potential partner increases. The same conditions will also reflect positively on the firm's capability to access and internalize knowledge from its partner (Grant & Baden-Fuller, 2004) and, in so doing, may enhance social capital. This has longer-term implications, in that it may add to the propensity for partner collaboration. It will also give the alliancing firms a potential opportunity to establish routines that may facilitate their collaboration.

Finally, alliance management learning relates to a firm's ability to manage alliances effectively. Following Zollo and Winter (2002), one can conceive of alliance management learning as "a dynamic capability . . . through which the organization systematically generates and modifies its operating routines in pursuit of improved effectiveness" (p. 340). The authors suggest that the development of dynamic capability is dependent on the amount of learning investment that the member firms are willing to make.

Alliance management learning is significant because it is an essential ingredient for enhancing an organization's competitive ability over the long haul (Ireland, Hitt, & Vaidyanath, 2002). It also forms the basis for the concept of alliance capability that is gaining increasing research attention. The concept has two major components; namely, alliance experience and organizational processes that may allow the firms to profit from such experience (De Man, 2005). Although it is intuitively clear that prior experience may enhance a firm's alliance capability, some recent work has proposed boundary conditions on the transferability of this experience. For example, according to Hoang and Rothaermel (2005), "It appears that to reap benefits from prior alliance experience, a firm needs to possess absorptive capacity, the potential capacity to acquire and assimilate new knowledge and the realized capacity to transform and exploit the new knowledge (Zahra & George, 2002)" (p. 342). We would surmise that firms with higher levels of alliance capability may be more effective in managing the learning process. They are also likely to have structured their alliance in a manner that mitigates any potential problems and are likely to have well-developed institutionalized mechanisms for managing conflict with their alliance partner. De Man (2005) points out that American companies have made greater efforts to develop their alliance capability in contrast to their European partners. Alliance management learning may also make a member firm more accepting of an exploratory intent in fashioning an alliance with a partner. Furthermore, the firm may become more adept at screening potential partners and in making certain that the alliance develops as intended.

LEARNING AND ALLIANCE PROCESS MODELS

When firms enter into alliances, they do so on the basis of certain native attributes that make it easier for them to engage in the process of value creation. Theorists have emphasized the importance of a firm's preexisting competitive position and the nature of its resource profile (Das & Teng, 2000a, 2003) in explaining the success of partner firms in value creation. Also, adopting a process perspective, a number of researchers have sought to explain how an alliance develops over time (e.g., Das & Teng, 2002; Doz, 1996; Kumar & Nti, 1998; Ring & Van de Ven, 1994).

While the notion of learning processes shaping alliance processes and outcomes is implicitly embedded in processual frameworks, only Doz (1996) and Kumar and Nti (1998) explicitly deal with the impact of learning on alliance evolution. In Doz's (1996) framework, a set of alliance conditions—task definition, partner routines, interface structure, and expectations of performance, behavior, and motives—determine how the learning process evolves in the alliance, prompting changes in conditions that in turn shape subsequent behavior. Kumar and Nti (1998) argue that learning-related discrepancies may pose a major problem for one or all of the partners because these cannot be evaluated objectively. As they note, "There is an ever-present hazard that a learning related discrepancy may be emerging locally, threatening to set in motion forces that can destroy commitment and trust in the relationship" (p. 363). Both these frameworks stress content learning, noting that the differential ability of the partner firms in content learning may generate forces that may be detrimental to the relationship.

Alliance Development Stages

Although the frameworks noted above stress the importance of learning-related discrepancies in shaping alliance processes and outcomes, none of these are explicitly dynamic—that is, they do not explicate how the learning processes unfold through the different stages of alliance development (Das & Teng, 2002). A dynamic perspective is useful for not only understanding how the learning processes change over time, but also how the different types of learning (content, partner-specific, alliance management) may be differentially salient in these different developmental stages.

Das and Teng (2002) argue, for example, that all alliances proceed through a formation stage, an operation stage, and an outcome stage.

During the formation stage the alliance partners seek to negotiate the alliance and begin implementing the agreement that they have entered into. The formation stage is marked by the calculated expectation that the alliance partners will not experience inordinate degrees of relational risk and performance risk (Das & Teng, 1996) as well as inefficiency and inequity (Ring & Van de Ven, 1994). At the operation stage, the alliance partners implement the contractually binding commitments they have made. Implementing the agreements may be either a smooth or a conflict-prone affair. This stage enables member firms to solidify their perceptions (either positive or negative) about their partner. It also may lead one or both of the member firms to engage in content learning, while simultaneously promoting alliance management learning. The success or failure of an alliance is determined at the outcome stage, where it can either be stabilized, reformed, enter a state of progressive decline, or eventually be terminated (Das & Teng, 2002). The particular outcome would depend, first, on whether the alliance has experienced a learning related discrepancy and, second, on the ability of the members to effectively cope with that discrepancy.

While these stages are sequential, there are also interdependencies among them. In other words, what transpires at the formation stage may affect what happens at the operation stage. Similarly, what happens at the outcome stage may induce the alliance partners to reinterpret their earlier experiences at the formation and operation stages. It may also initiate a process of renegotiation, should one or the other partner consider it desirable at that juncture. Moreover, the time duration of these stages may also exhibit considerable variability. It may be the case, for example, that the formation stage takes a long time, but if a good and solid understanding has been achieved here, the operation stage may unfold rather smoothly. One might surmise, for example, that at the formation stage partner-specific learning may be crucial, whereas at the operation stage the relative importance of content learning increases, and at the outcome stage alliance management learning may acquire decided salience.

We may also note that the unit of analysis in most of the existing work on explaining learning processes has been the individual member firms rather than the relationship between these firms and the strategic alliance. That current focus in the literature, once again, neglects the dynamic aspects of alliance evolution without which it would be difficult to understand how the alliancing firms deal with the inherent tensions in alliances (Das & Teng, 2000b).

Alliance Conditions

In our attempt to understand alliance learning, we need also to recognize that the different stages of alliance evolution (formation, operation, outcome) describe unique sets of alliance conditions (e.g., Doz 1996; Das & Teng, 2002). These alliance conditions are well captured by three categories: (a) collective strengths of the alliance, (b) interpartner conflicts, and (c) the pattern of interdependencies among the alliance partners (Das & Teng, 2000a). Collective strengths define the extent of value creation by the alliance partners as they work together. This requires the willingness and the ability to learn from one's partner while also assisting the partner to learn. The alliancing firms may be able to maximize value creation through their interactions. The greater the difference in the absorptive capacities of the member firms, the lower would be the collective strengths of the alliance. However, if a focal firm with a higher absorptive capacity can provide the right incentives to the partner with a lower absorptive capacity, the collective strengths of the alliance may well be augmented (Nti & Kumar, 2000).

Interpartner conflicts stem from differences in strategic objectives among partner firms (e.g., Khanna, Gulati, & Nohria, 1998), incompatibility in national and corporate cultures of the parent organizations (e.g., Ariño & de la Torre, 1998; Kumar & Nti, 2004; Parkhe, 1991), differing alliance horizons (Das, 2004, 2006), political activity among the alliance management team members (e.g., Pearce, 1997), and their experience in managing alliances. These conflicts generate process as well as outcome discrepancies (e.g., Kumar & Nti, 1998). Unfavorable process discrepancies reflect the fact that the member firms are dissatisfied with their pattern of interaction, whereas unfavorable outcome discrepancies reflect the inability of the alliance partners to achieve their learning-related objectives. Unfavorable process discrepancies reduce the psychological commitment of the partners to the alliance. While conflict resolution may well be the way to rebuild and reestablish trust among the members, it also increases the coordination costs in making an alliance function effectively.

Interdependencies define the extent to which the alliance members can benefit from their cooperation. The interdependencies may be either symmetric or asymmetric. When symmetric, there are benefits for both members in continuing with the alliance. In the symmetrical condition, the alliance members learn from each other in ways that are both equitable and efficient and, hence, conducive to mutual value creation. However, over time, relationships among the members may become either symmetrical or less so and, in the process, may either enhance or lessen the stability of the alliance.

THE DYNAMICS OF ALLIANCE LEARNING

In this section we discuss the role and implications of the different types of learning as the alliance goes through its developmental stages, basing our discussion on the significant changes in the alliance conditions.

Formation Stage

In the formation stage the prospective partners sound each other out about the possibility of entering into an alliance. If negotiations are successful the partners proceed with the task of implementing the agreed-upon commitments. The formation stage is critical because the partners are usually unfamiliar with each other and for that reason are likely to scrutinize each other's behavior particularly carefully.

This stage of the alliance provides some opportunity for partner-specific learning. Partner-specific learning affects the judgments made by a firm about the relational risk and the performance risk inherent in entering into an alliance with the prospective partner. Relational risk focuses on the opportunistic behavior of one's partner whereas performance risk focuses on the alliance's ability to achieve its objectives (Das & Teng, 1996, 1999). Although these judgments may not be made very explicitly at this stage, they are likely to subtly influence the subsequent pattern of interactions among the partners. A good example of this is in the sensemaking process that occurred in the alliance between Renault and Nissan. The partners acted in ways that strengthened the relationship between them. No attempt was made by either partner to act opportunistically or to withhold commitment. Both by acts of commission, as well as by acts of omission, the partners facilitated judgments that lowered the perception, both of performance and relational risk (Korine, Asakawa, & Gomez, 2002).

> **Proposition 1:** *The greater the ability of the partner firms to learn about each other at the formation stage of the alliance, the more confident they will be about the relational risk and performance risk inherent in the venture.*

Whether or not the partners form a positive or a negative assessment of these two kinds of risk at this stage is dependent on the negotiation strategies pursued by the partner firms. Integrative negotiation strategies (win–win) may promote information sharing and trust, while distributive negotiation strategies (win–lose) may prevent information from being shared and may heighten distrust among the parties.

Operation Stage

During the operation stage the alliance partners begin to translate their contractual commitments into concrete reality. The alliance takes on the task of achieving its negotiated objectives. The operation stage of the alliance offers the opportunity to the partner firms to learn from each other as well as to mutually influence each other's perceptions about their desirability as a partner. Content learning will affect the competitive positioning of both firms while partner-specific learning will affect their reputations.

A number of scholars have noted that content learning among alliance partners may significantly alter the competitive positions of the partner firms (e.g., Hamel, 1991; Nti & Kumar, 2000). Learning allows a partner firm to access critical technologies that can then be deployed effectively vis-à-vis competitors. Although learning undoubtedly has the potential for altering the competitive position of the firms, whether or not this potential is realized in practice depends on a number of factors. Lane and Lubatkin (1998) note, for example, that a focal firm's ability to learn from its partner is dependent on the similarity between the firms' knowledge bases, organizational structures, compensation policies, and dominant logics. The greater the similarity of the partners on these dimensions, the greater would be the likelihood of learning to occur. For Lane and Lubatkin (1998), it is, therefore, the relative absorptive capacity, and not the absolute absorptive capacity *a la* Cohen and Levinthal (1990), that is the key determinant of learning. Anand and Khanna (2000) note that alliance capabilities are an important determinant of whether or not learning occurs. Alliance capability presupposes the existence of organizational mechanisms that systematize the learning from every alliance and allow for the dissemination of such knowledge within the organization.

> **Proposition 2:** *The greater the content learning among the partner firms at the operation stage of the alliance, the more significantly will their competitive position shift vis-à-vis external competitors.*

When firms form an alliance they do so on the basis of "resource alignment" among the partners (Das & Teng, 2000a, 2003), in order clearly to collectively utilize the resources that they contribute to the alliance. Das and Teng (2000a) note that there are four kinds of interpartner resource alignment—namely, supplementary, surplus, complementary, and wasteful. Supplementary alignment implies that the firms are contributing similar resources that are being utilized effectively, whereas surplus alignment means that these similar resources are not fully utilized. Complementary alignment implies that the resources contributed by the partners are dissimilar, and utilized well, while wasteful alignment occurs when the dissimilar resources of the partner firms cannot be effectively utilized.

The operation of the alliance may result in the resource profiles of the partners becoming progressively divergent. This may occur for a number of reasons. First, the partner firms may differ in their orientation towards the alliance. Partner firms that have an exploratory intent, as opposed to an exploitative intent, may be more motivated and capable of harnessing knowledge to enhance their own organizational capabilities. Hamel's

(1991) study demonstrated that the alliance partners often differed in their strategic intent. Second, partner firms may differ in their ability to manage alliances, with the partner having the higher capability being more effective in utilizing the alliance for its own advantage. The partner firms may also differ in their organizational cultures and routines, some of which may be more conducive in acquiring and utilizing knowledge effectively. The divergence in the resource profiles of the partner firms may heighten alliance instability either due to a shift in the bargaining power of the partners, or due to opportunistic behavior, as the weaker firm tries to acquire its partner's valuable resources, or due to the perception of inequity that may emerge when it becomes apparent that contributions are not commensurate with outcomes. At the very least, divergence in the resource profiles will lead the partner firms to renegotiate the terms of their cooperative agreement.

The operation stage is also marked by the emergence of interpartner conflicts. Interpartner conflicts may stem from factionalism and heightened political activity among members of the alliance management team, differences in cultures (corporate and national) among alliance partners, and the relative inexperience of the partner firms in managing alliances. Interpartner conflicts may also arise when the strategic directions of the partner firms are incongruent. Both Ariño and de la Torre (1998) and Doz (1996) provide illustrative cases of alliances that broke down when the strategic direction of the partner firms began to exhibit incongruencies. Disagreement over the allocation of benefits is yet another reason for conflicts among partner firms (Ring & Van de Ven, 1994).

Finally, Ariño (2001) notes that interpartner conflicts are likely to be exacerbated when a partner firm engages in noncooperative behavior by commission rather than by omission. A noncooperative behavior enacted through commission invites attributions of intentionality that shape the evolving relationship among the partner firms. Although our discussion suggests that interpartner conflicts are inevitable when partners engage in the process of joint value creation, the extent of dysfunctionality of the conflicts depends on how well the partners manage the conflict. For example, in the process of resolving interpartner conflicts, the partner firms may be able to use their latent knowledge to construct novel alternatives that may heighten the interdependencies among the partner firms and be beneficial for the alliance. As Hargadon and Fanelli (2002) observe, "Plurality provides members of knowledge-brokering firms with latent knowledge that may be more flexible in its abilities to interpret problematic situations and recognize useful combinations of past ideas" (p. 299). This is most likely to occur if the partner firms construe the conflict in positive rather than negative terms. Kale et al. (2000) note, for example, that integrative management of conflicts (a win–win approach) enhances the relational capital among the partners while at the same time it lessens the motivation for the partners to behave opportunistically. An illustration of divergent resource profiles can be found in the alliance between Borden and Meiji Milk (Cauley de la Sierra, 1995). At the onset of the alliance the resource profiles of the partner firms were complementary, in that the Japanese firm, Meiji Milk, was providing local market knowledge, while Borden was contributing critical competencies. Over time, as Meiji internalized these competencies, and Borden's learning declined or stagnated, the resource profiles of the partners began to diverge and an intensification of conflict ensued.

> **Proposition 3:** *The greater the divergence of the resource profiles among the partner firms during the operation stage of the alliance, the greater will be the potential for conflict and instability in the alliance.*

The operation stage of the alliance provides a basis for it to develop its collective strengths. As outlined earlier, the collective strength of an alliance describes its overall strategic capability. The strategic capability may manifest itself, for example, in a dominant market share, rapid pace of new product development, or entry into new markets. The collective strength of an alliance is very dependent on the partners' ability to jointly generate relational rents. Relational rent is defined by Dyer and Singh (1998) as "supernormal profit jointly generated in an exchange relationship that cannot be generated by either firm in isolation and can only be created through the joint idiosyncratic contributions of the specific alliance partners" (p. 662). The authors argue that the ability to maximize relational rents is dependent on the alliance partners' investment in relation-specific assets, their ability to develop interorganizational processes that would facilitate the access and transfer of knowledge among partner firms, the possession of complementary resources and capabilities, and effective governance. The development of interorganizational processes and governance mechanisms that enhance the collective strengths of an alliance are facilitated at moderate levels of cultural disparity and hindered when the disparity crosses a critical threshold (Phan & Peridis, 2000).

> **Proposition 4:** *The greater the content and alliance management learning during the operation of the strategic alliance, the greater will be its collective strength.*

As a consequence of alliance operation, the competitive positioning of one or all of the partner firms may either strengthen or weaken their position relative to their competitors. Whether a positive or a negative outcome occurs depends, first, on the collective strength of the alliance and, second, on the ability of the partner firms to access that collective strength for their strategic positioning. The financial interdependencies between the partner firms refer to the degree to which the alliance enables the firms to strengthen their resource accumulation via the alliance. It may also be that the alliance provides little or no financial benefit, or even becomes a drain on the partner firms' resources.

Finally, technological interdependencies indicate the degree to which the alliance's technological capability becomes crucial for the partner firms in strengthening their own technological capability. Again, one can envisage two contrasting situations. In the first situation, the partner firms are not dependent on the technological strength of the alliance, whereas in the second there is a high level of dependence. A good example of a negative strategic interdependency between the partner firm and the alliance is the alliance between Borden and Meiji Milk that we mentioned earlier (Cauley de la Sierra, 1995). The partners in this case had entered into an alliance in Japan, with the Japanese partner marketing Borden's products in Japan. For a couple of decades the alliance performed reasonably well. However, over a period of time Meiji was able to internalize critical competencies from the alliance, and once this internalization had occurred the Japanese partner started introducing its own products that competed with those of Borden. Clearly, the Japanese partner was now no longer as dependent on the alliance, and for that reason could undertake strategic initiatives of its own. Borden, by contrast, was still very dependent on the alliance, and reacted very negatively to Meiji's actions. Eventually, the 20-year old relationship between the partners broke down amidst considerable acrimony.

An example of a lack of positive financial interdependency between the alliance and the partner firm is the alliance between Rover and Honda (Alvarez Gil & Gonzalez de la Fe, 1999). Rover had entered into an alliance with Honda with the goal of learning Honda's manufacturing techniques. Honda, by contrast, wanted to use the alliance to expand its geographical coverage, gain economies of scale, and strengthen links with local suppliers. Alvarez Gil and Gonzalez de la Fe (1999) suggest that in this alliance Rover failed to realize its objective of learning about Honda's manufacturing techniques. It only succeeded in "Roverising Honda models," and while this had some learning effect it failed to translate into adequate financial returns. One consequence of this was that Honda gained little positive financial synergy from the alliance, thereby lessening its commitment to the alliance.

Proposition 5: *During the operation stage of the alliance, the greater the degree of content learning among the partner firms, the greater will be the interdependency between the partner firms and the overall learning within the strategic alliance.*

Outcome Stage

In the outcome stage, the performance of an alliance can be evaluated with some clarity. We already noted that there are four possible outcomes at this stage: stability, reformation, decline, or termination (Das & Teng, 2002). If the alliance has met the expectations of its partners it will be stable and may even expand. An alliance may need to be restructured or reformed if the expectations of the alliance partners are not met. Decline may well call for similar actions although it may be a prelude to termination.

The outcome stage may affect both the partners' reputations and their competitive positions vis-à-vis external competitors. If the alliance generates positive outcomes for both partners it would tend to reaffirm their trust and commitment to each other. However, as Selnes and Sallis (2003) note, this may not always happen, as trust has hidden costs that may impede the functioning of a partnership. These hidden costs take the form of relaxing partner controls, loss of creativity due to groupthink, and the reluctance of the partners to convey negative information to each other. If the alliance does not produce positive outcomes for one or both of the partners, but the partners can handle their complaints in an amicable manner, no harm will be done to their reputation. Stuart (2000), in a study of alliances in the semiconductor industry, notes that a small or a relatively young partner benefited from an alliance with a partner that had a higher stature even though the alliance did not meet its objectives. The reputation of a smaller partner usually gets enhanced when it enters into an alliance with a more reputed partner. The troublesome scenario is where the outcomes are negative and the partners are not able to cope with such results effectively.

Competitive positions can be strengthened when one or both of the partners are able to gain access to new technologies and deploy them effectively. Perhaps the optimal situation is where there is reciprocal learning because such a situation tends to reinforce the relationship among the partners. Since both the partners are learning from each other and maximizing value creation, there is the natural propensity to continue with the relationship. Relationships can become unstable when a partner outlearns its counterpart or where neither learns from the other. An alliance that was characterized by positive learning outcomes was the Renault–Nissan alliance mentioned earlier. At the time of the alliance formation, Nissan was on the verge of bankruptcy while Renault was looking to strengthen its global position. Nissan's strengths lay in engineering while Renault's strengths were in styling and design. This useful complementarity and the ability to translate it into positive synergies were unique aspects of the alliance (Yoshino & Fagan, 2003).

In sum, the learning dynamics of the partner firms is a process characterized by considerable ambiguity. This would be particularly true of firms with little prior experience in managing alliances, so that they would be essentially working with their expectations about the alliance. The challenges of drawing reliable and valid conclusions about learning are likely to be particularly acute if the expectations of the alliance partners are not met.

Proposition 6: *At the outcome stage of the alliance, the more positive the partner-specific learning, the greater will be the collective strength of the alliance.*

Also, during this outcome stage, the alliance partners evaluate how successful or unsuccessful the alliance has been. Conflicting perceptions at this stage may intensify interpartner conflicts. Indeed, at this stage, one or all of the partners may either decide to reevaluate the wisdom of continuing with the alliance or call for readjustments in the strategic direction and the governance mechanisms. The inclination to reevaluate and renegotiate the alliance is likely to be further intensified if there is "divergent development" among the alliance partners, that is, a situation where the technological overlap among the partner firms declines during the course of the alliance (Nakamura, Shaver, & Yeung, 1996). A study of alliances by Mowery, Oxley, and Silverman (1996) found that increased diversity in the partner firms' resource profiles characterized a substantial subset of alliances that they studied. The attempted renegotiation may not always be successful and for this reason may lead to termination of the alliance. This dynamic is evident, for example, in the alliance between Alpha motorized systems, a U.S.-based motorcycle and moped equipment manufacturer, and Kai Li Machine, a Chinese manufacturer of gearing systems (Everatt, 1999). Owing to a substantial gap in the strategic, organizational, and the cultural contexts of the partners, the partners not only failed to learn from each other, but more to the point, their relationship deteriorated substantially with the American company becoming increasingly skeptical of their Chinese counterpart's intentions. The relationship was eventually dissolved.

The learning evolution in the relationship between the partner firms may make the partners more cognizant of their abilities to jointly create value in an efficient manner, and the extent to which their capabilities are complementary. This learning is crucial because the relationship among the partner firms is likely to determine their commitment to the alliance. While this is not the only determinant of alliance evolution, the learning that occurs here may play an important role in that evolution.

Proposition 7: *At the outcome stage, the level of confidence among the member firms about the ability of the alliance to create value will be dependent on the content, partner-specific, and alliance management learning.*

Also, at the outcome stage, the collective strength of an alliance manifests itself in the ability of the alliance to compete effectively, accumulate financial resources in order to undertake new ventures, and enhance its managerial and technological capabilities. An alliance that possesses high collective strength will likely continue to prosper, whereas one whose collective strength is low may need to be restructured, or may simply be terminated.

The critical question to be addressed here is whether an alliance has developed the collective strength that is essential for the alliance to survive and prosper. While the answer to this question has an important bearing on the strategies of the partner firms, it is also important for assessing the viability of the strategic alliance as an independent entity. And, as the collective strength of the alliance grows, it is more likely than not that the alliance will prosper.

It is during the outcome stage that the alliance partners may begin to rethink and reevaluate their alliance strategy, depending upon the pattern of interdependencies that come to characterize the relationship between the partner firms and the alliance. Positive strategic, financial, and technological interdependencies will enhance the commitment of the partner firms to the alliance whereas negative interdependencies may lower their commitment. The critical issue here is whether there is a positive or a negative interdependence between the strategic alliance and the partner firms. This issue has the most fundamental bearing on whether the alliance partners will enhance their commitment to the alliance or will seek to exit from it.

> **Proposition 8:** *During the outcome stage of the alliance, the greater the degree of interdependence between the partner firms, the greater will be the degree of commitment of the partners to the alliance.*

DISCUSSION

We have highlighted the nature and the consequences of the three types of learning that gets accomplished during the formation, operation, and outcome stages of an alliance. The formation stage marks the emergence of a possible relationship between potential partner firms. This is a phase marked by extensive sensemaking in which the intent is to enter into a contractual agreement, should that be feasible. An important decision variable in this context is the reputation of the potential partner. Learning about a partner is critical at this juncture. Given that a relationship is just being initiated at this stage, the other learning components are not relevant here.

The operation stage is where the alliance partners, having successfully completed negotiations, start translating the agreed upon commitments into concrete reality. We have argued that at this stage content learning initially becomes salient, both for the individual partner firms and the strategic alliance as a whole. When the alliance becomes operational, content learning may also become an important issue in shaping the interdependencies between the partner firms and the alliance.

The evolution of the relationship between the partner firms during the operation stage leads to further partner-specific learning that may encompass both learning from a partner and learning about a partner. We would argue that whether or not content learning occurs, and the degree to which it does occur, depends most critically on the preexisting reputations of the partner firms. If the partner firms enter into an alliance with positive reputations, they are likely to pursue integrative learning strategies, that is, strategies providing for "maximum transparency, receptivity, and thus interorganizational learning" (Larsson, Bengtsson, Henriksson, & Sparks, 1998, p. 292). Integrative learning strategies will maximize the collective strengths of the alliance while also allowing the individual partner firms to benefit in the process. The preexisting reputations with which the partner firms entered into the alliance may be further strengthened in the process. As the operations unfold over time, the first signs of positive interdependencies between the partner firms and the strategic alliance may begin to emerge if the partners have pursued integrative learning strategies. The initiation of positive interdependencies may also enhance the confidence of the partner firms in managing the alliance, with the consequence that the firms may be more willing to subsequently form additional alliances with the same or other partners. If, by contrast, the partners initiate the operation stage with somewhat negative perceptions of each other, they are likely to pursue competitive learning strategies that may, in turn, engender a self-destructive relationship.

In the outcome stage, the performance of the alliance and its implications for the partner firms become clear. The outcome stage is also likely to be influenced by the mode of interaction that transpired during the operation stage. If integrative learning strategies have been pursued in the operation stage, the competitive positions of the partner firms are likely to be strengthened vis-à-vis their external competitors. The impact of content learning on the partner firms may be most directly visible at this stage. Although integrative learning strategies may change the competitive positions of the partner firms, it is conceivable that not all of the partner firms may benefit equally, and this may sow some seeds of distrust in the relationship between the partner firms. However, this potential negative outcome may not occur if the partners have a positive reputation and a long-term orientation, and are cognizant of the vantage point from which they entered the relationship.

Content learning is salient for the strategic alliance, and there is no denying that the collective strength of the alliance may increase, which in turn may accentuate the positive interdependencies between the partner firms and the alliance. Partner-specific learning is likely to be prominent in the interactions between the partner firms, as the partners are likely to learn much more about each other as they seek to develop shared routines to maximize relational rents. Integrative learning strategies will undoubtedly facilitate this process considerably. The emergence of positive interdependencies between the strategic alliance and the partner firms may further reinforce alliance management learning whose roots probably lie in the earlier stage. The inter-relationships between the different coevolving components underscore the complexity of the learning dynamics in strategic alliances. Initial conditions matter, but the interplay between them is no less crucial. Thus, in summary, the formation stage of the alliance will be marked by the saliency of learning about a partner, the operation stage by the saliency of content learning, and the outcome stage by the saliency of the cumulative product of all three types of learning.

In this paper we have attempted to outline the dynamics of learning in the alliance development process. First, we have suggested that the different alliance conditions that impact upon the learning evolution are collective strengths, interpartner conflicts, and interdependencies. While collective strengths and interdependencies are associated with the strategic alliance and the relationship between the partner firms, interpartner conflicts are associated with the partner firms and the relationship between them.

Second, we have made a distinction between different types of learning and their associated strategic significance for the development of the alliance. In particular, we have underscored the fact that different types of learning are either more or less relevant for the different coevolving components in the alliance learning system. For purposes of our analysis here, we have adopted three different types of learning that occur in strategic alliances; namely, (a) content learning, (b) partner-specific learning, and (c) alliance management learning.

Third, we have noted that the different types of learning have different strategic implications. We have discussed how the strategic significance of the different types of learning may shift as the alliance progresses from the formation to the operation and the outcome stages. Briefly, partner-specific learning (learning about a partner) is crucial in determining whether or not an alliance gets formed, content learning determines the collective strengths of the alliance, and alliance management learning helps build the confidence of the partners to manage alliances.

Fourth, our framework draws attention to the fact that learning dynamics in alliances encompass both the level of the individual partner firms as well as the relationships with each other and the alliance. One implication is that the nature of the learning dynamics may not be consistent across all these different levels. For example, at the operation stage, an enhancement of the competitive position of a partner firm may be associated with heightened interpartner conflicts, and lowered collective strengths of the alliance. Similarly, at the outcome stage, an increase in the divergence of the resource profiles of the partner firms may accentuate interpartner conflicts while simultaneously enhancing the potential for the collective strengths of the alliance to increase, if the conflicts can be reasonably contained.

And lastly, we have noted that the learning process occurs within a highly interdependent system. The existing work on alliances has focused primarily on the unique characteristics of the alliances in explaining how an alliance as an entity evolves over time (e.g., Das & Teng, 2002; Doz, 1996; Ring & Van de Ven, 1994). A crucial implication of the interactive system perspective discussed here is that whether an alliance prospers or falters depends significantly on what happens among the different learning components within the confines of that alliance. The specific outcome depends, importantly, on the evolution of the interdependencies between the partner firms and the strategic alliance. Thus, for instance, even though an alliance may be functioning smoothly for a time, it may not survive if the interdependencies wither between one or more of the partner firms and the alliance.

In sum, we have made the argument that appreciating the dynamics of learning in alliances, in terms of three types of learning, advances our understanding of the alliance developmental processes. This dynamic perspective brings to the fore the importance not just of the quality of managerial intervention, but also its timing in determining whether a troubled alliance can be rescued. In particular, our framework reveals that while learning is always elusive, drawing valid inferences about learning is quite complicated when there are multiple processes at play. Nevertheless, such learning is required for alliance management to be effective, even as one appreciates that drawing appropriate lessons from the proposed learning framework is likely to be at once a complicated and worthwhile endeavor.

Process-based frameworks for understanding alliance development are rare, and rarer still are frameworks that jointly incorporate dynamic interactive learning processes and alliance development processes. Thus, having both these kinds of processes in a framework offers distinct theoretical advantages, while also yielding practical insights for managers that may not be available otherwise.

Managerial Implications

The dynamic learning framework outlined here has important managerial implications. It has been noted that "very little research has been devoted to how interorganizational relationships are managed" (Barringer & Harrison, 2000, p. 396). While this is indeed a pertinent issue, our framework suggests that the management of alliance-based relationships is likely to be determined by how effectively the alliance partners manage the three types of learning—namely, content, partner-specific, and alliance management learning. It is the ability to productively manage all the three types of learning that would impact on how the partners interact and determine how the alliance will evolve over time.

For instance, our framework suggests that the collective strengths of an alliance depend on the learning strategies (e.g., integrative vs. distributive, as in Larsson et al., 1998) pursued by partner firms and their ability to maximize relational rents (Dyer & Singh, 1998). We would also argue that integrative learning strategies and the maximization of relational rents are, in turn, dependent on learning about a partner. As we mentioned earlier, the literature has under-emphasized learning about a partner as against learning from a partner. If the alliance partner is perceived as having a positive reputation, it is likely that the focal firm will pursue integrative learning strategies that should enhance the collective strengths of the alliance. Too, a positive reputation will promote mutual responsiveness and adaptability among the member firms, and also a greater willingness to tolerate adverse performance during the operation of the alliance. The development of shared routines, critical to the maximization of relational rents, is a more likely outcome under these circumstances.

Second, the framework suggests that managers need to recognize the relative saliencies of the learning types in the different developmental stages. There are thus contingencies that managers must appreciate and incorporate in their thinking. Third, given the fluidity of the learning dynamics in a multi-actor system setting, managers involved in alliances must constantly monitor the ever-changing environment and be prepared to rapidly reorient their strategy and its implementation. This requires creative judgment, and while this judgment may not be pre-programmed in any deterministic fashion, it is vital for ensuring optimal adaptation in a changeful environment. There is also the simultaneous need to strengthen the capabilities of the partner firms, independent of the alliance. Thus, alliance managers need to optimally balance cooperation and competition, rigidity and flexibility, and short-term and long-term orientation (Das & Teng, 2000b).

The ability to manage the organizational learning process is becoming an important strategic asset, and this ability assumes an added level of complexity in the arena of alliances by virtue of the unique problems arising from having multiple organizations working together cooperatively for both individual and joint value creation. We have attempted to sketch the complex dynamics of learning in alliances against the backdrop of an increasingly competitive environment.

Future Research

Future research would obviously need to empirically assess the learning dynamics in strategic alliances. The propositions developed in this article should be of help in this endeavor. Research is also needed to study the intricacies of the coevolving learning components within an alliance; namely, the partner firms considered individually and the strategic alliance entity itself. That is, even as each component itself evolves in terms of learning, all of them also evolve simultaneously in the alliance, constituting the alliance learning system. As we noted earlier, the literature thus far has paid insufficient attention to the interactive character of the alliance learning process. One might also want to study the learning dynamics in alliances across industries and across different institutional environments. There are undoubtedly methodological issues that need to be addressed along the way, given the multidirectional causalities to contend with in this type of research. As a modest contribution toward that end, our attempt here has been to propose an initial framework for understanding the nature of the dynamics of learning in the alliance development process.

ACKNOWLEDGMENT

This chapter, save some minor changes, was earlier published as Das, T. K., & Kumar, R. (2007). Learning dynamics in the alliance development process. *Management Decision, 45*, 684–707.

REFERENCES

Ahuja, G. (2000). The duality of collaboration: Inducements and opportunities in the formation of interfirm linkages. *Strategic Management Journal, 21*(3), 317–343.

Alvarez Gil, M. J., & Gonzalez de la Fe, P. (1999). Strategic alliances, organizational learning, and new product development: The cases of Rover and Seat. *R&D Management, 29*(4), 391–404.

Anand, B. N., & Khanna, T. (2000). Do firms learn to create value: The case of alliances. *Strategic Management Journal, 21*, 295–315.

Argote, L., McEvily, B., & Reagans, R. (2003). Managing knowledge in organizations: An integrative framework and review of emerging themes. *Management Science, 49*(4), 571–582.

Ariño, A. (2001). To do or not to do: noncooperative behavior by commission and omission in interfirm ventures. *Group & Organization Management, 26*(1), 4–23.

Ariño, A., & de la Torre, J. (1998). Learning from failure: Towards an evolutionary model of collaborative ventures. *Organization Science, 9*(3), 306–325.

Balakrishnan, S., & Koza, M. (1993). Information asymmetry, market failure, and joint ventures: Theory and evidence. *Journal of Economic Behavior and Organization, 20*(1), 99–117.

Barringer, B. R., & Harrison, J. S. (2000). Walking a tightrope: Creating value through interorganizational relationships. *Journal of Management, 26*(3), 367–403.

Bell, S. J., Whitwell, G. J., & Lukas, B. A. (2002). Schools of thought in organizational learning. *Journal of the Academy of Marketing Science, 30*(1), 70–86.

Cauley de la Sierra, M. (1995). *Managing global alliances: Key steps for successful collaboration.* Wokingham, England: Addison Wesley.

Cohen, W. M., & Levinthal, D. A. (1990). Absorptive capacity: A new perspective on learning and innovation. *Administrative Science Quarterly, 35*(1), 128–152.

Crossan, M. M., Lane, H. W., & White, R .E. (1999). An organizational learning framework: From intuition to institution. *Academy of Management Review, 24*(3), 522–537.

Das, T. K. (2004). Time-span and risk of partner opportunism in strategic alliances. *Journal of Managerial Psychology, 19*(8), 744–759.

Das, T. K. (2005). Deceitful behaviors of alliance partners: Potential and prevention. *Management Decision, 43*(5), 706–719.

Das, T. K. (2006). Strategic alliance temporalities and partner opportunism. *British Journal of Management, 17*(1), 1–21.

Das, T. K., & Teng, B. (1996). Risk types and inter-firm alliance structures. *Journal of Management Studies, 33*(6), 827–843.

Das, T. K., & Teng, B. (1999). Managing risks in strategic alliances. *Academy of Management Executive, 13*(4), 50–62.

Das, T. K., & Teng, B. (2000a). A resource-based theory of strategic alliances. *Journal of Management, 26*(1), 31–61.

Das, T. K., & Teng, B. (2000b). Instabilities of strategic alliances: An internal tensions perspective. *Organization Science, 11*(1), 77–101.

Das, T. K., & Teng, B. (2002). The dynamics of alliance conditions in the alliance development process. *Journal of Management Studies, 39*(5), 725–746.

Das, T. K., & Teng, B. (2003). Partner analysis and alliance performance. *Scandinavian Journal of Management, 19*(3), 279–308.

De Man, A.-P. (2005). Alliance capability: A comparison of the alliance strength of European and American companies. *European Management Journal, 23*(3), 315–323.

Doz, Y. L. (1996). The evolution of cooperation in strategic alliances: initial conditions or learning processes? *Strategic Management Journal, 17*(Summer Special Issue), 55–83.

Dussauge, P., Garrette, B., & Mitchell, W. (2000). Learning from competing partners: Outcomes and durations of scale and link alliances in Europe, North America and Asia. *Strategic Management Journal, 21*(2), 99–126.

Dyer, J. H., & Singh, H. (1998). The relational view: Cooperative strategy and sources of interorganizational competitive advantage. *Academy of Management Review, 23*(4), 660–679.

Edmondson, A., & Moingeon, B. (1996). When to learn how and when to learn why: Appropriate organizational learning as a source of competitive advantage. In

B. Moingeon & A. Edmondson (Eds.), *Organizational learning and competitive advantage* (pp. 17–37). London, England: Sage.

Everatt, D. (1999). *Alpha Gearing Systems Shanghai Co., Ltd.* (Case # 99C014). Ontario, Canada: Ivey Management Services.

Grant, R. M., & Baden-Fuller, C. (2004). A knowledge accessing theory of strategic alliances. *Journal of Management Studies, 41*(1), 61–84.

Hamel, G. (1991). Competition for competence and inter partner learning within strategic alliances. *Strategic Management Journal, 12*(4), 83–103.

Hargadon, A., & Fanelli, A. (2002). Action and possibility: Reconciling dual perspectives of knowledge in organizations. *Organization Science, 13*(3), 290–302.

Hoang, H., & Rothaermel, F. T. (2005). The effect of general and partner-specific alliance experience on joint R&D project performance. *Academy of Management Journal, 48*(2), 332–345.

Holmqvist, M. (2003). A dynamic model of intra- and interorganizational learning. *Organization Studies, 24*(1), 95–123.

Huber, G. P. (1991). Organizational learning: The contributing processes and the literatures. *Organization Science, 2*(1), 88–115.

Inkpen, A. C., & Beamish, P. W. (1997). Knowledge, bargaining power, and international joint venture stability. *Academy of Management Review, 22*(1), 177–202.

Ireland, R. D., Hitt, M. A., & Vaidyanath, D. (2002). Alliance management as a source of competitive advantage. *Journal of Management, 28*(3), 413–446.

Kale, P., Dyer, J. H., & Singh, H. (2002). Alliance capability, stock market response, and long term alliance success: The role of the alliance function. *Strategic Management Journal, 23*(8), 747–767.

Kale, P., Singh, H., Perlmutter, H. (2000). Learning and protection of proprietary assets in strategic alliances: Building relational capital. *Strategic Management Journal, 21*(3), 217–237.

Khanna, T., Gulati, R., & Nohria, N. (1998). The dynamics of learning alliances: Competition, cooperation, and relative scope. *Strategic Management Journal, 19*(3), 193–210.

Korine, H., Asakawa, K., & Gomez, P.-Y. (2002). Partnering with the unfamiliar: Lessons from the case of Renault and Nissan. *Business Strategy Review, 13*(2), 41–50.

Kumar, R., & Nti, K. O. (1998). Differential learning and interaction in alliance dynamics: A process and outcome discrepancy model. *Organization Science, 9*(3), 356–367.

Kumar, R., & Nti, K. O. (2004). National cultural values and the evolution of process and outcome discrepancies in international strategic alliances. *Journal of Applied Behavioral Science, 40*(3), 344–361.

Lane, P., & Lubatkin, M. (1998). Relative absorptive capacity and interorganizational learning. *Strategic Management Journal, 19*(5), 461–477.

Larsson, R., Bengtsson, L. Henriksson, K., & Sparks, J. (1998). The interorganizational learning dilemma: Collective knowledge development in strategic alliances. *Organization Science, 9*(3), 285–305.

Levitt, B., & March, J. G. (1996). Organizational learning. In M. D. Cohen & L. S. Sproull (Eds.), *Organizational learning* (pp. 516–540). Thousand Oaks, CA: Sage.

Lubatkin, M., Florin, J., & Lane, P. (2001). Learning together and apart: A model of reciprocal interfirm learning. *Human Relations, 54*(10), 1353–1382.

Makhija, M. V., & Ganesh, U. (1997). The relationship between control and partner learning in learning-related joint ventures. *Organization Science, 8*(5), 508–520.

Mody, A. (1993). Learning through alliances. *Journal of Economic Behavior and Organization, 20*(2), 151–170.

Mowery, D. C., Oxley, J. E., & Silverman, B. S. (1996). Strategic alliances and interfirm knowledge transfer. *Strategic Management Journal, 17*(1), 77–91.

Nakamura, M., Shaver, J. M., & Yeung, B. (1996). An empirical investigation of joint venture dynamics: Evidence from US-Japan joint ventures. *International Journal of Industrial Organization, 14*(4), 521–541.

Nti, K. O., & Kumar, R. (2000). Differential learning in alliances. In D. O. Faulkner & M. de Rond (Eds.), *Cooperative strategy: Economic, business, and organizational issues* (pp. 119–134). Oxford, England: Oxford University Press.

Parise, S., & Henderson, J. C. (2001). Knowledge resource exchange in strategic alliances. *IBM Systems Journal, 40*(4), 908–924.

Parkhe, A. (1991). Interfirm diversity, organizational learning, and longevity in global strategic alliances. *Journal of International Business Studies, 22*(4), 579–601.

Pearce, R. J. (1997). Toward understanding joint venture performance and survival: A bargaining and influence approach to transaction cost theory. *Academy of Management Review, 22*(1), 203–225.

Phan, P. S., & Peridis, T. (2000). Knowledge creation in strategic alliances: Another look at organizational learning. *Asia Pacific Journal of Management, 17*(2), 201–222.

Reich, R. B., & Mankin, E. D. (1986). Joint ventures with Japan give away our future. *Harvard Business Review, 86*(2), 78–86.

Ring, P. S., & Van de Ven, A. H. (1994). Developmental processes of cooperative interorganizational relationships. *Academy of Management Review, 19*(1), 90–118.

Selnes, F., & Sallis, J. (2003). Promoting relationship learning. *Journal of Marketing, 67*(3), 80–95.

Stuart, T. E. (2000). Interorganizational alliances and the performance of firms: A study of growth and innovation rates in a high technology industry. *Strategic Management Journal, 21*(8), 791–811.

Yoshino, M. Y., & Fagan, P. L. (2003). *The Renault-Nissan alliance* (Case # 9-303-023). Boston, MA: Harvard Business School.

Zahra, S. A., & George, G. A. (2002). Absorptive capacity: A review, reconceptualization, and extension. *Academy of Management Review, 27*(2), 185–203.

Zajac, E. J., & Olsen, C. P. (1993). From transaction cost to transactional value analysis: Implications for the study of interorganizational strategies. *Journal of Management Studies, 30*(1), 131–145.

Zollo, M., & Winter, S. G. (2002). Deliberate learning and the evolution of dynamic capabilities. *Organization Science, 13*(3), 339–351.

CHAPTER 8

THE INFLUENCE OF ALLIANCE AND PARTNER CHARACTERISTICS ON TENSIONS IN CONTRACTUAL ALLIANCES IN TECHNOLOGICALLY TURBULENT ENVIRONMENTS

Diana Marie De Silva
Matthias Vermeiren
Ernst Verwaal

ABSTRACT

The chapter explores the behaviors of partners in technologically turbulent environments that influence the strategic alignment in contractual alliances. In the context of high technological turbulence, the competitive landscape of a firm and its partners in an alliance changes, which requires them to adapt their strategies in order to regain fit. However, little is known about how part-

Managing the Partners in Strategic Alliances, pages 195–221

ner firms in alliances individually and collectively strategize in a turbulent environment. We investigate competing views in the literature and offer propositions which explain how a strategy of an alliance to adapt is contradicted by the partners' tendency to protect the individual interests during turbulent times. Building on the resource-based view and dynamic capabilities theory, we look at alliance and partner characteristics and behaviors that can be associated with their strategic decisions. The chapter reports the findings of a qualitative multiple case study of 10 contractual alliances. The investigation focuses on behavioral, structural, and psychological tensions potentially leading to strategic misalignment. In the final section, we offer solutions to manage the predicted partner behaviors to prevent strategic misalignment and alliance instability.

INTRODUCTION

Recent decades have shown an exponential increase of technological innovations which spread quickly across global markets. This high rate of technological turbulence "arises from changes in the underlying technologies of products or services and their (increasing) rates of obsolescence" (Kandemir, Yaprak, & Cavusgil, 2006, p. 330). This will have a profound influence on how firms do business as the competitive position of a firm is more likely affected, and the competitive landscape of a firm and its competitors is more easily reshaped under conditions of high technological turbulence (Jaworski & Kohli, 1993). Technological turbulence leads to modifications in the dominant design and the alteration of industry standards (Chen, Li, Chen, & Ou, 2018; Kandemir et al., 2006; Tushman & Anderson, 1986) and firms are under pressure to continuously innovate because earlier developed knowledge and technology are not necessarily useful in new market conditions (Amankwah-Amoah, 2017; Chen et al., 2018). Under technological turbulence, alliances are particularly important as they can aid to gain access to new knowledge, pool resources, accelerate time to market, and reduce risk (Anand, Oriani, & Vassolo, 2010; Chatterjee, 2004; Jaworski & Kohli, 1993). The resource-based view (Barney, 1991; Grant, 1991; Wernerfelt, 1984) is appropriate for looking into the formation of strategic alliances because firms often use alliances to gain access to strategic and valuable resources they do not own, but also to protect and leverage their own valuable resources (Das & Teng, 2000a). More particularly relevant in environments of rapid technological change, the dynamic capabilities theory builds on the resource-based view that focus on a firm's access to complementary assets (Teece, Pisano, & Shuen, 1997) and the value captured from innovations (Anand et al., 2010). Particularly for the case of small firms, the study of Rashidirad, Soltani, and Salimian (2015) suggest that a sustained competitive advantage does not come from the formation of the strategic alliances per se but rather on the ability of the firm to align its externally competitive position with its internal possessions through a proper use of strategic alliances.

In comparison to equity alliances, non-equity alliances do not require many alliance-specific investments and they are easier to dissolve, which makes them a better setting to observe the shifting of different strategies. Furthermore, non-equity alliances do not involve the sharing of equity and instead are based on the sharing of resources with different risks attached and their values may be perceived differently by the partners. These contract-based alliances are divided into two types: exchange—and integration alliances (Chen & Chen, 2003) signifying two main motives to explain strategic alliance decisions. The first motive in an exchange alliance is to simply acquire the resources of others' and to utilize them independently with little concern that one partner will influence the competitive position of the other partner in the market. Resources such as knowledge sometimes lose much of their value when moved from their organizational context. Resource imperfect mobility, imperfect imitability, and imperfect substitutability refers to the barriers to obtaining similar resources from other firms (Dierickx & Cool, 1989). Many resources are thereby not tradable at all or not perfectly tradable (Dierickx & Cool, 1989), which still grants its original owner competitive advantages. The second motive in an integration alliance is to retain and develop its own resources by combining them with the resources of others. There is a cooperation between the different firms to achieve synergies or shared advantages for both parties. Note that there is more need for control and structure compared to exchange alliances as the risks of opportunistic behavior or spillovers to competition are higher (Chen & Chen, 2003). This view suggests that the resource profiles of partner firms may influence their structural preferences and the choice between different forms of contractual alliances (Chen & Chen, 2003). The resources a firm possesses are often not precisely definable due to the large variety of resource types and resource combinations. A number of resource typologies exist to make a distinction between different resource types. The typology of Miller and Shamsie (1996) identifies two major categories of resources for non-equity alliances: property-based and knowledge-based resources. In their study, knowledge-based resources proved more valuable in the more uncertain environment than property-based resources which are better in driving financial performance in stable environments.

For a firm in an alliance, the rapid changes in products and services with varying degrees of technological sophistication and engineering content, requires different coordination techniques throughout the related processes, as well as constantly adjusting the coordination to cope with the technological turbulence (Iyer, 2014). Earlier studies have shown the positive impact of strategic alignment of firms and the alliance they are in (Henderson &

Venkatraman 1993; Raymond & Bergeron, 2008) as relationships are perceived more important when the missions of each firm are strongly aligned with the alliance (Austin & Seitanidi, 2012). However, organizations wanting to be adaptive in a fast-changing technological environment are hindered because they are tied to a strategy that is aligned with other organizations in an alliance. Maintaining strategic alignment over the life of an alliance is a challenge. Goal disparity is apparent in the different phases of the alliance. In the onset of alliance formation, individual partners have their own private goals for venturing in the alliance. The alliance progresses to the next phase only when partners agree on a common alliance goal that is strategically aligned with that of the firms. At this early phase, goal disparity could be partially or completely resolved, but over the life of the alliance, a disruptive phase could affect this alignment. A turbulent environment could yield emergent goals that differ from the initial private firm goals and common alliance goals. According to Ariño (2003), the degree of accomplishment of all these goals, be it common or private, initial or emergent, largely defines the performance of the strategic alliance.

In this light, we find it relevant to explore the formation of disparate goals and associate the change in strategic behavior on certain alliance and partner characteristics. The relevance of our contribution in this study lies in the explanation of the dilemma faced by alliance partners as they try to adapt their individual strategies during technologically turbulent periods while maintaining a healthy alliance relationship. Our objective is to identify observable alliance and partner characteristics rooted on the resource profiles and dynamic capabilities that potentially lead to strategic misalignment during increased technological turbulence. In this way, alliance managers will know what strategic behaviors to expect from partners possessing such characteristics, allowing them to deal with and prevent potential alliance instability in the face of uncertainty.

CONCEPTUAL FRAMEWORK: STRATEGIC MISALIGNMENT AS A RESULT OF TENSIONS

Das and Teng (2000b) introduced the internal tensions framework in strategic alliances which describes three key pairs of opposing strategies—namely, cooperation versus competition (behavioral tensions), rigidity versus flexibility (structural tensions), and short-term versus long-term orientation (psychological tensions). These tensions are seen as essential which are necessary and persistent contradictions (Turner, Benessaiah, Warren, & Iwaniec, 2015) therefore a balancing strategy is used to manage the tensions without trying to eliminate them. However, the emergence of tensions also implies a "potential conflict" which when triggered poses the risk

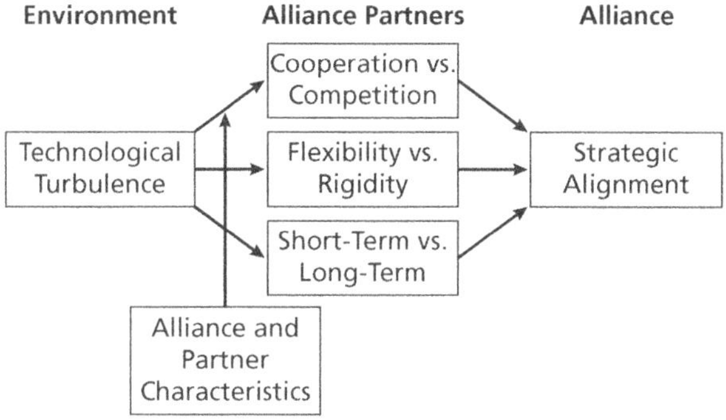

Figure 8.1 Conceptual framework.

of instability. Our conceptual framework in Figure 8.1 adopts the internal tensions framework and introduces technological turbulence as an environmental shock expected to influence shifts on the alliance and partner strategies. Their strategic behavior is predicted based upon their individual firm characteristics and the characteristics of the alliance as a whole. We investigate how strategic alignment is affected when partners have to deal with technological turbulence.

Technological Turbulence on Competition Versus Cooperation

A cooperative behavior is naturally expected from partnering firms in an alliance but if partners cooperate too much, they risk the loss of their individual competitive advantage (Das & Teng, 2000b). When partners are too competitive, they risk the lack of transfer and integration of their know-how. Cooperation supports knowledge integration towards the achievement of alliance goals, but competition is needed to keep vision on the firm-specific advantage of an alliance. When technological turbulence comes into play, the alliance as a whole and the individual partners are faced with a dilemma whether to adopt a cooperative or competitive strategy.

Some studies favor a more cooperative approach when dealing with a high technological turbulence in alliances. According to Iyer (2014), "high levels of technological turbulence and product complexity promote the positive influence of collaboration on operational performance" (p. 395). Also, it appears from previous research that when technological turbulence exists, even the dominant firm within an alliance relationship is more likely to stay in that partnership and is less likely to pursue opportunistic behavior (Chatterjee, 2004). The need for new ground-breaking knowledge and information is critical (Das, 2006; House, Hanges, Javidan, Dorfman,

& Gupta, 2004), to keep up with the changing technological landscape. Hence, in a technological turbulent environment, the alliance is expected to favor a cooperative strategy.

To the contrary, a more competitive strategy also makes sense between the partners when high technological turbulence occurs. House et al. (2004) explain that a turbulent business environment triggers a more competitive behavior among firms in general, which could also manifest within an alliance relationship. A firm may risk going out of business if they do not act aggressively either to adapt or to take advantage of opportunities brought by the disruption. Opportunistic behavior may come unplanned and may be seen in the form of violation, avoidance, forced renegotiation, and even unwillingness to adapt in an alliance. Partners can become more protective of the resources they hold as a means of self-preservation. This will result in a decrease of knowledge and information sharing (Delerue & Lejeune, 2011), which would have been necessary to adapt to the rapidly changing industry.

In terms of dynamic capabilities, there are key differences between big and small partners such as decision making speed, attitude towards risk, and the prioritization of resource allocation. Smaller partners can make quicker decisions, are high risk takers and are likely to protect scarce resources which all drive competitive behavior. Since small firms have limited financial capacity to recover from losses during a major disruption they need access to a variety of resource alternatives that can be adopted and abandoned, regardless of the nature of the contract. Commitment becomes in question when a partner fails to fulfill certain expectations which in turn affects the commitment of other partners. The perceived risk of opportunistic behavior and inter-firm competition is therefore strongly tied to the size of a partner.

Furthermore, the risks for behavioral tensions tend to be higher when R&D resources are shared in integration alliances compared to exchange alliances. Knowledge-based resources are more difficult to integrate when firms protect them from each other through legal contracts (Das & Teng, 1996). Whereas property-based resources in the form of physical, financial, and human resources are protected by legal rights of the original owner which make unintended transfers little concern in exchange alliances (Das & Teng, 2000a). Hence, we deduced the following proposition.

> **Proposition 1:** *In a technological turbulent environment, small partners in an integration alliance are more inclined towards a competitive strategy.*

Technological Turbulence on Rigidity versus Flexibility

Das and Teng (2000b) refer to rigidity as "the characteristics of mutual dependence and connectedness," whereas flexibility "enhances the ability of partners to adapt" (p. 85). The tension between rigidity and flexibility represents a structural tension that determines how strategy is placed into action. According to the internal tensions framework, alliances can only be successful when neither rigidity or flexibility is dominant. Leaning to one extreme can either result in poor performance because of insufficient detail on how to manage the alliance or otherwise suffer from limited creativity because of too much structure. Hence, a durable alliance can be obtained by nurturing both its flexible and rigid aspects. Despite the fact that they are competing forces, a balance of both features will serve the alliance best. In particular, the major advantage of contractual alliances is their flexibility; however, from a dynamic capability perspective, such flexibility would reduce the co-alignment of assets.

Under conditions of high technological turbulence, previous studies have shown that flexibility is commonly adopted by alliances (Buganza, Dell'Era, & Verganti, 2009; MacCormack, Verganti, & Iansiti, 2001) as a way to conquer the external pressures (Candi, van den Ende, & Gemser, 2013). Lee and Cavusgil (2006, p. 900) argued that "flexibility enables firms to adapt to problems raised from unforeseeable technological changes," which is the primary motivation to favor flexibility over control and commitment (van de Vrande, Vanhaverbeke, & Duysters, 2009). Santoro and McGill (2005) support this claim by indicating that under the condition of high technological turbulence, rather small, reversible investments should be made to remain flexible. Furthermore, Rashidirad et al. (2015) suggest that higher flexibility results in less time and resources needed to align the partners competitive strategies and resources. Similarly, other studies have shown that a more rigid strategy, in a high technological turbulent environment, will have a negative impact on the alliance performance (Crocker & Masten, 1988; MacCormack et al., 2001). Santoro and McGill (2005), for instance, found that a higher turbulence of technology negatively affects the use of more hierarchical (i.e., rigid) alliance forms. Inflexible strategies are found to be risky and disadvantageous in conditions of high environmental turbulence (Lee & Cavusgil, 2006). Young-Ybarra and Wiersema (1999) noticed that many firms have found that it is almost impossible to overcome the rapid technological change without major structural adjustments providing greater strategic flexibility and that the success of a strategic alliance is closely related to its strategic flexibility. Akgün, Lynn, and Byrne (2006, p. 75) argued that "Rigid product development procedures and group beliefs, as well as the preservation of routines and mindsets (i.e., being imprisoned by routines and habits), inhibit the reception and evaluation of new technology information and reduce the value of perceived new information." In other words, such a rigid and narrow strategy will reduce the chances of a successful new product in a turbulent environment. Furthermore, de Vaan (2015) stated that in periods of high technological turbulence that require identification and exploration of new ideas and information, stable and routinized behavior is more likely to be a weakness than a strength. He warns that "these strongly tied partners may become a liability rather than an asset" (p. 1669).

However, we posit that under conditions of high technological turbulence, a partner who has developed alliance capabilities prefers rigidity over flexibility. A partner's capability to handle technological change, translates dynamic capability into a higher-order alliance capability (Kale & Singh, 2007). Such competences are only able to provide competitive advantage and generate rents only if they are based on a collection of routines, skills, and complementary assets that are difficult to imitate (Dierickx & Cool, 1989; Teece et al., 1997) thus implying a sense of rigidity. Bilateral contracts in integration alliances are usually incomplete and open-ended (Mowery, Oxley, & Silverman, 1996), for which a higher degree of either control or trust is necessary. Feelings of uncertainty, loss of confidence, and distress arise during turbulent times, and those emotions trigger a greater lack of trust. In turn, a lack of trust signals greater desire for control. The desire for control can be defined as "the ambition of a firm to exercise control and dominance over the alliance's strategic decisions and operating procedures" (Musarra, Robson, & Katsikeas, 2016, p. 10). When a partner has gained alliance management know-how over prior alliance relationships, the partner has a higher propensity to manage a turbulent situation by installing governance structures.

Furthermore, the threat-rigidity theory from Staw, Sandelands, and Dutton (1981) suggests how changes in the environment can lead to a psychological reaction within the firm that can lead to forms of rigidity. Rigidity effects have their origin in the form of confusion, fast response incapability, information insufficiencies, blame avoiding, and misallocation of attention between internal and external environments from organizational members (Barnett & Pratt, 2000). Previous studies have shown that fear, anxiety, and stress are factors that can cause a form of rigidity (Barnett & Pratt, 2000), which are emotions associated with risk aversion. Risk aversion can be described as the behavior where someone in an uncertain environment perceives a higher risk than its expected value and will try to reduce that risk (Holt & Laury, 2002). Hartley and Phelps (2012) suggest that in psychological tests, anxiety and fear is associated with heightened risk aversion. Moreover, Calantone, Garcia, and Dröge (2003) argue that risk aversion can cause paralysis in decision-making in high technological turbulent environments, which can be linked to the threat-rigidity theory from Staw et al. (1981). All these arguments align with the stream of literature on managerial cognition as a core underpinning of dynamic capabilities (Helfat & Peteraf, 2015) where the foundation of strategic change is rooted on the cognitive ability of the individual manager. Over gained alliance experience, this managerial cognitive capability is foreseen to transform from an automatic mental activity into a type that is more controlled or deliberate. Stanovich and West (2000) make distinctions between these two types of mental activity but identify clear resemblances. From having initial quick reactions to risk stimuli, the alliance manager learns to rely on more defined and calculated strategies. From this, we arrived with the following competing proposition:

> **Proposition 2:** *For integration alliances in a technological turbulent environment, partners who are either risk averse or have greater alliance capabilities will favor a rigid structure.*

Technological Turbulence on Short-Term Versus Long-Term Orientation

Psychological tensions arise in the alliance when perceived timelines for the achievement of goals do not match. Ideally, a balance between long-term and short-term orientation should bring stability to an alliance (Das & Teng, 2000b). In a high technological environment, a short-term orientation seems more logical when dealing with high technological turbulence. Time is normally a constraint in a technologically turbulent environment where some partner firms may be under pressure to deliver outcomes within strict deadlines or shorter cycles. In contractual alliances, a couple of reasons support a short-term orientation. First, building an alliance is a risky undertaking and an incremental approach can help to control this risk. Such an approach could be achieved, for instance by using recurrent contracts that could be repeated based upon its satisfactory performance. Secondly, a short-term orientation prevents the alliance from turning into a liability for the partners due to increased commitment. Contractor, Woodley, and Piepenbrink (2011), argue that “short term strategic alliances are more flexible and keep future options more open, which is preferred when environmental uncertainty is high” (p. 73). This view is consistent with our earlier discussion on a flexible approach as a favorable option for alliances in turbulent environments. To survive industry turbulence, Duysters and deMan (2003) recommend the creation of transitory alliances which are “short-lived non-equity alliances that focus on completing narrowly defined tasks in a very short time frame” (p. 49). Therefore, a short-term orientation is more likely adopted by an alliance in a technological turbulent environment, as it is necessary to be able to timely change partners and to obtain new state-of-the-art knowledge. Hence, in a technological turbulent environment, contractual alliance partners that lean towards short-term orientation are more likely to stay strategically aligned.

In contrast, a partner could opt for a long-term orientation, even when confronted with high technological turbulence when one feels a strong dependency on its partners (Ganesan, 1994) particularly for co-specializing and the co-alignment of assets. Ideally, high interdependency among partners or symmetrical interdependence lead to stable alliances as technological innovation requires the recombination of partners complementary assets. This co-specialization in an alliance is developed over a period of sensing–seizing–reconfiguring (Helfat & Peteraf, 2015; Teece, 2007) which are functions that define dynamic capability. Monczka, Peterson, Handfield, and Ragatz (1998) suggest that "Interdependence exists when one actor does not entirely control all of the conditions necessary for achievement of an action or a desired outcome" and consider it as a form of relational management (p. 558). Therefore, if a partner is dependent on the other alliance partner, it will try to hold on to a long-term orientation especially during turbulent times when resource depletion is a concern. Hence, we derive the following competing proposition:

Proposition 3: *In a technological turbulent environment, partners in integration alliances with high interdependency will more likely lean towards a long-term orientation.*

EMPIRICAL FINDINGS

So far, our arguments have presented competing views, which require a more in-depth analysis of the strategic behavior of firms in an alliance, and how they individually and collectively adapt their strategies in a changing business landscape. To build upon the current theories, a case study research is best employed to explain strategic decisions: why they are made, how they are implemented, and the results they lead to (Yin, 2014). It is a practical method of extracting explicit and implicit information which are essential for the purpose of describing the situations and gain insights on a particular practice to gain better understanding of the context, people, and their interactions. In-depth explanatory data from a small sample are organized using a coding process. Later, the analysis draws out patterns from the codes, then insights and results are reported through illustrative narratives.

Methodology

We report the findings of a qualitative multiple case study (Vermeiren, 2019) that explored the multiple forces leading to strategic (mis)alignment in alliances. The data used to test our propositions was collected by a group of student researchers who conducted individual interviews using a common interview protocol from February to May 2019. Workshops were organized to arrive at a common understanding of the questions and the terminologies used in the protocol. A central data repository is created to organize the collection and storage of evidences from the cases. The use of both a protocol and a database reflect transparency in conducting the research and thereby contribute to increasing reliability (Yin, 2014). The case criteria guided the selection of non-equity contractual alliances involving three to six partner firms operating in Europe (particularly limited to partner firms located in Belgium or the Netherlands). At least two alliance partners had to participate in the interview in order to gain insight on multiple firm-perspectives. The interviewees were assured of anonymity (if desired) to reduce the potential social desirability bias. The interview protocol was designed to include a set of open-ended questions, and another set of closed-ended questions intended for clear-cut identification of alliance and partner characteristics and to validate the informants' narratives by triangulation. The semi-structured interviews gave the opportunity to clearly align the research but still give space to the interviewee to go deeper into matters that they consider important.

Analysis of Cases

The multiple case study is composed of 10 cases which are summarized in Table 8.1. It is essential to gain a basic understanding of the nature of the alliances, the individual partner firms, and the position of the individuals who participated in this study. Applying literal and theoretical replication (Yin, 2014), seven cases selected are active in technologically turbulent environments whereas the remaining three cases are part of a reference group where little to no technological turbulence is observed. Three cases are integration alliances and the rest are exchange alliances. In this way, it can be assessed whether the observed phenomenon is unique in a technological turbulent environment, for partners in a specific alliance type, or just typical for alliance partners in general. This cross-case analysis technique makes it possible to challenge or confirm the propositions and the initial findings from conducting a within-case analysis. Understanding the unique features of each case helps explain how the phenomenon of interest may work differently given different scenarios. In this way, the results of the within-in case analysis later on complement the cross-case analysis in explaining certain peculiarities.

The transcripts and the archival documents collected were analyzed using NVivo 12, a qualitative data analysis software performing a coding process for text analysis. Passages taken from the transcripts and archival documents

TABLE 8.1 Summary of Observed Cases

Case	Technological Turbulence	Alliance Type	Industry	Partner Respondent	
				Firm Size	Position of Interviewee
A	high	exchange	biotechnology	large	Senior director alliance manager
				large	Alliance manager R&D
B	high	exchange	software technology	small	Alliance manager
				large	Partner development manager
C	high	exchange	software technology	medium	Managing partner
				large	Alliance manager
D	high	exchange	software technology	large	Channel officer
				small	Unit director
E	high	exchange	automotive	large	e-mobility manager
				large	General manager e-mobility
F	high	integration	research/ academia	medium	Research lead
				small	R&D director
G	high	integration	telecom	large	Account manager
				large	CEO
H	low	exchange	construction	large	CEO
				large	CEO
I	low	exchange	real estate	large	Real estate manager
				medium	CEO
J	low	integration	utilities	medium	CEO
				large	Production manager

are assigned into codes that are straightforward and self-explaining to signify a named concept. These codes are equivalent to nodes when using NVivo 12. Figure 8.2 exhibits the node hierarchies to show how the abundant data have been organized to derive meaningful information. The theme nodes are based upon the relevant concepts taken from literature study and the propositions. Child nodes are further aggregated into parent nodes for categorization. This method makes it possible to link similar statements from different interviews to conduct the within- and cross-case analyses.

In our investigation, we sought to catch the interplay of how actors respond to technological turbulence given certain conditions, understand what caused those behaviors, and to what consequences those actions lead to. To do this, we assigned relationship nodes to show their connections using a coding paradigm illustrated in Figure 8.3. The coding paradigm gave

- PARTNER'S CHANGE IN STRATEGY *(core category)*
  - **Behavioral Change** *(P1)*
    - Causes *(R1)*
      - *Exchange alliance (c1)*
      - *Integration alliance (c2)*
      - *SME (c3)*
      - *Large firm (c4)*
    - Conditions *(R2)*
      - *Low turbulence (c10-S)*
      - *High turbulence (c11-S)*
    - Actions *(R3)*
      - *Cooperative (c12)*
      - *Competitive (c13)*
    - Consequences *(R4)*
      - *Aligned (c19-S)*
  - **Structural Change** *(P2)*
    - Causes *(R1)*
      - *Integration alliance (c2)*
      - *SME (c3)*
      - *Large firm (c4)*
      - *Risk aversion (c5)*
      - *Alliance experience (c6)*
      - *Alliance management know-how (c7)*
      - *Resource contribution (c8)*
    - Conditions *(R2)*
      - *High turbulence (c11-S)*
    - Actions *(R3)*
      - *Flexible (c14)*
      - *Rigid (c15)*
    - Consequences *(R4)*
      - *Misaligned (c20-S)*
  - **Psychological Change** *(P3)*
    - Causes *(R1)*
      - *Integration alliance (c1)*
      - *SME (c2)*
      - *Large firms (c3)*
      - *Resource contribution (c8)*
      - *Partner dependence (c9)*
    - Conditions *(R2)*
      - *High turbulence (c11-S)*
    - Actions *(R3)*
      - *Short-term orientation (c16)*
      - *Long-term orientation (c18)*
    - Consequences *(R4)*
      - *Aligned (c19-S)*

Figure 8.2 Node hierarchy.

the codes greater explanatory power by classifying them under four dimensions; namely, causes, actions, conditions, and consequences. The use of a coding paradigm gives definition and specificity to the categories. Most of these nodes have been revisited and revised to reflect consistency in their

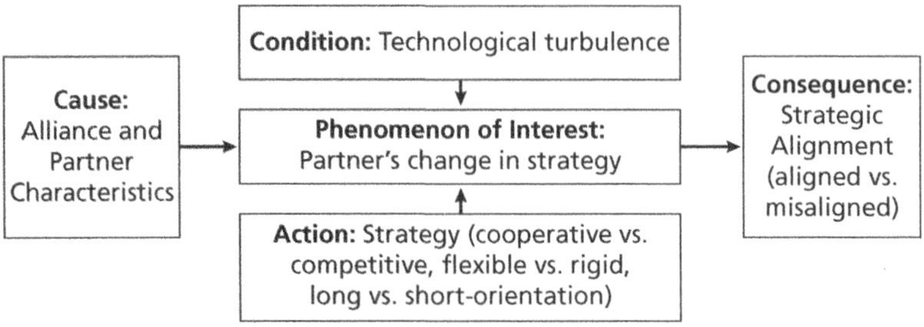

Figure 8.3 Coding paradigm for the relationship nodes.

meanings. This step is a thinking process that requires creating some sense or patterns out of each collection of codes. From here, statements can be drawn from the relationship of the causes, actions, conditions, and consequences to create scenarios that are comparable with the propositions.

The challenge for most case study researchers is to depart from the subjective judgments that may influence how the concepts are operationalized (Yin, 2014). To mitigate subjectivity and bias, the study relies on multiple sources of evidence (i.e., work manuals, contracts, observational data), taking multiple perspectives from different stakeholders in the alliance, and by establishing a chain of evidence using the coding paradigm. Moreover, the results from one interview will not only be compared to the other interviews, but also with the literature. The results from the in-depth interviews are compared against the answers to the close-ended questions. This helps to make sure that a firm truly exhibits the partner characteristic that is observed in the interview. This triangulation process should help to improve the validity of the research (Silverman, 2013).

RESULTS AND DISCUSSION

We begin by presenting some case evidences that indicate technological turbulence in the first seven cases. Competition in the biotechnology sector fuels technological turbulence in Case A, as one of the partners describes: "What we continuously do is screen who is still working on the same mode of action and where they are approximately in their research, what results they generate... because that greatly influences us." This partner speaks of its exposure to a different degree of technological turbulence compared to their partners as they are on constant lookout for the competitors' latest technology developments. For Cases B, C, and D, the shift towards cloud-based solutions have forced organizational changes which not every partner wants. Individual firms had to deal with transitioning from traditional IT systems to a cloud-based system. "The change of technology causes you to go from a very complex product for which you had to make a very large investment, towards a system in which you can buy relatively easy," a partner in Case C describes. Case E in the automotive sector is an exchange alliance that has been experiencing high technological turbulence due to the rise of electric cars. Most of the car companies want to offer an electric car with the mandatory charging options provided by their partner utility companies. Case F is a case of an integration alliance between a university and a research center. "As we do research and develop technology, we respond to that [technological turbulence]. Our research changes fairly quickly." Case G, is an integration alliance between two telecommunications companies aiming to digitalize all their services to capture a bigger share of the market. Digitalization however has brought greater technological turbulence to their already turbulent environment. Lastly, Cases H, I, and J are not active in a high technological turbulent environment and are assigned to the reference group.

For Proposition 1, we investigate behavioral tensions. Evidences from the within-case analyses show that alliance partners are mostly aligned with a cooperative strategy. Most alliance managers even choose to be more open and cooperative than what is necessary in most alliance scenarios. However, contrary to the proposition, the cross-case analyses reveal that leaning towards a cooperative strategy is not unique to cases in a technologically turbulent environment. Within the reference group, alliance partners also opt for a cooperative strategy and it did not matter whether the firms were part of integration or exchange alliances. Figure 8.4 shows the set of nodes that explain a partner's behavioral change as the phenomenon of interest.

In a few cases, we find evidence which partially supports Proposition 1. Instead of a case of an integration alliance, a large firm in an exchange alliance provides accounts of its smaller partner's competitive behavior. The informant recalls:

> As a partner you can sometimes identify opportunistic behavior in which the path of least resistance is chosen by the counterparty because they want to generate turnover as quickly as possible, certainly in the case of [our partner] and similar organizations that have to raise revenue and cash quickly.

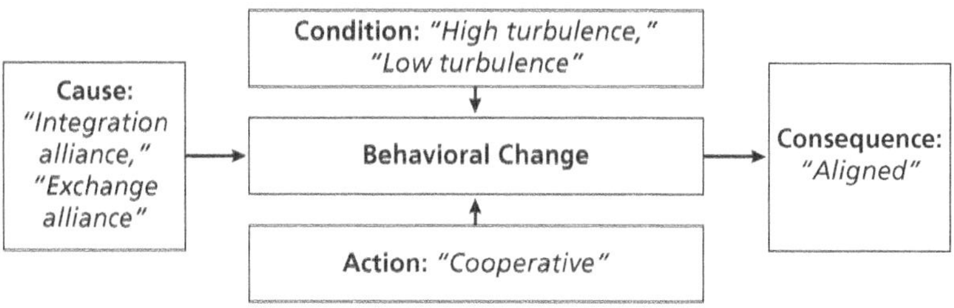

Figure 8.4 A sample of a collection of nodes on behavioral change.

Seemingly, the pressure to timely deliver triggered the partners change in behavior. But likewise, the bigger partner themselves claim, "We have limited resources and we need to see that we use them as profitably as possible, so today we will definitely focus on the things that bring return." Firms operate based on their relative size and excess working capital is not entirely dependent on firm size. However, it remains true that smaller partners aim for quick turnover than their larger counterparts as they may not have the same cushion to cope with unexpected financial losses in a turbulent environment. Firm size also made a difference in the cases of exchange marketing alliances where small partners make indirect sales through the bigger partners' channels. As the smaller partner gains wider reach, they are able to grow an "abundance of options" that trigger a competitive behavior as they develop more alternate routes to grow their business. Steering a smaller company towards a new direction is much easier than for a larger company. In an isolated situation in Case G, partners having to work on separate R&D phases led to a possible misalignment in integration alliance because of self-interest, as some partners are much closer to delivering the technology to market.

In the case of Proposition 2, we investigate structural tensions. It remains generally correct that partners will prefer flexibility to deal with technological turbulence. Our investigation aims to find those unique situations that could explain why this general accepted relationship does not fit a particular case. A number of evidences were found to support our competing proposition that display a partner's tendency to lean towards rigidity. For cases operating in the pharmaceutical and biotechnology industries, their elaborate legal requirements lay down a fairly strict relationship guide—"In general, we have documented 90% in guidance[s], also because we have to be able to prove everything from a regulatory perspective." A turbulent environment prompts partners to regularly revisit these guidelines to ensure that they continue to operate within the agreement and abide by regulation.

Moreover, having integrated systems in place have also contributed to preserving rigidity. One of the partners in Case G mentioned, "We—our company—are very conservatively organized... Everything must be exactly in the schedule. This also removes a lot of flexibility from our partners"—since some of their systems are tied to each other. Partners whose firm performance is dependent on the performance of the alliance have established more formal governance systems for monitoring and measuring performance. It appears that partners who opt to move towards structural rigidity struggle to cope but, in the end, succeed in dealing with turbulence. Besides, it is difficult to be flexible when uncertain times lead to a lack of mutual trust between the partners. This lack of mutual trust directs our analysis toward alliance capabilities as a partner's desire to control increases. Codes such as "alliance experience" and "alliance management know-how" reveal the preference for rigidity. When events happen out of the ordinary, partners will try to control the situation in the manner most familiar to them. Therefore, a partner having developed greater alliance capabilities may be more motivated to exercise greater control and even dominate over its partners.

Our competing proposition mentions "risk aversion" as a potential partner characteristic that determines preference for structural rigidity, however, the cross-case analyses do not reveal enough support. A few of the cases describe "risk aversion" as being associated with "firm size." In this proposition, "firm size" arrives as an emergent concept. Larger partners tend to be more risk averse than its smaller partner with bigger risk appetite as one of the partners in Case A described—"We are a rather small company, with the result that we dare to take a lot of risks. But look at large companies... They can cause damage to their entire company and portfolio. So, they think in a very different way." The structural misalignment is common due to the fact that small partners are way more agile and flexible in comparison with bigger partners especially when quick decisions have to be made during turbulent times. A respondent in Case D explained—"If you work as a small company with a large Mastodon, we are sometimes approached from different angles within that conglomerate, which can be very frustrating." A respondent from Case B adds:

> If you want to announce your partnership and you want to do a press release for it. With us, that press release is ready tomorrow and signed off by the CEO. But if you want to do that at the other company then you know that it should probably go through a hundred processes to get legal sign offs, iterations, and more. A speedboat turns at the moment it wants to run, whereas a tanker is not so easy to turn.

The scenarios described no longer present a case of preference, but acknowledgement. The smaller partner usually waits, adapts, and "you can anticipate on some things, which comes with experience. But on other things, it's just taking how it is" (a respondent from Case B explains). Therefore, it can be concluded that, in a technological turbulent environment even if flexibility is preferred, "firm size" intertwined with "risk aversion" can lead to strategic misalignment. In an environment with low technological turbulence as that of the cases in the reference group, partners are more likely to stay strategically aligned despite differences in firm size. In conclusion, Proposition 2 may be partially accepted. Figure 8.5 shows the set of nodes that explain a partner's change in structural preference as the phenomenon of interest.

Finally, analyzing the cases for Proposition 3 reveal partners' strong orientation towards a long-term strategy with exposure to high technological turbulence. It appears that the partners rather opt for building trust between

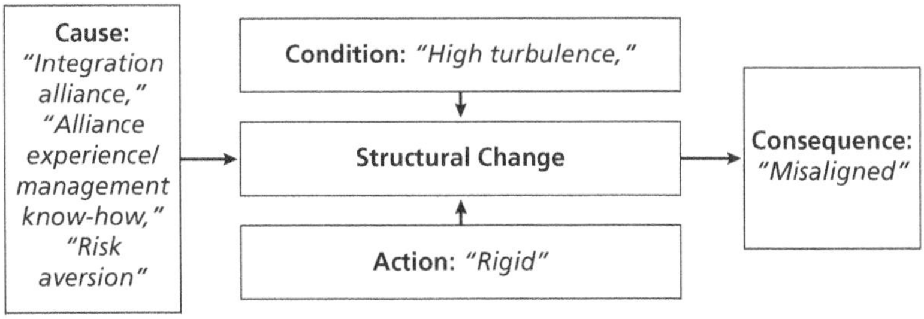

Figure 8.5 A sample of a collection of nodes on structural change.

the alliance partners and the uncertain and turbulent circumstance they are in presents the best opportunity to build legitimacy. In the same way, the alliance collectively prefers a long-term orientation which challenges the current literature. Our findings therefore do not show a strategic misalignment in terms of psychological tensions between the alliance strategy and the individual firm strategies. Under high technological turbulence, both the alliance and the partner firms shift towards a long-term orientation. Accounts from a partner in Case C describes, "I don't believe in short alliances with an end date. Short-term alliances . . . it means that something goes wrong, which has to do with trust." In the same way, a partner in Case B expresses, "It may be opportunistic, but not for just three months and after those three months, we have done one deal and we stop." In a technological turbulent environment, where investments are required, it is counter-intuitive to do these for a short period of time when resources are limited. Interestingly, the respondents do not see the usefulness of short-term investments in an alliance. Although they entered into a non-equity alliance, they intend to establish long-lasting relationships with their partners.

Under normal conditions, it is not a matter of choosing one of both sides. The alliance partners opt for a long-term orientation as this makes the most sense for even entering an alliance. However, they still keep an eye on the short term, so the predefined goals are met. This balance can be further explained by the following quotes of the respondents of Case B: "Your vision and strategy must be based on the long term, but your practical decisions and your tactics must of course be able to be controlled in the short term"; and Case E: "From the beginning I had clearly expressed a short-term tactic and long-term strategy, which was in line with the partner." So, under turbulent environments, the partners maintain the long-term mindset. The plan could be to consider waiting before critical decisions are made, allow the disruptive phase to pass and from the experience build stronger tested relationships.

Most evidences support the competing proposition which finds evidence of strong "partner dependence" in Cases B, C, D as small companies in the

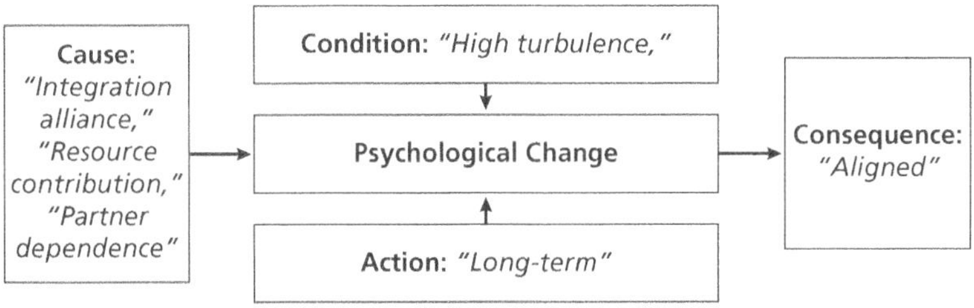

Figure 8.6 A sample of a collection of nodes on psychological change.

technology sector were involved. They are dependent upon their bigger partners in terms of utilizing their distribution channels. This interdependency led our analysis to an emergent concept that saturates toward value-adding "resource contribution." Codes such as "technological resource" and "physical resource" have emerged as partners' resource contribution that favors a long-term orientation. It suggests that a partner's structural preference does not only consider what its firm is getting from its partners in the alliance but also considers the protection of the resource it is contributing. The type of resource a partner is contributing and the amount of value it adds to the relationship could determine temporal orientation and also the degree of structural rigidity. Figure 8.6 shows the set of nodes that explain a partner's change in psychological orientation as the phenomenon of interest.

In summary, our results find sufficient support for Propositions 2 and 3 in terms of identifying the associated alliance and partner characteristics that lead to a strategic preference in a technologically turbulent environment. In addition to Proposition 3, our results find emergent characteristics such as a partner's "resource contribution" that further rationalizes the tendency of a partner to change their strategy.

Our results also provide support for some but not all current literature findings. For Proposition 1, we found insufficient evidence for our competing proposition, but we were able to confirm what the extant literature suggests on cooperative alliance strategies. This is in contrast to our findings in Proposition 3, where although we were able to confirm our competing proposition on long-term partner strategies, our findings do not align with a short-term alliance strategy, as the extant literature suggests.

RESEARCH AGENDA ON DEALING WITH PARTNERS DURING TECHNOLOGICAL TURBULENT TIMES

Typically, studies perceive the formation of an alliance as a strategy to cope with business risk and uncertainty. From a different angle, we show how an existing alliance could struggle to cope with technological turbulence potentially leading to alliance failure which is far more damaging to a partner firm. Maintaining strategic alignment is crucial to the success of the alliance. It is important to maintain the alignment of the goals of the partners, as well as the complementarity of their resources and capabilities. Unfortunately, aligning strategies in an alliance is not a walk in the park, but in many situations is looking a storm straight in the eye. Every turn of events in the life of an alliance can trigger a change in strategy of the individual partners. Our study finds it useful to understand what alliance and partner characteristic could signal a possible misalignment so that preventive actions can be taken in anticipation of highly turbulent conditions. Maintaining strategic alignment involves a stream of decisions taken to obtain the best possible fit between the external environment and a firm's structure and process (Venkatraman & Camillus, 1984). This implies that strategic alignment has a dynamic nature where internal and external strategic choices should be linked, interdependent, and consistent (Rashidirad et al., 2015) in a way that optimizes the contribution of those involved (Yarbrough, Morgan, & Vorhies, 2011).

Dealing With Partner Differences

Inherent to alliances are partner differences. Firms select partners because they are able to fill roles that they themselves are not able to fill. Khanna, Lavie, and Haunschild (2013) outlined typologies of differences between alliance partners and demonstrated that even interpartner differences exist, their negative effects on relational mechanisms can be minimized by proactively identifying those differences. Therefore, instead of calling out obvious differences, discussions should shift toward complementarities and how to recognize them. Partner differences not backed by complementarities are likely to result in flawed relationships. Seeking complementary resources requires a vision of the end-product as being a combination of distinct, and not merely accidental elements. In the same light, for firms selecting partners based on similarities, we can turn our questions on how one partner supplements or build on top what a partner already has and how that reciprocates back.

One of the reoccurring patterns recognizable from the analysis of our data was the difference of the partners' firm size. For instance, when dealing with partner size difference in contractual alliance, the partners have to bridge the disconnect between what is perceived as an innovation between a small and large partner. For a start-up, the new technology drives their whole business and for which their operations are built around, whereas, for large companies it is important for a big breakthrough to build on top of existing products. True innovation often requires a company to embrace something totally new which can be difficult for large companies because of their reluctance to take any sort of risk associated with entering a new business. If the partners differ in terms of what type of innovation they should seek—breakthrough versus incremental—and if technological turbulence constantly redefines technological standards, this can cause integration alliances to fail. Large companies are often very risk averse which make it difficult to adopt an innovation that is not exactly in their market or technology comfort zone. This scenario links risk aversion to firm size. Likewise, firm size associates to partner differences in spending. Small firms may not have enough financial cushion to cope with losses and delays and they may not understand that even large partners have their own limitations which make adjustments difficult for the alliance as a whole.

Initial insights point to the importance of openness, embracing partner differences and working together despite those differences. We then ask what partners can do to prevent alliance instability given the knowledge that certain inherent firm and alliance characteristics may lead to strategic misalignment during turbulent times. The answer could encourage new research to look more meticulously on governance mechanisms and develop new ways of dealing with partner differences.

Partner Assessment Tool

Our results have implications on the process of partner selection especially on the assessment of certain partner characteristics. During alliance formation, a structured partner selection process may prove beneficial (Dekker, 2008; Duisters, Duysters, & deMan, 2011; Mitsuhashi & Greve, 2009;) where an assessment tool could help gauge whether potential partners are likely to strategize against the alliance in the event of technological turbulence. Once assessed, the goal is not to reject a partner but to initiate conversations for setting up arrangements for all parties in the event of strategic misalignment.

Writing Alliance Contracts and Amendments

Although verbal agreements are legally binding, they are difficult to enforce especially when turbulent environments have already stirred confusion and disagreements. A written agreement is able to spell out the goals, duties of the individual parties, and their individual obligations in the case of non-conformance. In the onset of an alliance, contracts aid partners in strategic alignment. Typically, the common goal is clearly stated in the agreement, with little to no consideration on the private goals and emergent goals of the partners. Incorporating them however is a devious task but might be of great importance if the aim is to protect the respective parties' interests. So far, the clause describing another party's obligation in the case of non-conformance partly covers for the private interests of the partners.

Future strategic alliance research should delve more into the details of writing contracts (e.g., Crocker & Masten, 1988), and particularly important in the case of turbulent environments, would be writing amendments. The stream of decisions and organizational actions for ensuring strategic alignment could include revisiting contracts or recontracting, and making adjustments based on the most recent developments in the business landscape. Particularly, contracts for non-equity alliances can be divided into two categories—unilateral contract-based alliances and bilateral contract-based alliances (Das & Teng, 1998; Mowery et al., 1996) used commonly for exchange alliances and integration alliances respectively. To bring more specificity into these contracts, an assessment of the partners characteristics relating to firm size, risk aversion, optional business tracks, alliance capability, resource contribution, and partner dependence could guide what should be solidified in writing.

Periodical Goal Re-Alignment

Similar to partner selection, the process of goal alignment typically happens during alliance formation. This process links individual private firm interests toward a common alliance goal. However, repeating the process of goal alignment at a later stage in the life of an alliance is not a customary practice. Because relationship-specific investments are only possible when using a long-term vision (Das & Teng, 2000b), it may be necessary to conduct periodical goal re-alignment to deliberate the emergence of new goals, and from that form a basis of the next stream of investment decisions toward a long-term orientation. Similarly, Eisenhardt and Tabrizi (1995) proposed to operationalize innovation projects in terms of multiple design iterations, extensive testing, frequent milestones to assess project progress, and powerful project leadership, which enables quick strategic responses. Implementing a periodical goal re-alignment process recognizes and respects the development of emergent goals. In this way, disparity issues are not reconciled only to arrive at an agreement at the onset of an alliance, but to maintain the same agreement over the life of the alliance.

CONCLUSION

The great alliance success stories are those that endured instability and pushed through the slim odds of success. They shine because most alliances are not able to. Our attempt to answer why alliances fail brought in our view the most obvious up to the most subtle and natural reasons that lead to instability. We contribute by aiming for a higher level of research maturity as we do not simply attribute instability to the turbulent and uncertain environment, inflexibility, partner differences, or factors no single entity has control of. We pay attention to the firm and our investigation reveals inherent alliance and partner characteristics as potential causal factors that lead to strategic misalignment during high technological turbulence. The next step is to test the inter-relationship of these factors and address the methodological limitations of this study. Future research can also move forward by designing more dynamic organizational processes necessary for dealing with technological turbulence and to activate the potential value of resources partners share (Chen, Park, & Newburry, 2009) before they begin to lose hope on each other.

REFERENCES

Akgün, A. E., Lynn, G. S., & Byrne, J. C. (2006). Antecedents and consequences of unlearning in new product development teams. *Journal of Product Innovation Management, 23*(1), 73–88.

Amankwah-Amoah, J. (2017). Integrated vs. add-on: A multidimensional conceptualization of technology obsolescence. *Technological Forecasting and Social Change, 116*(3), 299–307.

Anand, J., Oriani, R., & Vassolo, R. S. (2010). Alliance activity as a dynamic capability in the face of a discontinuous technological change. *Organization Science, 21*(6), 1213–1232.

Ariño, A. (2003). Measures of strategic alliance performance: An analysis of construct validity. *Journal of International Business Studies, 34*(1), 66–79.

Austin, J. E., & Seitanidi, M. M. (2012). Collaborative value creation: A review of partnering between nonprofits and businesses–Part 2: Partnership processes and outcomes. *Nonprofit and Voluntary Sector Quarterly, 41*(6), 929–968.

Barnett, C. K., & Pratt, M. G. (2000). From threat-rigidity to flexibility–Toward a learning model of autogenic crisis in organizations. *Journal of Organizational Change Management, 13*(1), 74–88.

Barney, J. (1991). Firm resources and sustained competitive advantage. *Journal of Management, 17*(1), 99–120.

Buganza, T., Dell'Era, C., & Verganti, R. (2009). Exploring the relationships between product development and environmental turbulence: The case of mobile TLC Services. *Journal of Product Innovation Management, 26*(3), 308–321.

Calantone, R., Garcia, R., & Dröge, C. (2003). The effects of environmental turbulence on new product development strategy planning. *Journal of Product Development and Management, 20*(2), 90–103.

Candi, M., van den Ende, J., & Gemser, G. (2013). Organizing innovation projects under technological turbulence. *Technovation, 33*(4/5), 133–141.

Chatterjee, P. (2004). Interfirm alliances in online retailing. *Journal of Business Research, 57*(7), 714–723.

Chen, D., Park, S. H., & Newburry, W. (2009). Parent contribution and organizational control in international joint ventures. *Strategic Management Journal, 30*(11), 1133–1156.

Chen, H., & Chen, T. J. (2003). Governance structures in strategic alliances: Transaction cost versus resource-based perspective. *Journal of World Business, 38*(1), 1–14.

Chen, T., Li, F., Chen, X. P., & Ou, Z. (2018). Innovate or die: How should knowledge-worker teams respond to technological turbulence? *Organizational Behavior and Human Decision Processes, 149,* 1–16.

Contractor, F. J., Woodley, J. A., & Piepenbrink, A. (2011). How tight an embrace? Choosing the optimal degree of partner interaction, in alliances based on risk, technology characteristics and agreement provisions. *Global Strategy Journal, 1*(1/2), 67–85.

Crocker, K. J., & Masten, S. E. (1988). Mitigating contractual hazards: Unilateral options and contract length. *Rand Journal of Economics, 19*(3), 327–343.

Das, T. K. (2006). Strategic alliance temporalities and partner opportunism. *British Journal of Management, 17*(1), 1–21.

Das, T. K., & Teng, B. (1996). Risk types and inter-firm alliance structures. *Journal of Management Studies, 33*(6), 827–843.

Das, T. K., & Teng, B. (1998). Between trust and control: Developing confidence in partner cooperation in alliances. *Academy of Management Review, 23*(3), 491–512.

Das, T. K., & Teng, B. (2000a). A resource-based theory of strategic alliances. *Journal of Management, 26*(1), 31–61.

Das, T. K., & Teng, B. (2000b). Instabilities of strategic alliances: An internal tensions perspective. *Organization Science, 11*(1), 77–101.

de Vaan, M. (2015). Interfirm networks in periods of technological turbulence and stability. *Research Policy, 43*(10), 1666–1680.

Dekker, H. C. (2008). Partner selection and governance design in interfirm relationships. *Accounting, Organization, and Society, 33*(7/8), 915–941.

Delerue, H., & Lejeune, A. (2011). Managerial secrecy and intellectual asset protection in SMEs: The role institutional environment. *Journal of International Management, 17*(2), 130–142.

Dierickx, I., & Cool, K. (1989). Asset stock accumulation and sustainability of competitive advantage. *Management Science, 35*(12), 1504–1511.

Duisters, D., Duysters, G., & deMan, A. (2011). The partner selection process: Steps, effectiveness, governance. *International Journal of Strategic Business Alliances, 2*(1/2), 7–25.

Duysters, G., & deMan, A. (2003). Transitory alliances: An instrument for surviving turbulent industries? *R&D Management, 33*(1), 49–58.

Eisenhardt, K. M., & Tabrizi, B. N. (1995). Accelerating adaptive processes: Product innovation in the global computer industry. *Administrative Science Quarterly, 40*(1), 84–110.

Ganesan, S. (1994). Determinants of long-term orientation in buyer-seller relationships. *Journal of Marketing, 58*(2), 1–19.

Grant, R. M. (1991). The resource-based theory of competitive advantage: Implications for strategy formulation. *California Management Review, 33*(3), 114–135.

Hartley, C. A., & Phelps, E. A. (2012). Anxiety and decision-making. *Biological Psychiatry, 72*(2), 113–118.

Helfat, C. E., & Peteraf, M. A. (2015). Managerial cognitive capabilities and the microfoundations of dynamic capabilities. *Strategic Management Journal, 36*(6), 831–850.

Henderson, J. C., & Venkatraman, H. (1993). Strategic alignment: Leveraging information technology for transforming organizations. *IBM Systems Journal, 32*(1), 4–16.

Holt, C. A., & Laury, S. K. (2002). Risk aversion and incentive effects. *The American Economic Review, 92*(5), 1644–1655.

House, R. J., Hanges, P. J., Javidan, M., Dorfman, P. W., & Gupta, V. (2004). *Culture, leadership, and organizations: The GLOBE study of 62 nations.* Thousand Oaks, CA: Sage.

Iyer, K. (2014). Operational impact of collaboration and resource specificity: The moderating role of technology context. *Journal of Business & Industrial Marketing, 29*(5), 387–399.

Jaworski, B. J., & Kohli, A. K. (1993). Market orientation: Antecedents and consequences. *Journal of Marketing, 57*(3), 53–70.

Kale, P., & Singh, H. (2007). Building firm capabilities through learning: The role of the alliance learning process in alliance capability and firm-level alliance success. *Strategic Management Journal, 28*(10), 981–1000.

Kandemir, D., Yaprak, A., & Cavusgil, T. S. (2006). Alliance orientation: Conceptualization, measurement, and impact on market performance. *Journal of the Academy of Marketing Science, 34*(3), 324–340.

Khanna, P., Lavie, D., & Haunschild, P. R. H., (2013). Operating routines, cultural alignment, and relational mechanisms in alliances. In T. K. Das (Ed.), *Interpartner dynamics in strategic alliances* (pp. 27–54). Charlotte, NC: Information Age.

Lee, Y., & Cavusgil, S. T. (2006). Enhancing alliance performance: The effects of contractual-based versus relational-based governance. *Journal of Business Research, 59*(8), 896–905.

MacCormack, A., Verganti, R., & Iansiti, M. (2001). Developing products on "internet time": The anatomy of a flexible development process. *Management Science, 47*(1), 133–150.

Miller, D., & Shamsie, J. (1996). The resource-based view of the firm in two environments: The Hollywood film studios from 1936 to 1965. *Academy of Management Journal, 39*(3), 519–543.

Mitsuhashi, H., & Greve, H. (2009). A matching theory of alliance formation and organizational success: Complementarity and compatibility. *Academy of Management Journal, 52*(5), 975–995.

Monczka, R. M., Peterson, K. J., Handfield, R. B., & Ragatz, G. L. (1998). Success factors in strategic supplier alliances: The buying company perspective. *Decision Sciences, 29*(3), 553–557.

Mowery, D. C., Oxley, J. E., & Silverman, B. S. (1996). Strategic alliances and interfirm knowledge transfer. *Strategic Management Journal, 17*(Winter Special Issue), 77–91.

Musarra, G., Robson, M., & Katsikeas, C. (2016). The influence of desire for control on monitoring decisions and performance outcomes in strategic alliances. *Industrial Marketing Management, 55*(May), 10–21.

Rashidirad, M., Soltani, E., & Salimian, H. (2015). The role of strategic alliances in developing strategic alignment in SMEs. In T. K. Das (Ed.), *Strategic alliances for SME development* (pp. 223–244). Charlotte, NC: Information Age.

Raymond, L., & Bergeron, F. (2008). Enabling the business strategy of SMEs through e-business capabilities: A strategic alignment perspective. *Industrial Management and Data Systems, 108*(5/6), 577–595.

Santoro, M. D., & McGill, J. P. (2005). The effect of uncertainty and asset co-specialization on governance in biotechnology alliances. *Strategic Management Journal, 26*(13), 1261–1269.

Silverman, D. (2013). *Doing qualitative research: A practical handbook* (4th ed.). London, England: Sage.

Stanovich, K. E., & West, R. F. (2000). Individual differences in reasoning: Implications for the rationality debate? *Behavioral and Brain Sciences, 23*(5), 645–665.

Staw, B. M., Sandelands, L. E., & Dutton, J. E. (1981). Threat-rigidity effects in organizational behavior: A multilevel analysis. *Administrative Science Quarterly, 26*(4), 501–524.

Teece, D. J. (2007). Explicating dynamic capabilities: The nature and microfoundations of (sustainable) enterprise performance. *Strategic Management Journal, 28*(13), 1319–1350.

Teece, D. J., Pisano, G., & Shuen, A. (1997). Dynamic capabilities and strategic management. *Strategic Management Journal, 18*(7), 509–533.

Turner, V.K., Benessaiah, K., Warren, S., & Iwaniec, D. (2015). Essential tensions in interdisciplinary scholarship: Navigating challenges in affect, epistemologies, and structure in environment–society research centers. *Higher Education, 70*(4), 649–665.

Tushman, M. L., & Anderson, P. (1986). Technological discontinuities and organizational environments. *Administrative Science Quarterly, 31*(3), 439–465.

Van de Vrande, V., Vanhaverbeke, W., & Duysters, G. (2009). External technology sourcing: The effect of uncertainty on governance mode choice. *Journal of Business Venturing, 24*(1), 62–80.

Venkatraman, N., & Camillus, J. C. (1984). Exploring the concept of "fit" in strategic management. *Academy of Management Review, 9*(3), 513–525.

Vermeiren, M. (2019). *The effect of technological turbulence on strategic alignment: A study on strategic non-equity alliances* [Unpublished master's thesis]. KU Leuven, Antwerp, Belgium.

Wernerfelt, B. (1984). A resource-based view of the firm. *Strategic Management Journal, 5*(2), 171–180.

Yarbrough, L., Morgan, N. A., & Vorhies, D. W. (2011). The impact of product market strategy, organizational culture fit on business performance. *Journal of the Academy of Marketing Science, 39*(4), 553–573.

Yin, R. K. (2014). *Case Study research, design and methods* (5th ed.). Thousand Oaks, CA: Sage.

Young-Ybarra, C., & Wiersema, M. (1999). Strategic flexibility in information technology alliances: The influence of transaction cost economics and social exchange theory. *Organization Science, 10*(4), 439–459.

CHAPTER 9

BEHAVIORAL FACTORS FOR EFFECTIVE PARTNER MANAGEMENT IN INTERNATIONAL STRATEGIC ALLIANCES

Saleema Kauser

ABSTRACT

International strategic alliances between firms have become an important part of many firms' international business operations and strategies. However, studies of international strategic alliances show that they face a number of challenges that can often result in their premature demise. How can executives reduce the high rate of international alliance failure? Recent research conducted on international alliances suggests that building the right type of inter-firm relationship helps improve the chances of success. The evidence highlights several ways managers of firms can actively manage their working partnerships with their alliance colleagues.

Managing the Partners in Strategic Alliances, pages 223–244

INTRODUCTION

Strategic alliances have become an increasingly important part of many organization's strategies and in today's highly complex and competitive, global business environment, they have grown in importance as a means of doing business across national boundaries. No matter how strong and resourceful companies have become, they are no longer able to maintain a competitive advantage at every step in the value chain in all national markets, nor are they able to maintain a cutting edge in the wide range of technologies required for the design, development, manufacture and marketing of new products. International strategic alliances have become an important means of affecting transactions between partners in most industries (Gulati, Khanna, & Nohria, 1994; Park & Russo, 1996). Given their competitive importance in the global marketplace, "Why do a number of alliances break down or fail?"

Effective partner management of international strategic alliances has proven to be difficult because of the problems associated with the running of these ventures (Anderson, 1990; Lorange & Roos, 1991; Parkhe, 1991). Empirical evidence suggests that more than half of strategic alliances fall short of expectations or fail (Bleeke & Ernst, 1991; Das & Teng, 2000; 1999; Park & Ungson, 2001). While these failures certainly have many potential causes, experience with strategic alliances has shown that dissatisfaction with the relationship and alliance failure has been fuelled by a range of factors such as conflict, poor perceived performance, poor communications, opportunism, and incompatible objectives (Geringer & Herbert, 1991; Gugler & Dunning, 1993; Parkhe, 1993). These factors would appear to adversely affect the successful implementation of international alliances (Das & Teng, 2000). It is, therefore, not surprising that manager's and academics have a limited understanding of what makes an international strategic alliance successful. Effective partner management can avoid the number of failures that occur. Efforts are being made to understand the ingredients for successful strategic alliances, but the findings are far from conclusive (Park & Russo, 1996). In most cases, the problems in managing alliances stem from a lack of attention to relationship issues between partner firms (Kauser & Shaw, 2004; Ring & Van de Van, 1994). Building and maintaining close relationships between partners such that they demonstrate flexible, trusting, and committed attitudes towards each other are the most important factors necessary for the development of a successful alliance (Kauser & Shaw, 2004; Mohr & Spekman, 1994). In such relationships there exist a set of behavioral characteristics that help guide the flow of information between partners, manage the depth and breadth of interaction and capture the complex and dynamic interchange between partners. The assumption is that the existence of behavioral characteristics implies that partners within an alliance acknowledge their mutual dependence and their willingness to work for the survival of the relationship and thereby reducing the potential for opportunistic behavior. Generally, to date evidence suggests that the primary cause of alliance breakdowns are the result of poor and damaged relationships between partners. A breakdown in trust, communication, and commitment to the partnership festered by conflicts have resulted in severed relationships between partners. Empirical research has linked alliance success to commitment, trust, and coordination interdependence and communication and conflict resolution. (Kauser & Shaw, 2004; Mohr & Spekman, 1994; Monckza, Peterson, Handfield, & Ragatz, 1998).

Drawing on this stream of research the aim of this chapter is to determine the importance of a number of behavioral characteristics for the effective partner management of international strategic alliances. In this chapter, effective partner management is contained in the concept of a close relationship between partners, such that they demonstrate flexible, trusting, and committed attitudes towards each other. The assumption here is that there exists a set of attributes that help guide the flow of information between partners and manage interactions for the survival of the relationship.

The chapter will consider key behavioral traits for the effective management of international strategic alliances, drawing on a number of conclusions concerning the lessons that can be learned from international strategic alliances. The emphasis will be on how executives can coordinate their activities; develop a sense of trust and commitment to the relationship; have mutual interdependence and good communication through jointly resolving conflicts in order to gain maximum benefit from the relationship and reduce risk.

The chapter will start with an explanation of what strategic alliances are; then consider the behavioral characteristics associated with alliance success reflected in the literature with an emphasis on commitment, trust, coordination, interdependence, communication, and conflict resolution mechanisms. Finally the chapter will highlight several ways in which managers can weather the inevitable storms of conflict, through actively managing their working partnerships with their alliance colleagues.

DEFINING INTERNATIONAL STRATEGIC ALLIANCES

There is some confusion as to exactly what constitutes an international strategic alliance. A manifestation of terminology has resulted in a number of definitions and characteristics of strategic alliances, ranging from the most commonly used terms "strategic alliance" and "joint venture" which have been used interchangeably in the literature to refer to all types of interfirm agreements (Culpan, 2009; Hagedoorn & Sadowski, 1999; Harrigan,

1985, 1988; Hennart, 1988; Kogut, 1988; Ohmae, 1989; Pucik, 1988; Terpstra & Simonin, 1993; Yoshino & Rangan, 1995). To add to the confusion researchers have adopted the use of various other terms described in the literature which also refer to a range of inter-firm agreements, such as international cooperative arrangements (Root, 1988), international collaborative arrangements (Hergert & Morris, 1988), hybrid arrangements (Borys & Jemison, 1989), cooperative ventures (Buckley & Casson, 1988), coalitions (Porter & Fuller, 1986), partnerships (Mohr & Spekman, 1994; Perlmutter & Heenan, 1986), channel relationships (Anderson & Narus, 1990; Buchanan, 1992; Bucklin & Sengupta, 1993; Heide, 1994; Kumar, Scheer & Steenkamp, 1995), and cooperative agreements (Harrigan, 1988). Other forms of collaboration between independent firms, such as licensing agreements, franchising, cross-licensing, buy/sell contracts and mergers and acquisitions have also been described as a form of inter-firm arrangements (Harrigan, 1985; Yoshino & Rangan, 1995). All the above listed terminology is used to address inter-firm agreements ranging from contractual arrangements to a 50–50 joint venture (Yoshino & Rangan, 1995). It appears from this that the term strategic alliance uses different terminology for describing what appears to be the same thing. In spite of a lack of standardization in terminology strategic alliances reflect a wide range of inter-firm agreements that are aimed at achieving the strategic objectives of the partners, including, joint ventures, minority equity stakes and contractual arrangements (Das & Teng, 1998; Terpstra & Simonin, 1993; Yoshino & Rangan, 1995). However, in all instances the basic assumption of international strategic alliances is that cooperation between partners improves performance.

For the purposes of this study the term international strategic alliance will be used to describe both equity and nonequity arrangements (see Figure 9.1). As the objective of this chapter is to highlight how partners in international strategic alliances can effectively manage their working relationships with their alliance colleagues I adopt a broad alliance portfolio definition to include the different types of international alliances formed. As such the classification developed by Terpstra and Simonin (1993) will be adopted. They classify equity and non-equity arrangements into four types of international strategic alliances. These include contractual arrangements, joint ventures, equity participation, and consortia. International strategic alliances in this chapter include these four types of alliances. In this study contractual arrangements include international alliances that have been classified as "non-traditional contracts" (see Figure 9.1). These types of alliance are defined as non-equity formal agreements between two or more firms that pool resources or complement each other's strengths in various functions of business such as in R&D, manufacturing, marketing, and distribution (Contractor & Lorange, 1988; Hamel, Doz, & Prahalad, 1989; Ohmae, 1989; Terpstra & Simonin, 1993). A joint venture in this study falls

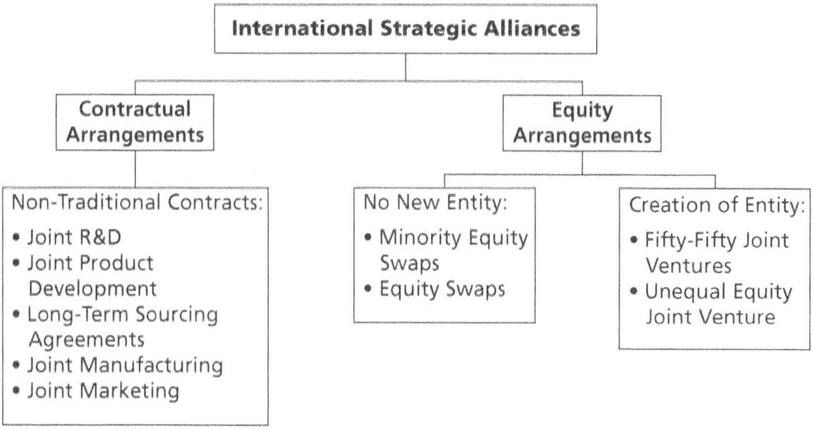

Figure 9.1 A range of international strategic alliances. *Note:* Adapted from Yoshino and Rangan (1995, Figure 1.1, p. 8).

under equity arrangements in Figure 9.1 and includes 50–50 joint venture types. A joint venture is defined as the establishment of a separate legal entity in which the equity is equally shared by both parties to the venture (Harrigan, 1985; Terpstra & Simonin, 1993; Yoshino & Rangan, 1995). Equity participation also falls under equity arrangements in Figure 9.1 and include what Yoshino and Rangan (1995) refer to as minority equity investments, equity swaps, and unequal equity joint ventures. International alliances of this type involve relationships between firms in which one firm purchases a minority or majority equity stake in the other firm in order to undertake joint activities (Killing, 1983; Terpstra & Simonin, 1993). Finally consortia are collaborative arrangements between three or more partners regardless of their equity structure. In this study consortia can range between "contractual arrangements" and "equity arrangement" depicted in Figure 9.1. Other types of cooperative agreements, such as licensing and franchising, cross-licensing, mergers and acquisitions, and subsidiaries of multinational corporations (MNCs) are not included because they do not involve for example pooling of resources, common objectives, sharing of costs and risks, commitment, and interdependency.

BEHAVIORAL DETERMINANTS OF INTERNATIONAL STRATEGIC ALLIANCES

Several dimensions of behavioral characteristics have been linked to alliance success (Cravens, Shannon, & Cravens, 1993; Kauser & Shaw, 2004; Mohr & Spekman, 1994; Monkcza et al., 1998). Research has shown that focusing on relationship issues can exert a dramatic impact on the contentment and success of the parties involved (Yang, 2009). Usually emphasis on these issues comes to light only after misunderstandings and antipathy grows, causing de-motivation of the parties involved.

Commitment

Organizational commitment has received a great deal of attention in organizational behavior where considerable attention has been given to examining the relationships between employee commitments to the organization in terms of job satisfaction (Mowday, Steers, & Porter, 1979). The study of commitment has also emerged in the marketing channel literature as a critically important element for channel survival and performance (Anderson & Narus, 1990; Anderson & Weitz, 1989; Kumar et al., 1994; Morgan & Hunt, 1994; Noordeweir, John, & Nevin, 1990). Here, commitment has been defined as an implicit or explicit pledge of relational continuity between exchange partners (Dwyer, Schurr, & Oh, 1988), with partners believing that the alliance is so important that it merits maximum efforts to maintain it (Morgan & Hunt, 1994). Partners demonstrate this commitment through their willingness to exert effort and commitment on behalf of the alliance and to adopt a long term perspective to the relationship.

Two views of organizational commitment are relevant to international strategic alliances (Anderson & Weitz, 1989; Morgan & Hunt, 1994). One view of organizational commitment emphasizes the economic costs of maintaining a relationship (Morgan & Hunt, 1994). The second view stresses the emotional ties to the relationship and is called affective commitment (Anderson & Weitz, 1989; Gundlach, Anchrol, & Mentzer, 1995) and is characterized as having three major components: (a) a strong belief in and acceptance of the organizational goals, (b) a willingness to exert considerable effort on behalf of the organization, and (c) a definite desire to maintain organizational membership (Mowday et al., 1979).

Several researchers have shown that partners who are affectively committed to the alliance partnership significantly influenced the level of success (Cullen, Johnson, & Sakano, 1995; Kauser & Shaw, 2004; Mohr & Spekman, 1994; Olson & Singsuwan, 1997). The level of commitment to the alliance on the goals and objectives, to the activities performed, the contractual terms of the agreement, the strategic direction of the alliance, how resources are allocated, to who makes decisions concerning roles and functions performed by each partner, and dealing with daily conflicts are strongly correlated with successful partnerships. Moreover, most of these commitment characteristics in high-performing alliances are related to the partners desire to maintain their relationships because they believe that the relationship is a necessity for the development and success of the relationship (Gundlach et al., 1995; Kauser & Shaw, 2004; Mohr & Spekman, 1994). These types of relationships show a strong sense of loyalty and belonging to the partnerships (Kauser & Shaw, 2004). They are more inclined to listen to their partners problems and try to help them solve them, by being patient with their partners if mistakes are made and making compromises to reach mutual objectives. Alliances are more willing to make an effort to meet the alliance's goals and interests on behalf of the relationship and partners tend to manage their relationships through mutual consent rather than relying on coercion through written contracts. It also means that commitment can help reduce the threat of opportunistic behavior, thereby reducing the costs associated with partnerships (Buckley & Casson, 1988).

Coordination

Coordination has been described as the extent to which two firms are integrated within an alliance relationship (Krapfel, Salmond, & Spekman, 1991). The process of interaction has been described as a social exchange process between two firms (Emerson, 1976; Thibaut & Kelley, 1959). Within this exchange process the firms coordinate their activities in order to achieve mutual outcomes (Anderson & Narus, 1990). The coordination of activities and resources can, therefore, lead to a better match between the firms (Hallen, Johansson, & Seyed-Mohamed, 1991). Studies have shown that partners who exchange ideas and keep each other informed about important decisions are more likely to coordinate their activities (Kauser & Shaw, 2004) and are a good predictor of successful partnerships (Mohr & Spekman, 1994). Coordination of activities between partner firms is critical because no firm is in complete control and because alliances cannot be "commanded" (Drucker, 1974). The two firms must work together. Thus strategic alliances achieve coordination by balancing the level of autonomy of each partner within the relationship (Pfeffer & Salancik, 1978).

Interdependence

Reciprocity between partners is an important dimension in evaluating the success of an alliance. Strategic dependence on the alliance determines the power structure, and an unequal power structure can lead to instability. Unlike traditional shareholders, partners in an alliance get involved in the day to day operations of the alliance. For this reason some partners may push for a dominant equity stake. However this link between equity distribution and success is far from conclusive and research suggests that there is a greater chance of success if the balance of power is shared (Anderson & Weitz, 1989).

The success rate of alliances with shared management is dependent upon the balance of power as all major decisions require consensus and because key areas allocated to each partner must be tightly controlled. This perspective flows directly from an exchange paradigm which is based on the assumption that firms must develop and maintain relationships with other firms because neither are self-sufficient or specialized to produce all their inputs or consume all their outputs (Pfeffer & Salancik, 1978). Resource dependency theory argues that firms that seek to reduce uncertainty and manage dependency by coordinating their activities will result in greater interdependence between the firms and a greater opportunity to coordinate their work (Pfeffer & Salancik, 1978). Pfeffer and Salancik (1978) suggest that greater coordination can be determined by each party's desire to balance dependence and autonomy. Each firm sees the other's work as an extension of its own, recognizes the joint benefits of coordinating work and strives to maximize the benefits of interdependence.

Gill and Butler (1996) identified three types of interdependencies and found that the pattern of interdependencies will affect the development of trust between the partners in joint venture relationships: (a) Within pooled interdependence in which both partners are expected to provide an output but have no direct dependence on each other, they found that direct competition will be less likely if there is no conflict which may stimulate the development of trust; (b) On the other hand, they found that in sequential interdependence which is the difference between the firm's dependence on its partner and the partner's dependence on the firm, both partners may come in to competition with each other and risk exploitation and thus lessen the degree of trust between the partners; and (c) reciprocal interdependence which occurs when there is mutual dependence and a balanced power between partners was found.

Research has shown that alliances with higher asymmetric interdependence are less stable and less trusting and more likely to be dysfunctional because of the exploitation opportunities that may result from the imbalance (Anderson & Weitz, 1989; Kumar et al., 1995). Partners equally dependent are also less likely to be opportunistic compared to alliances which are asymmetrical (Kauser & Shaw, 2004). This suggests that partners are more likely to value each other's resources and thus need to share their expertise and knowledge to achieve their mutual objectives. Buchanan (1992) and Kumar et al. (1995) also found that symmetrical interdependence enhances performance. Therefore managers need to understand that equal dependence between partners can be instrumental to the alliance's ability to improve its performance and thus should attempt to make sure that partners need to provide the critical resources that will enable each to achieve their performance goals and vice versa.

The degree of dependency can be determined by the balance of power. Firms that are highly dependent upon their partners for critical resources have less autonomy and control over their partners (Anderson & Narus, 1990; Anderson & Weitz, 1989; Gundlach et al., 1995) also found that symmetrical dependence in relationships results in greater stability and trust than relationships that are asymmetric in dependence. The symmetry of a relationship is determined by the extent to which trade partners value one another's resources. Symmetrical interdependence enhances performance (Buchanan, 1992; Kumar et al., 1995). If resources are valued equally by the two parties, the relationship is symmetrical; if the resources of one party are valued more than the other party's, the relationship becomes asymmetrical (Buchanan, 1992).

Trust

Trust has been defined as an essential element for the success of international strategic alliances (Das & Teng, 1998; Madhok, 1995; Mayer, Davies, & Schoorman, 1995; Ring & Van de Ven, 1992). In the strategic alliance literature trust has been viewed as "behavioral trust," in which one party willingly trusts the other party and involves vulnerability and uncertainty on the part of the trustier (Zand, 1972). Second, trust has been viewed as "intentional trust," in which trust results from reliability or intentional belief, confidence or expectation about an exchange partner's trustworthiness (Anderson & Weitz, 1989; Dwyer et al., 1988; Mayer et al., 1995). This view of trust has been defined as "the willingness to rely on an exchange partner in whom one has trust (Moorman, Desphande, & Zaltman, 1993, p. 82). Similarly Anderson and Narus (1990) have focused on this confidence aspect of trust by defining it as a "firm's belief that another company will perform actions that will result in positive outcomes for the firm as well as not take unexpected actions that result in negative outcomes" (p. 45). In the context of international strategic alliances this confidence element of trust is useful in maintaining an ongoing relationship, since cooperation is based on the confidence in the reliability and intentions of an exchange partner structural vulnerability (Aulakh, Kotabe, & Sahay, 1996).

The presence of trust has been a critical factor in the relational governance of strategic alliances because of problems coordination and mutual dependency (Anderson & Weitz, 1989; Aulakh et al., 1996; Monczka et al., 1998; Moorman et al., 1993; Morgan & Hunt, 1994; Nooteboom, 1999; Zaheer, McEvily, & Perrone, 1998). This is because trust has the ability to reduce transactions costs by deterring opportunistic behavior thus making partners take a long term perspective to the relationship (Beamish & Banks, 1987). Madhok (1995) suggested that the presence of trust develops tolerance to short-term losses in case of opportunistic behavior, reduces the potential for conflict and supports the belief among partners that they will be compensated by longer-term benefits. Beamish and Banks (1987) found that if trust is embedded in the alliance partnership, the incentive for opportunistic behavior is reduced and partners are more likely to take a long-term view concerning the alliance.

Similarly, trust based alliance relationships are seen as a substitute for hierarchical control when ownership-based control is not strategically viable or economically feasible (Aulakh et al., 1996). However, trust as a contract may be essential for the creation of a relationship, but not sufficient for its continuation. Trust has also been characterized as building and maintaining relationships within strategic alliances (Aulakh et al., 1996; Madhok, 1995; Parkhe, 1993). In this sense, trust is essentially dynamic and it develops over time in conjunction with the actions of the partners (Van de Ven & Walker, 1984). Badaracco (1991) suggests that when partners in an alliance trust each other, they are more inclined to grant substantial autonomy to managers, enabling them to respond more quickly to problems and opportunities and thereby raising the venture's success. Aulakh et al. (1996) suggest that trust is needed for a synergistic match, as well as for valued relationships in the long run and found the greatest obstacle to success to be a lack of trust. Buckley and Casson (1988) suggested that the higher the trust, the more efficient the international joint venture will be in transforming an input of cooperation into an output.

Several studies recognize trust to be a critical factor for successful collaboration where partners learn that joint efforts will lead to outcomes that exceed what the firm would achieve had it acted solely in its own best interests (Kauser & Shaw, 2004; Madhok, 1995; Mohr & Spekman, 1994). The success of a promising alliance can be endangered by the opportunistic behavior of partners. Lack of trust in the future behavior between partners can lead to the failure of the entire cooperation project or, at least, to the set-up of costly safeguards against opportunistic behavior, resulting in increased transaction costs. In Mohr and Spekman's (1994) study of successful partnerships trust was significantly associated with partner satisfaction in terms of profitability. They proposed that this significant relationship between trust and profitability suggested that trust was important in easing the dealer's fear of opportunistic behavior on the part of the vendor, thus leading to greater perceived satisfaction. Aulakh et al. (1996) investigated a sample of U.S. firms having distributor and licensing relationships with firms from Asia, Europe, and Central/South America. They empirically examined the direct association between trust and performance, as well as contingency effects. Although their findings indicated no direct relationship between trust and performance, their results support the notion that trust in international partnerships has positive implications for partnership performance when conditions exist for opportunistic behavior.

The literature suggests that confidence on the part of the trusting partner results from the belief, sentiment, or expectation that the partner's trustworthiness is reliable and intentional (Moorman et al., 1993; Morgan & Hunt, 1994). Thus, partners are marked by a high degree of harmony; open and informal, close personal ties; and make an effort to keep commitments. Mutual trust reduces the temptation for either partner to take advantage of the other, thus reducing opportunism.

Trust is undoubtedly the most important ingredient of success and a major reason for failure if it is absent. Trust can be competence based in the sense that each partner is confident that the other has the resources and competences to fulfill their part in the alliance. This means that each partner will promise to deliver what is expected. This trust and reciprocity is a dynamic concept and it is very tight. The tightness is apparent in each party agreeing to perform its known obligations. This has similarity to contracts in the sense that obligations are precisely understood. Moreover, this approach drastically reduces total control cost within the organization.

Communication Attributes

Communication is a central process in organizational activities and is critical to the success of organizations (Mohr & Nevin, 1990). Ineffective communication can reduce the effectiveness of strategic alliances and thus lead to conflict between partners (Jain, 1989). This suggests that an awareness of communication processes is essential within partnerships if maximum efforts are to be coordinated and directed towards the success of alliances. Because international strategic alliances involve companies of different nationalities, communication problems may arise because of cultural and language barriers, different working methods, and management styles. These differences and ineffective communication can lead to "misunderstandings, incorrect strategies, and 'mutual feelings of frustration'" (Mohr & Nevin, 1990, p. 36) which may reduce the effectiveness of the alliance, and thus lead to conflict between partners (Jain, 1989). This suggests that an awareness of communication processes is essential within alliances if maximum efforts are to be coordinated and directed towards the success of international strategic alliances.

Three aspects of communication behavior have been found to be critical to the success of partnerships: communication quality, extent of information sharing between partners, and participation in planning and goal setting (Kauser & Shaw, 2004; Mohr & Spekman, 1994; Monckza et al., 1998).

First, the quality of information has been measured in terms of the degree to which information exchanged between partners is shared in a timely, accurate, and credible manner. Timely, accurate, and relevant information between parties in a strategic alliance may be a significant factor in determining the degree to which each partner understands each other's goals and coordinates their efforts to achieve those goals (Mohr & Spekman, 1994). Meaningful and timely exchange of information may also result in a trusting relationship between firms (Anderson & Narus, 1990) and thus help partner firms to realize mutual benefits by reducing dysfunctional misunderstandings (Anderson & Narus, 1990; Dwyer et al., 1988). Timely, accurate, and relevant information is essential if the goals of the partnership are to be achieved (Mohr & Spekman, 1994; Monckza et al., 1998; Olson & Singsuwan, 1997). Second, the sharing of information refers to the extent to which critical information is communicated to one's partner (Badaracco, 1991). Huber and Daft (1987) suggest that closer ties result in more frequent and more relevant information exchanges between partners. By sharing information and by being knowledgeable about each other's business, partners are able to act independently in maintaining the relationship over time. Effective information sharing increases information value for all people in the organization (Glazer, 1991), is associated with increased levels of satisfaction (Schuler, 1979) and is an important predictor of partnership success (Devlin & Bleackley, 1988). Partnerships have been shown to develop trust (Anderson & Narus, 1990) and commitment (Anderson & Weitz, 1989) through the formal and informal sharing of timely information. Sharing information reduces the potential for conflict resolution and mistrust within collaborative relationships (Krapfel et al., 1991). Third, the extent of participation refers to the extent to which partners actively engage in planning and goal setting. When one partner's actions influence the ability of the other to effectively compete, the need for participation becomes necessary for defining roles and responsibilities (Anderson, Håkansson, & Johansson, 1994). Moreover, decision making and goal formulation are important aspects of participation that help partnerships to succeed.

Conflict Management

Harmony among partners is not necessarily a sign of a more successful alliance. Occasional conflict is a sign of an alliance with strong partners. As alliances evolve over time conflict is inevitable. What is important however is how conflicts are contained and resolved quickly before reaching further up the hierarchy? Conflict has been regarded as an important feature of international strategic alliances and arises when firms engaged in a partnership try to maintain their autonomy. Conflicts are an inherent element between units within a single organization and, therefore, are more likely to occur in the cooperation between people from different organizations (Child & Faulkner, 1998). Firms that engage in strategic alliances try to maintain their autonomy in an interdependent relationship, which gives rise to conflicts (Van de Ven & Walker, 1984). Partners within a strategic alliance relationship have a drive for both autonomy and cooperation, which results in the coexistence of cooperative and conflicting motives within the alliance (Aldrich, 1979).

Conflict has been specifically identified as a key reason for the failure of a number of strategic alliances as it can result in misunderstandings and distrust which in turn, lead to reduced cooperation and poor performance (Anderson & Narus, 1990). These misunderstandings can arise from differences in cultural values, management styles, operational methods and procedures, which may jeopardize the alliance (Jain, 1989). In international strategic alliances the presence of two parent firms can lead to differences between them in terms of management style, culture, communication, and operational practices which are conducive to conflict (Devlin & Bleackley, 1988; Jain, 1989; Killing, 1983). Given that a certain amount of conflict is expected, an understanding of how such conflicts can be resolved is also important (Borys & Jemison, 1989). Strategic alliances are encouraged to engage in joint problem solving, so that they are able to manage the uncertain environment that they are faced with. Joint problem solving allows a mutually satisfactory solution to be reached, thereby enhancing alliance success. Partners very often attempt to persuade each other to adopt particular solutions to the conflict situation, which appear to be more constructive than the use of coercion or domination. Domination or coercion are seen as being counterproductive and are likely to strain the fabric of the strategic alliance. In some strategic alliances conflict resolution is institutionalized, and third party arbitration is recommended (Anderson & Narus, 1990). However, it has been suggested that internal resolution is more likely to lead to long-term success. Other conflict resolution techniques such as smoothing over or ignoring and avoiding the issue are somewhat at odds with the norms and values advocated in more successful strategic alliances. Such techniques do not fit in with alliances in which the problems of one party become the problems affecting both parties.

Several studies of partnerships have identified that there is a negative relationship between conflict and alliance performance resulting in misunderstandings and distrust, leading to reduced cooperation between partners and thus the demise of the alliance. Frequent disagreements in a relationship tend to cause frustration and unpleasantness, and thus result in dissatisfaction (Anderson & Narus, 1990). In addition, conflict may harm accomplishment of the task of the relationships. Frequent disagreements may result in complex time consuming decision making or in obstructive behaviors that simply block any decision making (Killing, 1983). As a result time and resources are devoted to conflict resolution rather than activities productive for the alliance. Such situations may limit an alliance's ability to cope with and to respond to changes in its environment and thus to be successful in its business. Conflicts may also result in firms from cooperating and from withholding resources that may be required by the other partner to achieve its objectives (Buckley & Casson, 1988; Lane & Beamish, 1990). Transaction cost theory advocates that conflict breaks down trust and increases the potential for opportunistic behavior, thereby resulting in economically inefficient relationships (Beamish & Banks, 1987; Buckley & Casson, 1988).

Some studies have also shown that the manner in which conflicts are resolved has implications for the success of alliance relationships. Mohr and Spekman (1994) found successful partnerships were more likely to utilize problem solving techniques and less likely to use techniques such as smoothing over the problem, avoiding the issue, and domination and harsh words. Similar results were also noted by Monckza et al. (1998) who used the same measures of conflict resolution as Mohr and Spekman (1994).

HOW CAN EXECUTIVES REDUCE THE HIGH RATE OF INTERNATIONAL STRATEGIC ALLIANCE FAILURE?

The chapter has emphasized the importance of a number of behavioral characteristics of successful international strategic alliances. For managers in international alliances, it is imperative they focus their attention on the interpersonal relationships between partner firms if they want to be successful. This can be done through developing a greater level of coordination, interdependence, trust and commitment, communication, and the provision of measures to quickly defuse conflicts.

Coordinate Activities

Coordinate activities to achieve mutual objectives. Avoid ambiguous fuzzy goals and uncoordinated activities if you want to succeed. What you have to realize is both parties have to identify and agree on how to coordinate and adapt activities that are critical to the alliance. This means that you need to adopt similar or complementary goals and objectives, which have been defined and brought into operation by managers from both parties. If harmony and cooperation is what you're looking for then make sure that you are in complete agreement with your partner about the purpose of the alliance and the process by which your goals can be achieved (Kauser

& Shaw, 2004). Clarity of focus is vital. A successful alliance is one in which both parties' different groups work together toward achieving their goals and objectives—which will encourage a higher level of interaction between managers and heighten a regular exchange of ideas between partners (Mohr & Spekman, 1994).

Managing Mutual Interdependence

Value each other's resources and share expertise and knowledge to achieve mutual objectives. Your company can also help to enhance greater coordination with your partner firm by recognizing the benefits of mutual interdependence (Anderson & Weitz, 1989). Interdependence is fundamental to international strategic alliances. This means that managers must realize that each firm needs the other to provide the information and resources to complete their work. Each firm's research, production, finance, and marketing departments need to share their expertise and knowledge (Kauser & Shaw, 2004). This can also encourage the individuals and groups from each firm to interact with each other and coordinate their activities (Krapfel et al., 1991).

Developing Mutual Trust

Develop mutual trust towards achieving mutual objectives. In addition to helping guide coordination of alliance activities, managers can also assist in the development of mutual trust and commitment to the relationship. Building trust and commitment is essential for the long-term success of an international strategic alliance (Aulakh et al., 1996; Madhok, 1995; Mohr & Spekman, 1994; Parkhe, 1993). While the contractual terms of the relationship are important, the development of trust between partners should play a more significant role in the relationship's management. To enhance alliance performance and satisfaction, managers must demonstrate and reciprocate trusting behaviors by investing time and effort in partnership relationships. Several behaviors and actions associated with trust have been identified by alliance partners as having a positive effect on alliance performance. For example, the relationships that enjoy a high degree of harmony, loyalty, and sincerity have close personal ties with each other through commitments made; the partners are willing to offer each other support by sharing work-related problems; and they do not use each other for advantage by being opportunistic (Kauser & Shaw, 2004). These actions and behaviors support the development of trust. When there is trust between partners, both parties have the confidence that the other will be inclined to share and help solve work-related problems.

Building the Partnership Through Commitment

Identify with alliance goals and objectives; make an effort to invest in the relationship to achieve the goals and objectives; and maintain the relationship because you feel committed to the alliance goals (Mohr & Spekman, 1994; Monckza et al., 1998; Morgan & Hunt, 1994). Managers can facilitate the development of trust by institutionalizing commitment to the alliance relationship. This requires that both parties are in complete agreement about the purpose of the alliance and the process by which the goals can be achieved. Managers have to clearly define a number of important things for this to be effective: the goals and objectives of the alliance, the operational responsibilities of each party, authority over key decisions, and the way in which activities are to be performed. Details regarding resource commitments, daily operation, and resolution of conflicts should also be clearly stated. All these factors can be formalized in an alliance agreement to which both parties agree. However, this can only be effective to the extent that both parties share a strong mutual obligation to the alliance and understand each other and the extent to which they are willing and able to adopt each other's commitments. Once the agreement is formalized, efforts should be concentrated on listening to each other's problems, satisfying each other's needs, and compromising with each other to reach mutual objectives (Kauser & Shaw, 2004).

Frequent, Timely, and Shared Communication

Communication behavior also plays a significant role in determining international alliance success. Both the depth and breadth of information conveyed is important in managing the relationship. Sharing accurate and adequate information with partners in a timely manner should enable managers to interact and share ideas and information more effectively (Mohr & Spekman, 1994). Keeping each other informed about events and changes that may affect the other is especially important, and may lead to improved managerial decision making when planning activities and goal-setting. However, participation in planning and goal-setting should be rigorous and detailed enough to be effective. This again can be achieved by managers openly communicating their commitment to the alliance goals and objectives and participating in shared decision making on a regular basis. For effective alliance management communication must be frequent, on time, open, and shared (Kauser & Shaw, 2004).

Formulate an Effective Conflict Management Strategy

While this study has indicated that conflicts are characteristic of less successful international strategic alliances, it has been readily acknowledged that disagreements are inevitable in every alliance relationship. Each firm has its own agenda and goals for the alliance—which can result in conflicting goals. Differences between the partners' cultures can also lead to misunderstandings. Partners should work together to develop mediating mechanisms to defuse and settle their differences (Kauser & Shaw, 2004). Firms can train their personnel to be sensitive to and deal with such problems through using joint problem solving techniques. Managers can help blend the different cultures of the partners, helping phase in the relationship. But the complexities of managing cultural differences should be anticipated early on.

CONCLUSIONS

Research has shown the importance of behavioral characteristics in influencing the successful management of interorganizational relationships. While strategic alliances have been plagued by high failure rates, it has been generally recognized that building the right type of inter-firm relationship can improve the chances of success. Much of the current disenchantment with strategic alliances has been attributed to inadequate control processes, along with a failure to consider the role of interpersonal relations.

This chapter has built on that body of knowledge and has demonstrated that behavioral aspects of alliance relationships are needed to create the right environment and are the bond that holds an alliance together, particularly when conflicts arise. Partners in strategic alliances that are well integrated with each other by coordinating their activities, are more likely to have a higher level of performance and be more satisfied with their partnership. They are more likely to identify with and accept the goals and values of the partnership resulting in higher levels of commitment to achieving those goals and objectives. A trusting relationship that enjoys a high degree of harmony, loyalty, and sincerity is also shown to have a positive impact on the performance of international strategic alliances. Furthermore, the chapter has demonstrated that building connections between partners is about ensuring that information about the alliance is communicated and widely disseminated within the partnership. This lays the kind of groundwork that can help manage conflicts before they erupt.

The most important action to be taken by managers in building a successful international alliance is to foster and nurture the alliance relationship through the development of greater levels of coordination, commitment, trust, communication, and through the avoidance of frequent conflicts. This means that it is imperative for managers of alliances to focus their attention on the interpersonal relationships between partner firms if they want to be successful. Designing structures to fit the needs of the alliance will help partnerships to be managed more effectively through a system where authority is shared and decision making is more collaborative. If both parties strive for majority control, this may jeopardize their relationship and inhibit the success of their partnership. Partners in alliances need to arrive at a mutually acceptable solution. A balance may need to be struck between the need for control and the need to maintain a harmonious relationship. Though strategic alliances are not distinguished by their structure or control processes. Frequent participation in joint decision making appears to have more impact on the success of the alliance. Managers should help to design communication and administration structures that fit the needs of the alliance. While an administrative hierarchy with formalized systems of rules and procedures may erode the effectiveness of an alliance, too little formalization and centralization may result in each party behaving opportunistically. The alliance is best managed through a system where authority is shared and decision making is collaborative. Furthermore, control can be monitored through social interactions for maintaining partnerships such as regular reporting on performance, involvement in the planning process, and informal and formal contacts between managers. For instance regular reporting on the performance and progress of the alliance as a mechanism to monitor the alliance activities should be made available to management. The challenge lies in firms developing alliances in which the control and structure of the alliance can house these relationships.

ACKNOWLEDGMENT

This chapter, save some minor changes, was earlier published as Kauser, S. (2012). Behavioral factors for effective partner management in international strategic alliances. In T. K. Das (Ed.), *Behavioral perspectives on strategic alliances* (pp. 277–299). Charlotte, NC: Information Age.

REFERENCES

Aldrich, H. E. (1979). *Organizations and environments.* Englewood Cliffs, NJ: Prentice Hall.

Anderson, E. (1990). Two firms, one frontier: On assessing joint venture performance. *Sloan Management Review, 31*(2), 19–30.

Anderson, E., & Weitz, B. (1989). Determinants of continuity in conventional industrial channel dyads. *Marketing Science, 8*(4), 310–323.

Anderson, J. C., Håkansson, H., & Johansson, J. (1994). Dyadic business relationships within a business network context. *Journal of Marketing, 58*(4), 1–15.

Anderson, J. C., & Narus, J. A. (1990). A model of distributor firm and manufacturer firm working partnerships. *Journal of Marketing, 54*(1), 42–58.

Aulakh, P. S., Kotabe, M., & Sahay, A. (1996). Trust and performance in cross-border marketing partnerships: A behavioral approach. *Journal of International Business Studies, 27*, 1005–1032.

Badaracco, J. L. (1991). Alliances speed knowledge transfer. *Strategy and Leadership, 19*(2), 10–16.

Beamish, P. W., & Banks, J. C. (1987). Equity joint ventures and the theory of the multinational enterprise. *Journal of International Business Studies, 18*, 1–16.

Bleeke, J. & Ernst, D. (1991). The way to win in cross border alliances. *Harvard Business Review, 69*(6), 127–135.

Borys, B., & Jemison, D. B. (1989). Hybrid arrangements as strategic alliances: Theoretical issues in organizational combinations. *Academy of Management Review, 14*(2), 234–249.

Buckley, P. J., & Casson, M. C. (1988). A theory of cooperation in international business. In F. J. Contractor & P. Lorange (Eds.), *Cooperative strategies in international business* (pp. 31–53). Lexington, MA: Lexington Books.

Bucklin, L. P., & Sengupta, S. (1993). Organizing successful co-marketing alliances. *Journal of Marketing, 57*(2), 32–46.

Buchanan, L. (1992). Vertical trade relationships: The role of dependence and symmetry in attaining organizational goals. *Journal of Marketing Research, 29*(1), 66–75.

Contractor, F. J., & Lorange, P. (1988). Why should firms co-operate? The strategy and economics basis for cooperative ventures. In F. J. Contractor & P. Lorange (Eds.), *Cooperative strategies in international business* (pp. 3–20). Lexington, MA: Lexington Books.

Cullen, J. B., Johnson, J. L., & Sakano T. (1995). Japanese and local partner commitment to IJVs: Psychological consequences of outcomes and investments in the IJV relationships. *Journal of International Business Studies, 26*(1), 91–115.

Child, J., & Faulkner, D. (1998). *Strategies of cooperation: Managing alliances, networks and joint ventures.* Oxford, England: Oxford University Press.

Cravens, D. W., Shannon, H. S., & Cravens, K. S. (1993). Analysis of cooperative interorganizational relationships, strategic alliance formation and strategic alliance effectiveness. *Journal of Strategic Marketing, 1*(1), 55–70.

Culpan, R. (2009). A fresh look at strategic alliances: Research issues and future directions. *International Journal of Strategic Business Alliances, 1*(1), 4–23.

Das, T. K., & Teng, B. (1998). Between trust and control: Developing confidence in partner cooperation in alliances. *Academy of Management Review, 23*(3), 491–512.

Das, T. K., & Teng, B. (2000). Instabilities of strategic alliances: An internal tensions perspective. *Organization Science, 11*(1), 77–101.

Devlin, G., & Bleackley, M. (1988). Strategic alliances-guidelines for success. *Long Range Planning, 21*(5), 18–23.

Drucker, P. F. (1974). *Management: Tasks, responsibilities, practices.* New York, NY: Harper & Row.

Dwyer, F. R., Schurr, P. H., & Oh, S. (1988). A transaction cost perspective on vertical contractual structure and interchannel competitive strategies. *Journal of Marketing, 52*(2), 21–34.

Emerson, R. M. (1976). Social exchange theory. *Annual Review of Sociology, 2*, 335–362.

Geringer, J. M., & Hebert, L. (1991). Measuring performance of international joint ventures. *Journal of International Business Studies, 22*, 249–263.

Gill, J., & Butler, R. (1996). Cycles of trust and distrust in joint ventures. *European Management Journal, 14*(1), 81–89.

Glazer, R. (1991). Marketing in an information intensive environment: Strategic implications of knowledge as an asset. *Journal of Marketing, 55*(4), 1–19.

Gugler, P., & Dunning, J. H. (1993). Technology based cross border alliances. In R. Culpan. (Ed.), *Multinational strategic alliances* (pp. 123–165). New York, NY: International Business Press.

Gulati, R., Khanna, T., & Nohria, N. (1994). Unilateral commitments and the importance of process in alliance. *Sloan Management Review, 35*(2), 6–169.

Gundlach, G. T., Anchrol, R. S., & Mentzer, J. T. (1995). The structure of commitment in exchange. *Journal of Marketing, 59*(1), 78–92.

Hagedoorn, J., & Sadowski, B. (1999). The transition from strategic technology alliances to mergers and acquisitions: An exploratory study. *Journal of Management Studies, 36*(1), 87–107.

Hallén, L., Johansson, J., & Seyed-Mohamed, N. (1991). Interfirm adaptation in business relationships. *Journal of Marketing, 55*(2), 29–38.

Hamel, G., Doz, Y. L., & Prahalad, C. K. (1989). Collaborate with your competitors and win. *Harvard Business Review, 67*(1), 133–139.

Harrigan, K. R. (1985). *Strategic flexibility. A management guide for changing times.* Lexington, MA: Lexington Books.

Harrigan, K. R. (1988). Joint ventures and competitive strategy. *Strategic Management Journal, 9*(2), 141–158.

Heide, J. B., (1994). Interorganizational governance in marketing channels. *Journal of Marketing, 58*(1), 71–85.

Hennart, J.-F. (1988). A transaction costs theory of equity joint ventures. *Strategic Management Journal, 9*(4), 361–374.

Hergert, M., & Morris, D. (1988). Trends in international collaborative agreements. In F. J. Contractor & P. Lorange (Eds.), *Cooperative strategies in international business* (pp. 99–109). Lexington, MA: Lexington Books.

Huber, G., & Daft, R. (1987). The information environment of organizations. In F. M. Jablin, L. L. Putnam, K. H. Roberts, & L. W. Porter (Eds.), *Handbook of organizational communication* (pp. 130–164). Newbury Park, CA: SAGE.

Jain, C. S. (1989). Perspectives on international strategic alliances. *Advances in International Marketing, 2*(4), 103–120.

Kauser, S., & Shaw, V. (2004). The influence of behavioral and organizational characteristics on the success of international strategic alliances. *International Marketing Review, 2*(1), 17–52.

Killing, J. P. (1983). *Strategies for joint venture success.* New York, NY: Praeger.

Kogut, B. (1988). Joint ventures: Theoretical and empirical perspectives. *Strategic Management Journal, 9*(4), 319–332.

Krapfel, R. E., Salmond, D., & Spekman, R. E. (1991). A strategic approach to managing buyer-seller relationships. *European Journal of Marketing, 25*(9), 22–37.

Kumar, N., Scheer., L. K., & Steenkamp, J. E. M. (1995). The effects of perceived interdependence on dealer attitudes. *Journal of Marketing Research, 32*(3), 348–356.

Lane, H. W., & Beamish, P. W. (1990). Cross-cultural cooperative behavior in joint ventures in LDCs. *International Management Review, 30*(Special Issue), 87–102.

Lorange, P., & Roos, J. (1991). *Strategic alliances: Formation, implementation and evolution.* Oxford, England: Basil Blackwell.

Madhok, A. (1995). Opportunism and trust in joint venture relationships: An exploratory study and a model. *Scandinavian Journal of Management, 11*(1), 57–74.

Mayer, R. C., Davies, J. H., & Schoorman, F. D. (1995). An integrative model of organizational trust. *Academy of Management Review, 20*(3), 709–734.

Mohr, J., & Nevin, J. R. (1990). Communication strategies in marketing channels: A theoretical perspective. *Journal of Marketing, 54*(4), 36–51.

Mohr, J., & Spekman, R. (1994). Characteristics of partnership success: Partnership attributes communication behavior and conflict resolution techniques. *Strategic Management Journal, 15*(2), 135–152.

Monckza, R. M., Peterson K. T., Handfield R. B., & Ragatz G. L. (1998). Success factors in strategic supplier alliances: The buying company perspective. *Decision Sciences, 29*(3), 553–576.

Moorman, C., Desphande, R., & Zaltman, G. (1993). Factors affecting trust in market research relationships. *Journal of Marketing, 57*(1), 81–101.

Morgan, R. M., & Hunt, S. D. (1994). The commitment trust theory of relationship marketing. *Journal of Marketing, 58*(3), 20–38.

Mowday, R. T., Steers, R. M., & Porter, L. W. (1979). The measurement of organizational commitment. *Journal of Vocational Behavior, 14*, 224–227.

Noordeweir, T. G., John, G., & Nevin, J. R. (1990). Performance outcomes of purchasing arrangements in industrial buyer-vendor relationships. *Journal of Marketing, 54*(4), 80–93.

Nooteboom, B. (1999). *Interfirm alliances: Analysis and design.* New York, NY: Routledge.

Ohmae, K. (1989). The global logic of strategic alliances. *Harvard Business Review, 67*(2), 143–154.

Olson, L. B., & Singsuwan, K. (1997). The effect of partnership, communication, and conflict resolution behaviors on performance success of strategic alliances: American and Thai perspectives. In P. W. Beamish & J. P. Killing (Eds.), *Cooperative strategies: Asian Pacific perspectives* (pp. 245–267). San Francisco, CA: New Lexington Press.

Park, S. H., & Russo, M. V. (1996). When competition eclipses cooperation: An event history analysis of joint venture failure. *Management Science, 42*(6), 875–890.

Park, S. H., & Ungson, G. R. (2001). Interfirm rivalry and managerial complexity: A conceptual framework of alliance failure. *Organization Science, 12*(1), 37–53.

Parkhe, A. (1991). Interfirm diversity, organizational learning and longevity in global strategic alliances. *Journal of International Business Studies, 22*, 579–601.

Parkhe, A. (1993). Messy research, methodological predispositions and theory development in international joint ventures. *Academy of Management Review, 18*(2), 227–268.

Perlmutter, H. V., & Heenan, D. A. (1986). Co-operate to compete globally. *Harvard Business Review, 64*(2), 136–150.

Pfeffer, J., & Salancik, G. R. (1978). *The external control of organizations: A resource dependence perspective.* New York, NY: Harper and Row.

Porter, M. E., & Fuller, M. B. (1986). Coalitions and global strategy. In M. E. Porter (Ed.), *Competition in global industries.* Cambridge, MA: Harvard University Press.

Pucik, V. (1988). Strategic alliances, organizational learning and competitive advantage: The HRM agenda. *Human Resource Management, 27*(1), 77–93.

Ring, P. S., & Van de Ven, A. H. (1992). Structuring cooperative relationships between organizations. *Strategic Management Journal, 13*(7), 438–498.

Ring, P. S., & Van de Ven, A. H. (1994). Developmental processes of cooperative interorganizational relationships. *Academy of Management Review, 19*(1), 90–118.

Root, F. R. (1988). Some taxonomies of international cooperative arrangements. In F. J. Contractor & P. Lorange (Eds.), *Cooperative strategies in international business* (pp. 69–80). Lexington, MA: Lexington Books.

Schuler, R. S. (1979). A role perception transactional process model for organizational communication outcome relationships. *Organizational Behavior and Human Performance, 23*(2), 268–291.

Terpstra, V., & Simonin, B. L. (1993). Strategic alliances in the triad: An exploratory study. *Journal of International Marketing, 1*(1), 4–25.

Thibaut, J. W., & Kelley, H. H. (1959). *The social psychology of groups.* New York, NY: Wiley.

Van de Ven, A. H., & Walker, G. (1984). The dynamics of interorganizational coordination. *Administrative Science Quarterly, 29*(4), 598–621.

Yang, J. (2009). The determinants of supply chain alliance performance: An empirical study. *International Journal of Production Research, 47*(4), 1055–1069.

Yoshino, M. Y., & Rangan, U. S. (1995). *Strategic alliances: An entrepreneurial approach to globalization.* Boston, MA: Harvard Business School Press.

Zaheer, A., McEvily, B., & Perrone, V. (1998). Does trust matter? Exploring the effects of interorganizational and interpersonal trust on performance. *Organization Science, 9*(2), 141–159.

Zand, D. E. (1972). Trust and managerial problem solving. *Administrative Science Quarterly, 17*(2), 229–239.

CHAPTER 10

MANAGING ALLIANCE PARTNER ATTRIBUTES

Lessons From the Ericsson Case Study

Giulio Ferrigno
Andrea Piccaluga
Giovanni Battista Dagnino

ABSTRACT

Managing alliance partners has become a crucial issue for firms' competitiveness. Previous literature has provided a comprehensive understanding about how firms manage alliances. However, extant research has not yet developed a crystallized understanding about how firms can best manage their alliance partners. Drawing on the available management literature this chapter unveils three main features that characterize the management of alliance partners: (a) alliance partner size, (b) alliance partner diversity, and (c) alliance partner internationalization. Moreover, it analyzes these three key characteristics in a relevant alliance case study in the telecom industry such as Ericsson. We conclude the chapter by discussing theoretical and managerial implications and proposing future research directions for alliance literature.

Managing the Partners in Strategic Alliances, pages 245–269

INTRODUCTION

In order to compete in the current economic situation, firms establish strategic alliances, in some cases dozens of them. Consequently, so many strategic alliances originate with the challenge of how to manage simultaneously all these collaborative agreements (Ritter & Gemünden, 2003; Wassmer, 2010). Moreover, strategic alliances are becoming temporary organizations (Bakker & Knoben, 2014; Gomes-Casseres, 2015). Therefore, how to manage multiple strategic alliances per time has become a crucial condition for firms' competitiveness.

In an attempt to propose solutions to this critical challenge strategy scholars have suggested that the bundle of alliances in which a firm is involved should be considered from a portfolio perspective (Wassmer, 2010). These scholars have argued that firms must give more attention to the performance of their entire alliance portfolios rather than to individual strategic alliances (Bamford, Gomes-Casseres, & Robinson, 2003). Due to the synergies and cause-and-effect relationship among alliances that are and might be originated within (Hoffman, 2007; Sarkar, Aulakh, & Madhok, 2009) and from the alliance portfolio (Wassmer & Dussauge, 2012), firms must place the structure as well as the strategic orientation of their entire alliance portfolios at the center of their interests. In this vein, some scholars have conducted several empirical studies that analyze the relationship between alliance portfolios and firms' performance (Lee, Kirkpatrick-Husk, & Madhavan, 2017). However, scant attention has been devoted heretofore to how firms can manage the partners involved in their alliances (Hoffman, 2007). Given the reason above, the present study aims to enlarge the comprehension of alliance partner attributes by conducting a qualitative study that might help to shed light on this issue.

Drawing on the specific management literature, we identify three main features that characterize the management of alliance partners: (a) *alliance partner size*—the number of partners or alliances to which a firm is connected at a given point in time (Wassmer, 2010), (b) *alliance partner diversity*—the degree of variance in partners, alliances, and resources the focal firm has access to via its multiple alliances' links (Jiang, Tao & Santoro, 2010), and (c) *alliance partner internationalization*—the degree of foreign partners in a firm's collection of immediate alliance relationships (Lavie & Miller, 2008). On the basis of such literature, we explore the importance of these three alliance partner characteristics by conducting a representative alliance case study of the telecom industry, for example, Ericsson, a world-leading provider of communications technology and services. Specifically, we collected a large amount of primary and secondary information about the alliances formed by Ericsson from 1994 to 2014 and analyzed the relevance of alliance partner size, alliance partner diversity, and alliance partner internationalization over time.

The chapter is organized as follows. In the next section we review the alliance management literature and identify three main features (alliance partner size, alliance partner diversity, and alliance partner internationalization) that characterize the management of alliance partners. Then, we introduce the Ericsson case study and provide empirical evidence of the three alliance partner attributes in this case study from 1994 to 2014. Finally, we conclude the study by comparing the relevance of the three alliance partner attributes over time, thereby discussing theoretical and managerial implications for the alliance literature, and suggesting further research questions.

ALLIANCE PARTNER MANAGEMENT: MAIN FEATURES AND CHARACTERISTICS EXTRACTED FROM THE LITERATURE

The commitment of firms in simultaneously managing multiple strategic alliances has become a necessity in today's competitive setting (Blasingame, 2016; Pangarkar, Yuan, & Hussain, 2017). In particular, within the current importance of alliances for firms' strategies, an issue that has attracted attention is how these collaborative agreements can be managed (Hoffman, 2007; Ritter & Gemünden, 2003) and more precisely how can firms manage their partners. The answer that alliance scholars provide to this research question finds collocation in the concept of *dedicated alliance function.*

Alliance studies show that firms developing a function that is specifically dedicated to managing their alliance activities might gain several benefits. This is true at least for those alliances that involve two partners (Kale, Dyer, & Singh, 2002; Kale & Singh, 2009). Indeed, the presence of a dedicated alliance function allows firms to: (a) learn and leverage both explicit and tacit lessons from previous and current alliances, (b) keep firms' stakeholders well-informed about alliance activities, (c) improve internal coordination, and (d) maintain control in the evaluation of alliance performance (Kale et al., 2002).

While alliance studies have stressed the importance of a dedicated alliance function in managing alliances between two partners (Kale et al., 2002), other scholars have recently found that firms developing a dedicated alliance function might fall short to manage the alliances when these collaborative arrangements involve more than two partners (Dagnino & Ferrigno, 2015) or when the dedicated alliance function is used to manage the whole alliance portfolio (Sarkar et al., 2009).

With regard to multipartner alliances, Dagnino and Ferrigno (2015) found that when alliances involve three partners, the dedicated alliance function is barely appropriate to manage the complexities that emerge from four key aspects that epitomize this kind of alliances: (a) actor mindframes, (b) governance structure, (c) alliance learning problems and conflict management, and (d) strategic and operational problems. Drawing on a specific triadic alliance case study (i.e., the 3SUN alliance between Enel Green Power, Sharp, and STMicroelectronics), the authors also propose that such complexities can be managed when firms, involved in this kind of alliances, develop a set of contingent triadic alliance mechanisms that may be re-aligned to the design and installment of a flexible structure. Specifically, the authors surmise that firms involved in a triadic alliance should form a flexible structure, created ad hoc for the triadic alliance, that (a) fosters—in formal and informal ways—the dialogue among the three partners key managers and (b) ensures the rotation of partners in taking key roles pertaining to strategic and operational decisions.

Moving the focus to alliance portfolios, alliance research has not yet developed a crystallized understanding about how firms can manage the bundle of alliances in which they are involved. For instance, Sarkar et al. (2009) found that firms adopting a dedicated alliance function do not successfully manage the performance of their alliances. However, beyond this finding, the authors do not suggest any additional solution to the question under scrutiny. In parallel, some alliance studies call for a better comprehension of alliance partner management (Halinen & Törnroos, 2005).

To contribute to this debate, the present study aims to enlarge the comprehension of the alliance management phenomenon. In doing so, it explores the alliance literature and discloses three main features that characterize alliance partners: (a) *alliance partner size*—the number of partners or alliances to which a firm is connected at a given point in time (Wassmer, 2010); (b) *alliance partner diversity*—the degree of variance in partners, alliances, and resources the focal firm has access to via its multiple alliances' links (Jiang et al., 2010); and (c) *alliance partner internationalization*—the degree of foreign partners in a firm's collection of immediate alliance relationships (Lavie & Miller, 2008). Each of these alliance partners' characteristics will be discussed below.

Alliance Partner Size

Alliance partner size is the first feature that epitomizes alliance partner management. Alliance scholars conceive alliance partner size in two different ways: (a) the number of partners to which a focal firm is connected to (Hoffman, 2007) or (b) the number of alliances a focal firm is engaged in at a given point in time (Wassmer, 2010). Independently from the definition chosen or the dimension examined, what matters for the present study is that alliance research shows that the number of partners or alliances to which the focal firm is related to poses a trade-off for the focal firm. On the one hand, alliance research argues that a larger alliance offers a handful of advantages that might be beneficial to the focal firm. Accordingly, alliance scholars have found that a larger alliance partner allows the focal firm to: (a) access valuable resources, such as human resources, financial assets, marketing efforts, R&D investments and reputation, that enhance firm performance (Lahiri & Narayanan, 2013; Lavie, 2006) and (b) acquire the broad domain of knowledge encapsulated in the partner firms' organizational capital (Belgraver & Verwaal, 2018).

On the other hand, alliance research states that managing a larger alliance partner brings with it a set of challenges for the focal firm (Pangarkar et al., 2017): (a) value appropriation from alliances becomes difficult as large partner leverage bargaining power (Lavie, 2007) and (b) search, identification, and transfer of knowledge resources increase significantly when the alliance partner is large (Duysters, Kok, & Vaandrager, 1999; Lahiri & Narayanan, 2013).

Alliance Partner Diversity

Alliance scholars have pointed to the importance of a second characteristic that incarnates alliance partner management, that is, the multidimensional concept of alliance partner diversity (de Leeuw, Lokshin, & Duysters, 2014; Jiang et al., 2010; Lee et al., 2017). Alliance partner diversity refers to the degree of variance in partners, alliances, and resources that the focal firm has access to via its alliances (Jiang et al., 2010). Variance in partners has been studied in terms of partners' attributes (Oerlemans, Knoben, & Pretorius, 2013). Indeed, alliance scholars have explained alliance partner diversity by including in their empirical studies specific variables that are referred to specific partner attributes such as its size (Baum, Calabrese, & Silverman, 2000), its business activities (Dussauge, Garrette, & Mitchell, 2000) and also its country of origin (Lavie & Miller, 2008).

Drawing on the proliferation of studies on alliance partner diversity, some scholars have enlarged the contours of alliance partner diversity by investigating the diversity in terms of alliances and resources (Cui & O'Connor, 2012). These authors specifically credit attention to alliance resource diversity, that is, the degree to which the resources of different partners are different. Alliance literature suggests that managing a more diverse alliance implies that the focal firm must evaluate a series of benefits and drawbacks associated with the different degrees of variety of partners, alliances, and resources that the focal firm has access to.

On the one side, more variance in partners portrays an ample array of *benefits* associated with such heterogeneity (de Leeuw et al., 2014). Allying with diverse partners brings more opportunities in terms of (a) access to new resources (Swaminathan & Moorman, 2009); (b) development of new ideas, technologies, and products (Wuyts, Dutta, & Stremersch, 2004) as the focal firm is not locked into prior knowledge (Cohen & Levinthal, 1990); (c) reduction of coordination, monitoring, and communication costs (Oerlemans et al., 2013); and (d) more strategic flexibility to manage high technological uncertainty (Hoffmann, 2007).

On the other side, some scholars have pointed to the potential *drawbacks* connected to high levels of alliance partner diversity. Allying with different partners may (a) raise managerial challenges (Duysters & Lokshin, 2011), thereby inhibiting the exchange and integration of resources and information across alliance partners; (b) increase the costs associated with knowledge utilization (Parida et al., 2016; Vasudeva & Anand, 2011); and (c) nurture information overflow problem (Koput, 1997).

Alliance Partner Internationalization

Extant alliance literature states that another feature of alliance partners is relevant for alliance management: that is, alliance partner internationalization. This refers to the degree of foreign partners in a firm's collection of immediate alliance relationships (Lavie & Miller, 2008). The degree of foreignness is represented by cross-national cultural, geographical, institutional, and economic development divergences between the focal firm's home country and its partners (Ghemawat, 2001). Alliance research submits that managing an alliance with high levels of foreign partners is challenging because of the simultaneous presence of both advantages and disadvantages connected to different degrees of foreignness between the focal firm and its alliance partners. Some authors argue that an alliance with a high diversity of international partners provides several benefits to the focal firm. First, it gives the focal firm the possibility to obtain resources that are accessible through local partners, thus improving the firm's competitiveness (García-Canal et al., 2002). Second, a more foreign alliance can increase a focal firm's flexibility and its capacity to be responsive to turbulent and dynamic environmental changes (Eisenhardt & Schoonhoven, 1996). Finally, it allows the focal firm to allocate its activities over the globe in a way to improve its performance in technology-driven industries (Zaheer, 2000).

Nonetheless, other authors show that an alliance with a high diversity of international partners might also entail some challenges. First, managerial complexity emerging from acculturation issues between the focal firms and its foreign partners poses challenges that firms must be able to manage.

Second, learning becomes more difficult in the presence of international partners because the focal firm is required to invest larger amounts of resources in tools of communication and transportation to support interaction (Parkhe, 1991; Steensma & Lyles, 2000). Finally, misappropriation of value in foreign partners' home countries might occur as foreign partners possess more knowledge about shareholders in their countries of origin (Hamel, 1991; Lavie, 2006).

Summing up, extant alliance literature suggests that three main features characterize the management of alliance partners, that is alliance partner size, alliance partner diversity, and alliance partner internationalization. It also shows that these three alliance partner attributes are critical for alliance partner management because they present both benefits and challenges to the focal firm. In the following section, we explore the relevance of alliance partner size, alliance partner diversity, and alliance partner internationalization in a representative alliance case study of the telecom industry: Ericsson (1994–2014).

RESEARCH METHOD: IN-DEPTH CASE STUDY

To investigate the relevance of the three main alliance partner features that we have extracted from the alliance literature, we conducted an in-depth qualitative study that explores alliance partner characteristics within real-life context (Eisenhardt, 1989; Yin, 2003). In this vein, we performed an in-depth analysis of a single case (Eisenhardt & Graebner, 2007; Siggelkow, 2007).

Two reasons have driven us to conduct a single case study. First, the exploration of a single case study epitomizes a distinctive and critical case in challenging a well-formulated theory (Ravenswood, 2011; Yin, 2009). Second, since only limited theoretical understanding subsists about how firms handle their alliance partner, the benefits of extracting many details in a particular case (Eisenhardt & Graebner, 2007) allowing theory to emerge from the data can be a valuable starting point (Ravenswood, 2011; Siggelkow, 2007). Therefore, it seems that the alliance partner literature can benefit from the conduction of a single case as a revelatory case of how firms handle their alliance partners.

Theoretical Sampling: Ericsson

To conduct this study, we have selected the case by following the principles of theoretical sampling (Glaser & Strauss, 1967; Mason, 1996; Pettigrew, 1990). Three key motives have guided us to inspect Ericsson's alliances. First, Ericsson represents a case that is prototypical and paradigmatic of a successful

TABLE 10.1 A Snapshot of Ericsson

Business	Provider of communication technology and services
Firm foundation	1876
Headquarters	Stockholm, Sweden
Industry	Telecom industry
Net sales	2,373 ($ billion)
Operating income	175 ($ billion)
Operating margin	77 ($ billion)
Cash flow from operating activities	195 ($ billion)
Employees	114,340
Sales	35,320,543,689
Market capitalization	39,768,539,081

Note: The data in this table relates to the year 2014 and are available at Factiva database website (www.global.factiva.com)

key player in the European and global telecom industry (Di Minin & Bianchi, 2011). Founded in 1876 and with its headquarters in Stockholm, Sweden, Ericsson is a leading provider of communications technology and services in the world. It is among the three largest telecom firms in selling products and services to its customers, hiring employees, and involving a considerable number of shareholders in its businesses (see Table 10.1). Ericsson mostly provides services, software, and infrastructure in ICT for telecommunications operators. It also supplies traditional telecommunications and IP networking equipment, mobile and fixed broadband, operations and business support services, cable television, and video systems. These business activities involve more than 110,000 employees and lead Ericsson to play a key role in the telecom industry achieving $23,73 billion in net sales; $1,75 billions of operating income; and $1,95 billions of cash flow activities.

Second, we have reason to believe that Ericsson is a representative alliance case study because of its importance along the dimensions of interest (Gerring, 2007). From this perspective, the methodological value of the Ericsson case stems from its relevance along the three dimensions under scrutiny in this study (a) alliance partner size, (b) alliance partner diversity, and (c) alliance partner internationalization. Accordingly, prior studies show that over the last 2 decades Ericsson has announced 86 alliances, involving 134 different partners from 180 different countries (Ferrigno, 2017).

Finally, we have also decided to explore Ericsson's alliances thanks to data access. The possibility to leverage on a notable amount of data and information regarding the bundle of alliances in which Ericsson is involved offers a noteworthy opportunity to dig deeper into the understanding of the three main features of alliance partner management.

Data Source

As discussed earlier, the exploratory nature of this analysis implies the need to inspect the variety and richness of data that help to understand how firms manage their alliance partners.

To increase the evidence for the case study context and thus ameliorate the trustworthiness of the data (Lincoln & Denzin, 1994), as well as the comprehension of the sampling choice (Cook, Campbell, & Day, 1979), the analysis of the Ericsson's alliance case relies on a system of multiple data sources that combines a variety of information sources and allows the triangulation of data types (Jick, 1979). First, we have collected data from primary sources such as financial reports (annual reports, 10-Q reports, and 10-K reports from 1994 to 2014), and new releases available at the Ericsson website. Second, we have included in the data collection various secondary sources such as 92 alliance announcements press releases from two representative and complementary alliance databases (SDC Platinum and Factiva database) as well as an ample set of social networks (including Facebook, LinkedIn, Twitter, and Google plus) in which Ericsson has posted information about relationships with its alliance partners. Also, we have gathered data from 100 videos, posted on the Ericsson YouTube channel (section–networks), which have provided further information about the complementarities between Ericsson and its alliance partners. Third, we have integrated the previous sources by using 24 transcripts of interviews of Ericsson and its partners' executives. According to Ericsson website and press releases, the executives involved in the interviews collected are highly knowledgeable informants because they were positioned at various significant managerial levels or were involved in any of the alliances formed by the focal firm from 1994 to 2014. We summarize the main data sources used to analyze Ericsson's alliances in Table 10.2.

TABLE 10.2 Data Sources

Data Source	Details
Alliance announcements	92 press releases from SDC and Factiva database from 1994 to 2014
Ericsson website, and other online sources (e.g., SEC Edgar, Internet Archive)	SEC filings (annual reports, 10-Q reports and 10-K reports from 1994 to 2014). Ericsson news releases from founding to 2014.
Interviews	24 transcripts of interviews from Ericsson and alliance partners executives published in Factiva database.
Social networks	Ericsson posts on Facebook, LinkedIn, Twitter, Google plus about its relationships with alliance partners.
Videos	100 videos of Ericsson about its networks of partners on Ericsson YouTube channel (section networks) ranging from 1 to 6 minutes.

Temporal Bracketing

The focal period under inquiry ranges from 1994 to 2014. To better scrutinize the relevance of the three alliance partner characteristics across these 2 decades, we have analyzed the data through temporal bracketing (Langley, 1999; Van de Ven & Poole, 1995). By understanding the temporal progressions of alliance partner size, alliance partner diversity, and alliance partner internationalization, the case study led us to observe some interesting aspects of the relevance of these three alliance partner characteristics over time. To exemplify this, we have divided the 21 years under scrutiny into three temporal phases (i.e., Phase I, 1994–2000; Phase II, 2001–2007; and Phase III, 2008–2014). The methodological choice to partition Ericsson's alliance partner characteristics in the three phases is justified by three key reasons. First, making comparisons of alliance partner size, alliance partner diversity, and alliance partner internationalization across the three temporal phases is a particularly attractive approach for conducting a detailed appreciation of the relevance of these three alliance partner characteristics over time as each phase in which we observe alliance partner size, alliance partner diversity, and alliance partner internationalization comprises 7 years of observations. Thus, an appreciation of the relevance of these three alliance partner characteristics is not affected by differences in terms of years of observations among the three phases.

Second, temporal decomposition enriches the external validity of this study (Eisenhardt, 1989) because we consider as cut-off two external events that burst with marked economic implications for Ericsson: (a) the dot-com bubble in 2001 and (b) economic recession in 2007.

Finally, using temporal bracketing, we investigated how "actions of one period lead to changes in the context that will affect action in subsequent periods" (Langley, 1999, p. 703). In this sense, the research strategy to single out the time scale into successive periods is effectively suitable as it consents us to comprehend how Ericsson was able to shape its alliance partner over time by leveraging on its alliance partner characteristics.

DATA ANALYSIS OF THE ERICSSON CASE

The notable amount of data collected about Ericsson's alliance case study provides the basis to use an inductive case-based approach that allows us to offer a detailed analysis of the alliance partner management phenomenon in a real context. In this vein, the study seeks to offer a crystallized understanding of the relevance of the main features that, according to extant alliance literature, characterize alliance partners over time. Consequently, in the subsections that follow, we shall show empirical evidence of alliance partner size, alliance partner diversity, and alliance partner internationalization in

Ericsson's alliances. Then, we proceed by making a comparison of these three alliance partner characteristics across the three different temporal phases.

Ericsson's Alliance Partner Size

As previously argued, alliance research points to the importance of the alliance partner as one of the main features that characterize the alliance partner management phenomenon. Alliance partner size has been traditionally operationalized in two ways: (a) the number of alliances in which a focal firm is involved (Wassmer, 2010) or (b) the number of partners to which the focal firm is related to (Hoffman, 2007). Accordingly, in this study, we have calculated alliance partner size by considering both the number of alliances and the number of partners of Ericsson's alliances. As regards to the number of alliances, Table 10.3 shows that Ericsson has

TABLE 10.3 Ericsson's Alliance Partner Size (1994–2014)

Year	Number of Alliances	Number of Partners	Number of Alliances*	Number of Partners*
1994	0	0	0	0
1995	1	2	1	2
1996	1	2	1	2
1997	1	2	1	2
1998	1	2	1	2
1999	2	3	2	3
2000	14	25	13	23
2001	19	32	18	30
2002	27	48	26	46
2003	29	50	28	48
2004	39	67	37	64
2005	39	67	25	42
2006	43	72	24	40
2007	48	77	21	29
2008	56	90	27	40
2009	61	99	22	32
2010	66	105	27	38
2011	64	108	26	36
2012	66	110	23	33
2013	71	115	20	25
2014	74	118	18	19

* Indicates that we consider alive each alliance for 5 years (Stuart, 2000).

formed an increasing number of alliances over time. In particular, in the years 2000, 2004, and 2008, Ericsson has consistently enlarged the size of its alliance portfolio by forming 12, 10, and 8 alliances, respectively.

We found similar findings by considering the number of partners involved in Ericsson's alliances. Indeed, as Table 10.4 shows, in the years 2000, 2004, and 2008, Ericsson has enlarged the size of its alliance portfolio by involving respectively 22, 17, and 13 partners.

Hence, independently from the dimensions or the variable chosen to compute alliance partner size—that is, (a) the number of alliances in which a focal firm is involved (Wassmer, 2010) or (b) the number of partners to which the focal firm is related to (Hoffman, 2007)—what this analysis seems to show as unquestionable is that Ericsson has invested a lot of resources and efforts to enlarge its alliance portfolio over time. Accordingly,

TABLE 10.4 Ericsson's Alliance Partner Diversity (1994–2014)

Year	Number of Partners	Number of Different Partners	Number of Partners*	Number of Different Partners*
1994	0	0	0	0
1995	2	2	2	2
1996	2	2	2	2
1997	2	2	2	2
1998	2	2	2	2
1999	3	3	3	3
2000	25	25	23	23
2001	32	32	30	30
2002	48	47	46	45
2003	50	49	48	47
2004	67	63	64	60
2005	67	63	42	38
2006	72	66	40	34
2007	77	70	29	23
2008	90	81	40	32
2009	99	88	32	25
2010	105	92	38	29
2011	108	95	36	29
2012	110	97	33	28
2013	115	100	25	22
2014	118	101	19	16

* Indicates that we consider alive each alliance for 5 years (Stuart, 2000).

Ericsson's alliance partner case study seems to show that Ericsson involves large partners in its alliances. Thus, this finding seems to support the stream of alliance literature (Deeds, DeCarolis, & Coombs, 2000; Lahiri & Narayanan, 2013; Sampson, 2007) that argues that a large alliance partner might be beneficial for the focal firm performance.

Ericsson's Alliance Partner Diversity

Alliance research also suggests that alliance partner diversity is another feature that epitomizes the alliance partner management phenomenon. Alliance partner diversity relates to the degree of variance in partners, alliances, and resources that the focal firm has access to via its alliances (Jiang et al., 2010). Following previous literature, we have calculated alliance partner diversity by considering the degree of variance among alliance partners.

According to our data, we noted that Ericsson presents a wide array of diverse partners. Indeed, as Table 10.4 shows, the number of different partners involved by Ericsson does not appear to diverge significantly from the number of total partners which Ericsson is engaged with. Ericsson has devoted attention to maintain a certain level of partners' heterogeneity in its alliance portfolio over time, thereby gaining benefits that stem from such heterogeneity (Hoffmann, 2007; Swaminathan & Moorman, 2009; Wuyts et al., 2004). Notwithstanding that, the relevance of a high degree of variance among Ericsson's alliance partners does not indicate that Ericsson is not prone to repeat or renew its alliances with the same partners. For instance, Ericsson has formed five strategic collaborations with Telefonica (in the years 2000, 2001, 2005, 2010, and 2014), four strategic agreements with Microsoft (in the years 1999, 2000, 2003, and 2005), Motorola (in the years 2002, 2005, 2006, and 2010), and Samsung (in years 2002, 2005, 2008, and 2014). Beyond these collaborations, Ericsson's alliance case study seems to show that this focal firm has managed its alliances by relying on diverse partners over time, thereby supporting the stream of alliance literature that emphasizes the benefits that are associated with high degrees of alliance partner diversity among alliance partners.

Ericsson's Alliance Partner Internationalization

Alliance partner internationalization is the last feature that, according to extant alliance research, characterizes the alliance partner management phenomenon. It relates to the degree of foreign partners in a firm's collection of immediate alliance relationships (Lavie & Miller, 2008). Accordingly, we have calculated Ericsson's alliance partner internationalization by considering the country of origin of alliance partners.

We observed that Ericsson's alliances are characterized by the presence of an extensive array of foreign partners. Indeed, as Table 10.5 shows, regardless of the year we take into consideration, the number of foreign partners that are involved in Ericsson's alliances seems to converge significantly to the number of total partners to which Ericsson is connected to. In the years 1995, 1996, 1997, 1998, and 1999 the number of foreign partners in Ericsson's alliances seems to correspond to the number of total partners that are present in Ericsson's alliances. Thus, Ericsson's alliance case study seems to show that allying with foreign partners plays a central role in Ericsson's alliance partner management. In fact, as Table 10.5 shows, Ericsson has managed its alliances by involving a consistent number of partners from various countries

TABLE 10.5 Ericsson's Alliance Partner Internationalization (1994–2014)

Year	Number of Partners	Number of Foreign Partners	Number of Partners*	Number of Foreign Partners*
1994	0	0	0	0
1995	2	2	2	2
1996	2	2	2	2
1997	2	2	2	2
1998	2	2	2	2
1999	3	3	3	3
2000	25	22	23	20
2001	32	28	30	26
2002	48	44	46	42
2003	50	46	48	44
2004	67	63	64	60
2005	67	63	42	41
2006	72	68	40	40
2007	77	73	29	29
2008	90	86	40	40
2009	99	93	32	30
2010	105	99	38	36
2011	108	102	36	34
2012	110	104	33	31
2013	115	109	25	23
2014	118	112	19	19

* Indicates that we consider alive each alliance for 5 years (Stuart, 2000).

over the globe. Moreover, in Ericsson's alliance case study, we noted that Ericsson has formed only a few alliances with national partners. Indeed, Ericsson has created one strategic partnership with Investor AB, Industrivarden, and Swedbank (in 2000), one collaborative agreement with Skandia Insurance (in 2001) and, lastly, two strategic alliances with TeliaSonera (in 2009).

Hence, drawing on these results, this analysis seems to show that cross-national differences are relevant for the management of Ericsson's alliance partners. Thus, this insight seems to support the stream of alliance research that pinpoints the importance of the benefits associated with the presence of high degrees of international partners (Eisenhardt & Schoonhoven, 1996; García-Canal et al., 2002; Zaheer, 2000).

Summing up, the analysis of Ericsson's alliance case study sheds light on the relevance of the three main features that, according to extant alliance research, epitomize the management of alliance partners, that is, alliance partner size, alliance partner diversity, and alliance partner internationalization. Additionally, this analysis shows how Ericsson, a successful firm that operates in the telecom industry, manages its alliances by leveraging on the formation of several alliances with plenty of diverse and foreign partners over time.

DISCUSSION AND CONCLUSION

In the previous section, we have provided empirical evidence of alliance partner size, alliance partner diversity, and alliance partner internationalization in Ericsson's alliances. In this section, we will compare these three alliance partner characteristics over time.

To achieve this objective, we have decomposed the period of observation into three temporal phases: Phase I (from 1994 to 2000), Phase II (from 2001 to 2007), and Phase III (from 2008 to 2014); and we have juxtaposed the relevance of alliance partner size, alliance partner diversity, and alliance partner internationalization during each phase. The results of this analysis highlight two important aspects. First, alliance partner size, alliance partner diversity, and alliance partner internationalization present different levels of relevance across the three temporal phases. We observe that Phase I is characterized by the prominence of alliance partner diversity, while Phase II is epitomized by the prominence of alliance partner size, and Phase III is characterized by high levels of relevance of alliance partner internationalization. The findings of the temporal decomposition of Ericsson's alliance partner characteristics across the three phases are reported in Table 10.6. Second, we note that the different levels of relevance of alliance partner size, alliance partner diversity, and alliance partner internationalization across the three temporal phases are not random. Ericsson has changed its alliances over time by accruing the benefits and learning from the challenges that stem from high levels of

TABLE 10.6 A Comparison Among Ericsson's APS, APD, and API Over Time

Year	Alliance Partner Size: Number of Partners	Alliance Partner Diversity: Number of Different Partners	Alliance Partner Diversity: Number of Partners/Number of Different Partners	Alliance Partner Internationalization: Number of Foreign Partners	Alliance Partner Internationalization: Number of Partners/Number of Foreign Partners
Phase I (from 1994 to 2000)					
1994	0	0	0	0	0
1995	2	2	1	2	1
1996	2	2	1	2	1
1997	2	2	1	2	1
1998	2	2	1	2	1
1999	3	3	1	3	1
2000	25	23	1,09	22	1,14
Phase II (from 2001 to 2007)					
2001	32	32	1,00	28	1,14
2002	48	47	1,02	44	1,09
2003	50	49	1,02	46	1,09
2004	67	63	1,06	63	1,06
2005	67	63	1,06	63	1,06
2006	72	66	1,09	68	1,06
2007	77	70	1,10	73	1,05
Phase III (from 2008 to 2014)					
2008	90	81	1,11	86	1,05
2009	99	88	1,13	93	1,06
2010	105	92	1,14	99	1,06
2011	108	95	1,14	102	1,06
2012	110	97	1,13	104	1,06
2013	115	100	1,15	109	1,06
2014	118	101	1,17	112	1,05

alliance partner diversity (Phase I) as well as high levels of alliance partner size (Phase II). In doing so, Ericsson has progressively changed its alliances by shifting from an alliance partner diversity strategy (Phase I) to an alliance partner size strategy (Phase II), to an alliance partner internationalization strategy (Phase III). In the sections that follow, we discuss how Ericsson has successfully changed its alliances by managing these three alliance partner characteristics over time.

Phase I (from 1994 to 2000)

By comparing the relevance of alliance partner size, alliance partner diversity, and alliance partner internationalization in Phase I, we observe that Ericsson's alliance case study presents higher levels of alliance partner diversity than those of alliance partner size and alliance partner internationalization (Table 10.6). Table 10.6 also shows that Ericsson has established all alliances with diverse partners. The 25 partners involved in its alliances differ with regard to the knowledge and information they bring. This result suggests that in Phase I Ericsson has devoted its attention to involving different partners with different knowledge and information in its alliance alliances. By involving different partners in its alliances, Ericsson has leveraged on the benefits that stem from the heterogeneity of resources of its partners. Indeed, more variety of partners allowed Ericsson to access new resources (Swaminathan & Moorman, 2009) and to coordinate its internal R&D efforts (Noseleit & de Faria, 2013). For instance, this insight is apparent from the alliance that Ericsson has formed in 2000 with Telefonica Moviles:

> This joint venture will focus on the development of services and the creation and marketing of GSM, GPRS, and UMTS mobile telephony products. Ericsson and Telefonica Moviles plan to bring in a third partner specializing in information technology and an institutional investor, according to the statement, which provides no further details. Telefonica Moviles, Telefonica's mobile telephony subsidiary, will shortly float a part of its capital on the stock exchange. (Ericsson's Chief Operative Officer; Ericsson, 2000a)

Moreover, Ericsson's alliances inquiry also suggests that more variety in partners has allowed Ericsson to build new technologies and mobile products (Wuyts et al., 2004). In fact, in 2000 Ericsson has formed a multipartner alliance with Investor AB, Industrivarden, and Merrill Lynch to create new mobile products based on Internet technologies:

> "We expect more mobile Internet users than fixed Internet users already by 2003, and this means an incredible demand for building out networks and creating new services. By joining the knowledge of these four venture partners this initiative will provide a very strong drive for the creation of the mobile Internet." (Ericsson's Chief Executive Officer; Ericsson, 2000b)

Phase II (from 2001 to 2007)

In Phase I of our alliance case study it is apparent that Ericsson has devoted its efforts to forming alliances with different partners to access new resources and create new technologies and products. Thus, Ericsson has benefited from the heterogeneity of resources, knowledge, and information that is associated with high levels of alliance partner diversity. However, moving to Phase II of Ericsson's alliance study, we observe that Ericsson has changed its alliance partner strategy. In fact, in this period, which ranges from 2001 to 2007, Ericsson seems to have started to pay attention to the size of its alliance partners. More precisely, in Phase II Ericsson has enlarged its alliance partner size by forming a considerable number of alliances, thereby increasing the number of partners involved in its alliances. Indeed, as Table 10.6 shows, the Phase II of Ericsson's alliance case study presents high levels of alliance partner size. Accordingly, by comparing the number of partners involved at the end of Phase I (25 partners) with the number of partners at the end of Phase II (77 partners), we note that Ericsson has expanded its alliances by forming alliances with 52 additional partners. The strategic decision to focus on alliance partner size, rather than on alliance partner diversity and alliance partner internationalization, is due to two main reasons. First, Ericsson has involved several partners to leverage external knowledge (Bouncken & Fredrich, 2016) and to achieve economies of scale and volume flexibility from more than one alliance (Di Minin, Frattini, & Piccaluga, 2010; Lahiri & Narayanan, 2013). Accordingly, this insight is evident in the strategic alliance formed with Flextronics in 2001:

> In light of a significant change in the world market for mobile phones we have decided to fundamentally change the setup of our business...The alliance with Flextronics will enable us to achieve economies of scale and volume flexibility...We are committed to remain a top player in mobile phones...With this new set-up, we respond to a much tougher business environment, and we create a sound basis for long-term profitability. (Ericsson's Vice President; *EE Times*, 2001)

Second, Ericsson's alliance case study shows that in Phase II Ericsson has enlarged its alliance portfolio to develop a more comprehensive understanding of the diverse knowledge bases of its partners over time (Bouncken & Fredrich, 2016; Deeds et al., 2000). Indeed, at the end of 2004 Ericsson has formed an alliance with ParaRede and Cisco Systems to cross-leverage knowledge from a previous alliance with Cisco System:

> The companies plan to provide broadband Internet access featuring voice, data, and multimedia transmission via local fixed-line phone operators. Ericsson and Cisco Systems will provide the access technology and ParaRede will manage the implementation of the new technology in Portuguese fixed-line phone operators. ParaRede's partnership with Ericsson and Cisco Systems is a consequence of a strategic partnership established between Erics-

son and Cisco at the end of April 2004. (Ericsson's Chief Executive Officer; Ericsson, 2004)

Phase III (from 2008 to 2014)

In Phase III we note that it is alliance partner internationalization that assumes paramount importance *vis-a-vis* alliance partner size and alliance partner diversity. Hence, Ericsson's alliances inquiry suggests that, from 2008 to 2014, Ericsson has devoted its attention to include several foreign partners. Indeed, as Table 10.6 shows, in 2014 Ericsson involved 112 foreign partners. This result shows that, in Phase III, Ericsson has managed its alliance partners by leveraging on the cross-national cultural, geographical, institutional, and economic development divergences of its alliance partners (Ghemawat, 2001). Two reasons have led Ericsson to focus on alliance partner internationalization. First, a high degree of foreign partners has contributed to improving Ericsson's flexibility and its capacity to be responsive to turbulent and dynamic environmental changes (Eisenhardt & Schoonhoven, 1996). This insight is evident in the alliance formed with LG-Electronics in 2010:

> Korea is one of the largest telecom markets with advanced end-user demand for new services. A strengthening of our position through the collaboration with our new partner LG Electronics will enhance our position for future technology shifts such as LTE. (Ericsson's President; Ericsson, 2010)

Second, it allows Ericsson to allocate its activities over the world in a way to ameliorate its market position in technology-driven industries (Zaheer, 2000). This insight is evident in the alliance formed with T-Mobile in 2008:

> This strategic partnership is an important milestone in Ericsson's relationship with T-Mobile. It underlines our strong market position and means Ericsson is now a supplier to all Dutch operators. (President of Ericsson Netherlands; Ericsson, 2008)

Summing up, the comparison of the relevance among alliance partner size, alliance partner diversity, and alliance partner internationalization across the three phases of Ericsson's alliance study sheds additional light on how Ericsson has changed its alliance partner strategy over time. In Phase I (from 1994 to 2000), Ericsson has formed alliances with different partners, thereby benefiting from the heterogeneity of resources that stems from high levels of alliance partner diversity. In Phase II (from 2001 to 2007), Ericsson has changed its alliance partner strategy by giving more importance to the size of its partners. Accordingly, it has enlarged its alliance portfolio size by forming a considerable amount of alliances with several partners. In Phase III (from 2008 to 2014) Ericsson has paid specific attention to its alliance partner internationalization, thereby leveraging the cultural, geographical, institutional, and economic development differences of its alliance partners. Drawing on these findings, in the following section we discuss the theoretical and managerial implications and advance a few research questions that might stimulate additional research on alliance partner management.

THEORETICAL AND MANAGERIAL IMPLICATIONS

This study advances three theoretical implications for strategic alliance research. First, it provides a more comprehensive understanding of how alliances are constituted and how they function (Halinen & Törnroos, 2005). More specifically, this study unveils three main features (alliance partner size, alliance partner diversity, and alliance partner internationalization) that epitomize the management of alliance partners.

Second, this study discusses empirical evidence about these three alliance partner characteristics in a business context (Halinen & Törnroos, 2005). By conducting an in-depth longitudinal case study of the alliances that Ericsson has managed from 1994 to 2014, the study shows that alliance partner size, alliance partner diversity, and alliance partner internationalization are relevant for the management of Ericsson's alliance partners. Drawing on the analysis of Ericsson's alliances over time, this study also shows how this successful firm of the telecom industry has consistently devoted its resources and efforts in developing an alliance portfolio characterized by the presence of several alliances with an increasing amount of diverse and foreign partners over time. In doing so, the study enriches the array of qualitative studies on the evolution of alliance portfolios (Castro, Casanueva, & Galán, 2014; Lavie & Singh, 2011).

Finally, the study contributes to the stream of alliance literature that argues that three main characteristics are critical to the alliance partner management phenomenon as they present both benefits and challenges for the management of alliance partners. Indeed, by tapping into Ericsson's alliances, the study shows how Ericsson has managed its alliances by leveraging on the benefits that are associated with alliance partner size, alliance partner diversity, and alliance partner internationalization.

As concerns managerial implications, the study shows that alliance managers should pay attention to managing the attributes of the partners they ally with. By analyzing the alliances that Ericsson has formed in the last 2 decades, the study shows how a successful firm in the telecom industry faces the challenge of managing alliance partner attributes per time. Hence, how a focal firm can successfully manage alliance partner size, alliance partner diversity, and alliance partner internationalization is a significant question whose importance cannot be ignored by alliance managers.

Moreover, alliance managers need to develop a more comprehensive understanding of the main features that characterize the alliances they manage. Alliance partner size, alliance partner diversity, and alliance partner internationalization are three key characteristics that pose both benefits and challenges to the management of alliance partners. This study shows that alliance managers should pay considerable attention to the three key characteristics that epitomize their alliances: (a) the number of alliances they intend to form (as well as the partners they are willing to ally with); (b) the variety of partners, resources and alliances that might be present in their alliances; and (c) the differences that might exist between their company and its foreign partners' countries of origin.

Limitations and Future Research

This study offers new insights into the management of alliances subject to the caveat that it is based on observations regarding a single firm operating in the telecom industry. Nevertheless, future research can elaborate and formalize additional insights by leveraging multi-firm research designs (Eisenhardt & Graebner, 2007). In this vein, future studies may confirm, enlarge, or restrict the validity of the results of this study by conducting multiple comparative case studies research.

Moreover, we have focused our analysis on the three main features (i.e., alliance partner size, alliance partner diversity, and alliance partner internationalization) that, according to extant alliance literature, epitomize alliance partner management. To explore additional important features of alliance partner management phenomenon, future studies may investigate whether alliance portfolio structural characteristics such as alliance portfolio density, alliance portfolio cohesion, and alliance portfolio centrality might also be relevant for the management of alliance portfolio.

Finally, this study has not empirically analyzed the interrelationships between the three alliance partner characteristics. Since the analysis of interrelationships between alliance issues is gaining more importance in alliance research (Castro, Roldán, & Acedo, 2015), future studies may apply variance-based structural equation modeling to examine the relationships between the three alliance partner characteristics.

REFERENCES

Bakker, R. M., & Knoben, J. (2014). Built to last or meant to end: Intertemporal choice in strategic alliance portfolios. *Organization Science, 26*(1), 256–276.

Bamford, J. D., Gomes-Casseres, B., & Robinson, M. S. (2003). *Mastering alliance strategy.* San Francisco, CA: Jossey-Bass.

Baum, J. A. C., Calabrese, T., & Silverman, B. S. (2000). Don't go it alone: Alliance network composition and start-ups' performance in Canadian biotechnology. *Strategic Management Journal, 21*(3), 267–294.

Belgraver, H., & Verwaal, E. (2018). Organizational capital, production factor resources, and relative firm size in strategic equity alliances. *Small Business Economics, 50*(4), 825–849.

Blasingame, J. (2016). *Why strategic alliances are a 21st century imperative.* Retrieved from https://www.forbes.com/sites/jimblasingame/2016/12/10/why-strategic-alliances-are-a-21st-century-imperative/

Bouncken, R. B., & Fredrich, V. (2016). Learning in coopetition: Alliance orientation, network size, and firm types. *Journal of Business Research, 69*(5), 1753–1758.

Castro, I., Casanueva, C., & Galán, J. L. (2014). Dynamic evolution of alliance portfolios. *European Management Journal, 32*(3), 423–433.

Castro, I., Roldán, J. L., & Acedo, F. J. (2015). The dimensions of alliance portfolio configuration: A mediation model. *Journal of Management & Organization, 21*(2), 176–202.

Cohen, W. M., & Levinthal, D. A. (1990). Absorptive capacity: A new perspective on learning and innovation. *Administrative Science Quarterly, 35*(1), 128–152.

Cook, T. D., Campbell, D. T., & Day, A. (1979). *Quasi-experimentation: Design & analysis issues for field settings.* Boston, MA: Houghton Mifflin.

Cui, A. S., & O'Connor, G. (2012). Alliance portfolio resource diversity and firm innovation. *Journal of Marketing, 76*(4), 24–43.

Dagnino, G. B., & Ferrigno, G. (2015). The strategic management of multipartner alliances: Uncovering the triadic alliance problem. In T. K. Das (Ed.), *Managing multipartner strategic alliances* (pp. 135–169). Charlotte, NC: Information Age.

de Leeuw, T., Lokshin, B., & Duysters, G. (2014). Returns to alliance portfolio diversity: The relative effects of partner diversity on firm's innovative performance and productivity. *Journal of Business Research,* 67(9), 1839–1849.

Deeds, D. L., DeCarolis, D., & Coombs, J. (2000). Dynamic capabilities and new product development in high technology ventures: An empirical analysis of new biotechnology firms. *Journal of Business Venturing, 15*(3), 211–229.

Di Minin, A., & Bianchi, M. (2011). Safe nests in global nets: Internationalization and appropriability of R&D in wireless telecom. *Journal of International Business Studies, 42*(7), 910–934.

Di Minin, A., Frattini, F., & Piccaluga, A. (2010). Fiat: Open innovation in a downturn (1993–2003). *California Management Review, 52*(3), 132–159.

Dussauge, P., Garrette, B., & Mitchell, W. (2000). Learning from competing partners: Outcomes and durations of scale and link alliances in Europe, North America and Asia. *Strategic Management Journal, 21*(2), 99–126.

Duysters, G., Kok, G., & Vaandrager, M. (1999). Crafting successful strategic technology partnerships. *R&D Management, 29*(4), 343–351.

Duysters, G., & Lokshin, B. (2011). Determinants of alliance portfolio complexity and its effect on innovative performance of companies. *Journal of Product Innovation Management, 28*(4), 570–585.

EE Times. (2001). *Ericsson to cease production of mobile handsets.* https://www.edn.com/ericsson-to-cease-production-of-mobile-handsets/ (accessed June 15, 2021)

Eisenhardt, K.M. (1989). Building theories from case study research. *Academy of Management Review, 14*(4), 532–550.

Eisenhardt, K., & Graebner, M. (2007). Theory building from cases: Opportunities and challenges. *Academy of Management Journal, 50*(1), 25–32.

Eisenhardt, K. M., & Schoonhoven, C. B. (1996). Resource-based view of strategic alliance formation: Strategic and social effects in entrepreneurial firms. *Organization Science, 7*(2), 136–150.

Ericsson. (2000a). [Internal press release.] Unpublished internal company document.

Ericsson. (2000b). [Internal press release.] Unpublished internal company document.

Ericsson. (2004). [Internal press release.] Unpublished internal company document.

Ericsson. (2008). [Internal press release.] Unpublished internal company document.

Ericsson. (2010). [Internal press release.] Unpublished internal company document.

Ferrigno, G. (2017). Looking for alliance portfolio characteristics: The case of telecom industry. In T. K. Das (Ed.), *Managing alliance portfolios and networks* (pp. 177–201). Charlotte, NC: Information Age.

García-Canal, E., Duarte, C. L., Criado, J. R., & Llaneza, A. V. (2002). Accelerating international expansion through global alliances: A typology of cooperative strategies. *Journal of World Business, 37*(2), 91–107.

Gerring, J. (2007) *Case study research.* Cambridge, MA: Cambridge University Press.

Ghemawat, P. (2001). Distance still matters. *Harvard Business Review, 79*(8), 137–147.

Glaser, B. G., & Strauss, A. L. (1967). *The discovery of grounded theory: Strategies for qualitative research.* Chicago, IL: Aldine.

Gomes-Casseres, B. (2015). *Remix strategy: The three laws of business combinations.* Boston, MA: Harvard Business Review Press.

Halinen, A., & Törnroos, J. Å. (2005). Using case methods in the study of contemporary business networks. *Journal of Business Research, 58*(9), 1285–1297.

Hamel, G. (1991). Competition for competence and interpartner learning within international strategic alliances. *Strategic Management Journal, 12*(1), 83–103.

Hoffmann, W. H. (2007). Strategies for managing a portfolio of alliances. *Strategic Management Journal, 28* (8), 827–856.

Jiang, R. J., Tao, Q. T., & Santoro, M. D. (2010). Alliance portfolio diversity and firm performance. *Strategic Management Journal, 31*(10), 1136–1144.

Jick, T. D. (1979). Mixing qualitative and quantitative methods: Triangulation in action. *Administrative Science Quarterly, 24*(4), 602–611.

Kale, P., Dyer, J., & Singh, H. (2002). Alliance capability, stock market response and long-term alliance success: The role of the alliance function. *Strategic Management Journal, 23*(8), 747–767.

Kale, P., & Singh, H. (2009). Managing strategic alliances: What do we know now, and where do we go from here? *Academy of Management Perspectives, 23*(3), 45–62.

Koput, K. W. (1997). A chaotic model of innovative search: Some answers, many questions. *Organization Science, 8*(5), 528–542.

Lahiri, N., & Narayanan, S. (2013). Vertical integration, innovation, and alliance portfolio size: Implications for firm performance. *Strategic Management Journal, 34*(9), 1042–1064.

Langley, A. (1999). Strategies for theorizing from process data. *Academy of Management Review, 24*(4), 691–710.

Lavie, D. (2006). The competitive advantage of interconnected firms: An extension of the resource-based view. *Academy of Management Review, 31*(3), 638–658.

Lavie, D. (2007). Alliance portfolios and firm performance: A study of value creation and appropriation in the US software industry. *Strategic Management Journal, 28*(12), 1187–1212.

Lavie, D., & Miller, S. R. (2008). Alliance portfolio internationalization and firm performance. *Organization Science, 19*(4), 623–646.

Lavie, D., & Singh, H. (2011). The evolution of alliance portfolios: The case of Unisys. *Industrial and Corporate Change, 21*(3), 763–809.

Lee, D. D., Kirkpatrick-Husk, K., & Madhavan, R. (2017). Diversity in alliance portfolios and performance outcomes: A meta-analysis. *Journal of Management, 43*(5), 1472–1497.

Lincoln, Y. S., & Denzin, N. K. (1994). The fifth moment. In N. K. Denzin & Y. S. Lincoln (Eds.), *Handbook of qualitative research* (pp. 575–586). Thousand Oaks, CA: Sage.

Mason, J. (1996). *Qualitative researching*. Newbury Park, CA: Sage.

Noseleit, F., & de Faria, P. (2013). Complementarities of internal R&D and alliances with different partner types. *Journal of Business Research, 66*(10), 2000–2006.

Oerlemans, L. A., Knoben, J., & Pretorius, M. W. (2013). Alliance portfolio diversity, radical and incremental innovation: The moderating role of technology management. *Technovation, 33*(6), 234–246.

Pangarkar, N., Yuan, L., & Hussain, S. (2017). Too much of a good thing? Alliance portfolio size and alliance expansion. *European Management Journal, 35*(4), 477–485.

Parida, V., Patel, P. C., Wincent, J., & Kohtamäki, M. (2016). Network partner diversity, network capability, and sales growth in small firms. *Journal of business research, 69*(6), 2113–2117.

Parkhe, A. (1991). Interfirm diversity, organizational learning, and longevity in global strategic alliances. *Journal of International Business Studies, 22*(4), 579–601.

Pettigrew, A. M. (1990). Longitudinal field research on change: Theory and practice. *Organization Science, 1*(3), 267–292.

Ravenswood, K. (2011). Eisenhardt's impact on theory in case study research. *Journal of Business Research, 64*(7), 680–686.

Ritter, T., & Gemünden, H. G. (2003). Interorganizational relationships and networks: An overview. *Journal of Business Research, 56*(9), 691–697.

Sampson, R. C. (2007). R&D alliances and firm performance: The impact of technological diversity and alliance organization on innovation. *Academy of Management Journal, 50*(2), 364–386.

Sarkar, M. B., Aulakh, P. S., & Madhok, A. (2009). Process capabilities and value generation in alliance portfolios. *Organization Science, 20*(3), 583–600.

Siggelkow, N. (2007). Persuasion with case studies. *Academy of Management Journal, 50*(1), 50–24.

Steensma, H. K., & Lyles, M. A. (2000). Explaining IJV survival in a transitional economy through social exchange and knowledge-based perspectives. *Strategic Management Journal, 21*(8), 831–851.

Stuart, T. E. (2000). Interorganizational alliances and the performance of firms: A study of growth and innovation rates in a high-technology industry. *Strategic Management Journal, 21*(8), 791–811.

Swaminathan, V., & Moorman, C. (2009). Marketing alliances, firm networks, and firm value creation. *Journal of Marketing, 73*(5), 52–69.

Van de Ven, A. H., & Poole, M. S. (1995). Explaining development and change in organizations. *Academy of Management Review, 20*(3), 510–540.

Vasudeva, G., & Anand, J. (2011). Unpacking absorptive capacity: A study of knowledge utilization from alliance portfolios. *Academy of Management Journal, 54*(3), 611–623.

Wassmer, U. (2010). Alliance portfolios: A review and research agenda. *Journal of Management, 36*(1), 141–171.

Wassmer, U., & Dussauge, P. (2012). Network resource stocks and flows: How do alliance portfolios affect the value of new alliance formations? *Strategic Management Journal, 33*(7), 871–883.

Wuyts, S., Dutta, S., & Stremersch, S. (2004). Portfolios of interfirm agreements in technology-intensive markets: Consequences for innovation and profitability. *Journal of Marketing, 68*(2), 88–100.

Yin, R. K. (2003). *Case study research: Design and methods.* Thousand Oaks, CA: Sage.

Yin, R. K. (2009). *Case study research: Design and methods* (4th ed.). Newbury Park, CA: Sage.

Zaheer, S. (2000). Time zone economics and managerial work in a global world. In P. C. Earley & H. Singh (Eds.), *Innovations in international and cross-cultural management* (pp. 339–353). Thousand Oaks, CA: Sage.

CHAPTER 11

INTERPARTNER LEARNING DYNAMICS IN AN ALLIANCE CONSTELLATION

Megan Woods
Rob Hecker

ABSTRACT

Despite the widespread usage of strategic alliances and the complexity of their operation, the dynamics of alliance processes are still not well understood. Co-evolutionary perspectives of alliances suggest that alliances evolve through adaptive learning processes: as organizations learn about the alliance environment and their alliance partners, they adapt their understanding of both and adjust their contributions to the alliance accordingly. The focus of extant research on the learning undertaken at the firm level means the question of how partners' learning processes interact remains largely unexplored. This chapter advances understanding of interpartner learning dynamics by detailing the interactive learning processes that informed the evolution of an alliance constellation. The chapter reports a retrospective case study of a star-like alliance constellation which examined the adaptive learning processes experienced by the constellation manager and the 14 constellation members from 1992 to 2005. The study shows that partners' learning processes

Managing the Partners in Strategic Alliances, pages 271–298

interacted as they progressively developed and applied their knowledge about constellation management and constellation participation.

ALLIANCE CO-EVOLUTION

Despite the widespread usage of strategic alliances and the complexity of their operation, alliance processes are still not well understood (Bell, den Outen, & Ziggers, 2006; Ness, 2009). In recent years, alliance scholars have investigated alliance processes by adopting co-evolutionary perspectives (Wilson & Hynes, 2009). Co-evolution refers to the simultaneous evolution of parts of a system so a co-evolutionary view of alliances considers how alliance partners, alliance environments, and alliance activities influence each other as they develop over the course of the collaboration (Das & Teng, 2002). More specifically, co-evolutionary perspectives consider how alliance partners, alliance environments, and alliance activities co-evolve with alliance conditions. Alliance conditions are the characteristics of an alliance at any given point in its lifetime (Das & Teng, 2002). Alliance conditions incorporate elements such as the levels of trust and relational capital between alliance partners (Ariño, de la Torre, & Ring, 2001; Inkpen & Currall, 2004), the nature of the alliance contract (Lee & Cavusgil, 2006; Reuer & Ariño, 2002), the structures established to facilitate alliance activities (Doz, 1996), and the mechanisms used to facilitate knowledge-sharing between partners (Woods & Hecker, 2011).

Scholars of alliance co-evolution suggest that alliance environments co-evolve with alliance conditions. Das and Teng (2002) proposed that changes in the organizational alliance environment (defined as the partner firms' characteristics) influence the alliance conditions by affecting the collective strengths, interpartner conflicts, and interdependencies of the alliance. Conversely, changes to the alliance conditions affect the alliance environment by affecting the characteristics of the partner firms. Other scholars have examined the co-evolution of alliances and their environments and found that market conditions and competitive dynamics also co-evolve with alliance conditions. Market conditions and competitive dynamics affect alliance evolution by affecting the goals and nature of alliance activity (Koza & Lewin, 1998). Correspondingly, alliance activities affect market conditions and competitive dynamics by affecting the competitive positions of alliance and partner firms (Browning, Beyer, & Shetler, 1995).

Studies of alliance evolution have also found that alliances co-evolve with alliance partners. Research examining the co-evolution of alliances and alliance partners suggests that over the course of their collaboration, alliance partners co-evolve with each other through continuous cycles of actions and reactions (Lui & Ngo, 2005). As they engage in collaboration partners adjust their contributions to alliance activities as they respond to each other, to the outcomes produced from alliance activities, and to the benefits they receive from the collaboration (Das & Kumar, 2007). More specifically, alliance partners co-evolve with each other and their alliance relationship as a consequence of adaptive learning.

ADAPTIVE LEARNING IN STRATEGIC ALLIANCES

As partners collaborate they engage in iterative cycles of adaptive learning through which they develop their understanding of effective alliance operation (D'Aunno & Zuckerman, 1987). Partners form alliances with expectations about each other, future actions and future benefits, which they enact when executing their commitments to the relationship (Ring & Van de Ven, 1994). An initial trial of interorganizational collaboration provides feedback about collaboration effectiveness upon which partners' base decisions about continuing to collaborate and/or adapting their commitments and actions (Kumar & Nti, 1998; Van de Ven & Walker, 1984; Zajac & Olsen, 1993). Consequently, alliances evolve as partners learn about alliance performance and adapt their contributions to the alliance accordingly.

In other words, alliances evolve as alliance partners develop their theories of action about collaborating in alliance relationships. Theories of action refer to the understandings which individuals develop about the actions that produce desired outcomes in given situations (Argyris & Schon, 1996). Theories of action about collaboration combine mental models about the alliance environment and action routines for engaging in alliance activities. Individuals construct mental models of how the world operates (Senge, 1990), which they use to understand organizational situations (Weick & Boughton, 1986). They continuously develop knowledge about interacting with their environment through cycles of abstraction and reflection (Kolb, 1984). They predict from their cognitive maps the actions they need to interact successfully with their environment and judge from their experience the relevance and effectiveness of their models (Lembo, 1972). Confirmatory feedback strengthens the cause–effect beliefs based on current mental models and the expectation that models will effectively guide future action (Barr, Stimpert, & Huff, 1992). Contradictory feedback prompts re-evaluation of mental models and the development of new constructs to explain anomalous experiences (Laszlo, 1972). In this way, the adaptive learning in which alliance partners engage helps them to test and refine theories of action about collaboration.

Effective collaboration requires that alliance managers can develop their theories of action about collaboration and develop action routines for enacting such theories in their organizations. In a study acclaimed as the gold standard of alliance process research (Hennart, 2006; Salk, 2005), Doz (1996) found that this requires two forms of adaptive learning: cognitive learning about the factors key to the collaboration's success, and behavioral learning about how to achieve those success factors. Specifically, Doz found that partners' cognitive and behavioral learning experiences determined the developmental pathway for successful and unsuccessful alliances. In successful alliances, cognitive learning prompted subsequent behavioral learning cycles. Realizing what was needed to enhance alliance performance, partners learned how to take the actions necessary to fulfill success requirements. In unsuccessful alliances, the partners learned cognitively what was required for success but were unable to translate their cognitive learning into behavioral learning. Recognizing that they could not make the adaptations required, they terminated the alliance project.

Subsequent studies have confirmed Doz's (1996) findings that partners' learning informs the co-evolutionary pathway of their alliance and the theories of action they develop about collaboration. Ariño and de la Torre (1998) explored how learning about alliance equity and efficiency influenced alliance evolution by examining the 4-year life cycle of a failed international joint venture. They found that as partners worked together, external changes, learning about each other and learning about working together prompted periodic assessments of the efficiency, equity, and relationship quality of the venture. Perceptions of imbalances in relationship equity and efficiency motivated corrective action. Buchel's (2000, 2002) examination of a research and development joint venture between Ericsson and Hewlett Packard similarly found that the venture evolved through periodic sequences of convergence and divergence as partners interpreted new information, and converged with or diverged from each other as they renegotiated the venture on the basis of the new information. Both studies demonstrated that adaptive learning by the alliance partners affected the alliance's evolution by producing changes to the alliance conditions and to subsequent evaluations of the alliance.

Despite research evidence that partner learning processes interact and co-evolve (Ariño & de la Torre, 1998; Buchel, 2002; Doz, 1996) such interactions have yet to be integrated into conceptual models or frameworks about alliance co-evolution. Consequently, how partners affect each other's learning and the consequences this may have for learning and evolutionary processes is not well understood. This presents a research opportunity to investigate and model the interactive learning processes underpinning alliance evolution, which we have addressed by studying the evolution of an alliance constellation. In the following sections we present the method adopted and the research findings about the constellation's evolution. We conclude by presenting a conceptual model of the iterative and interactive adaptive learning processes through which the alliance constellation evolved and suggesting avenues for future research.

METHOD

To investigate how alliance partners' adaptive learning processes might interact and how this may affect alliance evolution we undertook an exploratory retrospective case study. The study examined the historical development of a hub-and-spoke alliance constellation known as the Aurora Preferred Suppliers Constellation that operates in Tasmania, an island state located off the south coast of Australia. The Aurora Preferred Suppliers Constellation comprises dyadic alliances between Aurora Energy (hereafter Aurora) and retailers of electrical heating appliances. The study examined the operation of the constellation over the 13-year period between its creation in 1992 and Tasmania's connection to the Australian national electricity grid in mid-2005. During the period examined by this study, Aurora was the only electricity retailer operating in Tasmania and hence the only energy company with whom constellation members could ally. Consequently, the study was able to isolate and explore learning outcomes which resulted exclusively from participants' experiences of the alliance constellation, enhancing the accuracy and strength of the research findings.

Four objectives framed data collection and analysis: determining the constellation's chronological history; determining the constellation's organizational design; identifying adaptations made by Aurora and constellation members to their collaboration; and determining the learning that informed these adaptations. To achieve these objectives, the study utilized data from interviews, documentation, and secondary data sources (see Table 11.1). Data were collected between September 2004 and June 2005. Secondary data sources such as newspaper articles, marketing publications, and Aurora's company documents were used to develop the initial time line of the constellation's development and identify issues for investigation in interviews. Primary data were collected through 25 semi-standardized interviews with the members of Aurora's constellation management team and managers from each of the 14 preferred supplier businesses that comprised the constellation at the time. Interviews addressed three major themes of participants' experiences: the events they experienced, their expectations for and understanding of the constellation operation, and their evaluations of constellation involvement.

QSR International's N-Vivo software program supported each phase of data analysis. Interview recordings, document extracts, and research notes were transcribed into Microsoft Word™ documents and imported into N-Vivo. Data categories ("nodes") specific to each research objective were

TABLE 11.1 Data Sources

Interview Participants	When Interviewed	Documents	Number of Pages
Aurora		Legislation & govt. reports	51
Constellation Manager	September 2004	News articles	14
	November 2004	Annual reports	180
	December 2004	Retail strategy documents	11
	April 2005	Constellation management documents	220
New Constellation Manager	January 2005	Promotional materials	96
	April 2005	Web pages	5
	June 2005	Preferred suppliers advertising	50
Constellation Marketing Manager	February 2005		
Training Officer	December 2004		
Constellation Administration Officer	December 2004		
Quality Assurance Officer	December 2004		
Preferred Suppliers			
Preferred Supplier 1	January 2005		
Preferred Supplier 2	December 2004		
Preferred Supplier 3	January 2005		
Preferred Supplier 4	December 2004		
Preferred Supplier 5	February 2005		
Preferred Supplier 6	February 2005		
Preferred Supplier 7	January 2005		
Preferred Supplier 8	March 2005		
Preferred Supplier 9	December 2004		
Preferred Supplier 10	January 2005		
Preferred Supplier 11	January 2005		
Preferred Supplier 12	December 2004		
Preferred Supplier 13	February 2005		
Preferred Supplier 14	February 2005		
Total Interviews	**25**	**Total Pages**	**627**

Source: Adapted from Woods & Hecker (2011, p. 96)

established and document contents were coded exhaustively into all relevant categories (see Table 11.2).

To optimize the study's validity and reliability we used triangulation, checks for coding accuracy, and peer review. Gathering data through

TABLE 11.2 Hierarchical Systems of Data Categories Developed to Achieve Each Analytical Objective

Major and Subsidiary Data Categories	Analytical Objective			
	Determine the constellation's chronological history	*Determine constellation conditions*	*Identify the adaptations made by Aurora and preferred suppliers to their collaboration*	*Determine the learning that informed adaptations to the collaboration*
	Aurora Preferred Suppliers Constellation 1 (1993–1997) 1993 1994 1995 1996 1997	Initial Constellation Conditions • Task definition • Interface structures • Action routines – Aurora internal routines – Preferred suppliers' internal routines • Interorganizational routines • Expectations – Aurora – Preferred suppliers	Aurora • Change alliance conditions • Change task definition • Change interface structures • Change action routines • Change expectations	Aurora Learning • Environment • Task • Partner/members • Process of working together • Constellation performance • Success factors • Self
	Aurora Preferred Suppliers Constellation 2 (1998–2005) 1998 1999 2000 2001 2002 2003 2004 2005	Adapted Constellation Conditions • Task definition • Interface structures • Action routines – Aurora internal routines – Preferred suppliers' internal routines – Interorganizational routines • Expectations – Aurora – Preferred suppliers	Preferred Suppliers • Join constellation • Utilize formal conditions • Comply with constellation conditions • Redress performance problems • Improve own capacity to benefit from constellation • Create new opportunities to benefit from constellation • Accommodate/respond to Aurora's changes • Counter interference from other preferred suppliers	Preferred Suppliers' Learning • Environment • Task • Partner/Aurora • Constellation performance • Success factors • Self

Source: Adapted from Woods & Hecker (2011, p. 98)

interviews and secondary data sources facilitated methodological triangulation. Using data from documents and participant interviews facilitated source triangulation to verify event occurrences. Executing distinct coding and interpretative stages to achieve each research outcome enabled analytical triangulation. Comparing analytical outputs and conclusions for each stage enabled checking of coding rigor and support for conclusions, as did peer review of coding accuracy. Project logs recorded the audit trail of research steps, enhancing the reliability of the research process.

THE AURORA PREFERRED SUPPLIERS CONSTELLATION

Aurora is an energy company located in Tasmania, Australia, and owned by the Tasmanian state government. Aurora was formed in 1998 when the Tasmanian government disaggregated the former Hydro Electric Commission and established Aurora as an energy retailing business. The company generates, distributes, and retails electricity and natural gas in Tasmanian and across mainland Australia as well as providing wholesale telecommunications services using optical fiber networks (Aurora Energy, 2011). In 2010–2011, Aurora employed over 1400 people across Tasmania and sold AU$1.305 billion worth of energy to customers in Tasmania and interstate (Aurora Energy, 2011).

Aurora (then known as the Hydro Electric Commission) established the Preferred Suppliers Constellation in 1993 to promote purchases of electric heating appliances, and, by extension, of electricity for heating purposes. At the time, only 27% of Tasmanian consumers utilized electric space heating (Hydro Electric Commission, 1993) due to the popularity of alternatives (such as gas and wood heating) and the high cost for electricity. To increase the appeal of electric space heating and promote sales of electricity for residential heating purposes, Aurora introduced a new electricity product which offered electricity for the operation of permanently installed residential heating appliances (e.g., air conditioners) at a rate approximately 25% cheaper than the standard light and power tariff (Hydro Electric Commission, 1992). Aurora predicted that the new product would create substantial demand for heating appliance retail channels as consumers investigated and adopted electric heating. To promote appliance purchases, Aurora established their Heating Advisory Service, a team of consultants who provided free in-home assessments of consumers' heating needs and advice about heating-related issues. Aurora also established alliance relationships with selected retailers of electric heating appliances, endorsing them as Aurora Preferred Suppliers while also promoting them to consumers as suppliers of heating appliances suitable for Tasmanian conditions.

Preferred suppliers' sales of heating systems increased, in turn, consumer uptake of the heating electricity tariff.

During 1996 and 1997, Aurora re-developed their collaborative strategies for the Aurora Preferred Suppliers Constellation in response to changing environmental conditions and strategic imperatives to increase revenues and reduce operating costs. To increase revenues, Aurora resolved to increase market share in the residential heating energy market, which in 1996 reached 45% (Hydro Electric Commission, 1996). Recognizing that advising customers about electric heating was strategically crucial to increasing market share for the residential heating tariff, Aurora reestablished the Preferred Suppliers Constellation in 1998 to establish members as Aurora-substitutes in heating advice provision. Consumers contacting Aurora for heating-related advice were directly referred to constellation members for an in-home assessment of their needs, who provided the in-home assessments of customer needs and advice about heating issues as well as selling and installing heating appliances. Under the "Aurora Preferred Suppliers" endorsement Aurora guaranteed the quality of constellation members' customer service, investigating customer complaints against preferred suppliers, and ensuring problems were rectified. Figure 11.1 illustrates the two operational models for the constellation.

Refocusing the constellation on superior customer service established new constellation conditions, performance standards, and a smaller membership of 15 preferred suppliers, two of whom later merged to establish a constellation of 14 members. Between 1998 and 2005 the constellation operated in the Tasmanian residential heating appliance market as a retail channel differentiated by superior customer service.

ADAPTIVE LEARNING IN THE ALLIANCE CONSTELLATION

During the course of establishing and operating the constellation, Aurora and the preferred suppliers developed and refined two distinct forms of knowledge. Aurora, through their alliance management team, learned how to manage an alliance constellation. Preferred suppliers learned how to operate as constellation members. Figure 11.2 illustrates the adaptive learning interactions through which developed their knowledge over the constellation's lifetime.

Interactive Learning Through the Creation of the Constellation

Creating the constellation instigated the first phase of Aurora's and the constellation members' learning about the constellation's operation.

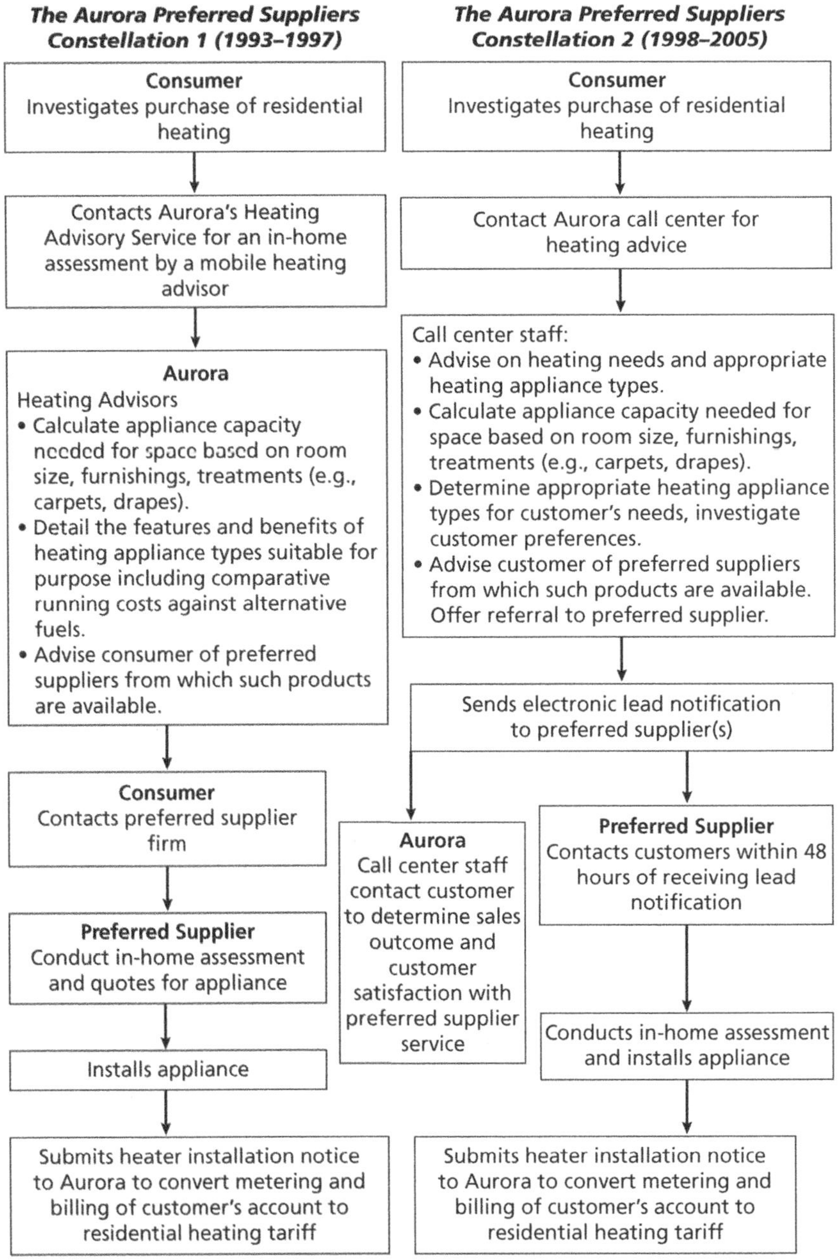

Figure 11.1 Operation of the preferred suppliers constellation as a retail channel for electric heating appliances. *Source:* Adapted from Woods & Hecker (2011, p. 100).

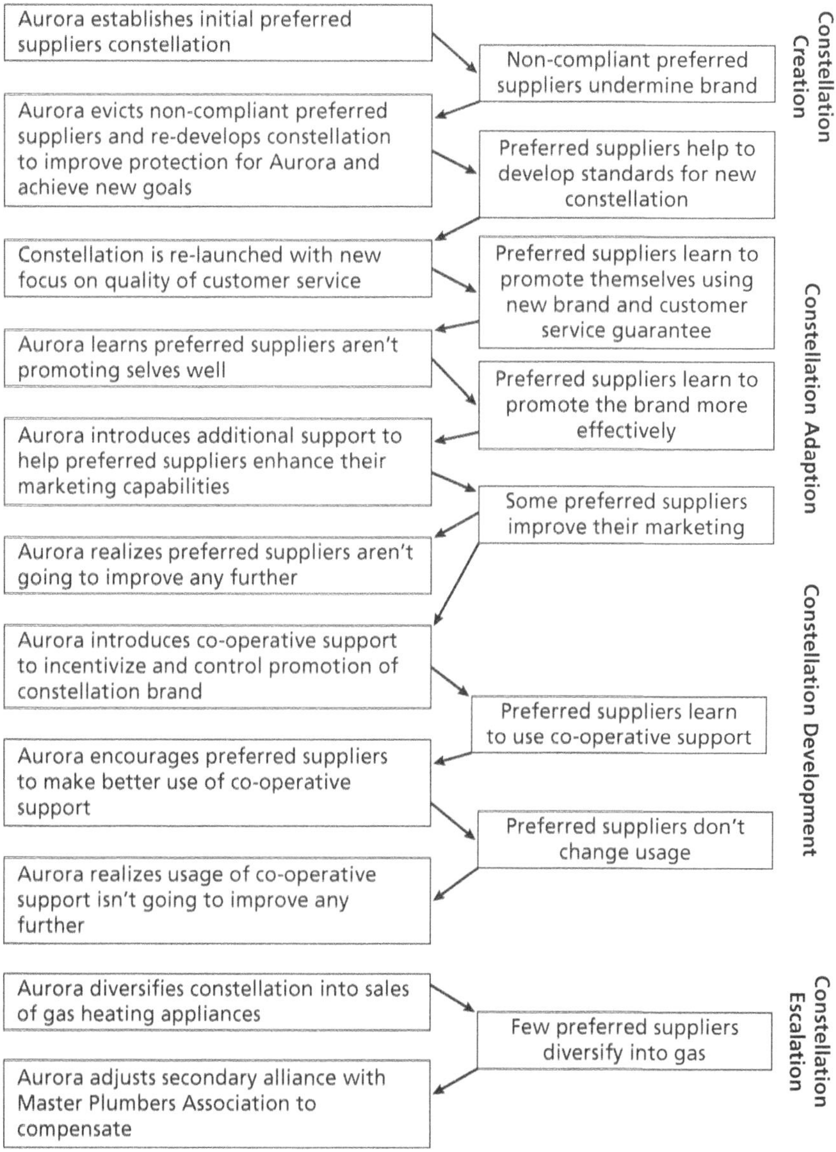

Figure 11.2 Adaptive learning in the Aurora preferred suppliers constellation.

Aurora's constellation management team began learning about the constellation's operation when they first conceptualized how the constellation would operate as a sales channel for electric heating appliances. Drawing on their knowledge of the market environment and the constellation's strategic purpose they designed the constellation's original operational structure to promote sales of residential heating appliances. Through the constellation's participation criteria and code of practice Aurora's team communicated their ideas about the constellation's operation to the constellation members.

Learning about the constellation's purpose, focus, and operational model from Aurora's constellation management team instigated the preferred suppliers' learning about how the constellation would operate and how they would contribute to its operation. They learned from the participation criteria and code of practice how Aurora and constellation members would each contribute to the constellation's operation. In this way they engaged in their initial cognitive learning about how the constellation would operate and how they would operate as constellation members.

Forming alliances and establishing the constellation's operations enabled Aurora and the constellation members to further their learning by testing and refining their ideas. Implementing the alliance conditions provided early feedback about the practicality of the constellation's design and its effectiveness in achieving the desired outcomes. From this feedback, Aurora and the preferred suppliers learned how effectively the constellation operated and where adaptations were required.

Interactive Learning Through the Adaptation of the Constellation

Feedback from the constellation's initial operations led Aurora to refine and extend their cognitive learning about managing an alliance constellation. In late 1995, Aurora evicted two constellation members for "failing to comply with requirements" for constellation membership (Davis, 1995, p. 1). To identify the commercial and legal liability to which members' dysfunctional behavior exposed Aurora, the alliance constellation's operating model was formally reviewed (Davis, 1995). The review specifically focused upon determining the extent to which existing alliance conditions protected Aurora from liability as the constellation's endorser. Through the review process Aurora's constellation management team learned that they needed to adjust the constellation conditions to operate more effectively. Legal advice confirmed that "by virtue of [Aurora's] endorsement and promotion of Preferred Supplier firms" (Hydro Electric Commission, 1995a, p. 2), Aurora was exposed to legal liability "where the Preferred Supplier does not live up to the product or service quality image promoted under that scheme" (Hydro Electric Commission, 1995a, p. 2). Specifically, the review identified that preferred suppliers' behavior could make Aurora liable through the areas of negligent misrepresentation and of misleading and deceptive conduct under the *Trade Practices Act* (1974; Hydro Electric Commission, 1995a). The review identified a need to provide "legal protection for [Aurora] but equally importantly... the protection of [Aurora's] reputation and good will with the community" (Hydro Electric Commission, 1995a, p. 2). The review also noted that "it cannot be stressed too strongly that any successful strategy really depends on how well provision is made for the prevention (insofar as possible) of such occurrences" (Hydro Electric Commission, 1995a, p. 2).

Under this advice, Aurora's Retail Services Group concluded that a new collaborative strategy and a new constellation design were needed to better accommodate the interdependent positions of Aurora and its alliance partners. The new strategy and design would focus on establishing proactive constellation governance to "put in place the appropriate accreditation, monitoring and reward schemes to ensure that there is two way value and control in the Preferred Supplier arrangements" (Davis, 1995, p. 1).

To increase Aurora's control over the constellation's performance, the review recommended restricting the channel's operation to sales of "[Aurora] approved products only" and to "[Aurora] approved electrical product installers only" (Hydro Electric Commission, 1995a, p. 6). To improve member's sales performance, Aurora would establish "compulsory initial and ongoing training/minimum standard requirements for Preferred suppliers and their staff" (Hydro Electric Commission, 1995a, p. 6). To improve Aurora's control over member compliance the review also recommended that Aurora introduce conditions "to approve/supervise, complete/rectify work at the Preferred Supplier's expense" (Hydro Electric Commission, 1995a, p. 6).

Through the review process, Aurora's constellation management team learned how they would need to adapt the constellation's operations to operate more successfully. By developing new constellation conditions and communicating these to constellation members, Aurora's team also promoted members' learning to adapt their constellation participation. Revisions to alliance terms re-defined expectations for member performance by defining and prohibiting specific forms of dysfunctional behavior by member firms or their sub-contracted appliance installers. The revised code of practice explicitly specified that preferred suppliers "display team spirit by working in a positive and co-operative manner with [Aurora] at all levels" (Hydro Electric Commission, 1995b, p. 3). Pursuant to that provision, the revised conditions specified that

> neither Preferred Suppliers or their nominated Contractors will make representations to customers deliberately suggesting or implying the non-compliance with any provision of the By-Laws (for example, connection of a heater of less than 3.5kW in capacity to [Aurora's residential heating tariff]). (Hydro Electric Commission, 1995b, p. 4)

To monitor member compliance, the revised conditions extended Aurora's control over preferred suppliers by establishing more specific expectations for the preferred suppliers' governance of this secondary relationship. Under the revised code of practice, preferred suppliers were required "to ensure the lodgment of paperwork on installation by their nominated contractors" (Hydro Electric Commission, 1995b, p. 5) following installation of appliances qualifying for Aurora's residential heating tariff.

Environmental changes also informed Aurora's re-development of its collaborative strategies for the Aurora Preferred Suppliers Network. In 1995, the Tasmanian Government legislated the de-regulation of the Tasmanian energy market and Aurora's entry into the Australian national energy market by 2005. Preparatory to Aurora's competition in the national market, the Tasmanian energy regulator was charged with regulating the commercial competitiveness of Aurora's pricing by reviewing Aurora's tariffs and retail margins every 3 years. In mid-1996 the Tasmanian energy regulator conducted its first review of Aurora's pricing strategies and capped Aurora's retail margins on energy sales at 10%, eliminating AU$10 million from Aurora's projected operating revenue. This established two new strategic goals for Aurora: increase revenues by increasing sales of electricity for residential heating, and reduce costs by replacing the Heating Advisory Service with the Aurora Preferred Suppliers constellation as the source of advice and assistance to consumers about electric heating alternatives. Consequently, in 1998, Aurora reestablished the Aurora Preferred Suppliers to establish members as Aurora-substitutes in heating advice provision.

During the process of re-designing and re-establishing the constellation, Aurora's alliance team learned that improving and enforcing performance requirements would also be crucial to attracting and retaining constellation members. The training officer recalled when the Aurora team initially canvassed preferred suppliers about participating in the new constellation, concerns about service quality made many members reluctant to commit.

> A lot of preferred suppliers... said, "Well I don't want to be a [member of the new constellation] because it is detrimental to our business. Every man and his dog is a preferred supplier and that guy down the road who's giving that customer really bad service is branding me a preferred supplier as well." (Training Officer)

To improve the constellation's operations and reputation Aurora developed the new operational model for the Aurora Preferred Suppliers Constellation in consultation with a retail management consultancy and with industry leaders of heating appliance retailing. Quality standards for customer service delivery by constellation members combined performance elements from Aurora's Heating Advisory Service and recommendations from industry-leading constellation members on reasonable and achievable standards for good customer service. The consultation process incorporated practices used at the time by the firms consulted, as well as service standards that could underpin the quality assurance and control mechanisms used in the constellation. Aurora also used the consultation process to demonstrate to the preferred suppliers Aurora's commitment to improving customer service and performance throughout the constellation. As the training officer explained:

> We sort of pushed them and said, "Well you are the better operators, we want you on board, we want you to help us with these standards. Being the better operators we know how you felt with other people being branded the same as you were and how you went through the same hassles as we did but we are going to fix this but we need your help with that." And those people were quite happy to help because there was already that relationship there. (Training Officer)

Through the consultation process, input from preferred suppliers enhanced Aurora's learning about improving the constellation's operational design and enhancing performance standards. This learning enhanced Aurora's cognitive learning about designing and managing the constellation. Designing and implementing the new constellation conditions enabled the Aurora team to correspondingly engage in behavioral learning about enhancing the constellation's operations.

The consultation process and the development of new conditions also enabled the preferred suppliers to learn how to improve their participation in and benefit from the constellation. Through the constellation participation requirements they learned how the constellation's operations would be adjusted and about the new expectations for their behavior as constellation members.

As Aurora and the preferred suppliers implemented the new constellation, Aurora realized they needed to adapt the constellation's marketing practices. As Aurora and the preferred suppliers implemented the new constellation Aurora's constellation management team learned that nonmembers' responses to the constellation were threatening its brand value. The constellation manager recollected that unendorsed heating appliance retailers would say to customers: "No I'm not a preferred supplier but you don't have to be one of them," threatening the perceived value of Aurora's endorsement. Aurora also learned that preferred suppliers' promotion of themselves as constellation members was undermining the constellation's brand value. The training officer explained that learning how preferred suppliers promoted their constellation membership to customers prompted Aurora to re-train members about marketing the constellation to consumers and emphasize that being a constellation member meant they had customer service standards which were enforced and guaranteed by Aurora.

Monitoring the preferred suppliers' promotional strategies allowed Aurora to learn how well constellation members were leveraging the "Aurora Preferred Suppliers" brand. By providing feedback to constellation members Aurora helped members learn to improve their promotional activities. Preferred Supplier 13 recalled learning from Aurora's feedback why and how he needed to improve his promotion of the constellation brand.

> We used to have great arguments about why it was called "preferred suppliers" as opposed to "preferred supplier." . . . And until someone sat down and told me exactly why I thought it was stupid to put an S onto it. . . . [The difference is that] if we state that we are a preferred supplier, it's different to the scheme. What they have is this brand called the preferred suppliers, as a brand, as opposed to a preferred supplier. So while we are a member of the "preferred suppliers" scheme, we are not actually a preferred supplier. As in a buying group. (Preferred Supplier 13)

Through Aurora's feedback, constellation members learned about the purpose and function of promotional conditions which enhanced their understanding of why and how to correctly project the constellation brand image and identity.

Implementing the Aurora Preferred Suppliers Customer Service Guarantee also provided a mechanism for Aurora and the constellation members to improve the constellation's customer service processes and outcomes. Members learned to promote the guarantee as a distinct benefit of purchasing from their firms and found that emphasizing the guarantee helped their firms close sales for electric heating appliances (Preferred Suppliers 3, 9, 13). They also learned to use the Aurora team's assistance in complaint investigations (Preferred Suppliers 1, 5, 7, 13) to improve the outcomes for their firms. Moreover, preferred suppliers learned from Aurora's feedback how successfully they were meeting the constellation's performance requirements and how to improve their customer service and sales performance. From Aurora's feedback members learned to improve their after-sales service and resolution of customer issues (Preferred Supplier 4), and adapt their record-keeping practices to better document their customer service practices in the event of a complaint investigation (Preferred Suppliers 6, 14).

Complaint investigation processes also enabled Aurora to learn from preferred suppliers' knowledge and experience. When investigating complaints about a constellation member's installation of a heating appliance Aurora would confer with other constellation members about industry standards and practices. In this way, preferred suppliers helped Aurora to realistically evaluate the behavior of constellation members and helped Aurora learn how to enhance their investigation processes.

Interactive Learning Through the Development of the Constellation

As the Aurora team learned about constellation members' promotional activities they developed new resources and routines for helping constellation members improve their marketing capabilities. In consultation with their advertising agency, Aurora produced an information booklet about enhancing advertising effectiveness. The booklet detailed steps in advertising planning, evaluating advertising alternatives, and media selection (Mazengarb Leo-Burnett, 2000). To enhance members' media selection, Aurora also collated and distributed information about effective radio and television advertising from the Radio Marketing Bureau and the Television Advertising Association. Aurora's Marketing Services department, led by the constellation marketing manager, provided individualized assistance with creative concepts and layouts for advertisements and signage. As the constellation marketing manager explained:

> A lot of these guys were in back streets, they didn't advertise much at all.... They didn't really know what to do.... I developed a little handbook for them on how to do advertising.... We even offered an advertising service here.... We try and encourage them to be professional and do the right thing.... And as their businesses have grown they've obviously understood that a bit more [and] been able to employ people to understand it a bit more. Which is good, because that's what we want. We want the whole level of professionalism to increase. (Constellation Marketing Manager)

By sharing their marketing knowledge Aurora helped constellation members improve their firm's marketing performance. Two preferred suppliers acknowledged that they improved their marketing activities by working with Aurora's Marketing Services department to develop advertisements (Preferred Supplier 1) and using Aurora's information booklets to improve their advertising and marketing planning (Preferred Supplier 6). From the responses of other constellation members, the Aurora team also learned that members' willingness to accept assistance mediated development of their marketing capabilities. The constellation marketing manager recollected offering "to do floor plans for them free of charge to get the stock and everything looking right" but recalled that "no-one took us up on that offer. I couldn't believe it." The constellation manager learned similarly that developing preferred suppliers' marketing activity would be mediated by the members' perceptions of their own firms. The constellation manager explained that one constellation member initially requested help developing signage for new business premises but subsequently rejected ideas developed by Aurora's Marketing Services department because they were "really fancy." From the member's responses, the constellation manager learned that the value of assistance for members depended upon fit with existing business practices. When the constellation manager subsequently learned that the constellation member intended to relocate their business premises, he offered again to arrange signage assistance through Aurora's Marketing Services. He recalled the member responding "I know what [they] will come up with and I think it's fantastic but I don't know that we're ready for that as a business just yet." From this experience the constellation manager learned that members' business circumstances would limit the further development of the constellation's marketing activity.

Implementing the new constellation also identified the need to effectively manage Aurora and preferred suppliers' complementary marketing of the constellation brand. An internal memo written by the constellation marketing manager highlighted the importance of monitoring usage of the Aurora Preferred Suppliers brand.

> We'd need to be assured [constellation members] would be tagging their own ads with the Aurora Preferred Suppliers line.... Therefore I'd like to suggest before any of our money goes into producing radio advertising, I'd need to be assured the scripts they'd use were correct and acceptable. In my role as "Brand Custodian" I need to get schedules from all of those likely to participate so I could see how and if we could align our ads to theirs, with the messages complementary and consistent, at the different times and geographic locations across the state. (Constellation Marketing Manager)

To incentivize and monitor the use of the constellation brand, Aurora created a co-operative advertising scheme in 1999 which partially reimbursed preferred suppliers for promotional activities incorporating the Aurora Preferred Suppliers brand. As the constellation manager explained:

> [As members improved their advertising] the challenge for me was then to have messages that were consistent on the capability of the business but still representing Aurora. So the way we got Aurora represented was saying "well if you're going to have ads, show us the scripts, show us how they refer to the Aurora Preferred Supplier customer quality outcomes and then we'll talk about what our co-operative support would be for that advertising. (Constellation Manager)

To qualify for co-operative advertising, support members submitted advance plans for advertising activities to the constellation's quality assurance officer. Assessment against policy guidelines evaluated fit with Aurora's corporate and brand objectives and the exposure achieved for the constellation (Aurora Energy, 1999). To accommodate the diverse range and nature of preferred suppliers' promotional activities, advertising that increased brand exposure or brand value was reimbursed on a proportional basis.

Reimbursement depended upon appropriate brand use in advertising that was likely to increase the constellation's profile.

Aurora's introduction of co-operative advertising prompted constellation members to learn how to leverage their membership to achieve new forms of value. Some members learned to adapt their constellation participation to benefit financially from Aurora's co-operative advertising support (Preferred Suppliers 1, 3, 4, 5, 6, 8, 9, 13, 14). Others learned that their firm's own marketing practices limited this value of constellation membership for their organizations. Preferred Supplier 10 and Preferred Supplier 2 learned that being state branches of national companies prevented them from qualifying for advertising support due to budgetary constraints outside their control (Preferred Supplier 10) and the use of global advertising campaigns which precluded the development of Tasmanian-specific advertisements incorporating the Aurora Preferred Suppliers brand (Preferred Supplier 2). Some preferred suppliers (Preferred Suppliers 1, 12) also learned that the ad hoc nature of their advertising activity stopped them from better utilizing co-operative advertising support because being unable to submit plans for Aurora's approval disqualified them from financial support.

Learning about preferred suppliers' use of co-operative advertising, Aurora's constellation management team realized that preferred suppliers' business operations limited the usefulness of the co-operative advertising support scheme and Aurora's assistance could "only go so far" in developing the constellation's operations.

> [Co-operative advertising] is one of the areas that I think has never worked as well as it could, because they all go and advertise and promote, forget to tell us, don't get the message quite right in their ads so we can't fix it before they've gone out and done it and therefore we don't get as many requests for co-operative advertising as we possibly could or should.... Sometimes I think a few of the preferred suppliers miss out.... despite [our] going out again in May and saying "... best you get your co-operative advertising [applications] in to us before the end of the month," they still don't.... [and] they miss out on financial support from Aurora.... I keep saying to them "look you could actually sit down and package this up in a hour or two and you could get AU$1000." [They say] "Oh yeah but we're so busy doing this and that." (Constellation Manager)

Interactive Learning Through the Escalation of the Constellation

During 2005, Aurora amended constellation conditions to diversify the Aurora Preferred Suppliers Constellation into sales of gas heating appliances. The completion of the Basslink natural gas pipeline linking Tasmania to the Australian mainland facilitated Aurora's entry into the Australian national energy market and diversification into selling natural gas. The first phase of pipeline construction made piped gas available to 36,000 households around Tasmania, presenting a market opportunity to diversify the Aurora Preferred Suppliers into selling gas heating appliances.

Aurora negotiated the constellation's diversification into sales of gas heating appliances through an ongoing process of briefings and consultation with constellation members. During discussions, Aurora canvassed preferred suppliers on their diversification intentions. Twelve members signaled intentions to retail gas heating appliances and support constellation diversification.

In early 2005, Aurora amended constellation participation standards and operational structures to include provisions for selling gas heating appliances. Aurora incorporated advice about natural gas availability and gas heating into training and operational routines for their call center and for training and quality-assuring preferred suppliers. The constellation's sales lead referral system was also adapted to capture and direct referrals for gas heating enquiries to preferred suppliers, and marketing routines incorporated gas heating into promotions of the constellation.

To support preferred suppliers' expansion into selling gas heating appliances, Aurora also negotiated a secondary alliance with the Master Plumbers Association. The secondary alliance established a pool of gas fitters to whom constellation members could sub-contract gas appliance installations. Aurora quality-assured gas fitters sub-contracted through the Master Plumbers Association to *constellation* performance standards. The alliance enabled constellation members to diversify into gas installations without needing to permanently employ tradespeople for whom demand was uncertain.

Aurora's escalation of constellation activities into gas appliance sales provided opportunities for all preferred suppliers to diversify their businesses and increase the constellation's sales activities. However, by May 2005 only two constellation members escalated their own business activity in this way. Preferred suppliers' reluctance prompted Aurora's constellation management team to realize they needed to escalate the constellation's activity through other means. Consequently, Aurora further amended the secondary alliance with the Master Plumbers Association to compensate for constellation members' strategic choices, approving nine Master Plumbers to receive sales leads through the constellation's lead referral system.

Aurora's escalation of the constellation's operations prompted new learning about constellation management. Expanding constellation operations to support sales of gas heating appliances tested and refined knowledge about constellation marketing, management, and development. Aurora's constellation management team used their experience of the constellation's previous operations to frame strategies for establishing secondary alliances with gas fitters that, in turn, established new resources to support constellation expansion. Diversifying the preferred suppliers constellation into gas heating appliance sales also prompted additional learning about constellation members and constellation operations. Slower-than-expected diversification by preferred suppliers revised Aurora's understanding of members' operational contexts and developmental capacity. Accommodating unmet demand for gas heating generated new insights into adapting constellation operation to unexpected outcomes.

Aurora's escalation of the constellation into sales of gas heating appliances also prompted additional learning about constellation participation by preferred suppliers. They learned from Aurora about new opportunities to expand into selling gas heating appliances. As Aurora adapted the constellation's conditions to support escalation, preferred suppliers learned that new conditions introduced new value creation opportunities and they learned how they needed to adapt their constellation participation to leverage potential benefits. Some preferred suppliers (Preferred Suppliers 5, 9, 11) concluded that Aurora's diversification would increase the value of constellation membership for their firms. Members anticipated that the constellation's escalation would prove beneficial by providing access to Aurora's information about the market (Preferred Suppliers 1, 11) and supporting the diversification of preferred suppliers' product range (Preferred Suppliers 5, 9). Other preferred suppliers concluded diversification opportunities offered insufficient benefits to offset the investments required (Preferred Suppliers 3, 6, 10).

INTERPARTNER LEARNING DYNAMICS IN THE CONSTELLATION

The case history of the Aurora Preferred Suppliers alliance constellation illustrates that over the course of their collaboration, the constellation manager and constellation members engaged in recurring cycles of adaptive learning. Aurora engaged in cycles of adaptive learning about marketing and managing the constellation as a sales channel for electric heating appliances. Preferred suppliers engaged in cycles of adaptive learning about operating and marketing themselves as constellation members. During these cycles they developed their knowledge about constellation management and participation by testing and refining their understanding of effective constellation operation. During the first cycle they engaged in their initial cognitive learning about how the constellation would operate, which they translated into behavioral learning by establishing the constellation as an operating sales channel. During each subsequent learning cycle they used feedback from constellation operations to develop new insights about improving the constellation's performance. They translated their new cognitive learning about improving constellation performance into behavioral learning by adapting their alliance behavior. Implementing new alliance behavior generated, in turn, feedback they used to further refine their knowledge about constellation management and participation. The learning cycles depicted in Figure 11.3 demonstrate how Aurora and the preferred suppliers progressively developed their knowledge over the course of the constellation's lifetime.

The research shows that the constellation's evolution was also influenced by Aurora and the preferred suppliers' adaptation to their alliance environment. Specifically, the research found the alliance environment affected the constellation's evolution by triggering adaptive learning cycles. The research found that cycles were triggered by elements in the external market, industry and regulatory environments, and by elements in the constellation's internal environment. New market opportunities, such as growing consumer interest in electric heating and the development of the natural gas pipeline, affected the constellation's evolution by causing Aurora to adopt new strategic goals which framed the constellation's operations. Changes to the regulatory environment, most notably the regulation of Aurora's pricing strategies, affected the constellation's evolution by prompting Aurora to redefine the constellation's contributions to Aurora's strategic goals. The industry environment influenced the constellation's operation

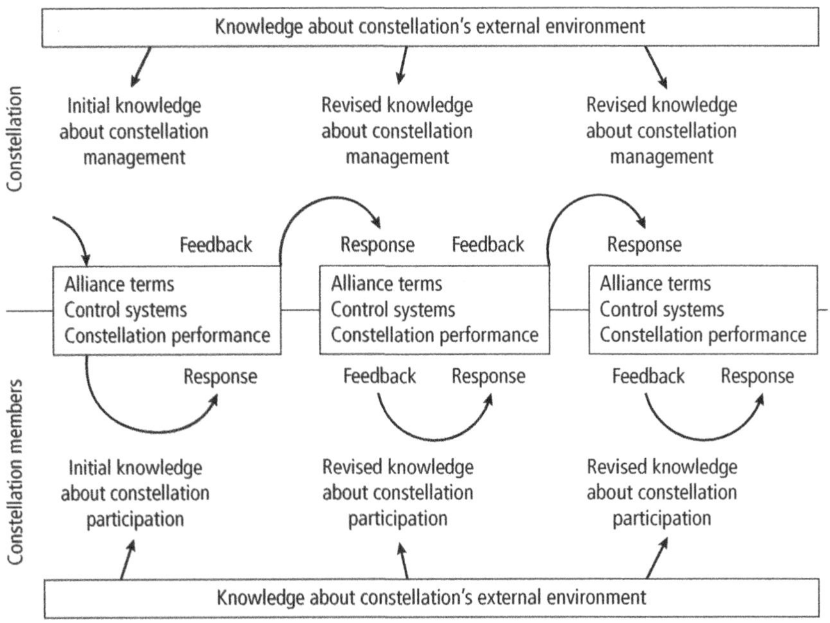

Figure 11.3 A model of interpartner learning dynamics in an alliance constellation.

by promoting learning about elements which were undermining the constellation's performance, such as non-members undermining the constellation's brand value. Finally, the network environment influenced the constellation's operation by promoting learning about ways in which members' own behavior undermined the constellation's operations. In all cases, environmental changes prompted adaptive learning cycles from which Aurora generated new insights about how the constellation's operations could be enhanced and generate more beneficial outcomes. New insights then led to adaptive responses which altered alliance conditions.

Figure 11.3 also illustrates the interdependent nature of the learning dynamics that underpinned the constellation's evolution. As Aurora and the preferred suppliers tested and refined their practical knowledge about constellation operation their actions triggered adaptive learning by the other. Aurora's adaptations to alliance conditions triggered learning cycles in which preferred suppliers learned about Aurora's action, interpreted feedback about the impact of those actions on constellation operations, and adapted their own understandings and actions accordingly. Likewise, preferred suppliers' actions triggered learning cycles in which Aurora's constellation management team learned about preferred suppliers' behavior, interpreted feedback about the impact of those actions on constellation operations, and adapted their own understandings and actions accordingly. The study found that these cycles were often concurrent but they are depicted as successive in Figure 11.3 to highlight their interactive nature.

The study also found that the alliance conditions of the constellation were the linchpin of the evolutionary learning process. The alliance conditions created the learning system through which Aurora learned about constellation management and the preferred suppliers learned about constellation participation. The conditions created a learning system by providing the mechanisms through which Aurora and the preferred suppliers exchanged information about the constellation's operations. This facilitated learning in several ways. Firstly, it enabled Aurora to communicate their ideas about operating the constellation to the preferred suppliers, instigating their learning about what the constellation's operations would entail. Secondly, the constellation's conditions created the structures and routines through which the constellation operated, facilitating the development of cognitive and behavioral learning about constellation management and operation as constellation members. Thirdly, the constellation conditions created the performance management system through which Aurora and the preferred suppliers received feedback about the constellation's operations and each other's behavior. This feedback facilitated, in turn, the reflective learning process by which each party evaluated performance information, tested and refined their existing ideas about constellation management and participation, and developed action responses. Fourthly, constellation conditions provided the context for trial-and-error learning as Aurora and the constellation members tested the efficacy of new routines and action responses.

As depicted in Figure 11.3, the alliance conditions also provided the point of connection between Aurora's and preferred suppliers' learning cycles. Specifically, the constellation's conditions provided the mechanism through which learning was triggered, undertaken, and applied. Constellation conditions acted as a learning trigger when they provided feedback about constellation operations or about environmental conditions. When this occurred, it triggered a reflective learning cycle in which Aurora and the constellation members used their knowledge of constellation operations to review and reconsider their alliance behavior. Since the constellation's conditions created the control systems and performance information which generated such feedback, the constellation conditions also provided the mechanisms for undertaking learning. Finally, as Aurora and the constellation members concluded each learning cycle with an action response, the alliance conditions became the point of learning application.

DISCUSSION AND CONCLUSIONS

This research explored the evolution of an alliance constellation and found that the constellation evolved as a consequence of successive, interactive cycles of adaptive learning by the constellation manager and constellation members. Specifically, it found that the constellation's evolutionary pathway resulted from the progressive development of Aurora's knowledge about constellation management, and of the preferred suppliers' knowledge about constellation participation. By producing a conceptual model of these evolutionary processes, the research advances our understanding of alliance co-evolution, and the development of alliance knowledge.

This research and the conceptual model in Figure 11.3 advance theories of alliance co-evolution by demonstrating the mechanisms and processes by which the alliance partners evolved in response to each other and their environment. Specifically, the research highlights the important role of alliance conditions in co-evolutionary learning processes as learning triggers, learning mechanisms, and points of learning application. The demonstrated role of alliance conditions as a learning system suggests that future research which explores how specific conditions mediate learning and how this impact might vary for different alliance forms, could generate valuable insights into the ways in which alliance conditions could be designed for specific learning outcomes.

The research also advances our understanding of the development of alliance knowledge in several key ways. Firstly, the model acknowledges the temporal dimension of knowledge development by depicting how knowledge developed progressively over the constellation's lifetime. Introducing temporal considerations paves the way for future research to explore the potential interactions between when learning occurs and what learning occurs. For example, future research could explore whether organizations develop different knowledge during the early stages of a collaboration than they do during later stages. More explicit consideration of when learning occurs may also facilitate more precise identification of learning events and the knowledge they produce. This would enhance recent research into the development of collaborative capabilities by enabling research that considers how and when the knowledge which underpins collaborative capabilities might develop.

Secondly, by distinguishing between the knowledge which Aurora developed as a constellation manager and which preferred suppliers developed as constellation members, the research identifies that collaborative activities can produce different types of collaborative knowledge. Researchers have acknowledged that different forms of collaboration (e.g., equity-based alliances) may require different skills and expertise and consequently firms wishing to use such forms successfully should deliberately build experience with the forms they intend to use in the future (Anand & Khanna, 2000; Draulans, de Man, & Volberda, 2003; Zollo, Reuer, & Singh, 2002). However, this view is premised on the assumption that participating in an alliance with a specific form will generate knowledge which can later be transferred into managing an alliance with that form. This research showed that the knowledge produced from a collaborative experience is determined by the role that is adopted: Aurora developed knowledge about constellation management that was quite different to the knowledge developed by the preferred suppliers about constellation participation. This finding paves the way for future research that explores how the roles adopted within an alliance might produce specific learning pathways and the implications these have for developing and subsequently applying knowledge about collaboration.

Future research could also explore how the processes described in this study might be influenced by interpartner competitive dynamics. The competitive context of the research participants established two factors that may have influenced the evolution of the Aurora Preferred Suppliers Constellation. The first factor is the balance of power between Aurora and the preferred suppliers. Aurora's monopoly over the Tasmanian electricity market during the study period may have enhanced the organization's bargaining power in the alliance relationship. As noted earlier, Aurora was the only electricity company operating in Tasmania at the time and therefore controlled the only alliance constellation in which constellation members could participate. This may have influenced adaptive learning within the alliance constellation in two ways. As the constellation manager, Aurora had almost full control over the constellation's conditions and over the constellation as a learning system. Consequently, Aurora was able to strongly influence the areas and nature of constellation members' learning. The willingness to maintain a positive relationship with Aurora, and access to the benefits of constellation participation, may also have increased preferred suppliers' willingness to share knowledge and to accept Aurora's learning influence. These possibilities suggest that future theorizing and research into the evolution of alliance constellations should consider the potential influences of power dynamics between collaborative partners.

The second factor which may have influenced the constellation's evolution is the nature of the relationships between Aurora and constellation members. Aurora and the preferred suppliers had a vertical relationship in the sense that customers buying heaters from preferred suppliers subsequently became consumers of Aurora's heating energy tariff. A common interest in promoting purchases of heating appliances motivated knowledge-sharing about customer needs and preferences in order to improve marketing efforts and sales outcomes. Operating in complementary industries reduced the risk that Aurora and the preferred suppliers could learn how to neutralize each other's competitive positions, which may have increased their willingness to share knowledge and heightened learning outcomes about improving constellation operations. Future studies should therefore explore the potential influences of competitive tensions on adaptive learning in alliance constellations.

ACKNOWLEDGMENT

This chapter, save some minor changes, was earlier published as Woods, M., & Hecker, R. (2013). Interpartner learning dynamics in an alliance constellation. In T. K. Das (Ed.), *Managing knowledge in strategic alliances* (pp. 159–186). Charlotte, NC: Information Age.

REFERENCES

Anand, B. N., & Khanna, T. (2000). Do firms learn to create value? The case of alliances. *Strategic Management Journal, 21*(3), 295–316.

Argyris, C., & Schon, D. A. (1996). *Organizational learning: A theory of action perspective.* Reading, MA: Addison-Wesley.

Ariño, A., & de la Torre, J. (1998). Learning from failure: Towards an evolutionary model of collaborative ventures. *Organization Science, 9*(3), 306–325.

Ariño, A., de la Torre, J., & Ring, P. S. (2001). Relational quality: Managing trust in corporate alliances. *California Management Review, 44*(1), 109–131.

Aurora Energy. (1999). *Co-operative advertising evaluation criteria* [checklist]. Hobart, Australia: Aurora Energy.

Aurora Energy. (2011). *Aurora Energy annual report 2010–2011.* Hobart, Australia: Aurora Energy.

Barr, P. S., Stimpert, J. L., & Huff, A. S. (1992). Cognitive change, strategic action, and organizational renewal. *Strategic Management Journal, 13*(Summer Special issue), 15–36.

Bell, J., den Outen, B., & Ziggers, G.W. (2006). Dynamics of cooperation: At the brink of irrelevance. *Journal of Management Studies, 43*(7), 1607–1619.

Browning, L. D., Beyer, J. M., & Shetler, J. C. (1995). Building cooperation in a competitive industry: SEMATECH and the semiconductor industry. *Academy of Management Journal, 38*(1), 113–142.

Buchel, B. (2000). Framework of joint venture development: Theory-building through qualitative research. *Journal of Management Studies, 37*(5), 637–661.

Buchel, B. (2002). Joint venture development: Driving forces towards equilibrium. *Journal of World Business, 37*(3), 199–207.

D'Aunno, T. A., & Zuckerman, H. S. (1987). A life-cycle model of organizational federations: The case of hospitals. *Academy of Management Review, 12*(3), 534–545.

Das, T. K., & Kumar, R. (2007). Learning dynamics in the alliance development process. *Management Decision, 45*(4), 684–707.

Das, T. K., & Teng, B. (2002). The dynamics of alliance conditions in the alliance development process. *Journal of Management Studies, 39*(5), 725–746.

Davis, P. (1995). *Review of preferred suppliers network* [internal office memo]. Hobart, Australia: Hydro Electric Commission.

Doz, Y. L. (1996). The evolution of cooperation in strategic alliances: Initial conditions or learning processes? *Strategic Management Journal, 17*, 55–83.

Draulans J., de Man, A.-P., & Volberda, H. W. (2003). Building alliance capability: Management techniques for superior alliance performance. *Long Range Planning, 36*(2), 151–166

Hennart, J.-F. (2006). Alliance research: Less is more. *Journal of Management Studies, 43*(7), 1621–1628.

Hydro Electric Commission. (1992). *Hydro Electric Commission annual report 1991–1992.* Hobart, Australia: Hydro Electric Commission.

Hydro Electric Commission. (1993). *Hydro Electric Commission annual report 1992–1993.* Hobart, Australia: Hydro Electric Commission.

Hydro Electric Commission. (1995a). *Summation of legal advice received on Preferred Supplier scheme.* Hobart, Australia: Hydro Electric Commission.

Hydro Electric Commission. (1995b). *HEC Preferred Supplier code of practice.* Hobart, Australia: Hydro Electric Commission.

Hydro Electric Commission. (1996). *Hydro Electric Commission annual report 1995–1996.* Hobart, Australia: Hydro Electric Commission.

Inkpen, A. C., & Currall, S. C. (2004). The coevolution of trust, control, and learning in joint ventures. *Organization Science, 15*(5), 586–599.

Kolb, D. A. (1984). *Experiential learning: Experience as the source of learning and development.* Englewood Cliffs, NJ: Prentice-Hall.

Koza, M. P., & Lewin, A. Y. (1998). The co-evolution of strategic alliances. *Organization Science, 9*(3), 255–264.

Kumar, R., & Nti, K. O. (1998). Differential learning and interaction in alliance dynamics: A process and outcome discrepancy model. *Organization Science, 9*(3), 356–367.

Laszlo, E. (1972). *Introduction to systems philosophy.* New York, NY: Gordon and Breach.

Lee, Y., & Cavusgil, S. T. (2006) Enhancing alliance performance: The effects of contractual-based versus relational-based governance, *Journal of Business Research, 59*(8), 896–905.

Lembo, J. M. (1972). *When learning happens.* New York, NY: Schocken Books.

Lui, S. S., & Ngo, H. (2005). An action pattern model of inter-firm co-operation. *Journal of Management Studies, 42*(6), 1123–1153.

Mazengarb Leo-Burnett. (2000). *How to make your advertising work.* Hobart, Australia: Mazengarb Leo-Burnett.

Ness, H. (2009). Governance, negotiations, and alliance dynamics: Explaining the evolution of relational practice. *Journal of Management Studies, 46*(3), 451–480.

Reuer, J. J., & Ariño, A. (2002). Contractual renegotiations in strategic alliances, *Journal of Management, 28*(1), 47–68.

Ring, P. S., & Van de Ven, A. H. (1994). Developmental processes of cooperative interorganizational relationships. *Academy of Management Review, 19*(1), 90–118.

Salk, J. E. (2005). Often called for but rarely chosen: Alliance research that directly studies process. *European Management Review, 2*(2), 117–122.

Senge, P. M. (1990). *The fifth discipline: The art and practice of the learning organisation.* Sydney, Australia: Random House.

Trade Practices Act of 1974, No. 51 (1974). https://www.legislation.gov.au/Details/C2010C00331

Van de Ven A. H., & Walker, G. (1984). The dynamics of interorganizational coordination. *Administrative Science Quarterly, 29*(4), 598–621.

Weick, K. E., & Boughton, M. (1986). Organizations as cognitive maps: Charting ways to success and failure. In H. P. Sims, D. A. Gioia, & Associates (Eds.), *The thinking organization* (pp. 95–120). San Francisco, CA: Jossey-Bass.

Wilson J., & Hynes, N. (2009). Co-evolution of firms and strategic alliances: Theory and empirical evidence. *Technological Forecasting and Social Change, 76*(5), 620–628.

Woods, M., & Hecker, R. (2011). Helping to learn: Governance of knowledge-sharing in the Aurora Preferred Suppliers alliance network. *International Journal of Strategic Business Alliances, 2*(1/2), 91–112.

Zajac, E. J., & Olsen, C. P. (1993). From transaction cost to transactional value analysis: Implications for the study of interorganizational strategies. *Journal of Management Studies, 30*(1), 131–145.

Zollo, M., Reuer, J. J., & Singh, H. (2002). Interorganizational routines and performance in strategic alliances. *Organization Science, 13*(6), 701–713.

CHAPTER 12

MANAGING INTERPARTNER DIVERSITIES FOR ALLIANCE PERFORMANCE

Hiroshi Yasuda

ABSTRACT

This research analyzes diversity between partners in strategic alliances from a number of different points of view, and attempts to understand how this diversity influences the performance of alliances. The chapter presents a model which comprehensively shows this influence on performance, and also shows the role of alliance governance in this relationship. Hypotheses are formulated reflecting this model, and they are empirically tested using the data collected from a survey of alliance managers. It is clarified that the diversity of capabilities and viewpoints has a positive influence on alliance performance through promoting the creation of new knowledge, while the diversity of corporate culture and operating routines has a negative influence on alliance performance through impeding the efficient management of alliances. The study also discusses the role of alliance governance in moderating the negative influence of diversity, and the moderating effects of relational governance are confirmed. In order to achieve good performance in alliances, it is necessary to design an appropriate relational governance structure which

Managing the Partners in Strategic Alliances, pages 299–318

can make use of the diversity in capabilities and viewpoints that each partner brings to the project, while overcoming the difficulties entailed by the diversity of corporate culture and operating routines.

INTRODUCTION

Strategic alliances are voluntary arrangements between firms that involve the exchange, sharing, or co-development of products, technologies, or services (Gulati, 1998). In recent years, many alliances have been formed on a global basis, reflecting the progressive globalization of markets (Silva, Bradley, & Sousa, 2012). As firms from different countries collaborate in alliances, the features of their interpartner relationships are characterized by a high level of diversity, which has a significant influence on the alliance performance. For example, corporate culture is subject to the influence of country culture, which is specific to the country in which the firm is operating (Parkhe, 1991). Due to the distance between corporate cultures, inconsistency of recognition will easily occur with foreign firms, and this will cause misunderstanding and distrust between partners. It has been pointed out that this distance between corporate cultures is a major cause of failure of international alliances (Lavie, Haunschild, & Khanna, 2012).

On the other hand, international alliances are also characterized by different resources and capabilities brought by partners. A firm's resources and capabilities are built in response to the influence of conditions and institutions which are specific to the country in which the firm operates (Porter, 1990). As a result, firms which are based in different countries have different strengths. Many international alliances have achieved outstanding performance, taking advantage of the complementarities of such strengths between partners.

The interpartner diversity corresponds to the various different characteristics between partners in alliances (Bruyaka, Caner, & Prescott, 2011). This chapter will capture the interpartner diversity from various viewpoints, and analyze how such diversity influences the performance of alliances. In prior literature, various forms of diversity between partners have been discussed, such as diversity of corporate culture (Parkhe, 1991), diversity of operating routines (Lavie et al., 2012), diversity of management resources (Lee, 2007), diversity of technology (Sampson, 2007), and diversity of industries (Goerzen & Beamish, 2005), and so on. However, most of these studies have paid attention only to specific factors of diversity, such as the corporate culture or resources, and research which considers the issue of interpartner diversity from multiple viewpoints is scarce.

In order to further develop alliance research, this study aims to comprehensively consider interpartner diversity from various viewpoints, and to provide an understanding of the mechanism by which it influences the alliance performance using empirical data gained from a survey of alliance managers. Among many types of alliances, the scope of this study is limited to technology alliances because their interpartner relationships have more direct effects on their performance compared with other types of alliances (Sampson, 2007). For example, if alliances are of the sales collaboration type, their performance will be greatly influenced by the market conditions of the partners' businesses. In the case of technology alliances, the influence of such market factors is slight and their performance is mainly influenced by the relational factors between partners.

The outline of this chapter is as follows. The next section will review prior literature and formulate hypotheses about how the interpartner diversity influences the performance of alliances. Subsequently, the methodology to test the validity of the hypotheses will be introduced. Following that, the results of an empirical survey and their analysis will be presented. Finally, the last section will summarize the findings of this study, discuss their implications, and present the issues left for future research.

THEORY AND HYPOTHESES

Two theoretical perspectives—namely, the resource-based perspective and the transaction-cost perspective—will be used to formulate hypotheses in this chapter. According to the resource-based perspective, a firm's competitive advantage is attributable to the unique resources owned by the firm, which are valuable, rare, and costly to imitate (Barney, 1991). The primary purpose of alliances is to obtain these resources from partners, because they are not available in the market transactions (Das & Teng, 2000). In technology alliances, a key to success is to create new knowledge and innovation by combining partners' technical know-how. In the creation of such new knowledge, the acquisition of external knowledge beyond the technical domain of the firms involved is needed. That is, the fusion of heterogeneous and varying capabilities is required (Phene, Lindquist, & Marsh, 2006). The originality of the research team increases as the capability of the team members becomes more diversified (Yano, 1997). In the same way, the performance of alliances improves as the capabilities of alliance partners become diversified and their diversified capabilities are complementarily combined (Das & Teng, 2003; Lin, Yang, & Arya, 2009). In research on bio-medical technologies, it has been reported that firms show better performance if they form alliances with partners having different capabilities from their own (Bruyaka et al., 2011).

Moreover, in conducting the research and development activities, the results are influenced by the viewpoints of the firm's members on the measures required to solve problems. Excellent results can be expected if partners bring various viewpoints and conceptions to the alliance so that they are complementarily united (Yasuda, 2012). The diversity of viewpoints as well as diversity of capabilities must be considered in analyzing the alliance performance. Firms' primary tendency is for a "local search," by which they try to find new knowledge near their technical domains and areas (Stuart & Podolny, 1996). However, the fusion of external knowledge across their domains creates innovation, which produces a source of new competitive power (McEvily & Zaheer, 1999; Rosenkopf & Nerkar, 2001). In this sense, alliances can expect better performance if they try to ally with technically and geographically distant partners, and utilize the heterogeneity of capabilities and viewpoints. In aiming for a competitive advantage on a global level, firms need to utilize various capabilities and management resources from all over the world, without relying solely on the predominant capabilities and resources of their own countries. In order to promote this kind of management, firms are required to combine different viewpoints and conceptions through international alliances, and this leads them to the creation of new knowledge (Asakawa, 2006). Based on the above discussion, the following hypothesis is formulated:

> **Hypothesis 1:** *The interpartner diversity of capabilities (H1a) and viewpoints (H1b) leads to the creation of new knowledge in alliances. As a result, such diversity has a positive influence on the alliance performance.*

In considering the above hypothesis based on the resource-based perspective, there was discussion about whether interpartner diversity improves the alliance performance by enhancing complemental advantages of resources and viewpoints. On the other hand, from the viewpoint of the transaction-cost perspective, there was discussion about whether the difference in recognition and mismatch in operations due to interpartner diversity may induce opportunistic behaviors, increase the transaction costs of control and coordination, and thus hamper the performance of alliances (Folta & Ferrier, 2000). According to the transaction-cost perspective, the most efficient structure of inter-firm relationships is determined by the costs required to perform transactions between firms (Williamson, 1975). Alliances will be formed when the transaction cost is not so high as to justify the hierarchical relationships, while it is not so low as to justify the market-based transaction (Das & Teng, 2000). However, if the transaction cost increases due to the high level of interpartner diversity, the optimum conditions to justify alliance relationships will not hold any more, and performance of alliances will be hampered (Park & Russo, 1995).

Many prior studies have pointed out that differences in corporate culture are major reasons for alliance failures. These can induce misperception and misunderstanding (Lane & Beamish, 1990; Yan & Zeng, 1999), lack of a trustful basis (Doney, Canon, & Mullen, 1998), difference of recognition of risks (Delerue & Simon, 2009), and disagreement about solutions (Kogut & Singh, 1988). In order to make alliances successful, it is important that values and norms are shared among partners. However, if there is a difference of corporate culture, partners are likely to recognize different problems, as well as act differently towards the same problems (Kumar & Anderson, 2000). Furthermore, a combination of firms with different cultures will increase the chances of opportunism and conflicts of interest, and management of alliances will become extremely difficult (Kumar & Nti, 2004). The major causes of alliance failures actually originate in the mismatching of corporate cultures (Lavie, Haunschild, & Khanna, 2012).

Differences in operating routines also make the alliance management unstable. The routine of how employees carry out everyday operations differs between firms (Datta, 1991). Each firm has its own business routine; for example, some firms usually make top–down decisions while other firms respect the bottom–up consensus. Since the manager in alliances expects that the partner will act similarly, if the partner does not respond to this expectation, disappointment and frustration will prevent the cultivation of trustful relationships (Lavie et al., 2012). The mismatching of operating routines restricts mutual communication and commitment, and hampers the efficient management of alliances (Cullen, Johnson, & Sakano, 1995).

As shown above, the interpartner diversity of corporate culture and operating routines makes the alliance management difficult. This will have a negative influence on the alliance performance. Therefore, the following hypothesis is formulated:

> **Hypothesis 2:** *The interpartner diversity of corporate culture (H2a) and operating routines (H2b) makes the efficient management of alliances difficult. As a result, such diversity has a negative influence on the alliance performance.*

As stated above, the interpartner diversity makes the alliance management difficult, and increases the transaction cost borne by partners. In this situation, the inter-firm efficiency can be optimized by shifting to a more hierarchical structure, which can be realized by strengthening the alliance governance. Alliance governance is the mechanism of governing each partner's actions so that the mutual contribution is defined, conflicts of interest are minimized, and opportunism is controlled (Pateli & Lioukas, 2011). Alliances involve both contractual governance and relational governance (Hoetker & Mellewigt, 2009). Contractual governance controls the alliance through clarifying the structure of project organization, rules for decision making, and distribution of rights and obligations by specifying detailed conditions in the alliance contract. On the other hand, relational governance bases its authority on mutual trustful relationships, and establishes the routines of frequent communication, regular meetings, joint problem-solving, after-work socialization, and so on.

The importance of governance in alliances has been pointed out by many studies. Effective governance can remarkably enhance the joint performance of alliances (Dutta & Weiss, 1997). Hierarchical and compulsory governance is more effective if the alliance is more complicated (Oxley, 1997). Especially in technology alliances, as tacit knowledge shared by partners plays an important role, changing to new partners is associated with high cost. Therefore, it is necessary to reduce the threat of partners' opportunism, and governance must be established to achieve this (Folta, 1998). As stated previously, diversity of corporate culture produces misunderstanding and disagreements between partners, and induces conflicts of interest and opportunism. Diversity of operating routines also disturbs the communication between partners, impedes collaborative relationships, and makes the alliance management difficult. However, these management problems can be overcome by establishing a strong governance structure to cope with them. Of course, the level of interpartner diversity differs from one alliance to another since the number of partners, their countries, and their characteristics are different. Therefore, governance needs to be established according to the level of diversity in the alliance. If the alliance is successful in doing this, it will overcome the difficulties arising from diversity and make efficient management feasible. The following hypothesis is formulated from the above argument.

> **Hypothesis 3:** *The negative influence of interpartner diversity of corporate culture and operating routines on the efficient management of alliances is moderated by strengthening alliance governance (contractual governance [H3a], and relational governance [H3b]).*

METHODOLOGY

Samples and Data

The theoretical framework is summarized in Figure 12.1. For the purpose of testing the formulated hypotheses, a survey was conducted on technology alliances which Japanese manufacturing firms had formed with foreign as well as domestic partners.[1]

In the case of technology alliances, it is difficult to measure their performance because there are no objective performance indicators in this type of alliance (Dussauge & Garrette, 1995). Therefore, this survey requested

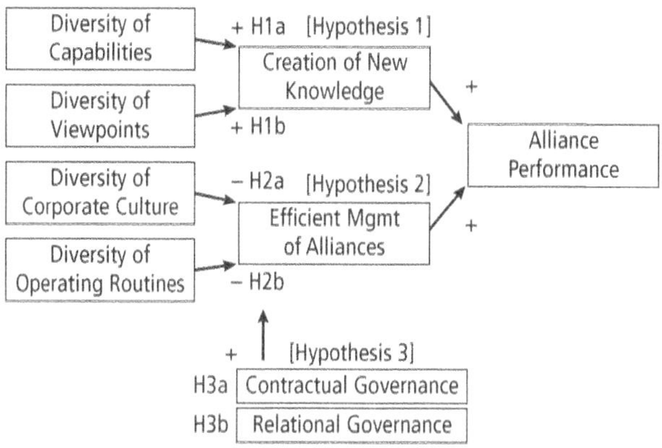

Figure 12.1 Theoretical framework.

alliance managers of firms to evaluate their experienced alliance projects, and then used their evaluation as a measure of alliance performance. Alliance managers are familiar with alliance projects and are the most suitable respondents for a survey on alliances (Kale, Singh, & Perlmutter, 2000). Although the measurements are based on the managers' subjective evaluation, they are strongly correlated with the objective performance (Chandler & Hanks, 1993; Faem, Alberink, Jong, Groen, & Woolthuis, 2012). Therefore, it is appropriate to evaluate the alliance performance using the responses of alliance managers (Geringer & Hebert, 1991; Yan & Gray, 1994).

The survey was conducted using an online survey system offered by NTT Communication Inc. Alliance managers of major Japanese manufacturing companies registered in the system were selected as respondents. They were requested to choose one international alliance and one domestic alliance of which they had experience, and respond to questionnaires for both of them. If they had experience of only one type of alliance, they responded in regard to that one alliance. Effective responses were obtained from 342 managers, and the response rate was 22.6%. In total, data for 497 alliance samples became available, of which 180 samples (36.7%) were international alliances between a Japanese firm and a non-Japanese firm, and 317 samples (63.8%) were domestic alliances between two Japanese firms.[2]

Measures

Scale items for constructs of hypotheses were formulated by referring to prior literature, and confirmed by two alliance managers in the preliminary tests. Based on these results, ambiguous items were clarified, overlapping items were integrated, and the number of items was narrowed down so that the respondents could answer all questions in a reasonably limited time. Items were measured using a five-point Likert scale ranging from 1 (*strongly disagree*) to 5 (*strongly agree*), except for some items requesting description. The constructs and scale items used in the survey were as follows.

Interpartner Diversity

Diversity of corporate culture was measured by four items in reference to Calori and Sarnin (1991; i.e., "The partner is different from our firm in the attitude to accepting the challenge of new projects and taking risks"). Principal components factor analysis yielded a single factor with a scale reliability of Cronbach's α of 0.81. In the same manner, *diversity of operating routines* was measured by four items in reference to Lavie et al. (2012; i.e., "The partner is different from our firm in the decision-making style, such as formal or informal"), *diversity of capabilities* was measured by three items in reference to Tomita (2010; i.e., "The partner has different technical capabilities from our firm"), and *diversity of viewpoints* was measured by three items in reference to Kale et al. (2000) (i.e., "The partner has different viewpoints from our firm in solving problems"). The scale reliabilities of Cronbach's α were 0.84, 0.80, and 0.84, respectively.[3]

Efficient Management of Alliances

Trustful relationships and close communication between partners are important to make the alliance management efficient. The scale of *efficient management of alliances* was measured by four items in reference to Lavie et al. (2012; i.e., "Our firm and the partner openly discuss opinions and thoughts with each other"). The scale reliability of Cronbach's α was 0.76.

Creation of New Knowledge

In technology alliances, the creation of new knowledge and innovation through combining capabilities and knowledge between partners will lead to good performance. The scale of *creation of* new *knowledge* was measured by four items in reference to Kale et al. (2000; i.e., "The alliance has created new knowledge which could not be produced without the partner"). The scale reliability of Cronbach's α was 0.82.

Alliance Performance

Many prior studies have evaluated the alliance performance by assessing the degree of achievement and the level of overall satisfaction. Following this approach, the scale of *alliance performance* was measured by four items in reference to Arifio (2003; i.e., "The alliance has achieved its goal"). The scale reliability of Cronbach's α was 0.90.

Contractual Governance

The scale of *contractual governance* was measured by three items in reference to Nielsen (2010; i.e., "Rights and obligations of partners are specified in detail in the alliance contract"). The scale reliability of Cronbach's α was 0.75.

Relational Governance

The scale of *relational governance* was measured by three items in reference to Hoetker and Mellewigt (2009; i.e., "A steering committee was organized for executives of both partners to regularly meet and discuss the outstanding issues"). The scale reliability of Cronbach's α was 0.60.

International Alliances

The scale to indicate *international alliances* was coded as "1" if the alliance was international between a Japanese firm and a non-Japanese firm, and as "0" if it was domestic between two Japanese firms.

Control Variables

Business categories and sales amounts were controlled by adding dummy variables. Business categories were classified into four: (a) electronics, precision, communication, and information; (b) automobile, machinery, and ship-building; (c) material and energy; and (d) medical supplies, chemistry, food, and others. Two dummy variables (*Business Dummy I* and *Business Dummy II*) were introduced to specify one of these four categories. A firm's annual sales amounts were classified into four levels: (a) more than 1 trillion yen, (b) less than 1 trillion yen and more than 100 billion yen, (c) less than 100 billion yen and more than 10 billion yen, and (d) less than 10 billion yen. Two dummy variables (*Sales Dummy I* and *Sales Dummy II*) were introduced to specify one of these four sales amounts.

Table 12.1 provides the zero-order correlations among major variables in this study. Multicollinearity does not influence the results, as the variance inflation factor (VIF) scores are all well below 10.

RESULTS

Hypothesis 1 predicts that *diversity of capabilities* (H1a) and *diversity of viewpoints* (H1b) promote the *creation of new knowledge,* which accordingly has a positive influence on the *alliance performance.* Moreover, Hypothesis 2 predicts that *diversity of corporate culture* (H2a) and *diversity of operating routines* (H2b) will hamper the *efficient management of alliances,* which accordingly has a negative influence on the *alliance performance.* In order to verify the mediating effects described in each hypothesis, mediated regression analyses in three steps were conducted following Baron and Kenny (1986). In

TABLE 12.1 Correlations Between Variables

Variables	1	2	3	4	5	6	7	8	9	10	11	12	13	14
1. Diversity of Capabilities	—													
2. Diversity of Viewpoints	.49**	—												
3. Diversity of Corporate Culture	.21**	.34**	—											
4. Diversity of Operating Routines	.24**	.38**	.71**	—										
5. Creation of New Knowledge	.49**	.44**	.01	.06	—									
6. Efficient Management of Alliances	.13**	.13**	–.16**	–.17**	.41**	—								
7. Alliance Performance	.23**	.27**	–.10*	–.08	.61**	.42**	—							
8. Contractual Governance	.23**	.34**	.12**	.12**	.52**	.33**	.54**	—						
9. Relational Governance	.09**	.13**	.19**	.18**	.10*	.05	.04	.30**	—					
10. Business Dummy I	–.12**	–.08*	.00	.00	–.14**	–.04	–.07	–.05	.11*	—				
11. Business Dummy II	–.03	–.05	–.02	–.03	–.03	–.13**	–.03	–.01	–.02	.49**	—			
12. Sales Dummy I	.02	.04	.06	.06	.02	.01	–.05	–.08*	–.06	–.08	–.17**	—		
13. Sales Dummy II	–.01	–.03	–.03	–.06	.12	.06	.07	–.03	–.08*	–.10*	–.18**	.18**	—	
14. International Alliances	–.01	–.15**	–.18**	–.24**	.02	.01	.04	–.05	–.09*	–.04	–.03	.02	.12**	—

Note: ** $p < .01$; * $p < .10$; + $p < .10$ (SD)

verifying that an independent variable affects a dependent variable through a mediator variable, the following three steps need to be confirmed: (a) an independent variable affects a mediator variable in Step 1, (b) an independent variable affects a dependent variable in Step 2, and (c) a mediator variable affects a dependent variable and also the effect of an independent variable on a dependent variable is significantly reduced when a mediator variable is introduced in Step 3.

As for Hypothesis 1, *diversity of capabilities* and *diversity of viewpoints* are independent variables, *creation of new knowledge* is a mediator variable, and *alliance performance* is a dependent variable. Model 1, Model 3, and Models 4 and 5 in Table 12.2 test Step 1, Step 2, and Step 3, respectively. In Model 1, both *diversity of capabilities* and *diversity of viewpoints* have significant positive effects on *creation of new knowledge* ($r = .31$, $p < .01$; $r = .16$, $p < .01$). Both of them also have significant positive effects on *alliance performance* in Model 3 ($r = .09$, $p < .05$; $r = .16$, $p < .01$), and their effects become insignificant when *creation of new knowledge* is introduced as a mediator variable in Model 5 ($r = -.04$, $p > .10$; $r = .06$, $p > .10$). Accordingly, in regard to Hypothesis 1, both H1a (*diversity of capabilities*) and H1b (*diversity of viewpoints*) are supported.

As for Hypothesis 2, *diversity of corporate culture* and *diversity of operating routines* are independent variables, *efficient management of alliances* is a mediator variable, and *alliance performance* is a dependent variable. Model 2, Model 3, and Models 4 and 5 in Table 12.2 test Step 1, Step 2, and Step 3, respectively. In Model 2, both *diversity of corporate culture* and *diversity of operating routines* have significant negative effects on *efficient management of alliances* ($r = -.11$, $p < .05$; $r = -.14$, $p < .05$). Both of them also have significant negative effects on *alliance performance* in Model 3 ($r = -.15$, $p < .01$; $r = -.09$, $p < .10$), and their effects are reduced when *efficient management of alliances* is introduced as a mediator variable in Model 5 ($r = -.07$, $p < .10$; $r = -.06$, $p > .10$). Accordingly, in regard to Hypothesis 2, both H2a (*diversity of corporate culture*) and H2b (*diversity of operating routines*) are supported.

Hypothesis 3 predicts that the negative influence of *diversity of corporate culture* and *diversity of operating routines* on *efficient management of alliances* is moderated by the establishment of strong alliance governance. In order to test the effects of moderating variables, samples are divided into two groups based on the high or low value of moderating variables, and the significance of negative influence between these two groups is compared (Lee & Cavusgil, 2006). This study, in order to test the moderating effects of alliance governance, divides the alliance samples into two groups according to the level of governance, that is, whether it is higher or lower than average. The results are shown in Table 12.3.

As for the moderating effect of contractual governance, *diversity of operating routines* has a weaker negative influence under high ($r = -.03$, $p > .10$) than

TABLE 12.2 Results of Multiple Linear Regression Analysis for Hypotheses 1 and 2

	Creation of New Knowledge	Efficient Management of Alliances	Alliance Performance		
	Model 1	Model 2	Model 3	Model 4	Model 5
Diversity of Capabilities	.31 (.03)**		.09 (.04)*		–.04 (.04)
Diversity of Viewpoints	.16 (.04)**		.16 (.04)**		.06 (.04)
Diversity of Corporate Culture		–.11 (.05)*	–.15 (.05)**		–.07 (.04)+
Diversity of Operating Routines		–.14 (.05)*	–.09 (.05)+		–.06 (.04)
Creation of New Knowledge				.40 (.04)**	.41 (.04)**
Efficient Management of Alliances				.15 (.03)**	.12 (.03)**
Contractual Governance	.41 (.03)**	.37 (.04)**	.52 (.04)**	.30 (.04)**	.31 (.04)**
Relational Governance	–.05 (.03)	–.01 (.04)	–.08 (.03)*	.09 (.03)*	–.07 (.03)*
Business Dummy I	–.14 (.07)+	.10 (.09)	–.01 (.08)	.04 (.07)	.04 (.07)
Business Dummy II	.07 (.08)	–.31 (.09)**	–.02 (.08)	.01 (.08)	–.01 (.07)
Sales Dummy I	.07 (.07)	.01 (.08)	–.05 (.07)	.10 (.07)	–.08 (.06)
Sales Dummy II	.02 (.07)	.08 (.08)	.16 (.07*	.14 (.06)*	.14 (.06)*
International Alliances	.13 (.07)+	–.05 (.08)	.05 (.07)	.06 (.06)	.02 (.07)
Adjusted R Squared	.45**	.19**	.38**	.48**	.50**
Sample Numbers	**497**	**497**	**497**	**497**	**497**

Note: ** $p < .01$; * $p < .05$; + $p < .10$ (SD)

TABLE 12.3 Results of Multiple Linear Regressions Analysis for Hypothesis 3

	Contractual Governance		Relational Governance	
	Weak	Strong	Weak	Strong
	Efficient Management of Alliances			
	Model 2			
Diversity of Capabilities				
Diversity of Viewpoints				
Diversity of Corporate Culture	–.06 (.08)	–.15 (.07)*	–.17 (.08)*	–.04 (.08)
Diversity of Operating Routines	–.20 (.08)*	–.03 (.07)	–.22 (.08)**	.06 (.08)
Creation of New Knowledge				
Efficient Management of Alliances				
Contractual Governance	.10 (.12)	.36 (.08)**	.25 (.06)**	.46 (.05)**
Relational Governance	–.05 (.07)	–.01 (.05)	.26 (.44)	.05 (.07)
Business Dummy I	.13 (.15)	.07 (.11)	.04 (.12)	.01 (.15)
Business Dummy II	–.36 (.16)*	–.27 (.12)*	–.30 (.13)*	–.28 (.15)+
Sales Dummy I	–.20 (.13)	.16 (.11)	–.17 (.11)	.13 (.12)
Sales Dummy II	–.09 (.13)	.26 (.11)*	.29 (.11)*	–.14 (.12)
International Alliances	–.09 (.13)	.04 (.11)	–.08 (.11)	.01 (.12)
Adjusted R Squared	.11**	.18**	.22**	.25**
Sample Numbers	**245**	**252**	**256**	**241**

Note: ** $p < .01$; * $p < .05$; + $p < .10$ (SD)

low level of governance ($r = -.20$, $p < .05$) as hypothesized; however, *diversity of corporate culture* has a stronger negative influence under high ($r = -.15$, $p < .05$) than low level of governance ($r = -.06$, $p > .10$), contrary to the hypothesis. Accordingly, H3a was not supported. On the other hand, as regards the moderating effect of relational governance, both *diversity of corporate culture* and *diversity of operating routines* have weaker negative influences under high ($r = -.04$, $p > .10$; $r = .06$, $p > .10$) than low level of governance ($r = -.17$, $p < .05$; $r = -.22$, $p < .01$), as hypothesized, accordingly H3b was supported. As a result, the moderating effect was confirmed only for relational governance.

CONCLUSION

Summary of Findings

Most prior studies have discussed interpartner diversity by comparing international alliances with domestic alliances. Some research has emphasized the negative sides of these diversities, noting that the difference of corporate culture induces distrust between partners, or showing that inconsistency of operating routines impairs efficiency. On the other hand, other studies have pointed out the positive side of diversity by emphasizing that the fusion of heterogeneous capabilities promotes innovative ideas, or by indicating that the combination of different viewpoints contributes to problem-solving. Thus, since conventional studies have discussed the interpartner diversity from various different viewpoints, opposing views have been asserted about its influence on the alliance performance. In the fields of empirical studies comparing the performance between international alliances and domestic alliances, some studies have shown the predominance of the former, while others have insisted on the opposite conclusion. In the globalization of markets, the framework of alliances must be globally optimized. In many situations, it is unavoidable to ally with firms of varying diversity. Therefore, the issue is not whether the alliance with diversified partners is better or worse, but how to utilize the positive effects of interpartner diversity while overcoming its negative impacts.

Based on awareness of the issues described above, this study aimed to grasp, by comprehensively evaluating the various factors of interpartner diversity, how such diversity influences the performance of alliances, and how such influence is mediated or moderated. Hypotheses regarding these issues were formulated, and they were tested and verified by analyzing the results of a survey of alliance managers. As a result, it was shown that the diversity of capabilities and viewpoints has a positive influence on the alliance performance through promoting the creation of new knowledge, while the diversity of corporate culture and operating routines has a negative influence on the alliance performance through impeding the efficient management of alliances. Although these results are basically consistent with prior studies which have separately discussed each factor of diversity, the contribution of this study is that these results were verified using a theoretical model which comprehensively captured various factors of diversity. Moreover, this study also discussed the role of alliance governance in moderating the negative influence of diversity, and such effects of relational governance were confirmed.

Theoretical Considerations

I would like to consider the reasons why H3a was not supported. Contractual governance and relational governance play complementary roles in alliances (Poppo & Zenger, 2002); however, they have different features. Because contractual governance has compulsory power to control opportunistic behaviors and coordinate interests of conflict, it is an effective means of efficiently managing alliances. However, because it is impossible to prepare perfect contracts specifying all conditions under all situations, contractual governance has limitations in dealing with problems, especially if the environmental change is substantial and the level of uncertainty is high. In addition, excessively detailed specification of contracts will result in loss of flexibility and will induce suspicion between partners. On the other hand, the relational governance is grounded in trustful relationships through close communication and joint efforts between partners, and it can flexibly deal with environmental changes or unexpected situations. Although it takes time to construct trustful relationships, they will be steadily developed and strengthened as time goes on (Goerzen, 2007). In the test of Hypothesis 3, the effect of relational governance (H3b) was confirmed; however that of contractual governance (H3a) was not. These results show that relational governance is more effective in dealing with the issues related to interpartner diversity, especially for technology alliances in which the level of uncertainty is generally high. This study also shows the direct effects, not the moderating effects, of contractual governance on the efficient management of alliances. Contractual governance, with its compulsory power, may influence alliance management and alliance performance through different mechanisms to those related to interpartner diversity. Although it is beyond the scope of this study, this issue needs further consideration.

Managerial Implications

This study also has practical implications for alliance management. Although the number of international alliances is increasing, many firms still have a tendency to form domestic alliances. In the survey of alliance managers, they responded that the similarity of corporate culture and operating routines, as well as the ease of communication due to having the same language and customs, were the major reasons for selecting partners from the same country (Yasuda, 2012). They are likely to make this partner selection due to concern about the negative influence of interpartner diversity, although the merits of diversified capabilities and viewpoints are recognized. This study emphasizes the importance of having a comprehensive understanding of interpartner diversity, by showing that each factor of diversity has a different influence on the alliance performance based on the different mechanisms. This study also shows that the negative influence of diversity can be moderated by strengthening relational governance. With this understanding of interpartner diversity in mind, alliance managers will be able to promote international alliances with confidence, and utilize interpartner diversity for the achievement of good performance.

Suggestions for Future Research

Future research could address some of the limitations of this study. First, the measurement of each construct in this study is based on the subjective evaluation by alliance managers of the focal firm. This method is common in most prior studies; however it is likely that the results are influenced by the selection of respondents. While surveying respondents from both partners is challenging, future research may obtain measurements from both sides and enhance the reliability of analysis by confirming their consistency. Moreover, although this study does not compare the results between different industries, it is likely that the influence of interpartner diversity differs depending on the characteristics of the industries concerned. It would be an interesting research topic to evaluate the universality of results across different industries, and this would open the door to the new research field of comparative analysis between industries. Finally, this study uses a simplified model to analyze the influence of interpartner diversity on alliance performance. For example, the model assumes that the diversity of capabilities and viewpoints leads to the creation of new knowledge, which influences the performance of alliances. There may be more processes to mediate this influence other than the creation of new knowledge. Furthermore, this study examines the implications of limited elements of alliance governance, and it would also be meaningful to extend the scope of governance in the model. Future research may explore more factors in the model to explain their influence on alliance performance and deepen understanding about the interpartner diversity in alliances.

NOTES

1. Technology alliances are defined as cooperation between firms on matters related to technology, such as joint development, joint research, technology licenses, technology support, and so on.
2. Out of 180 international alliances, the following are the names of countries where the foreign partner is headquartered, and the number of international alliances with partners from such countries: the United States (57), China (30), South Korea (23), Germany (14), Taiwan (7), Vietnam (7), India (6), Thailand (6), Singapore (5), France (4), Italy (3), Canada (3), the United Kingdom (2), the Netherlands (2), Australia (2), Hong Kong (1), Chile (1), Russia (1), Brazil (1), the Philippines (1), South Africa (1), Finland (1), Malaysia (1), and Belgium (1).
3. A respondent was requested to evaluate the difference between his/her firm and its partner, not to evaluate his/her firm or its partner independently. For example, on the question of whether the decision process was formal or informal, the respondent evaluated the differences in the decision process between the two firms regardless of whether his/her firm was more formal or more informal.

ACKNOWLEDGMENT

This chapter, save some minor changes, is a translated version of the author's Japanese language article: Yasuda, H. (2015). [Influence of interpartner diversities on the performance of strategic alliances]. *Journal of Business Management, 35*, 16–27.

REFERENCES

Arifio, A. (2003). Measures of strategic alliance performance: An analysis of construct validity. *Journal of International Business Studies, 34*(1), 66–79.

Asakawa, K. (2006). Metanational management: Major issues and future research directions [in Japanese]. *Organizational Science, 40*(1), 13–25.

Barney, J. B. (1991). Firm resources and sustained competitive advantage. *Journal of Management, 17*(1), 99–120.

Baron, R. M., & Kenny, D. A. (1986). The moderator-mediator variable distinction in social psychological research: Conceptual, strategic and statistical considerations. *Journal of Personality and Social Psychology, 51*(6), 1173–1182.

Bruyaka, O. P., Caner, T., & Prescott, J. E. (2011, August). *Relative contribution of alliance ties and partner's diversity to firm performance.* Paper presented at the Academy of Management 2011 Annual Meeting, San Antonio, TX.

Calori, R., & Sarnin, P. (1991). Corporate culture and economic performance: A French study. *Organization Studies, 12*(1), 49–74.

Chandler, G. H., & Hanks, S. H. (1993). Measuring the performance of emerging business: A validation study. *Journal of Business Venturing, 8*(5), 391–408.

Cullen, J. B., Johnson, J. L., & Sakano, T. (1995). Japanese and local partner commitment to IJVs: Psychological consequences outcomes and investments in the IJV relationship. *Journal of International Business Studies, 26*(1), 91–115.

Das, T. K., & Teng, B. (2000). A resource-based theory of strategic alliances. *Journal of Management, 26*(1), 31–61.

Das, T. K., & Teng, B. (2003). Partner analysis and alliance performance. *Scandinavian Journal of Management, 19*(3), 279–308.

Datta, D. K. (1991). Organizational fit and acquisition performance: Effects of post-acquisition integration. *Strategic Management Journal, 12*(4), 281–297.

Delerue, H., & Simon, E. (2009). National cultural values and the perceived relational risks in biotechnology alliance relationships. *International Business Review, 18*(1), 14–25.

Doney, P. M., Cannon, J. P., & Mullen, M. R. (1998). Understanding the influence of national culture on the development of trust. *Academy of Management Review, 23*(3), 601–620.

Dussauge, P., & Garrette, B. (1995). Determinants of success in international strategic alliances: Evidence from the global aerospace industry. *Journal of International Business Studies, 26*(3), 505–530.

Dutta, S., & Weiss, A. M. (1997). The relationship between a firm's level of technological innovativeness and its pattern of partnership agreement. *Management Science, 43*(3), 343–356.

Faems, D., Alberink, R., Jong, G., Groen, A., & Klein Woolthuis, R. (2012). Contractual alliance governance: Impact of different contract functions on alliance performance. In T. K. Das (Ed.), *Strategic alliances in a globalizing world* (pp. 67–92). Charlotte, NC: Information Age.

Folta, T. B. (1998). Governance and uncertainty: The tradeoff between administrative control and commitment. *Strategic Management Journal, 19*(11), 1007–1028.

Folta, T. B., & Ferrier, W. J. (2000). The effect of national culture on partner buyouts in cross-border biotechnology alliances. *Journal of High Technology Management Research, 11*(2), 175–198.

Geringer, J. M., & Hebert, L. (1991). Measuring performance of international joint ventures. *Journal of International Business Studies, 22*(2), 249–264.

Goerzen, A. (2007). Alliance networks and firm performance: The impact of repeated partnerships. *Strategic Management Journal, 28*(5), 487–509.

Goerzen, A., & Beamish, P. W. (2005). The effect of alliance network diversity of multinational enterprise performance. *Strategic Management Journal, 26*(4), 333–354.

Gulati, R. (1998). Alliances and networks. *Strategic Management Journal, 19*(4), 293–317.

Hoetker, G., & Mellewigt, T. (2009). Choice and performance of governance mechanisms: Matching alliance governance to asset type. *Strategic Management Journal, 30*(10), 1025–1044.

Kale, P., Singh, H., & Perlmutter, H. (2000). Learning and protection of proprietary assets in strategic alliances: Building relational capital. *Strategic Management Journal, 21*(3), 217–237.

Kogut, B., & Singh, H. (1988). The effect of national culture on the choice of entry mode. *Journal of International Business Studies, 19*(3), 411–432.

Kumar, R., & Andersen, P. H. (2000). Inter-firm diversity and the management of meaning in international strategic alliances. *International Business Review, 9*(2), 237–252.

Kumar, R., & Nti, K. O. (2004). National cultural values and the evolution of process and outcome discrepancies in international strategic alliances. *Journal of Applied Behavioral Science, 40*(3), 344–361.

Lane, H.W., & Beamish, P.W. (1990). Cross-cultural cooperative behavior in joint ventures in LDCs. *Management International Review, 30*, 87–102.

Lavie, D., Haunschild, P., & Khanna, P. (2012). Organizational differences, relational mechanisms, and alliance performance. *Strategic Management Journal, 33*(13), 1453–1479.

Lee, G. K. (2007). The significance of network resources in the race to enter emerging product markets: The convergence of telephony communications and computer networking, 1989-2001. *Strategic Management Journal, 28*(1), 17–37.

Lee, Y., & Cavusgil, T. (2006). Enhancing alliance performance: The effects of contractual-based versus relational-based governance. *Journal of Business Research, 59*(8), 896–905.

Lin, Z., Yang, H., & Arya, B. (2009). Alliance partners and firm performance: Resource complementarity and status association. *Strategic Management Journal, 30*(4), 921–940.

McEvily, B., & Zaheer, A. (1999). Bridging ties: A source of firm heterogeneity in competitive capabilities. *Strategic Management Journal, 20*(12), 1133–1156.

Nielsen, B. B. (2010). Strategic fit, contractual, and procedural governance in alliances. *Journal of Business Research, 63*(7), 682–689.

Oxley, J. E. (1997). Appropriability hazards and governance in strategic alliances: A transaction cost approach. *Journal of Law, Economics, and Organization, 13*(2), 387–409.

Park, S. H., & Russo, M. V. (1996). When competition eclipses cooperation: An event history analysis of joint venture failure. *Management Science, 42*(6), 875–890.

Parkhe, A. (1991). Interfirm diversity, organizational learnings, and longevity in global strategic alliances. *Journal of International Business Studies, 22*(4), 579–601.

Pateli, A., & Lioukas, S. (2011). The choice of governance mode in ICT alliances: A property rights approach. *Information and Management, 48*(1), 69–77.

Phene, N., Lindquist, K. F., & Marsh, L. (2006). Breakthrough innovations in the U.S. biotechnology industry: The effects of technological space and geographic origin. *Strategic Management Journal, 27*(4), 369–388.

Poppo, L., & Zenger, T. (2002). Do formal contracts and relational governance function as substitutes or complements? *Strategic Management Journal, 23*(8), 707–725.

Porter, M. E. (1990). *The competitive advantage of nations.* New York, NY: Free Press.

Rosenkopf, L., & Nerkar, A. (2001). Beyond local search: Boundary-spanning, exploration, and impact in the optical disk industry. *Strategic Management Journal, 22*(4), 287–306.

Sampson, R. C. (2007). R&D alliances and firm performance: The impact of technological diversity and alliance organization on innovation. *Academy of Management Journal, 50*(2), 364–386.

Silva, S., Bradley, F., & Sousa, C. (2012). Empirical test of the trust-performance link in an international alliances context. *International Business Review, 21*(2), 293–306.

Stuart, T. E., & Podolny, J. M. (1996). Local search and the evolution of technological capabilities. *Strategic Management Journal, 17,* 21–38.

Tomita, K. (2010). Building trust in the strategic alliance between Japanese-American pharmaceutical companies [in Japanese]. *Organizational Science, 43*(3), 18–32.

Williamson, O. E. (1975). *Markets and Hierarchies.* New York, NY: Free Press.

Yan, A., & Gray, B. (1994). Bargaining power, management control, and performance in United States–China joint ventures: A comparative case study. *Academy of Management Journal, 37*(6), 1478–1517.

Yan, A., & Zeng, M. (1999). International joint venture stability: A critique of previous research, reconceptualization, and directions for future research. *Journal of International Business Studies, 30,* 397–414.

Yano, M. (1997). Heterogeneity and creativity of firms' research and development teams [in Japanese]. *Organizational Science, 31*(3), 61–73.

Yasuda, H. (2012). Influence of diversity between partners in global alliances [in Japanese]. *Journal of Business Management, 30,* 3–15.

Yasuda, H. (2015). Influence of interpartner diversity on the performance of strategic alliances [in Japanese]. *Journal of Business Management, 35,* 16–27.

CHAPTER 13

ALLIANCE CAPABILITY DEVELOPMENT THROUGH THE ADOPTION AND ADAPTATION OF INTRA- AND INTERORGANIZATIONAL MANAGEMENT CONTROL PRACTICES

Diana Marie De Silva
Ernst Verwaal

ABSTRACT

The cycle of adoption and adaptation of management control mirrors the dynamic and evolving nature of alliance capability development. It is possible to trace through a review of literature the evolution of management control from the transfer of best practices across interconnected organizations. This transformation process occurring between the (intra)organization and the interorganizational environment is the outcome of continual efforts to build

Managing the Partners in Strategic Alliances, pages 319–343

integrated management control systems for which the current literature does not provide sufficient guidance. The chapter offers propositions intended to advance current research in this unexplored area of management control and alliance capability development. We suggest that developments in alliance capability is displayed by the increased effectiveness in terms of output measurability and task programmability of managing a portfolio of alliances using new and sophisticated management control mechanisms. We develop a co-evolutionary framework that allows a cross examination of two separate organizational levels accounting for both the evolution of the firm and the alliance. The framework shows how the simultaneous and recursive adoption and adaptation of management controls across a network of organizations contribute to the development of alliance capability.

INTRODUCTION

Links between research on management control and alliance capability (Dekker & Van den Abbeele, 2010) unravel interesting dynamics between organizations and their alliances. The transfer of knowledge and competencies across epistemic and organizational boundaries facilitates evolutionary transformations that reshape how firms do business (Coad & Cullen, 2006). Repeated engagement in alliances allows firms to learn from their experiences and the experience of others (Findikoglu & Lavie, 2019). Some companies enter alliances with the intention to observe and imitate partners to acquire useful practices. Firms are motivated to engage in interorganizational relationships to access and combine distinctive resources or competencies, resulting in a stronger competitive position than could not be achieved independently (Dyer & Singh, 1998). But other than the alliance partners' desire to bank on new abilities, integrating management controls become an essential prerequisite for ensuring smooth firm (Eisenhardt, 1985) and alliance operations (Ricciardi, Zardini, & Rossignoli, 2018; X. Zhang, Van Donk, & van der Vaart, 2016). Management control in alliances increases response conformity, deter opportunistic behavior of alliance partners (Nooteboom, 1996), and improves consistency and transparency, which may enhance the co-alignment of assets developed by the alliance partners (Teece, 1986). As management control plays an essential role in the success of alliances, the competence to effectively operationalize control mechanisms is a key alliance capability. The studies shown in Table 13.1 provide evidence of the link of alliance capability and management control mechanisms. Generally, the level of alliance capability of a firm has been measured by the number of mechanisms the company has adopted, such as alliance manuals, tools, procedures, training programs, and codification of best practices (Draulans et al., 2003; Heimeriks & Duysters, 2007; Kale & Singh, 2007), which are all identifiable management controls.

TABLE 13.1 Potentially Relevant Literature That Links Alliance Capability Development and Management Control

Study	Links to Alliance Capability Development	Links to Management Control
Anderson (1990)	Improved understanding of the transformation process of input to output measures, and improved accuracy of measurements	Performance assessment
Ariño et al. (2001)	Facilitating the processes of collaboration through the transfer of relational capabilities	Complementarity of trust and formal governance mechanisms
Dekker et al. (2016)	Learning management skills as part of the learning objectives of collaboration	Collaborative performance management
Dekker & Van den Abbeele (2010)	Organizational learning	Interfirm control
Draulans, et al. (2003)	Building alliance capability	Management techniques, alliance management mechanisms
Findikoglu & Lavie (2019)	Alliance management capability gained from general partnering experience (GPE) and partner-specific experience (PSE)	Dedicated alliance function (DAF) as a key element of the formal alliance organization
Sluyts et al. (2011)	Alliance management capability	Alliance learning mechanisms—such as alliance manuals, tools, procedures, training programs, and codification of best practices

Control mechanisms are the means by which to exercise control and they have been described and classified similarly for firms (e.g., Merchant, 1998) and alliances (e.g., Dekker, 2004). Although the literature identifies the same set of control mechanisms, they operate differently in these two contexts particularly for performance measurement (Lehtinen & Ahola, 2010). One classification makes a distinction between formal and informal control mechanisms (Smith, Carroll, & Ashford, 1995). The organization theory and the strategic alliance literature suggest these institutions require both formal and informal controls (Almeida, Song, & Grant, 2002; Berry, Coad, Harris, Otley, & Stringer, 2009; Caglio & Ditillo, 2008; Dekker, 2004). Formal controls are identified as standard processes (e.g., how decisions are made, resources allocated and information processed), formalized organizational structures (e.g., how roles, responsibilities and power are assigned; Busco, Giovannoni, & Scapens, 2008), and legalized agreements in writing (Dekker, 2004). Whereas, informal or social control are described as unstructured processes and routines that enable self-regulation (Ouchi,

1979), grounded primarily on trust (Dekker, 2004), culture-based mechanisms (Geringer & Hebert, 1989), shared norms, values, and perceptions (Ariño, de la Torre, & Ring, 2001). The work of Anderson (1990) provides one of the earliest insights suggesting that performance assessment can be executed both formally and informally depending first on how well managers understand the transformation process of input to output measures, and second on how accurate they are with their measurements, both conditions gained over time and maturity. However, the evolution of management control has not been adequately explored in literature. Li, Tang, Okano, and Gao (2013) claim to have provided the first observation of evolutionary changes in management control by investigating how the shared and split control model provides the balance between stability and change in management control specific in international joint ventures. A shared but split control model allows alliance partners to share control over the entire range of activities of the alliance but each possesses dominant control only over certain specific activities. In an earlier study of Choi and Beamish (2004), the split management control system performed better than the shared management control and the partner-dominant management control system. This result highlights the importance of firm-specific abilities of organizations in alliance management to which several studies refer to as alliance capabilities.

Alliance capability (Draulans, de Man, & Volberda, 2003), alliance management capability (Kauppila, 2015; Sluyt, Matthyssens, Martens, & Streukens, 2011), alliance competence (Lambe, Spekman, & Hunt, 2002), and collaboration know-how (Simonin, 1997) have been given similar interpretations described as "the ability to create successful alliances, based on learning about alliance management and leveraging alliance knowledge inside the company" (Draulans et al., 2003, p. 152). From past experience, partnering firms learn skills for identifying potential partners, negotiating terms of the agreement, managing and monitoring the activities, knowing when to terminate, and transferring knowledge (Simonin, 1997). The highlight is on the firms' individual characteristics and capabilities to drive the performance of the strategic alliance and to combat the high-failure rate of alliances in general. This makes certain companies more attractive as alliance partners than others. Lambe et al. (2002) suggests that the best way to enhance alliance capabilities, other than having the right infrastructure, is to engage into more alliances and turn them into a learning experience. More recent trends focus on strategic alliance research on learning and capability development in order to foster innovation. In the past, innovation activities were kept within the boundaries of the firms which is why prior studies view learning as a firm-level construct (Jiang & Li, 2008).

The alliance capability is a result of past experiences and learning processes which are dynamic and path-dependent. We follow its development by looking into the evolution of management control both at the firm- and alliance-level. We perceive the evolution of interorganizational management controls to culminate towards increased alliance capability. Transforming alongside the evolution of alliances that follow a pattern of learning cycles (Doz, 1996), alliance partners progressively make improvements in the alliance conditions as they make irreversible commitments. The alliance goes through a series of transitions as they evolve over a cycle of learning, reevaluation, and readjustment. This study aims to establish the strong link between management control and alliance capability by integrating (intra)organizational and interorganizational perspectives.

THEORETICAL DEVELOPMENTS ON THE RELATIONSHIP OF INTRA- AND INTERORGANIZATIONAL MANAGEMENT CONTROL

Competing in today's global business environment pushes enterprises to go beyond the boundaries of the firm (Almeida et al., 2002; Dekker, 2016). Over the past 3 decades, many industries have become highly networked to take advantage of the benefits of building interorganizational relationships (Gomes, Barnes, & Mahmood, 2016). Dealing with interorganizational relationships has been challenged by the plethora of related terms such as inter-firm, network, collaboration, partnership, extended enterprise, joint venture, and alliance. With small differences in their definitions, these terms are conceptually alike, in the sense that they identify two or more business organizations that jointly define a strategy to pursue a set of private and common goals (Ariño et al., 2001). Among many examples include international joint venture (IJV) which is unique to cross-border relationships involving shared equity; public–private partnership (PPP) which is exclusive to partners coming from the public and private sectors with obvious diverse goals; and collaborative supply chains (SC) which are unique to closely cooperating companies in vertically structured relationships. The organizations remain autonomous and independent entities as they try to coordinate their business processes and share resources, knowledge, and risks. Maintaining control of the business becomes more challenging as firms expand their reach, therefore, in order to keep vision of the firm goals, distinct management control competences are necessary.

There is a limited yet relevant existing literature that appreciates the association of (intra)organizational and interorganizational management control. Studies on strategic alliances have largely advanced over the past decade with little recognition of their potential inter-relationships mostly accounted for by the difference in the level of analysis (Dekker, 2016). These are legitimate concerns raised regarding the validity of application of control frameworks as differences can be expected in the way management control is applied in different contexts. Differences are expected because a firm is governed by a hierarchical structure whereas an alliance involves multiple centers of legally independent organizations that have only partially overlapping objectives. This goal incongruence sets limitations that need to be addressed when examining the usefulness of management control mechanisms in the alliance context. Although seen from separate lenses, these management controls find its roots in organization theory with the goal of predicting behaviors driven by individual and collective interests.

Two streams of literature have separately developed which studied the dynamics of intra- and interorganizational control dynamics (Kraus & Strömsten, 2016). Part of the studies investigate how (intra)organizational control drive changes interorganizational management control (Coad & Cullen, 2006; Cuganesan & Lee, 2006; Mahama, 2006), whereas, the other stream looked at the opposite, which determined how interorganizational management controls drive changes in (intra)organizational management control (Mouritsen, Hansen, & Hansen, 2001). Altogether, these two perspectives reveal a co-evolving dynamic between them. A number of management control variables originally conceived for (intra)organizational analysis have been adopted for interorganizational analysis (Caglio & Ditillo, 2008; Dekker, 2016). Interorganizational management controls can be associated with multiple aspects of organizational practices where the translations of control, strategy, organization, and technology drive modes of dependence and autonomy, first at the interorganizational level and then later, in the partner firms (Mouritsen et al., 2001).

Prior management accounting researches have investigated inter-firm relationships aimed at aligning the interests and actions of boundary spanners (Dekker, 2016). Although constantly faced with the predicament on whose objectives should their decisions be aligned, boundary spanners are in the best position to move from a firm- to an alliance-standpoint to align individual and collective interest of the collaborating entities. Boundary spanner interactions enable coordinated adaptation between partners, reduce uncertainty, build trust, and learning (Dyer & Singh 1998; Kale & Singh 2007). Performance measurement, information sharing, and boundary spanner interaction are also found to be complementary practices in the management of inter-firm relationships (Dekker, Ding, & Groot, 2016). Furthermore, the management accounting literature recognizes open book accounting and cost management practices as an exercise of power to try to establish centers in relations beyond the firm's boundaries (Mouritsen et al., 2001). Kraus and Strömsten (2016) details how "accounting talk" determined the intra- and interorganizational control dynamics. Internal management accounting can affect firms' opportunities, choices and practices at the inter-firm level (Carlsson-Wall, Kraus, & Lind, 2011).

In this chapter, we first explore the collective design of interorganizational management control by initially assuming that authority relationships are different at the intra- and the interorganizational level. This difference has implications for the way in which a collective solves the problems related to the creation of a hierarchy between different bodies of appropriate knowledge. At the (intra)organizational level, control conflicts are solved by centralization and alignment with leaders who often have formal authority. At the interorganizational level, the absence of a formal hierarchy encourages partners to invest heavily in relational activity which allows them to keep their status in a context where conflicts are always present (Pina-Stranger & Lazega, 2010).

Dekker et al. (2016) and Larimo, Nguyen, and Ali (2016) identify motive or collaborative objectives as a key antecedent that determines the alliance choice of management control practices such as partner selection effort and formal governance extensiveness (Dekker, 2008) or performance measurement choice between financial and/or non-financial measures of performance (Larimo et al., 2016). Besides translating the firms' strategies, competencies, technologies, and products, management controls bridge the information gap between different organizations. "Management control could provide managers with a common language informed by accounting and non-accounting measures and information that are spread across the different parts of the organization" (Busco et al., 2008, p. 104). A firm in an alliance that possesses (intra)organizational control mechanisms different from its partners would likely prefer to adopt its own management controls at the interorganizational level. The desire to maintain control alignment may be warranted by the need to efficiently monitor the achievement of the private goals of the firm in relation to the alliance. If for example, one partner is concerned about the profitability of the alliance as it contributes to the profitability of the firm, then the partner will push for the monitoring of financial indicators to ensure output measurability. As Eisenhardt (1985) argues, the preference for a suitable control mode relies on two task features—output measurability and task programmability. Output measurability "refers to the ability to quantify outputs in an exact and objective manner" whereas task programmability "refers to the degree to which managers understand the transformation process in which appropriate behaviors are to take place" (Das & Teng, 2001, p. 259) both important for improving effectiveness of managing the task at hand. Increased output measurability and task programmability on both the firm and alliance end are indications of a strongly integrated management control system. Systematically relating control to operations management is quite useful for capturing the complexities of how intra- and interorganizational control interact (Kraus & Strömsten, 2016). The acquisition of comparative information during partner search facilitates interorganizational management control design, by providing organizations with knowledge of which performance levels and which behaviors are (un)desirable (Anderson & Dekker, 2005) to their partners. Providing this common language to agents with various backgrounds is a critical function of an effective and efficient knowledge-driven organization (Arrow, 1974) and is a requisite for the effective co-alignment of complementary knowledge assets (Teece, 1986).

Different information characteristics favor different types of controls (Ouchi, 1979). Knowledge of partners' processes and technology particularly facilitates use of behavior control mechanisms because it allows specifying in more detail desired behaviors and monitoring, evaluating, adjusting, and rewarding these behaviors. The future-oriented information about cooperation and dependence relates more strongly to use of outcome control mechanisms. Indeed, such information enables the partners to plan and set performance goals, as well as to monitor, evaluate, reward, and discuss performance outcomes (Dekker & Van den Abbeele, 2010). When partners in the alliance have similar (intra)organizational controls, they may comprehend better how each partner contributes to the achievement of the alliance goals. Partners may be able to integrate interorganizational controls and their (intra)organizational controls more efficiently as they see them fit their own private goals, standards, and way of doing. This leads us to our first proposition:

> **Proposition 1:** *Alliance partners that have common (intra)organizational management controls increase the output measurability and task programmability of interorganizational management controls.*

We argue however that not all alliance partners are willing to adopt new management control practices which do not align with their organization standards. We attribute this behavior to the partners' differences in epistemic and organizational frameworks. Research related to epistemic communities (e.g., Haas, 1992; Holzner, 1968) suggest that knowledge and competencies which are not applied or produced in line with the community's epistemic framework is not considered valid. Akgün et al. (2006, p. 75) argued that "group beliefs, as well as the preservation of routines and mindsets (i.e., being imprisoned by routines and habits), inhibit the reception and evaluation of new technology information and this reduces the value of perceived new information." The same may be the case across organizations that have their own established governance structures and management control practices associated with a set of problems to which their organizational competence is directed. According to Mørk, Aanestad, Hanseth, and Grisot, (2008), the complexity of the network of people, activities, and structures could explain why learning on the system level of epistemic communities can be challenging because it may lead to path-dependent learning processes, and radical change can become limited if the knowledge required by new and different practices is incompatible with the existing stock of knowledge. In effect, alliance capability development is slowed down by organizational differences. In alliances, Mowery, Oxley, and Silverman (1996) reiterates that the complementarity of partner expertise contributes to each firm's absorptive capacity that determines knowledge transfer and learning. Studies on the alignment and fit between partners (Moshtari, 2016; X. Zhang et al., 2016) investigate the effect of goal disparity, heterogeneity (Paul, Seetharaman, Samarah, & Mykytyn, 2004) and functional diversity (Mohr & Puck, 2005) on alliance performance. For Sluyts et al. (2011), the concept of alliance capability match between alliance partners offers interesting research opportunities to address questions related to whether a specific alliance can benefit from the "fit" between partners with regard to their alliance capability.

By free selection, firms tend to adopt the most effective practices that support the most frequent organizational tasks and address the most common problems in their respective firms (Dekker, 2016). During the transfer of management control knowledge and competencies from inter- to (intra) organizational levels, firms are under less pressure to adopt practices that challenge their traditional way of doing and may only choose those that serve them best. However, this selective behavior is a convenience that potentially slows down alliance capability development. To be able to develop a sharpened alliance management competence, firms should be willing to open their epistemic and organizational boundaries to external influences. This is possible as Berends, Garud, Debackere, and Weggeman (2011) describe an alternative mechanism for tapping into knowledge across boundaries called "thinking along." Unlike knowledge transfer and knowledge transformation, this interactive process allows a firm to tap into its partners' knowledge base without compromising its specializations. It is an interactive process that respects and simply eludes interpretative barriers so partners do not have to get in the way of each other's ways of knowing. This non-invasive process of tapping into knowledge across boundaries offers a preliminary approach towards reconciling differences critical for the establishment of integrated management control systems.

Recently, there has been an emphasis on integrating a company's internal and external activities which has become a major thrust in the development of integrated information systems (X. Zhang et al., 2016). Wong, Lai, Cheng, and Lun (2015) shows a positive structural relationship between interorganizational information integration and information and communication technology (ICT)-enabled collaborative decision making, leading to customer service performance, when a high level of ICT infrastructure development is present. By measuring and communicating the impact of any strategic decision, it is possible to create understanding, mold behavior and improve competitiveness, and its main ability is to link strategies with targets and goals. The importance of using performance information is explained by the fact that people in firms respond to measures; and the right measures not only offer a means of monitoring whether objectives are being implemented, but also a means of communicating strategy and encouraging its implementation. Cunha, Ferreira, and Macedo (2008) explain that in new forms of organization that are more demanding and complex than single organizations, such as integrated SC and production networks, information and communication play major roles for effective performance measurement. It is important to have a common information platform where partners can draw knowledge from performance data. Lohman, Fortuin, and Wouters (2004) point out various barriers to the design and implementation of performance measurement systems accounted to decentralized operational historical reporting, deficient insight in cohesion among metrics, uncertainty about what to measure, poor communication between reports and users, and dispersed information technology infrastructure. Zollo and Winter (2002) suggest that deliberate learning efforts to articulate and codify collective knowledge useful for handling complex organizational tasks act as a basis for improving a firm's skills to manage those tasks more effectively. From this, we derive our second proposition.

Proposition 2: *Firms deliberate efforts to establish integrated intra- and interorganizational management control systems speed up alliance capability development.*

In this respect, some partners will gain more alliance capabilities than others depending on the degree of partner difference and their willingness to align their way of doing with those of their partners. Having the ICT infrastructure also contributes to the efficiency of developing alliance capability; however, little attention has been paid to ICT and its impact on control system design and capability (Berry et al., 2009). Basing from prior management accounting literature, systems that integrate intra- and interorganizational management controls are limited to traditional information systems such as SC cost management practices (e.g., Wong et al., 2015), open book accounting and functional analysis (e.g., Mouritsen et al., 2001), and mechanisms that influence the behavior of boundary spanners (Dekker, 2016; Mahama, 2006). Berry et al. (2009) emphasize the importance of future research to stay grounded on real situations especially when dealing with integrative activities on management control design and use. It is an organizational reality that firms would prefer to remain independent, flexible, and confidential when it comes to their internal management control and strategies which is only logical for maintaining firm competitive advantage.

The growing interconnectedness of the business landscape has been accounted for through developments in ICT and the growth in the number of alliances formed over the years. Although a lot more failures than successes have been recorded over history, strategic alliances continue to grow in number (Gomes et al., 2016). Firms remain motivated to venture in alliances which demand for greater alliance capability to increase the chance of building successful relationships. Building from our first two propositions, the greater motivation to gain alliance capability should therefore encourage firms to increase integration efforts and become more open to their partners. In addition, we argue that direct and indirect transfers of alliance capabilities can be traced within the network of organizations. Direct transfers of management control knowledge and competencies can be traced from the relationship developed between two firms in an alliance. Indirect transfers are the result of organizational spillovers of management control competencies with firms having no form of history together. Prior studies indicate how interorganizational management control can have (sometimes unanticipated) effects on (intra)organizational practices (Dekker, 2016) and we posit that organizational spillovers contribute to this. Organizational spillovers are unintended and uncompensated flow of knowledge and competencies from a source firm to a recipient firm that then uses the knowledge and competencies for its own purposes (Phene & Tallman, 2014). It may be clear that increased social capital creates a basis of trust among the collaborating firms and that the increase of trust between partners influences the nature of information exchanged (Uzzi, 1997). When a focal firm involved in separate alliances has established social capital and relational proximity to its partners in those separate alliances, the connection established by the focal firm may potentially allow alliance management knowledge to flow from a partner in one alliance, to another partner in a separate alliance. The study of Phene and Tallman (2014) explored the conditions under which knowledge spillovers lead to alliance formation and discovered that source firms are motivated to establish alliances in those cases where they perceive the benefits from the spillover pool to be significantly larger than the potential costs inherent in an alliance and where they aim to transform vicarious learning to interactive and experiential learning by forging a formal connection with the recipient firm. From this we develop our third and final proposition.

Proposition 3: *The increasing alignment of management control allows the direct and indirect transfer of alliance management competencies.*

The above propositions are laid as a foundation for developing an evolutionary framework. We propose a framework that allows the iterative cross-level examination (Duysters, Heimeriks, & Jurriëns, 2004; Smith et al., 1995) using the firm and the alliance perspectives. Our insights hope to offer guidance for alliance managers in gaining alliance capability while growing their networks.

THE CYCLE OF ADOPTION AND ADAPTATION TOWARDS ALLIANCE CAPABILITY DEVELOPMENT: A CO-EVOLUTIONARY FRAMEWORK

Dyadic alliances, more than broader networks, have been the predominant research in alliance which has limited our view and the scope of our understanding on interconnectedness of alliances (Sydow, Müller-Seitz, & Provan, 2013). A broader view is essential when an evolutionary perspective is taken since influences coming from beyond the boundaries of the firm, and even those coming from the ecosystem surrounding an alliance create the changes that we observe. It is a process of taking-in external knowledge, and allowing that new knowledge to create internal transformation. The idea of progression is embedded in the concept of evolution and it is important to recognize periods when relevant transformations are identifiable. Leroi-Werelds, Pop, and Roijjakers (2017) conceived an evolutionary framework that oversees the phases of maturity beginning from a strategic alliance, to alliance portfolios, alliance networks, and ultimately into ecosystems. This progression happens as knowledge is accumulated over time through organizational learning (Zollo & Winter, 2002). Learning constructs are highly embedded in evolutionary frameworks and it is important to trace the source of new knowledge and the learning mechanisms that drive them.

The dynamic processes of adoption and adaptation are fit for an evolutionary approach as both processes imply a positive change of state towards development. However, adopting and adapting are two words often confused to be one and the same despite their big differences in meaning. Adoption is the act of taking ownership of something from another entity by duplication suggesting the transfer or acquisition of knowledge and competences. Whereas, the change process of adaptation requires adjustments to the current setting to integrate new influences that allows the entity to become better suited to a new environment. In the learning process, knowledge acquisition and knowledge integration may equally represent them respectively. We develop a conceptual framework that place these two processes iteratively in sequence to better explain the development of alliance capability as intra- and interorganizational management control competencies are exchanged. The different phases signify development as a positive progression over time, advancing alliance capability further at every cycle. This cyclical co-evolutionary framework is illustrated in Figure 13.1. The change process described here is consistent with the idea of

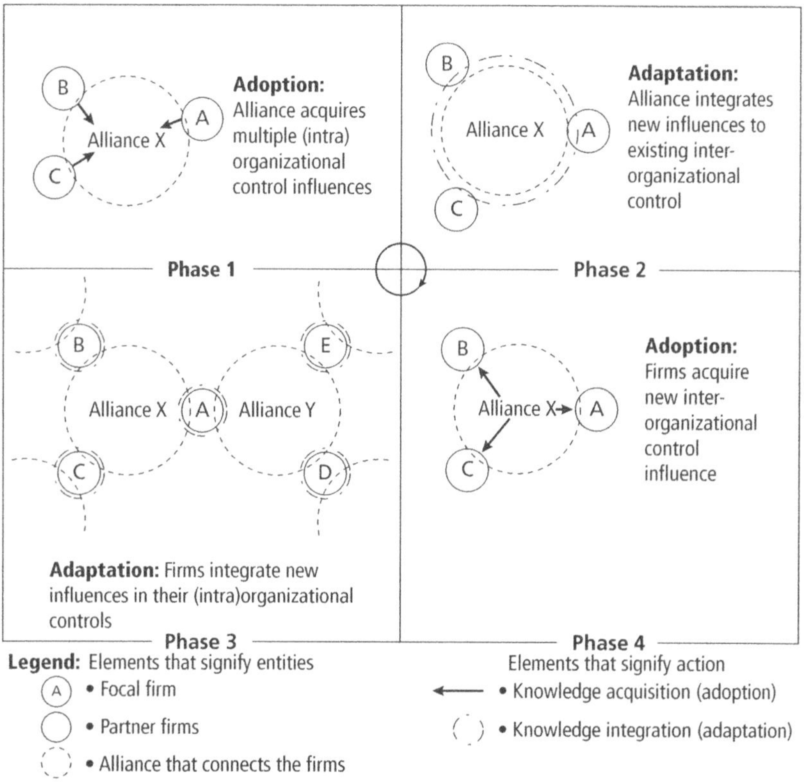

Figure 13.1 Alliance and firm co-evolutionary framework.

co-evolution of alliances and their partner firms (Das & Teng, 2002) where in this case, the particular interest is how alliance evolution affects partner firm evolution in terms of developing alliance capability. Co-evolution take place when different parts of a system evolve simultaneously and interact with each other so that one's evolution is affected by another's evolution and vice versa (Das & Teng, 2002)

Phase 1: Adoption of Different Organizational Management Control Practices (Transfer from Firms to Alliance)

During alliance formation, firms collectively bring in different organizational management control know-how hoping to find agreement on a common system that can support the achievement of their common goals as well as potential private goals different from that of the alliance. However, the design of the interorganizational control is not a simple collection of (intra) organizational practices. As more firms engage in an alliance, their different private objectives and management control know-how complicates the design of interorganizational management controls. Maintaining strategic, relational, and operational alignment among partners becomes a bigger challenge as the alliance grows in size. This pre-alliance process would involve the negotiation of roles and responsibilities in a context where no hierarchical authority can demand cooperation. Alliance formation processes explain the dynamic relationship between bargaining power and management control (Yan & Gray, 1994). The introduction of new management control at the interorganizational is motivated by questions on establishing centers and peripheries, or about who is able to act on others (Mouritsen et al., 2001). This view is consistent with the shared but split management control model (Li et al., 2013) which enacts the practices of the dominant partner in the area of its expertise leaving the general areas. Kraus and Strömsten (2016) urges a deeper understanding of power to be able to explain intra- and interorganizational management control dynamics because power is often at play among firms in an alliance context where an authoritative figure is absent. Underlying this phase of alliance capability development is the organizations' need to establish areas for integration and socialization.

Geringer and Hebert (1989) specified three particularly important dimensions; namely, extent of control, focus of control, and the different types of control mechanism. This phase is particularly concerned with establishing the extent of control (Choi & Beamish, 2004; Ding, 1997; Musarra, Robson, & Katsikeas 2016) which gives attention to the desire and exercise of control done by the individual partners. In this phase, a firm who desires more control in the alliance will have to dominate in terms demonstrating commanding alliance capabilities. The dominant alliance capabilities are the competencies more likely assumed at the interorganizational level. However, Musarra et al. (2016) argues that a partner firm's desire for control—taken as a dark personality trait—may negatively impact performance outcomes, and in our view, risks losing the opportunity to gain new alliance management knowledge from its partners. Moreover, at this point the dominant partner should already consider the potential spillover of its alliance management know-how to other firms in the later phases.

Phase 2: Adaptation of Interorganizational Management Control (Transformation in the Alliance)

In the second phase, our focus moves to the interorganizational management control and how it is shaped by external and internal influences over the life of the alliance. Cuganesan and Lee (2006) highlights the fluidity of interorganizational management controls that contradicts the notions of fit between control mechanisms and a given transaction. Since it is impossible to predict every possible scenario for which control needs to be exercised, it is important to understand and recognize the incompleteness of management controls at the onset of an alliance or even over the length of its lifetime. For instance, Dekker (2004) distinguishes between two control modes in ex-ante and ex-post mechanisms. The design of ex-ante mechanisms is intended to resolve problems by aligning the partner's interests and by reducing the coordination needs before engaging in the alliance, however, they are often unable to mitigate all problems that occur in the alliance. The problems that remain are resolved by applying ex-post control mechanisms. In this regard, interorganizational management controls are expected to constantly evolve as it is necessary to adapt to the dynamic and uncertain nature of alliances. Management controls should always give room for adaptations because changes, although expected, are difficult to predict. Håkansson and Lind (2004) demonstrated how management control systems with overlapping accountabilities in interorganizational environments created contradictions which required actors continuously to find provisional solutions to problems. In this manner, management control was implicated in orchestrating a dynamic interorganizational network that could develop and change despite the embeddedness of actors, activities, and co-specialized resources and the complexities of inter-dependence. The existing interorganizational management control is shaped by the standards of different interest groups participating in the alliance such as management accountant, human resources, information systems, marketing, and strategic management.

Interorganizational management control should be allowed to adapt to both positive changes brought about by growth and the discovery of new opportunities; and negative changes as a result of the volatility of the business environment and the ambiguity of the future attitude of the partner towards the relationship (Bidault, 2012). Likewise, changes in the alliance can be influenced either by internal factors like a change in strategy, external factors such as a change in legal policy, or temporal factors such as maturity.

Phase 3: Adoption of New Interorganizational Management Control Practices (Transfer from Alliance to Firms)

It is important to recognize that the evolution of operating routines is founded on learning mechanisms such as experience accumulation, knowledge articulation, and knowledge codification (Zollo & Winter, 2002). To understand better how knowledge on alliance management is transferred from the alliance to the different collaborating firms, we follow the alliance learning process described by Kale and Singh (2007) for building alliance capability. Alliance experience alone is insufficient to benefit from past collaborations, and Simonin (1997) suggests that the experience needs to be internalized and collaboration know-how developed for the experience to be useful for future alliance engagements. In their study, Kale and Singh (2007) do go in depth about management control but mention the use of formal mechanisms in the form of organized task force and committees that do periodical reviews to exchange alliance management experiences and best practices, as well as informal mechanisms in the form of casual conversations that stimulate the learning process. The alliance learning process involves articulation, codification, sharing, and internalization of alliance management know-how (Kale & Singh, 2007). We contribute to this framework by identifying its place within a larger alliance setting to specifically show where the learning process facilitates the adoption of interorganizational management control to (intra)organizational management controls. We elevate these learning processes to a higher-order dynamic capability by considering the other dynamics processes that simultaneously happen around it. In this way, a bigger understanding of the systematic generation and modification of skills and competencies can be gained from the framework.

The first step of the alliance learning process is "articulation" which involves "efforts of accessing and externalizing individually held knowledge into explicit knowledge" (Kale & Singh, 2007, p. 984). This phase focuses on the boundary spanners who are the individuals involved in the alliance exposed to external influences. These individuals might enjoy knowledge of management control that is used in the strategic alliance, but which is still unknown to the company itself. It is essential that the individual externalizes this information if the firms want to benefit from it. The second step is codification which "involves creating and using knowledge objects or resources such as alliance guidelines, checklists, or manuals to assist action or decision making in future alliance situations" (Kale & Singh, 2007, p. 985). Examples of these objects or resources are guidelines, checklists, or manuals which are management control mechanisms. By codifying, managers can obtain a common understanding of practices by making explicit the flow of exchanges of alliance management know-how. This stage focuses on formulating the knowledge to make it understandable and practical to apply. The third step of the alliance learning process is sharing which "involves exchanging and disseminating individually and organizationally held alliance management knowledge, which is both tacit and/or codified, through interpersonal interaction within the organization" (Kale & Singh, 2007, p. 985). At this point, the initiative lies on the firm to exert company-wide efforts to bring to its constituents the opportunity of greater learning. It is best to identify individuals who can potentially act as boundary spanners for the firm's future alliances. The final step "internalization" is essential for the retention of the knowledge gained and to actually apply it in practice. In this stage, the firm tries to ensure that employees, for whom certain know-how is relevant, have mastered the knowledge, gained competence, and achieved consecutive successes through application. Sluyt et al. (2011) analyzed the effects of the four separate types of learning mechanisms on alliance performance and find that only two types have a significant positive effect on alliance outcome; namely, alliance codification, and alliance sharing, recognizing that the two other processes, articulation, and internalization, might not be determinant factors to explain alliance performance, but might be important prerequisites to support codification and sharing processes. Information and communication technology significantly contribute to these two critical steps as ICT offers efficient dissemination capabilities for codified knowledge. As a measure of the degree of adoption of interorganizational management control practices, two interorganizational system (IOS) deployment dimensions: depth and breadth (C. Zhang, Xue, & Dhaliwal, 2016) showed significant positive effects on operational improvement and competitive performance of the partner firm. The "depth of the IOS refers to the scale of the firm's IOS usage that complements other organizational practices . . . and the breadth of the IOS refers to the scope of a firm's IOS usage" (C. Zhang et al., 2016, p. 80). The information systems literature recommends the implementation of IT-enabled business processes to take advantage of the benefits on operational improvement and improved business relationships but most studies are in the context of SC partners (Ricciardi et al., 2018; C. Zhang et al., 2016, X. Zhang et al., 2016).

Phase 4: Adaptation of (Intra)Organizational Management Control to Link with the Alliance (Transformation within the Firms)

As new knowledge and competencies are discovered from the interaction in the alliance, firms soon learn the challenge of including their partners into their activities realizing that they themselves were required to reorganize to be able to uphold the relationship that were set up, as Mouritsen et al. (2001) describes, "They themselves were not only effecting change, they were also affected by that change." (p. 241). A far greater challenge comes when a firm has to adapt to multiple external influences because of its likely association with multiple alliances at one time. At this point, the process of adaptation tries to accommodate all the knowledge and competencies that are transferred from the previous phase. In this process, the most dominant and effective alliance management practices may prevail and replace management control practices deemed ineffective in the past. The process is similar to benchmarking which is a set of activities that support and enhance strategies of imitation and/or collaboration (Drew, 1997) This selection process shows how traditional techniques are replaced by new and sophisticated management control practices which is evidence to alliance capability development. However, the origin of the prevailing alliance management practice may be difficult to trace given the possible transfers of alliance management know-how from organizational spillovers. On a positive note, the organizational spillovers signify the progressive spread of positive behaviors and with the systemic nature of alliance constellations, they contribute to the development speed of alliance capability. When prevailing management control practices vastly continue to dominate within a cluster of firms, these practices and routines could define new business cultures. Drew (1997) reveals how benchmarking can generate broadly based change in organizational thinking and action. If firms are better at integrating the alliance mindset into their corporate cultures then alliance capability could be more effective at driving alliance success (Sluyt et al., 2011). The conceived alliance ecosystem of Leroi-Werelds et al. (2017) is consistent with the environment described in this phase where each organization makes its own adaptations based on its unique connections with other organizations. In this phase, we demonstrate how different elements in an alliance ecosystem could evolve separately as well as interactively (Das & Teng, 2002).

GAINING FROM THE ALLIANCE EXPERIENCE OF OTHERS

This study tries to bring in a more diverse set of theoretical lenses to understand the forces shaping alliance capability development. From scanning the literature, we bring into the discussion the interesting link between alliance capability and management control studies. The interrelationship between these two concepts has not been made explicit so far in the academic literature. Furthermore, management scholars have also been constrained to investigate the dynamics of firms and alliances due to the necessary cross examination of intra- and interorganizational perspectives, therefore requiring two levels of analysis. Along this line, the challenge of designing management controls to fit intra- and interorganizational settings may be challenged by organizational heterogeneity and maintaining strategic alignment. There is the opportunity to look into the conflict between contingency and institutional fits (Volberda, van der Weerdt, Verwaal, Stienstra, & Verdu, 2012) in a network of organization. In this situation, the prioritization between individual private goals and the common goal of the alliance should be profoundly understood. The fact that partner organizations remain independent entities creates a risk that private goals may become more important than the common goal of the alliance. This can happen in time through preference reversal of the alliance partners, even in the full absence of opportunistic intent. Prioritization of goals could therefore have a critical influence on the design and use of management controls in alliance capability development. To be able to guide research towards this direction, we offer theoretical propositions that could challenge scholars to explore further this particular research area to address many interesting lines of inquiry. Building on our propositions, we developed an evolutionary framework that offers a perspective much larger than what is currently available in literature showing interactions that could explain how (intra)organizational practices might influence interorganizational practices, and vice versa, following dynamic learning processes that take place at different organizational levels.

Within the management control literature, we pay attention to conditions that lead to improved output measurability and task programmability of controls which are both indications of control effectiveness in Phase 1. A capable alliance manager is expected to access information that will help make better decisions for the firm he represents and for the alliance in general and to ensure the accomplishment of tasks towards the achievement of goals. High output measurability and task programmability are associated more to the use of formal control mechanisms. A known effective formal control mechanism for sharing codified knowledge comes in the form of ICT infrastructures. When firms in an alliance share the same interest on information related to outputs and tasks, then the partner firms are more willing to integrate systems. They are motivated to feed accurate information to support the system for their use in the alliance and for their individual firms' benefit. System compatibility among partners therefore contributes to increasing control effectiveness in terms of achieving high output measurability and task programmability at the interorganizational level. Along this line, we encourage deliberate efforts from partners to establish integrated management controls to favor alliance capability development in Phase 2. Deliberate actions are necessary to reverse the natural tendency of firms to protect its status quo in terms of its epistemic integrity and organizational balance because learning is about challenging the status quo and pushing boundaries.

The knowledge management literature offers knowledge "transfer" and "transformation" as mechanisms to tap into the diversity of knowledge that lies dispersed over organizations (Berends et al., 2011). The inter-connectedness of alliance constellations brings an advantage for channeling alliance management knowledge in Phase 3. Particularly interesting are transfers which are the result of organizational spillovers. Though unintended, these spillovers bring a benefit to both the recipient and the source as firms develop a better sense of what works and no longer works in alliance management. In the case that a prevailing management control continuously dominates and replaces current (intra)organizational management controls, the next cycle will witness a convergence of management controls for the firms in Phase 4. Every iterative cycle of the four phases brings a network of firms closer to a common set of alliance management competencies, and towards a common alliance culture.

We look forward to future research that could explain how far and widespread alliance management knowledge spillovers reach when institutionalizing best practices. The links we establish in this chapter are just preliminary efforts to advance our knowledge of management control systems and how alliance partners learn about them. Many research opportunities open up to further develop the concepts that emerged from our insights. In this regard, we see alliance portfolio analysis as an interesting avenue to explore (e.g., Duysters, Heimeriks, Lokshin, Meijer, & Sabidussi, 2012). Our insights imply going beyond managing the firms' internal alliance portfolios, but analyzing the alliance portfolios of potential partners to be able to get a share of their experiences. Alliance capability development depends on prior related knowledge of the firm to be able to assimilate and exploit new knowledge. This broad prior knowledge can be reflected in a potential partner's portfolio of alliances.

In addition, learning from intermediaries on alliance capability development may be an interesting avenue because the way intermediaries operate is mainly founded on their alliance capabilities. Intermediaries have increasingly gained recognition as platform providers for the coordination of the flow of innovation and solutions across heterogeneous settings. Intermediaries active in strategic alliances have gained competence, reach, and influence and have proven useful in the search for solutions outside partners' traditional collaborative relationships (Bidault, 2012). They have gained the ability to oversee the activities within its core industry, and this ability puts the intermediary in a position to take a coordinating role in the management of the relationship (Honig, 2004). Being brokers, they try to maintain a rich portfolio of alliances to manage. How do firms with higher alliance capabilities design and use management control? How different are the alliance capabilities of intermediaries from firms managing similar alliance portfolios? What can typical firms learn from intermediaries in terms of developing alliance capabilities? Part of our objectives is developing these new questions to stir interest for researchers to pursue a greater understanding of alliance capability development. Hopefully, the insights offered by our study could stimulate more fruitful discussions on the topic especially with the evolutionary framework serving as a useful starting point for future research to delve on a comprehensive study of the alliance revolution.

REFERENCES

Akgün, A. E., Lynn, G. S., & Byrne, J. C. (2006). Antecedents and consequences of unlearning in new product development teams. *Journal of Product Innovation Management, 23*(1), 73–88.

Almeida, P., Song, J., & Grant, R. M. (2002). Are firms superior to alliances and markets? An empirical test of cross-border knowledge building. *Organization Science, 13*(2), 147–161.

Anderson, E. (1990). Two firms, one frontier–on assessing joint venture performance. *Sloan Management Review, 31*(2), 19–30.

Anderson, S. W., & Dekker, H. C. (2005). Management control for market transactions: The relation between transaction characteristics, incomplete contract design and subsequent performance. *Management Science, 51*(12), 1734–1752.

Ariño, A., de la Torre, J., & Ring, P. S. (2001). Relational quality: Managing trust in corporate alliances. *California Management Review, 44*(1), 109–131.

Arrow, K. J. (1974). *The limits of organization.* New York. NY: W.W. Norton & Company.

Berends, H., Garud, R., Debackere, K., & Weggeman, M. (2011). Thinking along: A process for tapping into knowledge across boundaries. *International Journal of Technology Management, 53*(1), 69–88.

Berry, A. J., Coad, A. F., Harris, E. P., Otley, D. T., & Stringer, C. (2009). Emerging themes in management control: A review of recent literature. *British Accounting Review, 41*(1), 2–20.

Bidault, F. (2012). *Managing joint innovation: How to balance trust and control in strategic alliances.* London, England: Palgrave Macmillan.

Busco, C., Giovannoni, E., & Scapens, R. W. (2008). Managing the tensions in integrating global organizations: The role of performance management systems. *Management Accounting Research, 19*(2), 103–125.

Caglio, A., & Ditillo, A. (2008). A review and discussion of management control in inter-firm relationships: Achievements and future directions. *Accounting, Organizations and Society, 33*(7/8), 865–898.

Carlsson-Wall, M., Kraus, K., & Lind, J. (2011). The interdependencies of intra- and inter-organisational controls and work practices – the case of domestic care of the elderly. *Management Accounting Research, 22*(4), 313–329.

Choi, C. B., & Beamish, P. W. (2004). Split management control and international joint venture performance. *Journal of International Business Studies, 35*(3), 201–215.

Coad, A. F., Cullen, J. (2006). Interorganizational cost management: Towards an evolutionary perspective. *Management Accounting Research, 17*(4), 342–369.

Cuganesan, S., & Lee, R. (2006). Intraorganizational influences in procurement networks controls: The impacts of information technology. *Management Accounting Research, 17*(2), 141–170.

Cunha, P. F., Ferreira, P. S., & Macedo, P. (2008). Performance evaluation within cooperate networked production enterprises. *International Journal of Computer Integrated Manufacturing, 21*(2), 174–179.

Das, T. K., & Teng, B. (2001). Trust, control, and risk in strategic alliances: An integrated framework. *Organization Studies, 22*(2), 251–283.

Das, T. K., & Teng, B. (2002). The dynamics of alliance conditions in the alliance development process. *Journal of Management Studies, 39*(5), 725–746.

Dekker, H. C. (2004). Control of interorganizational relationships: Evidence on appropriation concerns and coordination requirements. *Accounting Organizations and Society, 29*(1), 27–49.

Dekker, H. C. (2008). Partner selection and governance design in inter-firm relationships. *Accounting, Organization, and Society, 33*(7/8), 915–941.

Dekker, H. C. (2016). On the boundaries between intra-firm and inter-firm management accounting research. *Management Accounting Research, 31*(June), 86–99.

Dekker, H. C., Ding, R., & Groot, T. (2016). Collaborative performance management in inter-firm relationships. *Journal of Management Accounting Research, 28*(3), 25–48.

Dekker, H. C., & Van den Abbeele, A. (2010). Organizational learning and inter-firm control: The effects of partner search and prior exchange experiences. *Organization Science, 21*(6), 1233–1250.

Ding, D. Z. (1997). Control, conflict, and performance: A study of U.S.–Chinese joint ventures. *Journal of International Marketing, 5*(3), 31–45.

Doz, Y. L. (1996). The evolution of cooperation in strategic alliances: Initial conditions or learning processes? *Strategic Management Journal, 17*(S1), 55–83.

Draulans, J., deMan, A. P., & Volberda, H. W. (2003). Building alliance capability: Management techniques for superior alliance performance. *Long Range Planning, 36*(2), 151–166.

Drew, S. A. W. (1997). From knowledge to action: The impact of benchmarking on organizational performance. *Long Range Planning, 30*(3), 427–441.

Duysters, G., Heimeriks, K. H., Lokshin, B., Meijer, E., & Sabidussi, A. (2012). Do firms learn to manage alliance portfolio diversity? The diversity-performance relationship and the moderating effects of experience and capability. *European Management Review, 9*(3), 139–152.

Duysters, G., Heimeriks, K. H., & Jurriëns, J. A. (2004). An integrated perspective on alliance management. *Journal on Chain and Network Science, 4*(2), 83–94.

Dyer, J. H., & Singh, H. (1998). The relational view: Cooperative strategy and sources of interorganizational competitive advantage. *The Academy of Management Review, 23*(4), 660–679.

Eisenhardt, K. M. (1985). Control: Organizational and economic approaches. *Management Science, 31*(2), 134–149.

Findikoglu, M., & Lavie, D. (2019). The contingent value of the dedicated alliance function. *Strategic Organization, 17*(2), 177–209.

Geringer, J., & Hebert, L. (1989). Control and performance of international joint ventures. *Journal of International Business Studies, 20*(2), 235–254.

Gomes, E., Barnes, B., & Mahmood, T. (2016). A 22-year review of strategic alliance research in the leading management journals. *International Business Review, 25*(1), 15–27.

Haas, P. M. (1992). Introduction: Epistemic communities and international policy coordination. *International Organization, 46*(1), 1–35.

Håkansson, H., & Lind, J. (2004). Accounting and network coordination. *Accounting, Organizations and Society, 29*(1), 51–72.

Heimeriks, K. H., & Duysters, G. (2007). Alliance capability as a mediator between experience and alliance performance: An empirical investigation into the alliance capability development process. *Journal of Management Studies, 44*(1), 25–49.

Holzner, B. (1968). *Reality construction in society*. Cambridge, MA: Schenkman.

Honig, M. I. (2004). The new middle management: Intermediary organizations in education policy implementation. *Educational Evaluation and Policy Analysis, 26*(1), 65–87.

Jiang, X., & Li, Y. (2008). The relationship between organizational learning and firms' financial performance in strategic alliances: A contingency approach. *Journal of World Business, 43*(3), 365–379.

Kale, P., & Singh, H. (2007). Building firm capabilities through learning: The role of the alliance learning process in alliance capability and firm-level alliance success. *Strategic Management Journal, 28*(10), 981–1000.

Kauppila, O. P. (2015). Alliance management capability and firm performance: Using resource-based theory to look inside the process black box. *Long Range Planning, 48*(3), 151–167.

Kraus, K., & Strömsten, T. (2016). Internal/inter-firm control dynamics and power-A case study of the Ericsson-Vodafone relationship. *Management Accounting Research, 33*(December), 61–72.

Lambe, C. J., Spekman, R. E., & Hunt, S. D. (2002). Alliance competence, resources, and alliance success: Conceptualization, measurement, and initial test. *Journal of the Academy of Marketing Science, 30*(2), 141–158.

Larimo, J., Nguyen, H. L., & Ali, T. (2016). Performance measurement choices in international joint venture: What factors drive them? *Journal of Business Research, 69*(2), 877–887.

Lehtinen, J., & Ahola, T. (2010). Is performance measurement suitable for an extended enterprise? *International Journal of Operations and Production Management, 30*(2), 181–204.

Leroi-Werelds, S., Pop, O-M., & Roijjakers, N. (2017). Value creation in alliance ecosystems: Insights from marketing. In T. K. Das (Ed.) *Managing alliance portfolios and networks* (pp. 1–31). Charlotte, NC: Information Age.

Li, P., Tang, G., Okano, H., & Gao, G. (2013). The characteristics and dynamics of management controls in IJVs: Evidence from a Sino-Japanese case. *Management Accounting Research, 24*(3), 246–260.

Lohman, C., Fortuin, L., & Wouters, M. (2004). Designing a performance measurement system: A case study. *European Journal of Operational Research, 156*(2), 267–286.

Mahama, H. (2006). Management control systems, cooperation and performance in strategic supply relationships: A survey in the mines. *Management Accounting Research, 17*(3), 315–339.

Merchant, K. A. (1998). *Modern management control systems*. Upper Saddle River, NJ: Prentice Hall.

Mohr, A. T., & Puck, J. F. (2005). Managing functional diversity to improve the performance of international joint ventures. *Long Range Planning, 38*(2), 163–182.

Mørk, B.E., Aanestad, M., Hanseth, O., & Grisot, M. (2008). Conflicting epistemic cultures and obstacles for learning across communities of practice. *Knowledge and Process Management, 15*(1), 12–23.

Moshtari, M. (2016). Interorganizational fit, relationship management capability, and collaborative performance within a humanitarian setting. *Production and Operations Management, 25*(9), 1542–1557.

Mouritsen, J., Hansen, A., & Hansen, C. Ø. (2001). Interorganizational controls and organizational competencies: Episodes around target cost management/functional analysis and open book accounting. *Management Accounting Research, 12*(2), 221–244.

Mowery, D. C., Oxley, J. E., & Silverman, B. S. (1996). Strategic alliances and interfirm knowledge transfer. *Strategic Management Journal, 17*(Special Issue), 77–91.

Musarra, G., Robson, M. J., & Katsikeas, C. S. (2016). The influence of desire for control on monitoring decisions and performance outcomes in strategic alliances. *Industrial Marketing Management, 55*(4), 10–21.

Nooteboom, B. (1996). Trust, opportunism, and governance: A process and control model. *Organization Studies, 17*(6), 985–1010.

Ouchi, W. G. (1979). A conceptual framework for the design of organizational control mechanisms, *Management Science, 25*(9), 833–848.

Paul, S., Seetharaman, P., Samarah, I., & Mykytyn, P. P. (2004). Impact of heterogeneity and collaborative conflict management style on the performance of synchronous global virtual teams. *Information & Management, 41*(3), 303–321.

Phene, A., & Tallman, S. (2014). Knowledge spillovers and alliance formation. *Journal of Management Studies, 51*(7), 1058–1090.

Pina-Stranger, A., & Lazega, E. (2010). Interorganizational collective learning: The case of biotechnology in France. *European Journal of International Management, 4*(6), 602–620.

Ricciardi, F., Zardini, A., & Rossignoli, C. (2018). Organizational integration of the IT-function: A key enabler of firm capabilities and performance. *Journal of Innovation and Knowledge, 3*(3), 93–107.

Simonin, B. L. (1997). The importance of collaboration know-how: An empirical test of the learning organization. *Academy of Management Journal, 40*(5), 1150–1174.

Sluyts, K., Matthyssens, P., Martens, R., & Streukens, S. (2011). Building capabilities to manage strategic alliances. *Industrial Marketing Management, 40*(6), 875–886.

Smith, K. G., Carroll, S. J., & Ashford, S. J. (1995). Intra- and interorganizational cooperation: Toward a research agenda. *Academy of Management Journal, 38*(1), 7–23.

Sydow, J., Müller-Seitz, G., & Provan, K. G. (2013). Managing uncertainty in alliances and networks. In T. K. Das (Eds.), *Managing knowledge in strategic alliances* (pp. 1–43). Charlotte, NC: Information Age.

Teece, D. J. (1986). Profiting from technological innovations – implications for integration, collaboration, licensing, and public policy. *Research Policy, 15*(6), 285–305.

Uzzi, B. (1997). Social structure and competition in inter-firm networks: The paradox of embeddedness. *Administrative Science Quarterly, 42*(1), 35–67.

Volberda, H. W., van der Weerdt, N., Verwaal, E., Stienstra, M., & Verdu, A. J. (2012). Contingency fit, institutional fit, and firm performance: A metafit approach to organization–environment relationships. *Organization Science, 23*(4), 1040–1054.

Wong, C. W. Y., Lai, K., Cheng, T. C. E., & Lun, Y. H. V. (2015). The role of IT-enabled collaborative decision making in interorganizational information integration to improve customer service performance. *International Journal of Production Economics, 159*, 56–65.

Yan, A. M., & Gray, B. (1994). Bargaining power, management control, and performance in United States–China joint ventures—A comparative case-study. *Academy of Management Journal, 37*(6), 1478–1517.

Zhang, C., Xue, L., & Dhaliwal, J. (2016). Alignments between the depth and breadth of interorganizational systems deployment and their impact on firm performance. *Information and Management, 53*(1), 79–90.

Zhang, X., Van Donk, D. P., & van der Vaart, T. (2016). The different impact of interorganizational and intraorganizational ICT on supply chain performance. *International Journal of Operations & Production Management, 36*(7), 803–824.

Zollo, M., & Winter, S. (2002). Deliberate learning and the evolution of dynamic capabilities. *Organization Science, 13*(3), 339–351.

CHAPTER 14

QUALITY OF PARTNER RELATIONS IN INTERNATIONAL CONSTRUCTION ALLIANCES

Beliz Ozorhon
David Arditi

ABSTRACT

Construction companies consider strategic alliances (SAs) as a vehicle to enter new markets and exploit business opportunities. Through such alliances, they take advantage of the distinctive competencies and the complementary resources of their partners. Such entities are very difficult to manage mainly due to their inherent complexity, involving a mixture of different cultures, managerial systems, philosophies, and attitudes. As a result, partners in SAs in international construction have a hard time figuring out how to achieve high levels of quality in interpartner relations. A better understanding is critical in selecting the right partners, in getting along well with partners, and in realizing anticipated synergies. In this chapter, the key factors that affect the quality of interpartner relations in SAs in international construction are explored. In this respect, the issues related to interpartner relations, that is,

Managing the Partners in Strategic Alliances, pages 345–365

(a) the strategic and organizational fit between partners, (b) the impact of cultural differences in national and organizational approaches, and (c) the structural characteristics of the SA, are operationalized and investigated. A framework for analyzing the relationship between interpartner relations and these three issues is presented. The research makes use of data collected from a questionnaire survey administered to 28 Turkish contractors that entered into a total of 68 SAss with non-Turkish partners. The data are analyzed by using structural equation modeling. It is expected that the information in the chapter will help professionals during the partner selection process and will result in a successful alliance that operates smoothly.

INTRODUCTION

Alliances improve the strategic position of firms in competitive markets by providing resources from other firms that enable them to share costs and risks in product design, production, marketing, and distribution. Doing business within a strategic alliance (SA) provides the partnering firms the opportunity to share costs and risks, to acquire knowledge, to enter new markets, and to gain economies of scale or to rationalize operations (Contractor & Lorange, 1988). Despite their benefits, such entities are difficult to manage because of the presence of two or more partner organizations usually with different managerial systems, philosophies, values, and attitudes, which may be competitors as well as collaborators (Janger, 1980; Killing, 1983; Tatoglu & Glaister, 1998). Previous studies have shown that SAs have a high failure record, reporting on the dissolution rate but also on the ineffectiveness and the inefficiency of the SA management. The nature of the relationship between SA partners is likely to affect SA operations (Buckley & Casson, 1988; Parkhe, 1993). Many factors have been suggested in the literature as factors affecting the quality of partner relations in international construction alliances including the fit between the partner companies and the structural characteristics of the alliances.

The quality of partner relations in international construction alliances was modeled in Ozorhon's (2007) research based on the experiences of Turkish contractors and their foreign partners. The aim of this research was to explore the impact of various factors on the quality of partner relations. In this respect, the research investigated the impact of strategic and organizational fit between alliance partners; national and organizational cultural fit between alliance partners; and the structural characteristics of the SA organization on the quality of partner relations. Based on the findings of this study partner selection and alliance formation stages will be discussed for the SAs in international construction.

PARTNER SELECTION AND PARTNER RELATIONS

With an increasing level of globalization in business, alliances between and among multinational firms have become popular. There are a number of overriding economic and political reasons for the rise in the popularity of SAs. These include the characteristics of foreign markets, such as access to suitable distribution channels, sharing heightened economic and political risks in new business ventures, government pressure, and technology transfer (Makino & Delios, 1996). Forging an alliance enables a firm to focus resources on its core skills and competencies while acquiring other components or capabilities it lacks from the marketplace (Zaman & Mavondo, 2002). Through the formation of SAs, companies are able to exploit business opportunities and enter new markets abroad. However, the benefits associated with SAs are counterbalanced by a wide range of problems. The failure rate of SAs, in general, is high (Makino & Beamish, 1998). Since SAs consist of at least two parent organizations, these entities may have different goals, management practices, and organizational cultures and it becomes difficult to manage these organizations and achieve critical success criteria. The good intentions and rational motives behind these alliances are not always congruent with the strategic direction of either firm on its own, let alone the strategic direction of both in unison. Like in other industries, achieving high levels of performance is difficult in the construction industry as performance is extensively dependent on several internal and external factors.

In order to identify those factors contributing to the success of SAs, each stage of an alliance process should be investigated. The process of an SA is generally distinguished in three stages; namely, partner selection, formation, and operation. The selection of the appropriate partner constitutes one of the major success factors for an SA. Partner selection determines an SA's mix of skills, knowledge, and resources, its operating policies and procedures, and its vulnerability to indigenous conditions, structures, and institutional changes (Geringer, 1991). SAs are formed based on strategies of how to manage environmental uncertainties, how to overcome lack of resources and, in particular, how to manage the firm's range of interorganizational relations. During the formation stage, potential partners spend considerable time to identify their common compatible interests in the task-related areas. Kwok, Then, and Skitmore's (2000) study identified a number of these critical factors, including negotiation, profit and loss distribution, clarity of contribution among partners, control and decision making policy, clarity of sharing of risks and liabilities, composition of decision making body, and dispute resolution procedures. During the operation of a project, it is important to enter into a fair engineering contract, employ qualified subcontractors and suppliers, maintain a good relationship with the host government and other parties, and adopt renegotiation as a dispute resolution and problem-solving technique (Bing & Tiong, 1999).

Geringer (1991) posits that the partner selection process is considered to be of crucial importance to the formation and operation of SAs. Partner consistency in terms of strategic goals and behaviors, cooperative culture, managerial philosophy, innovativeness, and long-term orientation influences mutual trust, commitment, and collaboration between parties (Parkhe, 1991). Killing (1983) states that it is impossible to identify an exhaustive list of criteria which an organization should meet when attempting to assess a potential complementary partner. Partner fit determines the extent to which partner firms can get along and realize anticipated synergies from the joint venture (Buckley & Casson, 1988; Hill & Hellriegel, 1994; Morris & Cadogan, 2001; Yan & Duan, 2003). The issue of partner fit has been widely discussed in the partner selection literature. For example, Geringer (1988) argues that selection of an SA partner needs to consider a fit in both task-related characteristics (e.g., resources and skills) and partner-related characteristics (e.g., size, objectives, and operating policies).

Most researchers suggest that a mismatch in terms of alliance fit is the most important reason for alliance failure. According to previous studies, the factors that affect interpartner fit commonly include strategic fit, resource fit, operational fit, organizational fit, and cultural fit (Luo, 1998; Morris & Cadogan, 2001; Ulijn, Duijsters, Schaetzlein, & Remer, 2005; Yan & Duan, 2003). According to Luo (1998), strategic, organizational, and financial attributes are all crucial to SA performance. A partner with superior strategic traits, but lacking strong organizational and financial characteristics, results in an unstable SA. The possession of desirable organizational attributes without corresponding strategic and financial competence leaves the SA unprofitable. A partner with superior financial strengths without strategic and organizational competencies can lead to an unsustainable venture.

The partner selection and venture formation processes set the basis of the relationship between the partners during the operation of the SA. The smooth operation of the SA is dependent mainly upon the interaction between the partners in making strategic and operational decisions (Sridharan, 1997). For SAs to survive, their parents must find a way to work together, that is, they must be able to agree on goals and policies, and to renegotiate them in response to changes in the environment (Doz, 1996).

MODELING INTERPARTNER RELATIONS IN INTERNATIONAL CONSTRUCTION ALLIANCES

This study is built upon the findings of a research by Ozorhon (2007) who proposed and tested a set of indicators and drivers for stronger partner relations in international construction alliances. The following sections present the research methodology, the data collection process, and the components of the framework developed by Ozorhon (2007).

The following five hypotheses were tested: the strategic fit between SA partners (H1), the organizational fit between SA partners (H2), the national culture fit between SA partners (H3), the organizational culture fit between SA partners (H4), and the effectiveness of structural characteristics of the SA organization (H5) have positive effects on the quality of partner relations.

Operationalization of the "Quality of Partner Relations" in SAs

Extant literature has focused on commitment, cooperation, collaboration, communication, trust, and conflict resolution as the important components of alliance relationships (Luo, 2002). In this study, "quality of partner relations" is defined by the six indicators discussed below (Ozorhon, 2007).

Commitment

Commitment can be described as the willingness of SA partners to exert effort on behalf of the SA (Mohr & Spekman, 1994). Committed partners are likely to consider long-term gains rather than short-term advantages. Committed partners are interested in creating and maintaining a good relationship with the other partners and thus are less likely to let differences in functional approaches result in conflicts and negatively affect SA performance. Committed partners are likely to be more cooperative, communicative, and flexible in accommodating conflict issues. When parties are committed to the relationship, cooperation evolves from "commitment to cooperation in its own right" (Buckley & Casson, 1988).

Effective Communication

Effective communication between the SA partners is important for good partner relations since partners do not usually start an SA with a full understanding of each other's goals, capabilities, and behaviors; in many instances, these are revealed when the SA starts operating (Doz, 1996). Communication allows the partners to understand the goals of the alliance, and the roles and responsibilities of all the actors. Failure by parents to quickly learn about each other may lead to misunderstandings and suspicion, and eventually to lower commitment, poor economic results, and dissolution (Doz, 1996; Shenkar & Zeira, 1992). Communication helps with the sharing and dissemination of individual experiences (Inkpen, 1996).

Cooperation

Cooperation is the key dimension of the SA relationship. Understanding the nature and scope of cooperation is essential in analyzing the operation and success of an alliance. Cooperation is a proxy for commitment, trust, and synergy. It is required to overcome the potential misunderstandings and coordination difficulties that can arise from differences in managerial or organizational practices (Das & Teng, 1998). Cooperation is critical to avoid possible conflicts (Ozorhon, Arditi, Dikmen, & Birgonul, 2010).

Previous Cooperation

Previous cooperation and experience earned from prior engagements between the partners allows the partners to justify subsequent risky steps (Das & Teng, 1998). In addition, prior relationships indicate a history of repeated interaction, which may lead to relational advantages and stability. Previous contact between partners also leads to the development of specialized skills and routines adapted to the exchange. These include specific knowledge about the structure and operation of the partner organization as well as familiarity with its executives and managers (Shenkar & Zeira, 1992). Previous cooperation also fosters a climate of openness that is essential for discussing behavioral problems that may be a barrier to learning (Doz, 1996).

Conflict Resolution

Conflict resolution refers to methods of resolving amicably the conflicts between partners. Fey and Beamish (1999) define SA conflict as the interaction between SA partners, where the actions of one partner prevent or compel some outcome against the resistance of another partner. Conflict between the partners can indicate disagreement over goals, operational and managerial expectations, send confusing signals to the parent managers and employees, and thereby hamper performance levels (Yan & Gray, 2001). Such circumstances may also limit an SA's ability to respond to environmental changes (Hebert, 1994). Conflict may also result in the unwillingness of parent firms to contribute resources that the IJV needs to achieve its goals (Killing, 1983). Since extensive conflict negatively affects SA performance, the amicable resolution of disputes is essential for the continuity of an SA in harmony.

Degree of Trust

The degree of trust between the partners is one of the most critical indicators affecting the quality of partner relations since trust provides for greater adaptability in an SA, and enhances the exchange of knowledge, a key component of organizational learning and SA success (Bing, Tiong, Fan, & Chew, 1999; Das & Teng, 1998; Park & Ungson, 1997; Parkhe, 1993).

Operationalization of the Variables Affecting the Quality of Partner Relations

The factors influencing the quality of partner relations were defined in terms of (a) strategic and organizational fit between SA partners, (b) national and organizational culture fit between SA partners, and (c) structural SA characteristics (Ozorhon, 2007).

Contextual Fit in SAs

In forming SAs in construction, the SA partners expose themselves to several internal and external risks. These include but are not limited to inheriting a partner's financial problems; having disagreements about accounting standards; distrust between partner employees; policy changes in parent companies affecting the project; lack of management competence; disagreements about staff allocation and positions in the project team hierarchy; disagreement on allocation of work to be done; and technology-transfer disputes (Bing et al., 1999). In this study, factors related to contextual fit are grouped as strategic and organizational fit.

Strategic fit. The strategic orientation of a partner firm is important for a successful alliance operation. In this study, "strategic fit" consists of goal congruency between SA partners, previous experience in the host country, previous experience with similar projects, adequacy of management skills, technical skills and human resources, and quality of relationship with the client.

- Goal congruency between partners is one of the primary factors in SA success (Inkpen & Currall, 1998; Tomlinson & Thompson, 1977). Conflict between partners that may result from goal incongruity can negatively affect partner relations (Fey & Beamish, 1999).
- Complementarity of partners in terms of previous experience in host country is an important strategic asset since in this experiential process, foreign firms develop a general knowledge about the political, social, economic, and cultural aspects of the SA location and specific knowledge about local business practices and local networks (Johanson & Vahlne, 1977). This acquired knowledge stimulates the trust and collaboration between partners (Beamish, 1987; Luo, 1997; Shenkar, 1990).
- Complementarity of partners in terms of previous project experience may be critical for achieving stronger partner relations. The partners' ability to acquire, learn, process, assimilate, integrate, deploy, and exploit an inflow of new knowledge and skills may depend on how these relate to the skills already established (Luo, 1997). As Gunhan and Arditi (2005) state, having a special expertise can be a major strength for a company operating in international markets.

- Compatibility of partners' managerial skills, technical skills, and human resources is important in that it allows a firm to complete a project successfully. Compatible management skills not only enable partners to operate the SA effectively but also help them maintain good relations with other project participants. Compatible technical skills are required to smoothly mitigate possible project risks that may lead to cost, time, and quality problems. Finally, human resources reflect the blending of partners' cultures and management styles, and as such affect the SA's joint human resources strategies.
- The quality of partners' relationship with the client is also a good indicator of strategic fit. Since client satisfaction is an important indicator of performance, strong relations with the client are useful in dealing with client-related issues.

Organizational fit. "Organizational fit" consists of complementarity/compatibility of partners' financial capabilities, company size, management systems, and national/international workload.

- Financial capability of partner firms is critical since a partner's profitability directly influences its ability to make a capital contribution, fulfill financial commitments, and dispense financial resources in the operation of the SA.
- Partner size may be a significant determinant of quality of partner relations and thereby SA performance (Hennart, Kim, & Zeng, 1998; Merchant, 2000; Pan & Chi, 1999; Pan & Li, 2000; Smith, Guthrie, & Chen, 1989). The literature suggests that asymmetry in partners' firm size has negative effects on the stability of an SA (Geringer, 1988; Gomes-Casseres, 1990; Harrigan, 1988; Killing, 1983).
- Similarity between partners' management systems is another important determinant of performance (Beamish, 1984; Killing, 1983). Differences in partners' management styles can result in conflict; nonresolution of such conflicts can eventually affect the success of SAs (Sridharan, 1997).
- Partners' national/international workload may influence the effort and time they allocate to the SA. A partner with extensive international spread tends to reduce its commitment to the SA (Beamish, 1984), which in turn may affect SA performance.

Cultural Fit in SAs

Cultural distance has received a great deal of attention in the international business literature (Barkema, Shenkar, Vermeulen, & Bell, 1997; Evans & Mavondo, 2002; Kogut & Singh, 1988; Morosini, Shane, & Singh, 1998; O'Grady & Lane, 1996; Park & Ungson, 1997). Culture has been referred to as a set of shared experiences, understandings, and meanings among members of a group, an organization, a community, or a nation (Hofstede, 1991; Mead, 1998). Culture is also that complex whole which includes knowledge, beliefs, arts, morals, customs, and any other capabilities and habits acquired by men and women as members of a society (Low & Leong, 2000). Culture is an ingrained behavioral influence which affects the way collective groups approach, evaluate, and negotiate opportunities for international business. The topics relating to the impact of culture on SAs span a number of areas such as national and organizational cultures.

It is hypothesized that cultural similarity increases harmony and reduces friction (Shenkar, 2001) in cross-cultural strategic partnerships. Arguments to support this proposition build on three primary insights. First, culturally similar managers are more likely to share the same attitudes, values, beliefs, knowledge, management systems (Lasserre, 1999), leadership styles and scripts of behavior, as well as business, organizational and administrative practices (Kogut & Singh, 1988). Second, such cultural similarities facilitate and enhance the ability to communicate, cooperate, integrate knowledge, and develop trust (Killing, 1983). Third, cultural dissimilarities increase the frequency and severity of communication difficulties (Brown, Rugman, & Verbeke, 1989), miscommunications (Park & Ungson, 1997), conflict (Sim & Ali, 2000), and misinterpretation of a foreigner's intentions, whether honest or opportunistic. In brief, past theoretical arguments can be captured in a single statement: cultural similarity increases harmony and decreases friction in cross-cultural interactions and vice versa.

National culture fit. Several researchers reported that differences in national cultures are a source of poor communication, inadequate cooperation, lack of commitment, and ineffective conflict resolution between SA partners (Mohr & Spekman, 1994; Parkhe, 1991). These problems occur because of the dissimilarities of partners' interpretation of and responses to strategic and managerial issues.

Hofstede (1991) developed a pioneering and widely accepted classification scheme which breaks national culture into the following five indicators. *Power distance* focuses on the degree of equality or inequality between people in a country's society. *Individualism-collectivism* focuses on the degree the society reinforces individual or collective achievement and inter-personal relationship. *Masculinity-femininity* focuses on the degree the society reinforces the traditional masculine work role model of male achievement, control, and power. *Uncertainty avoidance* focuses on the level of tolerance for uncertainty and ambiguity within the society, the extent to which rules are obeyed and risks are avoided. *Long-term orientation* focuses on the degree the society embraces long-term devotion to traditional, forward thinking values.

Organizational culture fit. Partners with dissimilar organizational cultures may expend time and energy to establish mutually agreeable managerial practices and routines to facilitate interaction (Park & Ungson, 1997), which can in turn lead to a significant negative influence on SA performance (Pothukuchi, Damanpour, Choi, Chen, & Park, 2002). Hofstede, Neuijen, Ohayv, and Sanders (1990) asserted that organizational culture is best measured by organizational practices instead of more abstract assumptions and values. Hofstede et al. (1990) empirically found six independent indicators that describe the numerous organizational practices. *Process-oriented vs. results-oriented culture* is related to the risk attitude of organizations; *employee-oriented vs. job-oriented culture* is about how the employees are valued; *professional vs. parochial approach* is related to how employees are identified; *open vs. closed system* refers to the perceived communication climate within the organization; *loose vs. tight control* dimension refers to the degree of internal structuring in the organization; and *normative vs. pragmatic* dimension considers the popular notion of customer orientation.

Structural Characteristics of the SA

The structural characteristics related to the SA organization include the extent of management control imposed on the SA, ownership distribution, and the completeness of the contract (Ozorhon, 2007).

The extent of management control. One of the most tested drivers of performance in the research on SAs. Control is defined as the influence exercised by the SA partners over the management of the SA (Geringer & Hebert, 1989; Killing, 1983). The exercise of managerial control has been one of the most important subjects in the SA literature (Parkhe, 1993; Yan & Gray, 1994). In this study, adopting the approach of Choi and Beamish (2004), management control is divided into three categories, including (a) shared management for all activities, (b) dominant management for all activities by one of the partners, and (c) split management of activities for which each partner has competence. To improve performance, Mjoen and Tallman (1997) proposed that the activities controlled by each partner should be matched with their respective firm-specific strengths.

Distribution of ownership. Involves an SA's equal or unequal division of ownership and has been found to affect its performance (Blodgett, 1992; Geringer & Hebert, 1989; Killing, 1983). The ownership of an SA may be dominated by the respondent company, by a foreign partner, or can be equally shared by the partners. According to Killing (1983), the dominance of one partner will increase stability avoiding the managerial costs inherent in an SA and potential conflicts between partners. However, Blodgett (1992) argued that roughly equal equity shares will result in greater stability because the partners are equally committed to the SA. It is proposed by Ozorhon (2007) that it is most advantageous when the partner from the host country has dominant ownership, and that the ownership structure has no effect on performance if the host is a third country.

The completeness of the SA contract. An essential success factor that can avoid a great deal of trouble and conflict in future SA operations (Bing & Tiong, 1999). An SA contract provides a legally bound, institutional framework in which each party's rights, duties, and responsibilities are codified and the goals, policies, and strategies underlying the anticipated SA are specified. Since there are many potential problems in construction projects, the contract between the SA partners should define the rights and responsibilities of each party clearly to ensure success (Luo, 2002). Basically, an SA should be established based on mutual trust and understanding, but the agreement must be more concrete and precise regarding liability (Bing & Tiong, 1999).

DATA ANALYSIS

A questionnaire survey was administered to the Turkish partners of SAs. Almost half of the projects were undertaken in 18 foreign countries including Afghanistan, Bulgaria, Jordan, Russia, Iraq, India, the United States, and so on, whereas the remaining projects were undertaken in Turkey. Considering the fact that medium-to-large companies are likely to undertake SAs with more frequency compared to smaller firms, the target population was set as the members of the Turkish Contractors Association (TCA). All of the respondents were upper-level managers of large contractors with an average age of 39 years, operating both in domestic and international markets, and having expertise mainly in general contracting and infrastructure construction. The number of SA projects completed by Turkish construction companies with foreign partners in the last 10 years is around 110 (TCA, 2005). A total of 68 completed questionnaires were returned for data analysis, 48 of which were administered through face-to-face interviews and 20 via e-mail. Around 60% of the target population was covered in this study. Data were collected from 28 Turkish partners that undertook 68 international construction projects. The choice of only one partner in an SA as opposed to all partners was motivated by the difficulties in obtaining data from all partners due to logistical and cost barriers. Survey respondents were asked to evaluate the level of the above mentioned determinants of partner relations as well as the quality of the partner relations in their SA on a 1–5 point Likert scale.

The data were analyzed using a software package called EQS 6.1, a structural equation modeling (SEM) tool. The general form of SEM consists of a measurement model that specifies how the hypothetical constructs are measured in terms of the observed variables, and that establishes the validity and reliability of the observed variables; and a structural model that explores the causal relationships between the validated constructs, and that tests the hypothesized causal effects (Bollen, 1989). In the first step, construct validity is tested through qualitative and empirical validity tests. Content validity is a qualitative test and refers to the degree to which the construct is represented by indicators that cover the domain of meaning of the construct (Dunn, Seaker, & Waller, 1994), whereas reliability, convergent and discriminant validity tests compose the empirical part of the construct validity.

RESULTS

Table 14.1 shows the factor loadings corresponding to the six constructs of the model. The factor loadings are important because indicators that do not have statistically significant loadings are to be deleted from the model.

TABLE 14.1 Variables of the Model

Variables	Factor Loading	Variables	Factor Loading
Quality of partner relations		*National culture fit*	
Commitment	0.901	Power distance	0.865
Communication	0.751	Individualism	0.541
Cooperation	0.796	Masculinity	0.688
Previous cooperation	0.939	Uncertainty avoidance	*(0.054)
Conflict resolution	0.651	Long-term orientation	*(0.138)
Trust	0.730		
Strategic fit		*Organizational culture fit*	
Goal congruency	0.336	Process vs. results-oriented culture	0.668
Host country experience	0.454	Employee vs. job-oriented culture	0.545
Similar project experience	0.734	Parochial vs. professional practice	0.712
Managerial skills	0.733	Open vs. closed system	0.799
Technical skills	0.892	Loose vs. tight system	0.780
Human resources	0.674	Normative vs. pragmatic orientation	0.674
Client relations	0.622		
Organizational fit		*Structural characteristics*	
Financial capability	0.693	Extent of management control	0.665
Size of partners	0.786	Distribution of ownership	0.620
Management systems	0.622	Contract satisfaction	0.533
Workload of partners	0.685		

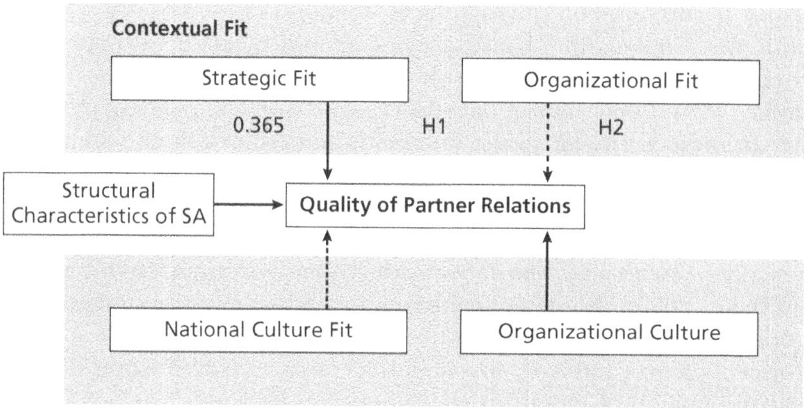

Figure 14.1 The structural equation model for quality of partner relations.
Source: Adapted from Ozorhon (2007).

In this respect, uncertainty avoidance and long-term orientation are deleted from the "national culture fit" construct. The analysis is performed using the statistically significant indicators. In the second step, SEM tests the hypotheses between the validated constructs.

Figure 14.1 shows the hypothesized relations between the constructs of the model. The numbers on the arrows represent the path coefficients that are equivalent to regression weights. The analysis suggests that "strategic fit between SA partners" is the main driver of "quality of partner relations" with a path coefficient of 0.365. "Organizational culture fit" has a moderate effect on partner relations (path coefficient: 0.268), which is followed by "structural characteristics of the SA" (0.212). On the other hand, no significant influence of "organizational fit" and "national culture fit" on the "quality of partner relations" was found. Links that are not statistically significant at $\alpha = 0.05$ were eliminated from the model (shown in dashed lines in Figure 14.1).

DISCUSSION

The model in Figure 14.1 indicates that previous cooperation between SA partners, commitment to the SA, cooperation of SA partners during strategic decision making, and communication are the major indicators of "interpartner relations."

The first hypothesis that strategic fit between SA partners has a positive effect on the "quality of partner relations" is verified by the data. Strategic fit has the highest influence on partner relations compared to other factors. If one relies on the high factor loadings of the variables that constitute the "strategic fit" construct, one should recommend that for better partner relations SA partners should have compatible technical (factor loading: 0.892) and managerial (0.733) skills and complementary experience in projects similar to the one being undertaken by the SA (0.734). It appears that SA partners that have complementary resources and skills enhance interpartner relations in terms of commitment, cooperation, communication, and trust in the operation of an SA. This finding also supports the earlier research by Luo (1998), Morris and Cadogan (2001) and Yan and Duan (2003) who stated that partner match in terms of strategic assets is critical for managing an SA since it increases the chance of achieving project objectives and leads to a high level of partner satisfaction. The strategic orientation of parent firms is important to venture success because how well it matches that of its partner influences interpartner consistency in terms of strategic goals and behaviors, cooperative culture, and investment commitment (Parkhe, 1991).

The second hypothesis that organizational fit between SA partners has a positive effect on the "quality of partner relations" is not verified by the data since the influence of the quality of partner relations fit was not significant at $\alpha = 0.05$. This finding is interesting since previous research indicated that organizational fit has a positive impact on partner relations. This difference might be due to the fact that in this research, strategic fit and organizational fit are investigated as two separate constructs and the impact of strategic fit on partner relations was found to be dominant. It could also be argued that similarities in parent firms' size, workload, management systems, and financial capability do not help achieve better partner relations.

The third hypothesis that national culture fit between SA partners has a positive effect on the "quality of partner relations" is not verified by the data either since the influence of national culture fit was not significant at $\alpha = 0.05$. In this study, the differences in the national cultures of two firms were measured in terms of power distance, individualism, and masculinity. Similarity in the national cultures of SA partners was not found to affect the "quality of partner relations." This finding is in line with the findings of the studies conducted by Beamish and Kachra (2004); Luo, Shenkar, and Nyaw (2001); Park and Ungson (1997); and Shenkar and Zeira (1992). However, it should also be stated that prior research has provided mixed empirical evidence regarding the specific influence of cultural distance on SA operation and performance (Brouthers & Brouthers, 2001). Although several researchers reported that differences in national culture are a source of poor communication, inadequate cooperation, lack of commitment, and ineffective conflict resolution between the SA partners (Harrigan, 1988; Mohr & Spekman, 1994; Parkhe, 1991) due to the dissimilarities of partners' interpretation of and responses to strategic and managerial issues; some argue that these differences may help SA partners learn how to operate with a foreign partner (Barkema & Vermeulen, 1997) and may enhance the firm's learning capabilities (Makhija & Ganesh, 1997). Other researchers like Beamish (1985) and Glaister and Buckley (1999) found no relation between the two variables.

The fourth hypothesis that organizational culture fit between SA partners has a positive effect on the "quality of partner relations" is verified by the data. Differences in the organizational culture of two SA partners are manageable, since a firm's organizational culture can always be modified. The positive influence of SA partners' organizational culture fit is supported by other studies in the literature (e.g., Brown et al., 1989; Pothukuchi et al., 2002). When partners in an SA differ in their organizational culture, these differences may result in conflicting behaviors, leading to misunderstandings and interaction problems, which may lead to lower partner satisfaction and difficulties in achieving project targets. Based on the high factor loadings of the variables that constitute the "organizational culture fit" construct, one should recommend that for better partner relations SA partners should have compatible cultures in terms of communication climate; internal structuring; and employee identification that are measured in this study by open vs. closed system (factor loading: 0.799); loose vs. tight system (0.780); and parochial vs. professional practice (0.712), respectively.

The fifth hypothesis that the effectiveness of the structural characteristics of an SA has a positive effect on the "quality of partner relations" is verified by the data. This finding also supports earlier research arguing that an appropriate structure allows the partner firms to integrate the SA's activities with their individual strategies and activities and protects against the loss of the venture's competitive advantage (Geringer & Hebert, 1989). This finding reveals the importance of the extent of management control (factor loading: 0.665), ownership distribution (0.620), and the completeness of the SA contract (0.533). Split management control is expected to increase the level of performance since the specific competencies of each partner could be utilized effectively. A home country partner that has majority ownership is likely to put into full use their being familiar with the conditions in the host country. For a successful SA organization, a complete contract should be prepared in which company and project objectives are reflected, roles and responsibilities of each party are defined and ownership distribution together with control mechanisms are arranged based on the specific needs of the project and contribution of partners. A balanced control of the management, a balanced distribution of ownership, and a complete and thorough SA contract lead to smooth operation and enhances interpartner relations as suggested by Ozorhon et al.'s (2010) findings.

CONCLUSION

SAs are effective ways of combining distinctive resources and capabilities of parent organizations to become more competitive in business. Such entities have been active for many years in the construction industry. Due to globalization, construction firms are forced to establish SAs so as to enter and compete in international markets. The main principle behind forming construction alliances is to share financial and human resources as well as managerial and technical skills that are critical for accomplishing a successful project. Despite their popularity, SAs are very difficult to operate; failure rates of SAs are reported to be high. Successful partner relations is one of the main determinants of SA success. In this chapter, factors contributing to the quality of partner relations are explored.

Partner selection and alliance formation are critical stages of an SA where better partner relations may be achieved. If compatible and complementary partners come together under a well-working structure, it is likely that the SA will operate smoothly. This study builds upon the findings of a research by Ozorhon (2007) to examine the determinants of the quality of partner relations in international construction alliances. The research used SEM to test the hypotheses relative to the factors contributing to better partner relations. In this respect, strategic and organizational fit between SA partners; national and organizational culture fit between SA partners; and structural characteristics of SAs are investigated and their impacts on partner relations are analyzed.

Based on the findings of the study, it is suggested that the main indicators of partner relations in an international construction alliance are previous and current cooperation, communication between partners, and commitment to the alliance. The factors governing the smooth working relations are the strategic fit between the parent firms, the organizational culture fit between the parent firms, and the structural characteristics of the SA. Strategic fit is the most influential factor among the three. Partners having complementary technical, managerial, and human resources and similar project experience are expected to maintain better partner relations. Organizational culture fit between partners moderately affects the quality of partner relations. The most important dimensions relate to the similarity between partners in terms of the communication climate; internal structuring; and employee identification within the parent firms. Finally, the structural characteristic of the SA have less effect on partner relations. All the indicators of structure—namely, extent of management control, ownership distribution, and a satisfactory contract—seem to somehow affect the quality of partner relations. It should also be noted that organizational fit and national culture fit between the partners have not been found to be related to partner relations.

The findings of the analysis indicate that for better working relations in an SA, construction companies should concentrate on selecting compatible partners that could best complement their capabilities in terms of strategic assets and organizational culture. In addition, they should establish an appropriate structure for the SA organization in which each partner controls the activities related to its core competency, and they should prepare a complete and thorough agreement that defines each partner's roles and responsibilities clearly. Ensuring good relations between partners will help companies achieve a higher business performance in the context of international construction alliances.

ACKNOWLEDGMENT

This chapter, save some minor changes, was earlier published as Ozorhon, B., & Arditi, D. (2013). Quality of partner relations in international construction alliances. In T. K. Das (Ed.), *Interpartner dynamics in strategic alliances* (pp. 233–253). Charlotte, NC: Information Age.

REFERENCES

Barkema, H. G., Shenkar, O., Vermeulen, F., & Bell, J. H. J. (1997). Working abroad, working with others: How firms learn to operate international joint ventures. *Academy of Management Journal, 40*(2), 426–442.

Barkema, H. G., & Vermeulen, F. (1997). What differences in the cultural backgrounds of partners are detrimental for international joint ventures? *Journal of International Business Studies, 28*(4), 845–864.

Beamish, P. W. (1984). *Joint venture performance in developing countries* (Unpublished Doctoral Dissertation). University of Western Ontario, Canada.

Beamish, P. W. (1985). The characteristics of joint ventures in developed and developing countries. *Columbia Journal of World Business, 20*(3), 13–19.

Beamish, P. W. (1987). Joint ventures in LDCs: Partner selection and performance. *Management International Review, 27*(1), 23–37.

Beamish, P. W., & Kachra, A. (2004). Number of partners and JV performance. *Journal of World Business, 39*(2), 107–120.

Bing, L., & Tiong, R. L. K. (1999). Risk management model for international construction joint ventures. *Journal of Construction Engineering and Management, 125*(5), 377–384.

Bing, L., Tiong, R. L. K., Fan, W. W., & Chew, D. A. S. (1999). Risk management in international construction joint ventures. *Journal of Construction Engineering and Management, 125*(4), 277–284.

Blodgett, L. (1992). Factors in the instability of international joint ventures: An event history analysis. *Strategic Management Journal, 13*(6), 475–481.

Bollen, K. A. (1989). Structural equations with latent variables. New York, NY: Wiley.

Brouthers, K., & Brouthers, L. (2001). Explaining the national cultural distance paradox. *Journal of International Business Studies, 32*(1), 177–189.

Brown, L. T., Rugman, A. M., & Verbeke, A. (1989). Japanese joint ventures with Western multinationals: Synthesizing the economic and cultural explanations of failure. *Asia Pacific Journal of Management, 6*(2), 225–242.

Buckley, P. J., & Casson, M. (1988). A theory of co-operation in international business. In F. J. Contractor & P. Lorange (Eds.), *Cooperative strategies in international business* (pp. 31–53). Lexington, MA: Lexington Books.

Choi, C. B., & Beamish, P. W. (2004). Split management control and international joint venture performance. *Journal of International Business Studies, 35*(3), 201–215.

Contractor, F. J., & Lorange, P. (1988). Why should firms cooperate? The strategy and economics basis for cooperative ventures. In F. J. Contractor & P. Lorange (Eds.), *Cooperative strategies in international business* (pp. 3–30). Lexington, MA: Lexington Books.

Das, T. K., & Teng, B. (1998). Between trust and control: Developing confidence in partner cooperation in alliances. *Academy of Management Review, 23*(3), 491–512.

Doz, Y. L. (1996). The evolution of cooperation in strategic alliances: Initial conditions or learning processes? *Strategic Management Journal, 17*(Special Issue), 55–83.

Dunn, S. C., Seaker, R. F., & Waller, M. A. (1994). Latent variables in business logistics research: Scale development and validation. *Journal of Business Logistics, 15*(2), 145–172.

Evans, J., & Mavondo, F. T. (2002). Psychic distance and organizational performance: An empirical examination of international retailing operations. *Journal of International Business Studies, 33*(3), 515–532.

Fey, C. F., & Beamish, P. W. (1999). *Joint venture conflict: The case of Russian international joint ventures* (Working Paper #99-104). St. Petersburg, Sweden: Stockholm School of Economics.

Geringer, J. M. (1988). *Joint venture partner selection: Strategies for developing countries.* New York, NY: Quorum.

Geringer, J. M. (1991). Strategic determinants of partner selection criteria in international joint ventures. *Journal of International Business Studies, 22*(1), 41–62.

Geringer, J., & Hebert, L. (1989). Control and performance of international joint ventures. *Journal of International Business Studies, 20*(2), 235–254.

Glaister, K. W., & Buckley, P. J. (1999). Performance relationships in UK international alliances. *Management International Review, 39*(2), 123–147.

Gomes-Casseres, B. (2000) Mastering management. *Financial Times, 16*(10), 14–15.

Gunhan, S., & Arditi, A. (2005). Factors affecting international construction. *Journal of Construction Engineering and Management, 131*(3), 273–282.

Harrigan, K. (1988). Joint Ventures and competitive strategy. *Strategic Management Journal, 9*(2), 83–103.

Hebert, L. (1994). *Division of control, relationship dynamics and joint venture performance* [Unpublished doctoral dissertation]. University of Western Ontario, Canada.

Hennart, J. F., Kim, D. J., & Zeng, M. (1998). The impact of joint venture status on the longevity of Japanese stakes in U.S. manufacturing affiliates. *Organization Science, 9*(3), 382–395.

Hill, R. C., & Hellriegel, D. (1994). Critical contingencies in joint venture management: Some lessons from managers. *Organization Science, 5*(4), 594–607.

Hofstede, G. (1991). Cultures and organizations: Software of the mind, intercultural cooperation and its importance for survival. New York, NY: McGraw-Hill.

Hofstede, G., Neuijen, B., Ohayv, D., & Sanders, G. (1990). Measuring organizational cultures: A qualitative and quantitative study across twenty cases. *Administrative Science Quarterly, 35*(2), 286–316.

Inkpen, A.C. (1996). Creating knowledge through collaboration. *California Management Review, 39*(1), 123–140.

Inkpen, A. C., & Currall, S. C. (1998). The nature, antecedents, and consequences of joint venture trust. *Journal of International Management, 4*(1), 1–20.

Janger, A. R. (1980). *Organisation of international joint ventures.* New York, NY: Conference Board.

Johanson, J., & Vahlne, J. E. (1977). The internationalization process of the firm: A model of knowledge development and increasing foreign market commitments. *Journal of International Business Studies, 8*(1), 23–32.

Killing, J.P. (1983). *Strategies for joint venture success.* New York, NY: Routledge.

Kogut, B., & Singh, H. (1988). The effect of national culture on the choice of entry mode. *Journal of International Business Studies, 19*(3), 411–432.

Kwok, H. C. A., Then, D., & Skitmore, M. (2000). Risk management in Singapore construction joint ventures. *Journal of Construction Research, 1*(2), 139–149.

Lasserre, P. (1999). Joint venture satisfaction in Asia-Pacific. *Asia-Pacific Journal of Management, 16*(1), 1–28.

Low, P. S., & Leong, C. H. Y. (2000). Cross-cultural project management for international construction in China. *International Journal of Project Management, 18*(5), 307–316.

Luo, Y. (1997). Partner selection and venturing success: the case of joint ventures with firms in the People's Republic of China. *Organization Science, 8*(6), 648–662.

Luo, Y. (1998). Joint venture success in China: How should we select a good partner? *Journal of World Business, 33*(2), 145–166.

Luo, Y. (2002). Contract, cooperation, and performance in international joint ventures. *Strategic Management Journal, 23*(10), 903–919.

Luo, Y., Shenkar, O., & Nyaw, M. K. (2001). A dual parent perspective on control and performance in international joint ventures: Lessons from a developing economy. *Journal of International Business Studies, 32*(1), 41–58.

Makhija, M. V., & Ganesh, U. (1997). The relationship between control and partner learning in learning-related joint-ventures. *Organization Science, 8*(5), 508–527.

Makino, S., & Beamish, P. W. (1998). Performance and survival of international joint ventures with non-conventional ownership structures. *Journal of International Business Studies, 29*(4), 797–818.

Makino, S., & Delios, A. (1996) Local knowledge transfer and performance: Implications for alliance formation in Asia. *Journal of International Business Studies, 27*(Special Issue), 905–928.

Mead, R. (1998). *International management: cross-cultural dimensions.* Malden, MA: Blackwell.

Merchant, H. (2000). Configuration of international joint ventures. *Management International Review, 40*(2), 107–140.

Mjoen, H., & Tallman, H. (1997). Control and performance in international joint ventures. *Organization Science, 8*(3), 257–274.

Mohr, J., & Spekman, R. (1994). Characteristics of partnership success: Partnership attributes, communication behavior, and conflict resolution techniques. *Strategic Management Journal, 15*(2), 135–152.

Morosini, P., Shane, S., & Singh, H. (1998). Cultural distance and cross-border acquisition performance. *Journal of International Business Studies, 29*(1), 137–158.

Morris, B., & Cadogan, J.W. (2001). Partner symmetries, partner conflict and the quality of joint venture marketing strategy: an empirical investigation. *Journal of Marketing Management, 17*(1–2), 223–256.

O'Grady, S., & Lane, H. W. (1996). The psychic distance paradox. *Journal of International Business Studies, 27*(2), 309–333.

Ozorhon, B. (2007). *Modeling the performance of international construction joint ventures* [Unpublished doctoral dissertation]. Middle East Technical University, Ankara, Turkey.

Ozorhon, B., Arditi, D., Dikmen, I., & Birgonul, M. T. (2010). The performance of international joint ventures in construction. *Journal of Management in Engineering, 26*(4), 209–222.

Pan, Y., & Chi, P. S. K. (1999). Financial performance and survival of multinational corporations in China. *Strategic Management Journal, 20*(4), 359–374.

Pan, Y., & Li, X. (2000). Joint venture formation of very large multinational firms. *Journal of International Business Studies, 31*, 179–189.

Park, S. H., & Ungson, G. R. (1997). The effect of national culture, organizational complementarity, and economic motivation on joint venture dissolution. *Academy of Management Journal, 40*(2), 279–307.

Parkhe, A. (1991). Interfirm diversity, organizational learning, and longevity in global strategic alliances. *Journal of International Business Studies, 22*, 579–601.

Parkhe, A. (1993). Messy research, methodological predispositions, and theory development in international joint ventures. *Academy of Management Review, 18*(2), 227–268.

Pothukuchi, V., Damanpour, F., Choi, J., Chen, C. C., & Park, S. H. (2002). National and organizational culture differences and international joint venture performance. *Journal of International Business Studies, 33*, 243–265.

Shenkar, O. (1990). International joint ventures' problems in China: Risks and remedies. *Long Range Planning, 23*(3), 80–90.

Shenkar, O. (2001). Cultural distance revisited: Towards more rigorous conceptualization and measurement of cultural differences. *Journal of International Business Studies, 32*, 519–535.

Shenkar, O., & Zeira, Y. (1992). Role conflict and role ambiguity of chief executive officers in international joint ventures. *Journal of International Business Studies, 23*(1), 55–75.

Sim, A. B., & Ali, M. Y. (2000). Determinants of stability in international joint ventures: Evidence from a developing country context. *Asia-Pacific Journal of Management, 17*, 373–397.

Smith, K. G., Guthrie, J. P., & Chen, M. (1989). Strategy, size and performance. *Organization Studies, 10*(1), 63–81.

Sridharan, G. (1997, December). *Factors affecting the performance of international joint ventures: A research model.* Paper presented at the First International Conference on Construction Industry Development, Singapore, Singapore.

Tatoglu, E., & Glaister, K. W. (1998). Performance of international joint ventures in Turkey: Perspectives of Western firms and Turkish firms. *International Business Review, 7*(6), 635–656.

TCA. (2005). *Turkish Contractors Association* [in Turkish]. Retrieved from http://www.tmb.org.tr/genel.php?ID=2.

Tomlinson, J. W. C., & Thompson, M. (1977). *A study of Canadian joint ventures in Mexico.* Ottawa, Canada: Office of Science and Technology, Department of Industry, Trade and Commerce.

Ulijn, J., Duijsters, G., Schaetzlein, R., & Remer, S. (2005). *Culture and its perception in strategic alliances, does it affect the performance? An exploratory study into Dutch-German ventures* (Working Paper 03.05). Eindhoven, Netherlands: Eindhoven Centre for Innovation Studies.

Yan, A., & Duan, J. (2003). Interpartner fit and its performance implications: A four-case study of U.S.-China joint ventures. *Asia Pacific Journal of Management, 20*(4), 541–564.

Yan, A., & Gray, B. (1994). Bargaining power, management control, and performance in United States-China joint ventures: a comparative case study. *Academy of Management Journal, 37*(6), 1478–1517.

Yan, A., & Gray, B. (2001). Antecedents and effects of parent control in international joint ventures. *Journal of Management Studies, 38*(3), 393–416.

Zaman, M., & Mavondo, F. (2002) *Measuring strategic alliance success: A conceptual framework.* Retrieved from http://smib.vuw.ac.nz:8081/WWW/ANZMAC2001/anzmac/AUTHORS/pdfs/Zaman.pdf.

ABOUT THE CONTRIBUTORS

David Arditi is professor of civil and architectural engineering, and the founder and director of the construction engineering and management program at the Illinois Institute of Technology, Chicago, IL. His area of expertise covers all aspects of construction management, engineering, and support. He conducted several funded research projects sponsored by federal and state agencies. He is the author of many papers published in refereed national and international journals and conference proceedings. He serves on the editorial board of 11 journals. He was elected to the College of Fellows of CMAA in 2013.

Email: arditi@iit.edu

Jeffrey L. Cummings is professor in the Sellinger School of Business at Loyola University Maryland, Baltimore, MD, where he teaches business and alliance strategy. He holds a PhD from George Washington University, USA, and is a certified strategic alliance professional (CSAP). His research and consulting focus on strategic analysis, alliance selection, and knowledge sharing processes. Recent alliance publications include those in *Behavioral Strategy for Competitive Advantage, Group and Organization Management, International Journal of Strategic Business Alliances, Long Range Planning,* and *ASAP Handbook of Alliance Management: A Practitioner's Guide.*

Email: jcummings@loyola.edu

Giovanni Battista Dagnino is chair of management and professor of digital strategy at the University of Rome LUMSA, Palermo Campus, Italy, where he is the founding director of the MSc program in economics and manage-

Managing the Partners in Strategic Alliances, pages 367–374

ment and chair of the scientific committee of LUMSA Digital Hub. His current research examines coopetition strategy dynamics, digital transformation strategy, the management of temporary competitive advantage, and the relationship between strategy, governance, and entrepreneurship. He is co-editor of the *Journal of Management and Governance* and authored/edited 13 books and over 40 articles in leading management journals, including *Academy of Management Perspectives, Global Strategy Journal, Organization Studies, Strategic Management Journal,* and *California Management Review.*

Email: g.dagnino@lumsa.it

T. K. Das is professor emeritus of strategic management at the City University of New York, NY, where he taught for over 3 decades and served concurrently as a member of the university's doctoral faculty. Prior to entering academic life, Professor Das had extensive experience as a senior business executive. Professor Das received his PhD in organization and strategic studies from the Anderson Graduate School of Management, University of California at Los Angeles, Los Angeles, CA (UCLA). He has a bachelor's degree in physics, two master's degrees in mathematics and management, and a professional certification in banking. His research interests are in strategic alliances, strategy making, organization studies, temporal studies, and executive development. Professor Das is the author or editor of 28 academic research books, mainly on strategy, organization, and management, and also 6 booklets on bank management for practicing executives. His research articles have appeared in over 45 journals, of which some of the later ones include *Academy of Management Executive, Academy of Management Review, Accounting, Organizations and Society, British Journal of Management, Cross Cultural Management: An International Journal, Entrepreneurship Theory and Practice, International Journal of Entrepreneurial Behaviour & Research, International Journal of Organizational Analysis, International Journal of Strategic Business Alliances, International Journal of Strategic Change Management, Journal of Business and Psychology, Journal of Business Ethics, Journal of General Management, Journal of International Management, Journal of Management, Journal of Management Development, Journal of Management Studies, Journal of Managerial Psychology, Long Range Planning, Management Decision, Management International Review, Organization Science, Organization Studies, Scandinavian Journal of Management, Strategic Management Journal,* and *Time & Society.* Also, by invitation, he has contributed book reviews in *Administrative Science Quarterly, Contemporary Psychology,* and *Journal of Management,* and authored the entry on "Strategic Alliances" in *Oxford Bibliographies in Management.* His work has been cited in over 1,500 journals published in a wide variety of disciplines. For a number of years now, he has been consistently ranked in the top 2% of scholars in his field of business & management in terms of research impact. Most recently, a Stanford University professor led a comprehensive study of the career-long research impact of more than 8 million researchers worldwide across 174 fields during the 60-year period 1960–2019, based on the article citations included in the well-known multidisciplinary citation database *SCOPUS*, and this study has ranked Professor Das among the top 1% of scholars (complete list published in the journal *PLOS Biology*). Professor Das is a former senior editor of *Organization Studies* and has previously served, or is serving, on the editorial boards of a number of other academic journals, and has been an *ad hoc* editorial reviewer for over 70 journals. He is the founding (and current) series editor of the three book series, *Research in Strategic Alliances, Research in Behavioral Strategy*, and *Research in Strategy Science* (all published by Information Age Publishing).

Email: TK.Das@baruch.cuny.edu

Diana Marie De Silva is Assistant Professor at the Department of Industrial Engineering, University of the Philippines Los Baños, Philippines. She recently earned joint degrees of PhD in Business Economics from KU Leuven, Belgium, and PhD in Management Engineering and Real Estate Economics from the University of Padua, Italy. She has a Master of Science in Finance from the University of the Philippines Diliman, Quezon City, Philippines, and a Bachelor of Science in Industrial Engineering from the University of the Philippines Los Baños, Laguna, Philippines. Her main research areas are in interorganizational networks, systems design, and project management. She has 10 years of work experience in academia and 2 years of applied industry work and has been able to acquire and manage government funded research projects in the Philippines.

Email: drdesilva1@up.edu.ph

Giulio Ferrigno is a postdoctoral scholar at Sant'Anna School of Advanced Studies, Pisa, Italy. He received his PhD in economics and management from the University of Catania, Italy. He has held visiting positions at Tilburg University, Netherlands, and University of Umea, Sweden. He has won the Best Paper award of the Academy of Management's Management History Division (2019), the Outstanding Reviewer award of Academy's Strategic Management Division (2015 and 2016), and the JMS and SMS Doctoral Workshop Scholarship (respectively in 2015 and 2016). His research interests include strategic alliances, value creation and appropriation, and open innovation. He has published articles in *Small Business Economics, Technological Forecasting and Social Change, International Journal of Management Reviews*, and *Journal of Business and Industrial Marketing*, as well as chapters in the volumes *Managing Multipartner Strategic Alliances* and *Managing Alliance Portfolios and Networks* in the book series Research in Strategic Alliances (Information Age Publishing).

Email: giulio.ferrigno@santannapisa.it

Rob Hecker is the academic director of postgraduate coursework programs in the faculty of business at the University of Tasmania in Australia. With a background in psychology and as a working manager, his research interests are in understanding the place of the individual both within (human resource management and development) and outside (consumer behavior) the organization. He contributes to journals such as *Journal of Small Business and Enterprise Development, Journal of European Industrial Training, International Journal of Service Industry Management,* and *Personality and Individual Differences,* and to international conferences.

E-mail: Rob.Hecker@utas.edu.au

Michael A. Hitt is distinguished professor of management at Texas A&M University and holds the Joe B. Foster chair in business leadership. He received his PhD from the University of Colorado. He has co-authored or co-edited 26 books and authored or coauthored many journal articles. A recent article in the *Journal of Management* listed him as 1 of the 10 most cited authors in management over a 25-year period. Additionally, the *Times Higher Education* in 2010 listed him among the top scholars in economics, finance, and management based on the number of articles with a high citation rate on the Web of Science. He has served on the editorial review boards of multiple journals and is a former editor of the *Academy of Management Journal* and the *Strategic Entrepreneurship Journal.* He is a fellow in the Academy of Management and in the Strategic Management Society, a research fellow in the National Entrepreneurship Consortium and received an honorary doctorate from the Universidad Carlos III de Madrid. He is a former president of the Academy of Management, a former president of the Strategic Management Society and a member of the Academy of Management Journals' Hall of Fame. He received awards for the best article published in the *Academy of Management Executive* (1999), *Academy of Management Journal* (2000), and the *Journal of Management* (2006). He received the Irwin Outstanding Educator Award and the Distinguished Service Award from the Academy of Management and the Falcone Distinguished Entrepreneurship Scholar Award from Syracuse University.

E-mail: mhitt@mays.tamu.edu

Saleema Kauser is a lecturer in the Organization Studies Group at Manchester Business School, UK. She earned her first degree in psychology from the University of London, a master's degree in information systems and technology from Cass Business School, an MBA from Aston Business School, and a PhD from the Warwick Business School, University of Warwick, all in the United Kingdom. She has been lecturing for many years on strategic and organizational management issues.

Email: saleema.kauser@mbs.ac.uk

Angelos Kostis is a PhD candidate at Umeå School of Business, Economics and Statistics, Umeå, Sweden. His research interest lies in behavioral strategy and uncertainty in interorganizational interactions. His research focuses on the dynamics of trust and distrust and on the role of digital artifacts in the context of interorganizational relationships involving coopetition and interdependence. He has published in *California Management Review, European Management Journal,* and *Journal of Trust Research.*

Email: angelos.kostis@umu.se

Rajesh Kumar is a strategy consultant who specializes in cross-cultural management and international negotiations. Earlier, he was professor of international management at Menlo College, Atherton, CA. He has a PhD degree from New York University, NY. He has published in leading international journals such as *Journal of Management, Journal of Management Studies, Organization Science, Journal of World Business, Industrial Marketing Management, Journal of Applied Behavioral Science, International Marketing Review,* and *International Journal of Conflict Management.*

Email: rjk499@yahoo.com

Dave Luvison is an executive in residence in the Sellinger School of Business at Loyola University Maryland, Baltimore, MD, USA, where he teaches courses in organizational behavior and collaboration. He has a DBA from Nova Southeastern University, USA, and is a certified strategic alliance professional (CSAP). His research focuses on alliance capability and organizational culture, as well as the implications of behavioral processes on strategic alliance performance. Recent alliance publications include those in *Behavioral Strategy for Competitive Advantage, Group and Organization Management, International Journal of Strategic Business Alliances, Management Decision,* and *Behavioral Perspectives in Strategic Alliances.*

Email: dluvison@loyola.edu

Alex Örtegren is a doctoral student at the Department of Applied Educational Science at Umeå University, Sweden. Amongst his research interests are technology in education, technology and literacy, and citizenship in a postdigital world.

Email: alex.ortegren@umu.se

Beliz Ozorhon is an assistant professor of construction management in the Department of Civil Engineering at Bogazici University, Turkey. Her research initiatives focus on innovation management, international joint ventures, strategic decision making, performance management, and knowledge management. Her recent projects investigate the sustainability issues in built environments, innovative project delivery and integration in construction, and investment decision making. She has published many papers in leading journals and international conference proceedings.

Email: beliz.ozorhon@boun.edu.tr

Andrea Piccaluga is full professor of innovation management at the Institute of Management and a delegate for Technology Transfer at Scuola Superiore Sant'Anna, Pisa, Italy. He is vice president of Netval (www.netval.it), the Italian network of University Technology Transfer Offices and Associate editor of the *R&D Management*. His research and teaching mainly deal with R&D and innovation management, open innovation, and the collaboration between firms and research institutions in the innovation process. He has published several articles in leading management journals, including *R&D Management, Small Business Economics, California Management Review, Journal of Technology Transfer, Journal of Knowledge Management, Technology Analysis & Strategic Management, European Management Journal,* and *Creativity and Innovation Management.*

Email: a.piccaluga@santannapisa.it

Nadine Roijakkers is the director of the Expertise Centre for Education and full professor of open innovation at the Open University of The Netherlands in Heerlen, Netherlands. Her research interests include open innovation, alliances, and ecosystems and her work has been published in journals such as *Long Range Planning, Research Policy, British Journal of Management, European Management Journal, Technological Forecasting and Social Change, Small Business Economics, California Management Review, Journal of Product Innovation Management,* and *R&D Management.* She is a co-editor of *Researching Open Innovation in SMEs* (World Scientific, 2018) and co-editor of *Sustainable Innovation: Strategy, Process, and Impact* (Routledge, 2021).

Email: nadine.roijakkers@ou.nl

Diana Rus is a senior lecturer in organizational psychology at the University of Groningen, Netherlands. Her research interests include open innovation, workplace innovation, and leadership. Her work has been published in journals such as *Leadership Quarterly, European Journal of Work and Organizational Psychology, Journal of Business Ethics,* and *Journal of Experimental Social Psychology.* She is the co-editor of the volume *Workplace Innovation: Theory, Research and Practice* (Springe, year?r) and also co-editor of the journal *European Work and Psychology in Practice.* She also works as an innovation management consultant focusing specifically on collaborative innovation and building collaborative innovation capability.

Email: d.c.rus@rug.nl

Timothy B. Steele is president and founder of ARM Partners, LLC, Leesburg, VA, USA, which assists technology executives to staff and operate partnerships and optimize their unique partnering challenges and opportunities. His earlier experience covered alliance leadership across sales, marketing, general management, alliances, business development and as a CEO. His experience includes working with both Fortune 50 companies, including CA Technologies, IBM, Motorola, and Siemens, and with entrepreneurial ventures and private equity-backed companies.

Email: tim.steele@armpartners.io

Matthias Vermeiren recently obtained a master's degree in business administration with a major in international business at KU Leuven, Belgium, and currently works as a junior auditor at RSM Belgium. His professional interest in the field of international business arose from his experience as a music producer. During his studies, he worked as a student-entrepreneur where he managed his own contracts, finances, and performances in countries such as Estonia and Czech Republic.

Email: matthiasvermeiren@hotmail.com

Ernst Verwaal is full professor of international business strategy in the Department of Management, Strategy and Innovation at KU Leuven, Belgium. His research interest focuses on the question: "Why do firms not fully realize and capture the value that is embedded in their knowledge resources?" His articles have been published in journals such as *Organization Science, Organization Studies, Journal of Management, Journal of World Business, Journal of International Business Studies,* and *Journal of Common Market Studies.* He serves as a reviewer for several research journals and book publishers. He received best research paper awards at the Academy of International Business and the American Marketing Academy Conferences. He acquired grants from public and private research funding organizations and advised public policy institutes in Belgium, Netherlands, the United Kingdom, and Brazil. His industry experience covers a broad range of research and consulting activities with governments. He advised the European Commission on the cross-border business transaction in the European Union. (e.g., EC documents SEC/2005/1543 and SEC/2006/566), and multinational companies, including Siemens, Philips, Royal Dutch Shell, ABN-AMRO, and Royal Vopak.

Email: ernst.verwaal@kuleuven.be

Megan Woods is a lecturer in management at the Tasmanian School of Business and Economics at the University of Tasmania, Australia. Her research interests include strategic management of organizations and human resources, qualitative research approaches, and organizational learning, with a particular focus on adaptive learning by individuals, groups, organizations, and communities in collaborative contexts. Her work has been published in journals such as *Academy of Management Learning and Education, International Journal of Social Research Methodology*, and *International Journal of Public Sector Management*. Her teaching is firmly grounded in applied learning contexts and focuses on helping learners synthesize their theoretical and practical experiences of management. This approach has informed her recent books *Management in Focus: The Global Financial Crisis* (Pearson Education Australia, 2010) and *Management: The Essentials* (Pearson Australia, 2014).

Email: Megan.Woods@utas.edu.au

Hiroshi Yasuda is a professor of the School of Business, Aoyama Gakuin University, Japan. He graduated from University of Tokyo, Japan, in applied physics and received his degree of Master of Science in management from Sloan School of Management at Massachusetts Institute of Technology, USA, and PhD in industrial engineering and management from Tokyo Institute of Technology, Japan. His main research interest lies in the analysis of strategic alliances, especially in the context of competitive strategies and management of technologies. His research has been published in refereed journals such as *International Journal of Business Performance Management, International Journal of Business and Systems Research, Technovation, Organizational Science, Journal of Business Management, Journal of Strategic Management Studies*, and *Japan Journal of Finance*. He has authored three books, *Strategic Alliances Under the Competitive Environment* [in Japanese] (NTT Publishing, 2006), *Strategies for Competitive Alliances* [in Japanese] (NTT Publishing, 2010), and *Alliance Strategies in the Competitive Environment* [in Japanese] (NTT Publishing, 2016).

Email: yasuda@busi.aoyama.ac.jp

INDEX

A

Managing the Partners in Strategic Alliances, pages 375–396

B

D

G

H

I

J

K

L

M

Q

R

T

U

V

W

X

Y

Z

Printed and bound by CPI Group (UK) Ltd, Croydon, CR0 4YY

15/09/2026

14962336-0005